THE COUNSELING
:: EXPERIENCE ::

THE COUNSELING
:: EXPERIENCE ::
A Theoretical and Practical Approach

MICHAEL E. CAVANAGH

WAVELAND
PRESS, INC.
Prospect Heights, Illinois

For information about this book, write or call:
Waveland Press, Inc.
P.O. Box 400
Prospect Heights, Illinois 60070
(708) 634-0081

To my wife, Marie,
and our children,
Michele, Christine, Janelle, and Michael,
and to all the people
with whom I lived the counseling experience

Preface

This book covers three dimensions in counseling: basic behavioral dynamics that are particularly relevant to counseling; an eclectic theoretical underpinning that accommodates many, if not most, specific theories of counseling; and practical approaches that flow from a combination of the first two dimensions. More specifically, the book presents 14 issues that are an integral part of counseling. When counseling progresses, it is because both the counselor and the person in counseling are handling these issues well; when counseling lags or regresses, it is because the counselor, the person, or both are mishandling one or more of these areas.

This book is unique in a number of ways. It not only presents the principles of effective counseling but discusses in depth why the principles are important, what effects they have on the counseling relationship, and what happens to both the person in counseling and the counselor when the principles are not followed. For example, it is said that warmth is a necessary quality in a counselor. But exactly why is it important? Are there times when warmth creates problems? And what interferes with counselors' feeling or expressing warmth?

The presentation is realistic. It discusses in detail not only the potential good of counseling but also its potential harm. It treats counselors as human beings who have limitations and weaknesses that need to be recognized if counselors are to evolve continually into more effective helpers. The book focuses on the principles of effective counseling but also details the behavioral dynamics of the person in counseling, the dynamics of the counselor, and the very complex dynamics that occur when the counselor and the person in counseling interact.

The topics are organized from simple to complex. The depth of the book is adjustable and relative to the reader's insight and experience. It is simple enough to be grasped by students in an introductory course and profound enough to be a challenge to sophisticated graduate students, paraprofessionals, and professionals.

The book is meant to be practical and down to earth, tailored to modern undergraduate and graduate programs. Many students today are involved in practicum experiences and need a book that is more than a compilation of theories and abstract principles. This book is written to help students face the daily challenges, confusions, problems, successes, and failures that arise when human beings try to help each other.

The book's theoretical underpinning is healthily eclectic. It does not follow one theoretical school, but it is not a hodgepodge of bits and pieces of theory thrown together as mortar to support the author's ideas. The theoretical consistency underlying the text is guided by a prudent and ethical pragmatism. In other words, the book holds that counselors should use what works and discard what does not work rather than adhere to a particular theoretical model, despite the fact that the person in counseling cannot be bent to fit it.

It is a book that counselors can recommend to people in counseling. Progress in counseling is often unnecessarily impeded because people have little or no knowledge of the process of counseling. They do not know what to expect from it, what it will require them to give, or how they can cooperate most fully. When people have a clear concept of counseling, they can more easily graduate from students participating in a mysterious phenomenon to partners involved in an understandable process.

I am grateful to the following reviewers for their constructive and helpful suggestions: Barbara D'Angelo of California State University at Fullerton, Elsie J. Dotson of Western Kentucky University, Mildred L. Fortner of Southwest Missouri State University, and David A. Kendall of the State University of New York at Brockport. I am also grateful to Claire Verduin and Fiorella Ljunggren, for their cooperation and support. Finally, I wish to express my appreciation to Liz Michael for her invaluable assistance in typing the manuscript.

Michael E. Cavanagh

Contents

CHAPTER 1

The Nature
of Counseling

Before beginning the discussion of the principles of counseling, it is helpful to understand some concepts. I will discuss these concepts in this chapter by considering the following questions:

1. What is counseling?
2. Does counseling differ from psychotherapy?
3. Does counseling work?
4. What is the place of research in counseling?
5. Is there a "best" theory of counseling?
6. What are the benefits of studying counseling?

A DEFINITION OF COUNSELING

There are many definitions of counseling, but the one I use and that best sets the stage for the theme and principles discussed in this book is the following: Counseling denotes a relationship between a trained helper and a person seeking help in which both the skills of the helper and the atmosphere that he or she creates help people learn to relate with themselves and others in more growth-producing ways. This definition contains seven key elements. If any one of these seven elements is absent, then counseling, as defined in this text, cannot take place and is not taking place, regardless of the good intentions of the people involved.

First, the helper is a *trained* professional. Trained counselors are not the only people who can help others, just as physicians are not the

1

only ones who can do cardiopulmonary resuscitation. However, the more academic and practical training a person has, the more he or she will be capable of dealing with a wide range of problems of varying degrees of severity.

Second, the counselor is in a *relationship* with the person being helped. This means that there is at least an adequate degree of mutual understanding, confidence, acceptance, and cooperation. A professional relationship can develop in one counseling session, or it may not develop in 20 visits. All other factors remaining the same, a counseling relationship will grow in depth as the number of sessions increases.

Third, a professional counselor needs *both* counseling skills *and* a helpful personality. Counseling skills alone cannot create a growth-producing atmosphere, and the atmosphere alone will not be sufficient to help a person grow. To the degree that both skills and atmosphere are present, a person can realistically expect to be offered maximum help.

Fourth, a counselor helps a person *learn.* This denotes that counseling is a learning process through which the person unlearns maladaptive behaviors and learns adaptive ones in their place. Maladaptive behavior may be either abnormal or normal, but in either case, it interferes with need fulfillment and growth.

Fifth, people learn to *relate with themselves and others*. This means that counselors help people relate with themselves better so that they become more integrated and less fragmented and conflictual. Learning to relate better with others is important because most basic psychological needs can be met only through interpersonal relationships. It is also important because human beings have not only a personal responsibility to grow but a social responsibility to help others grow or, at least, not to impede their growth.

Sixth, people learn to relate *in growth-producing ways. Growth-producing* has three meanings. First, it means that people grow in intrapersonal and interpersonal competencies. Second, it means that ordinarily counseling is aimed at personality growth and not merely symptom removal. Third, counseling is not solely for psychologically disturbed people; normal people who are experiencing an obstacle to their growth can also benefit from counseling.

And seventh, counseling connotes a relationship between a counselor and *a person seeking help*. It is necessary that the person who approaches counseling is actually seeking help. This is in contrast to people who don't feel they need help but contact a counselor because someone talked them into it or because they want to complain about the people in their lives.

COUNSELING AND PSYCHOTHERAPY

There is little agreement among counselors on whether and how counseling and psychotherapy differ. As M. E. Hahn writes,

> I know of few counselors or psychologists who are completely satisfied that clear distinctions [between counseling and psychotherapy] have been made. . . . Perhaps the most complete agreements are (1) that counseling and psychotherapy cannot be distinguished clearly, (2) that counselors practice what psychotherapists consider psychotherapy, (3) that psychotherapists practice what counselors consider to be counseling, and (4) that despite the above, they are different.[1]

Some people view the terms as synonymous, and others see differences. The following are some of the differences suggested in the literature:

1. Counseling deals mostly with normal people; psychotherapy deals primarily with those who are psychologically disturbed.
2. Counseling is more educative, supportive, conscious oriented, and short term; psychotherapy is more reconstructive, confrontive, unconscious oriented, and long term.
3. Counseling is more structured and directed toward limited, concrete goals; psychotherapy is purposely more ambiguous and has goals that change and evolve as the person progresses.

Although there may be legal reasons to make such distinctions, counseling and psychotherapy are viewed as basically synonymous for the purposes of this text. The reason for this is that there is so much overlap between the two that attempts to separate them would damage both concepts. Moreover, such a separation would unduly restrict a presentation that is equally relevant to both.

I chose the term *counseling* for this text because *psychotherapy* tends to connote a more restricted area of specialization. The principles elucidated in this book have a wide range of applicability that is equally valid across the continuum of the helping professions.

THE EFFECTIVENESS OF COUNSELING

The counseling literature presents studies that purport to show that counseling does not work; that counseling works but no better than any other kind of relevant help, such as medication; that counseling works but helps people no more than had they been left alone; that counseling

---

[1] Hahn (1953), p. 232.

works more often than it doesn't; and that counseling can do more harm than good.[2]

Which of these positions is correct? They are *all* correct, although not all of them stem from sound methodologies. Just as automobiles work or don't work, depending on the state of the vehicle, the skills of the driver, and the temperature of the environment, counseling works or does not work, depending on the relationship among many variables. Some of these variables are the duration, nature, and severity of the psychological disturbance; the motivation of the person and the quality of environmental supports; the degree of psychological health the person possessed before the presenting problem; the degree of psychological health the person possesses at the start of counseling; the general skills of the counselor and the specific skills that are required for a particular person and problem; and the motivation of the counselor and the quality of the therapeutic atmosphere he or she is able to create. The quantity and quality of these and other variables make it difficult to evaluate empirically the effectiveness of counseling, both as a discipline and as it applies to a specific person in counseling.

In addition to the problem of controlling confounding variables, problems exist concerning what constitutes effective treatment and who is to decide if the criteria have been met successfully. The person in counseling, the counselor, the person in counseling's family, the person in counseling's employer—all may offer widely different opinions.[3]

Since counseling can, at various times, be helpful, unhelpful, or harmful, it is the responsibility of counselors to acquire the personal qualities, academic knowledge, and practical skills necessary to increase the number of instances in which counseling will be the most helpful to the greatest number of people.

THE ROLE OF RESEARCH IN COUNSELING

Research is important in any field of endeavor, and it is no less important in counseling. There are two questions that arise when one considers the relationship between research and counseling: How much should a counselor base his or her approach on research findings? Should counselors proceed with theories and practices not yet validated by research? There are two points of view on the first question. One is

---

[2]For references that deal with the effectiveness of counseling, see Bergin (1971), Eysenck (1966), and Strupp (1971).

[3]For sources that deal with the multiple problems of accurately assessing the outcome of counseling, see Burck & Peterson (1975), Goldman (1976), and Osipow, Walsh, & Todi (1980).

that research in counseling has made important and significant contributions to the practice of counseling. The second is expressed by Belkin, who writes:

> The experimental method is faulty in not providing a reasonable facsimile of the dynamic counseling situation. No matter how many sophisticated scales we devise to measure empathy, genuineness, and concreteness, no matter how cleverly we test the counselor's efficacy and strategy, the fact remains that the hypothetical conditions of the experiment differ significantly from the unpredictable variables that occur in the counseling setting.[4]

Basically I agree with Belkin. Counseling is so complex that only bits and pieces of it can be studied, and even then, the results are often incomplete, conflictual, or inapplicable to many everyday counseling situations. This is not the fault of research but simply a reflection of the many and complex issues involved in counseling. Confounding and uncontrollable variables appear from all directions. There is the complexity of the person in counseling, the person of the counselor, the relationship between the person and the counselor, the environmental influences that affect both the person and the counselor, varying views of the nature and goals of counseling, the validity and reliability of measuring devices, and the complexities involved in studying counseling without significantly affecting the process.

This is not to say that research in counseling is meaningless. It has created interest and discussion in areas that have been taken for granted. It has made counselors more aware of the difficulties of counseling. It has stimulated a great deal of thought and discussion, which generates further ideas, hypotheses, and strategies. But to hold that research has reached a point where counselors should modify their theories and approaches according to the newest research findings is at least debatable, if not untenable.

There are also two positions concerning the second question, whether counselors should proceed with theories and practices not yet validated by research. One position states that it is perilous for counselors to proceed until there is scientific validation of their approaches. The second holds that it is perilous for counselors *not* to proceed until their approaches are empirically validated. I hold the latter point of view, which is expressed by Mahoney:

> As you might imagine, the bulk of today's therapists would be hard pressed if they were told to use only those techniques which have been

---

[4]Belkin (1980), p. 29. For authors who share the same concern, see Krumboltz (1967), Sprinthall (1975), and Goldman (1976).

experimentally examined. There are only a few such techniques and they are hardly sufficient for the wide range of problems which the therapist must face. . . . What do we do with the drug addict, the criminal, the schizophrenic? Can we ethically say, 'Listen, we're not ready for you yet—come back in about 20 years'? Or do we have the right, and perhaps the obligation, to offer them the best we have today, hoping that we can also learn from our experiences with them—so that today's best will be tomorrow's better?[5]

The theories and principles discussed in this book stem from an awareness of the relevant research and a reliance on clinical theory and experience.

COUNSELING THEORIES

Counselors who strongly identify with a particular theory might claim that their theory is the best theory of counseling. Others might say there is no "best" theory. What is "best" for one person in counseling may be "worst" for another. These counselors are likely to be eclectic; that is, they are very familiar with many theories and use them in conjunction with each other in ways that befit a particular person with a specific problem.

I think that counselors who are healthily eclectic are in a better position to deal with a wide range of people and problems than are those so immersed in one school of counseling that they exclude others. Being healthily eclectic means three things. It means that the counselor has a sound knowledge and understanding of the theories from which he or she draws. This is in contrast to a knowledge that is superficial, incomplete, or erroneous.[6] It means that the counselor has a basic philosophy of human behavior and uses it to tie the disparate parts of differing theories into a theoretical collage that is integrated and meaningful. And it means that the counselor fits his or her approach to the person in counseling and not vice versa. As Brammer states,

> Each helper must develop his or her own style and theory about helping because each person has had different life experiences and has different ways of looking at people. We may find others' assumptions similar to our own, but each helper must take responsibility for revamping them into his or her unique ideas and beliefs. Freud was not a Freudian, and Rogers was not a Rogerian; each was himself, and each built on the wisdom of the past. Admiring disciples of these men often gave their own explanations of the helping process a Freudian or Rogerian label.[7]

[5]Mahoney (1980), p. 498.
[6]For comprehensive discussions of the relationship between various personality theories and counseling, see Corsini and contributors (1979) and Sahakian (1976).
[7]Brammer (1979), p. 151.

For counselors who feel more comfortable and integrated adhering to one theoretical orientation, the principles discussed in this text are basic and underlie many, if not most, theoretical schools of thought. However, students and counselors who follow one theoretical approach to the exclusion of others must be careful to avoid the following pitfalls:

1. Perceiving the person and the person's problems in a manner that is restricted by one's own theoretical orientation. A person in counseling would be seen differently, and sometimes *very* differently, by a Freudian, Adlerian, Skinnerian, humanist, or Gestalt counselor. When a counselor sees only part of a person, the results of counseling can only be partial.
2. Stretching people in counseling so that they fit the theory, whether or not they do in reality. The causes and dynamics of all people's problems do not neatly fit any one theory. To insist that they do and to treat people accordingly can be countertherapeutic.
3. Turning counseling into an academic seminar in which people terminate counseling knowing more about a particular theorist than they know about themselves.

Interestingly, many of the founders of the major schools of counseling emphasized the tentative nature of their therapeutic approaches. They discouraged people from viewing theories and strategies as valid under every circumstance or with all people. For example, Freud wrote, "There are many ways and means of practicing psychotherapy. All that lead to recovery are good."[8] Jung wrote, "Theories in psychology are the very devil. It is true that we need certain points of view for orienting and heuristic value, but they should always be regarded as mere auxiliary concepts that can be laid aside at any time.... Learn your theories as well as you can, but put them aside when you touch the miracle of the living soul."[9]

THE BENEFITS OF STUDYING COUNSELING

There are numerous possible benefits of studying counseling, limited only by students' imaginations and resourcefulness. Most people who study counseling are planning to enter counseling as a profession. They have some idea of what counseling is and want to develop the competencies necessary to become effective counselors. Counseling courses and texts offer people the theories and principles necessary to

[8]Freud (1953), p. 259.
[9]Jung (1954), p. 7.

become effective counselors, and practicum experiences help them modify, test, and polish what they have learned in their courses.

Second, students may study counseling to become professional counselors but discover they no longer wish to pursue counseling as a career. Perhaps their personalities are better suited to a different kind of work or perhaps counseling is too challenging or isn't challenging enough for them. In any case, this insight is a worthwhile one and may save the person a great deal in terms of wasted time and energy.

A third benefit of studying counseling is that it includes many practical principles of human behavior. It encompasses theories of personality, principles of personal and social adjustment, dynamics of interpersonal relating, and elements of abnormal psychology. In studying how professional counselors function, people can learn how to relate with themselves and with other people more effectively. It is not unusual for a teacher of counseling to hear a student say "I took this course to learn how to help people but I think I learned as much about how to help *myself*." Whether a person chooses counseling as a career, the concepts learned in counseling can be personally helpful.

Another benefit occurs when people who study counseling decide that they could be helped by it. Counseling can help people with and without psychological problems. Many people who are studying counseling are in young adulthood, which is a very challenging period of development. During this time people are deciding on a career, whether to enter graduate school or work, whether to continue living at home or to move, whether to get married and, if so, to whom, whether to continue with a love relationship, or whether to pursue the values of society and their parents or to discard them for a less clearly defined but more personal value system. After studying counseling, one may decide that getting counseling at this time could help build a stronger foundation for life, regardless of whether one chooses counseling as a career.

No one can teach another how to do counseling, just as no one can teach another how to paint a beautiful picture. An art teacher can demonstrate how to mix colors, how to use different brushes for different effects, and how to use the canvas and lighting. Art teachers can *explain the principles* involved in art, but *they cannot teach* art. The same is true for counseling, because counseling is both a science and an art. The scientific principles can be taught, but it is up to the student to take these principles and put them on canvas.

This book presents and discusses many principles that underlie counseling. Each reader can take these principles, mix them with the dynamics of his or her personality, and eventually apply them. As with painting, the first efforts are rarely very good. What looked so simple in the book becomes very complex in the counseling room. But after a great deal of study and experience, the pictures begin to develop depth and beauty. And finally the counselor is no longer "painting by the numbers" but is painting with his or her being. At this point the counselor realizes two things: the paintings are getting progressively better, and there is an increasing awareness of how each painting could have been significantly improved. There is no perfect picture. That is the infinite challenge of counseling.

THOUGHT QUESTIONS

1. It is sometimes said that marriage can spoil a good friendship. It can also be said that learning techniques and theories of counseling can spoil a helpful personality. What does this statement mean, and what are your reactions to it?
2. Respond to the following statement: "Counseling doesn't help. I read that people on a waiting list at a mental health center did as well as, if not better than, the people who had received counseling."
3. A study has shown that counselors who sit with their back at a 30-degree angle to the back of their chair are judged to be more attentive and caring than those who sit in other positions. What does this finding mean to you on a practical basis?
4. Since counseling is more of an art than a science, counselors, as artists, are freer to "do their own thing" than are physicians or physicists. What is your response to this statement?
5. What could you discover about yourself or the field of counseling that would lead you to reevaluate your plan to become a counselor?

CHAPTER 2

Counseling as a New Experience

Counseling provides people with a new learning experience. For people whose behavior is in the normal range, counseling can provide a new environment that removes the blocks to better functioning. People whose problems stem from psychological disturbances can be helped by counseling to unlearn maladaptive ways of thinking, feeling, and responding and to learn adaptive ones. Referring to counseling, Jourard and Landsman write: "Humans have incredible learning capacity, and when environment changes, they have it in their power to learn new modes of conduct."[1]

If counseling fails to provide a new experience, it cannot be any more helpful than the person's previous experiences, which obviously weren't sufficiently helpful to keep the person out of counseling. To the extent that counseling is an echo of past advice, admonitions, encouragement, and feedback, it will be unhelpful. The fact that a professional counselor is the one providing the echoes does not mitigate, and perhaps may increase, the unhelpfulness of the situation.

Making counseling a different experience is more difficult than it sounds. If a person in counseling is 30 years old and the counselor is also 30, there are 60 years of echoes in the room. It is likely that each person has grown in the same social environment, which prescribes what people do when one of them has a psychological difficulty. It is no

---

[1]Jourard & Landsman (1980), p. 402.

wonder many people enter counseling with a look and an attitude that says "Here we go again." And, unfortunately, they are not always wrong in their assumption.

It takes great awareness and sensitivity for a counselor to rid the counseling room of echoes of the past. Counselors must be aware of how society reacts and responds to specific psychological problems. For example, what are depressed people in our society likely to hear and receive from others? When someone is having an extramarital affair, a homosexual experience, a difficult time at school or work, a stressful marriage, or a turbulent romance, what response is likely from his or her significant others?

Even when these people keep their problems quiet, what echoes are bouncing around in their heads about themselves and their behavior? Most unhelpful feedback that people receive comes from within them. As a result of these echoes, people tell themselves "There's no use talking to others about it; I already know what they're going to say," or "You can't tell me anything I haven't already told myself."

It also takes great awareness and sensitivity for counselors to recognize how *they* have been indoctrinated with echoes. As they listen to a person relate an extramarital affair, they may reflexively tell themselves, "Oh, this isn't good. How am I going to get him (her) to terminate it?" When they listen to somebody who is depressed, they ask themselves, "How can I assure this person things will turn out all right?" When a person shares a very complicated situation, the counselor asks himself or herself, "What answer can I give this person? How can I reduce the anxiety?" Yet these responses are the exact ones that these people have received from others they have known longer, loved more, and trusted more than this stranger, the counselor.

The challenge for counselors is to find the ongoing answers to two questions: How can I be a qualitatively different significant other to this person? How can I create an environment—a relationship—that is significantly different than any presently experienced by this person? Answering these challenges and putting the answers into behavior is a journey that is interrupted at every turn by the accumulated years of echoes in the lives of both the counselor and the person in counseling.

All theorists agree explicitly or implicitly that counseling must be a new experience that provides opportunities for people to perceive themselves and life differently, to experience and express their feelings differently, and to behave in ways that are new for them. I shall discuss some of the key ways counseling can provide a new experience that includes a new kind of environment and relationship for the person.

RECOGNIZING INTERNAL CONFLICTS

Counseling helps people recognize that the majority of their problems stem from unresolved internal conflicts rather than from external situations. The source of the vast majority of problems that bring people into counseling resides in the person's personality. Unfortunately, people usually think the cause of their problem lies outside themselves. Most people enter counseling with an attitude of "If it weren't for. . . . " They explicitly or implicitly state "If it weren't for my boss, my work would be a pleasure"; "If it weren't for my mother, I could move away and have a great life"; "If it weren't for my husband's drinking, we would have a very happy family"; "If it weren't for my wife's social aspirations, I could relax and enjoy life."

One of the first steps a counselor must take is to help the person realize that the counselor cannot do anything to help the person's boss, mother, husband, or wife. The focus must be on the person in counseling. The question for the person is "Are there some changes *you* can make in your behavior that will help alleviate the problem?"

Sometimes people answer with a very definite "No!" What they are saying is that they have no plans to change their behaviors, or at least not to do so until the other person does. Other people answer "I don't know. I've never thought of it that way." These people are often more willing to consider changing their behavior if it would prove helpful. Others may answer "Well, I guess I could be more patient" or "I guess sometimes I exaggerate the conflicts and don't see his (her) good points." This person may be the closest to the source of conflict, although he or she is still not on target. Some people attribute the cause of their distress to their symptoms: "If it weren't for my insomnia (depression, anxiety attacks, fears, insecurities, drinking), life would be great."

Before contacting a counselor, all these people discussed their problem with others or at least racked their brains for a solution. But their efforts were doomed to fail because they were asking the wrong question, which invariably elicited the wrong answer. This created a sense of frustration and sometimes despair. Usually the person doesn't make an appointment with a counselor until the frustration reaches a peak.

Counseling can teach people that most psychological problems emanate from within, and the environment is merely the arena in which the battles are waged. Many, if not most, situational and interpersonal problems are externalized manifestations and reflections of internal conflicts. This is not to say that external situations and relationships play no part in a person's problems. External factors activate the internal conflicts; that is, they act as grist for the mill. But the mill was there first. People misunderstand this dynamic, however, when they say "My job must be the cause of my problem because I was fine until I got promoted." More likely, the stress of the promotion activated an internal dynamic that was latent until that point. For this reason, counselors can recognize that removing a person from an environment rarely solves his or her problem. For example, if a woman is experiencing difficulties at work, the automatic solution is not to change jobs. If a man's marriage is causing him distress, the logical solution is not necessarily a separation. These people may experience great relief after a change of environments (which they inaccurately perceive as proof that they made the correct decision), but they are likely to carry their problem into the next environment.

There are times, however, when the environment has become so intractably destructive that no counseling can occur as long as the person remains in it. It is also possible, in some cases, that the environment is objectively damaging, and the person can be helped to make the appropriate changes.

The following are three internal factors that can cause conflicts that rebound off the environment, giving the appearance that they originated there.

Negative self-appraisal

When people consciously or unconsciously harbor negative feelings about themselves, they are vulnerable in their interactions with the environment. Examples of negative self-appraisal are "I am stupid," "I am unattractive," "I am unsophisticated," "I am immature," "I am lazy," "I am selfish," "I am uncaring," "I am cold," "I am needy," "I am weak," "I am sexually inadequate," "I am immoral," "I am insecure," "I am uninteresting."

Negative self-appraisals are like fuses waiting to be ignited by the environment. When a situation occurs that lights one of these fuses, it causes fight or flight behavior. For example, when a woman declines an invitation to go on a date with a man, she may ignite his "I am uninteresting" fuse, which causes him to "tell her off" or to vow never to ask another woman for a date. A man without negative self-appraisals would either not give the refusal a second thought or would have assumed that, whatever the woman's reasons were, they did not reflect negatively on him.

The more negative self-appraisals people have, the more problems they will experience for the following reasons. First, a significant amount of their time and energy will be spent fighting with or fleeing from people and situations. Second, their relationships with their environment will be increasingly combustible because as they fight or flee, they are creating objective problems with the environment. Third, because they see only the flame coming from the environment and not the fuse within themselves, they continually blame the environment for their problems, which ensures that the problems will continue unabated.

Psychological imperatives

Some people have psychological imperatives; that is, they have certain "musts" in life that are compelling and absolute. They feel that if they do not accomplish a "must," they will be less worthwhile and life will be less livable. There are four types of psychological imperatives: personal, interpersonal, social, and destructive.

The following are some examples of common personal imperatives: "I must be kind . . . attractive . . . strong . . . correct . . . sexual . . . asexual . . . loyal . . . unselfish . . . happy . . . carefree . . . successful . . . brave . . . loving . . . special."

Some examples of interpersonal imperatives are "I must be treated fairly . . . liked . . . loved . . . appreciated . . . rewarded . . . entertained . . . paid attention to . . . sought after . . . spoken well of . . . admired." "You must be perfect . . . docile . . . agreeable . . . sexual . . . kind . . . reliable . . . beautiful . . . interesting . . . industrious . . . religious."

Examples of social imperatives are "I must go to the right schools . . . have the right friends . . . enter a particular profession . . . be heterosexual . . . be promoted . . . make a certain salary . . . have a certain position . . . get married . . . have a family."

Destructive imperatives are generally the opposite of any of the previous ones. For example, "I must be stupid . . . unhappy . . . weak"; "I must be treated unfairly . . . ignored . . . rejected"; "I must fail in work . . . in school . . . in marriage."

People with psychological imperatives do not relate comfortably and realistically with their environment. They place undue pressure on themselves and expect people to treat them in ways that are inappropriate or unreasonable. The tension that "must" behavior creates both within them and within their environment causes problems. These people do not assume responsibility for the problems, but assure themselves that if only life met their "musts," everything would be fine.

Conflicting needs

Some people have contrary needs that are in conflict with each other. The more acceptable need is usually conscious, while the less acceptable one is subconscious or unconscious. The result is that these people are in conflict with themselves. In other words, need A is in conflict with need Z. Instead of recognizing the conflict as being waged within themselves, these people admit to need A and project need Z onto the environment. In this way they can deny responsibility for need Z and at times even be "forced" by the environment to get it met.

For example, a woman might have a strong need to be independent and an almost equally strong need to be dependent, which she represses. She protests that she does not want to remain at home with her parents, but they are putting so much pressure on her to remain that she feels she must. She blames her parents for manipulating her but at the same time accedes to their "manipulations" with only a token struggle. She may enter counseling to get help extracting herself from the clutches of her parents when in fact she is where she wants to be.

An example of conflicting needs simply generating heat in the environment without the repressed one being met is seen in a priest who consciously enjoys the priesthood but who unconsciously has a strong need to get married and have a family. In counseling, every time the counselor comes even remotely close to uncovering this need, the man projects it onto the counselor: "I know you think I should leave the priesthood and get married, and that concerns me because I need a counselor who respects my vocation and who wants to help me grow within that context." The priest is disowning his unconscious need and accusing the counselor of owning it. Brought to its logical conclusion, the projection will cause the priest to terminate counseling before he has to face his need and find a counselor who will be "more accepting" of who he is. Of course, he will never find an effective counselor who is "more accepting" and consequently gives up on counseling.

The following are some typical conflicting needs:

Independence versus dependence

Intimacy versus safety

Humility versus prestige

Sexuality versus chastity

Believing versus doubting

Belonging versus being free

Perseverance versus the need to get out of damaging situations

Altruism versus selfishness

Achieving versus relaxing

The inner tension these conflicts create spills onto the environment, and the environment is made into the antagonist. The person accuses the environment: "Why are you causing this stress in me?" In fact, the person is causing the stress within himself or herself.

Counseling can be a new experience for these people because they have lived their lives thinking that the cause of their problem was either their environment or some inherent, intractable defect within themselves. People are often surprised to learn that they created the vast majority of their conflicts and that they can learn to strengthen their inner weakness so the remainder of their lives can be significantly more satisfying and fulfilling.

DEALING WITH REALITY

Counseling is an opportunity for dealing more effectively with reality. Before entering counseling, many people have dealt poorly with reality. They think they are perceiving reality clearly and dealing with it well, but their problems contradict this belief. Not only have people who enter counseling been hiding from and manipulating reality to diminish their anxieties and meet their needs, but they have often been able to garner the support of significant others to help them avoid reality. There are three ways people commonly deal poorly with reality.

Avoidance

People become skilled at avoiding the present. Much of their time is spent reliving the past or planning the future. They revel in or mourn their pasts and fear or look forward to their futures. The past may be five years ago or five minutes ago, and the future can be five years from now or five minutes from now. Meanwhile, they never have a present because it continually slips into the past without being used. The more inept they are at dealing with the present, the more their past haunts them because they didn't handle it well when it was their present and the more they fear the future because they have no present upon which to build.

Commonly, when people enter counseling, all they can talk about is yesterday and tomorrow. They may fiercely avoid the present, especially as it exists between them and the counselor. Counselors can help introduce these people to the present. When people become aware of the here-and-now (this moment in time), they will begin to be aware of who they really are, who others really are, and what the situation really is. This is so because their whole being is now focused on the present instead of one eye on the past and one on the future. To do this, people must be totally open to their here-and-now experience: to see it with both eyes; to listen to it with both ears; to examine it with their brains; and to feel it with their hearts. This exquisite awareness causes them to react, and if they do so simply and naturally, growth will occur. In fact, the main way to grow is to deal with the present moment because the past is no more and the future is not yet. People get themselves and others into trouble when they avoid the present or react to it in an ingenuine way.

The significant others in people's lives usually have been unable to help them deal with the present because of their own inability to do so. The vast majority of the communication between people in counseling and their significant others has involved the past and the future. They have a tacit agreement not to bring up the present because it is too new, unchartered, and unsculpted. While significant others have asked the person "why" questions ("Why did you do that?"), counselors ask "what" and "how" questions to bring the person into the present. "What" questions are "What is going on inside of you right now?" or "What is going on between us right now?" A "how" question is "How are you avoiding thoughts and feelings that you find difficult to experience and to share?"

As people learn to stare unflinchingly at the present and deal with it effectively, the inappropriate anxiety attached to the past and future dissolves and is replaced by the real, constructive anxiety of the present. This anxiety is celebrated because it is the fuel that will help the individual take risks necessary to become a fuller person.[2]

Overgeneralization

People overgeneralize personal qualities to the extent that they violate reality. They view themselves as kind when they are also unkind. They view themselves as intelligent, but they are intelligent in some ways and stupid in others. They see themselves as altruistic when they are sometimes selfish, as open and freeing when at times they are closed and manipulative. They perceive themselves as uncaring when they sometimes care deeply, as impervious when they can be quite vulnerable, as cold when they possess genuine warmth as well.

They perceive others (parents, spouse, friends) as ideal when in fact they are only human. They see others as well-meaning when at times they are not, as trustworthy when they are sometimes untrustworthy, as beautiful when they are sometimes ugly. They also see others as hostile

---

[2]Further discussion of the importance of dealing with the present can be found in Perls (1969).

when they are benevolent, as manipulative when they are also freeing, as neurotic when they are not, as dishonest when they are also honest.

Blaming

People have blamed themselves or others for the stresses in their lives. Blaming is a very subtle way of avoiding reality. When people blame themselves for a problem, they need not confront the other people involved with their thoughts and feelings about the situation. When they blame others, they do not have to deal with their own part in contributing to the problem. When two or more people experience a problem, it is most likely that all of them are contributing to the situation in some active or passive way. In almost all human problems there is "contributory negligence" whereby the people involved are both perpetrators and victims, oppressors and oppressed.

Most people who enter counseling are either self-blamers or other-blamers and are unaware that they have a third option. The third option is to view their problematic situations realistically and address themselves to the mutuality of the problem. In other words, they can accept responsibility for contributing to the problem without accepting blame, and they can help others see their responsibility without forcing them to accept blame. The person's attitude is "If I do this differently and you do that differently, it may solve our problem" versus "I'm sorry; I won't do that again" or "Until you can see the situation is your fault, we can't resolve this problem." People can learn through counseling that blaming may temporarily reduce anxiety but, in the long run, it compounds problems.

DEVELOPING INSIGHT

Counseling is an experience that invites people to discover who they really are and to live accordingly. When people know who they really are, they are aware of their specific needs, values, attitudes, motives, strengths, and weaknesses. Because they know who they are, they can chart each day according to their own psychological map. This places them in a position for maximum growth and happiness. However, self-awareness in itself is not sufficient for growth. People must not know only who they are but also be able to relate with others according to this real self.

Most people enter counseling with one of three problems regarding who they are: Some know who they are, but have created a counterfeit image to present to others. Some think they know who they are, but really don't. Others are confused about who they are.

Counterfeit images

Those people who enter counseling *knowing* reasonably well who they are may lack the courage to put their real selves into action. They create an image or public self to present to others. Their image may be that they are generous, agreeable, strong, affectionate, good humored, industrious, logical, independent, or intelligent. They may even present different images to different people, which further compounds the problem.

These people believe their images, and not their real selves, have attracted people. They fear that if their real selves emerge, the significant others in their lives will see strangers who are less attractive, if not obnoxious.

Counseling can demonstrate not only the marked discrepancy between who these people really are and their images but also the discrepancy that often occurs among their various images. Counseling can also help people realize the tremendous psychological cost of trying to maintain and balance ill-fitting images. Once people recognize clearly what they have been doing and can appreciate how it has caused them unnecessary anxiety, they are in a better position to choose whether to allow their true selves to emerge or to continue with their images.

Psychological filters

Some people who enter counseling *think* they know who they are, but they really don't. Their real self has become buried beneath layers of psychological filters that have successfully sifted out their true identities.

One of the psychological filters is *indoctrination*, which comes generally from society and specifically from parents and teachers. Indoctrination is based on the injunction "This is who you are; this is who you will be; and this is what life is about." This injunction is taped and played an endless number of times until the child and adolescent can repeat it automatically and live it out. Indoctrination is different from education. Education is based on the attitude "Let's find out who you are so that you can decide who you want to become; you will learn about life as it evolves."

A person who has been indoctrinated may have been given the injunction "You *are* special, agreeable, asexual, religious, and athletic; you *will be* successful, industrious, cautious, obedient to the church, a leader, and a family man; and *life is* good, as long as you don't enjoy it." As this person develops, he recognizes that he can neither possess all these qualities nor possess any one of them to the degree to which he has been commissioned. He then starts pretending to others that he possesses these qualities. After pretending for a certain period of time, he begins to fool himself as well. By the time he is 25 years old, the indoctrination is complete; that is, he thinks he is what he pretends to be. He is like a person who has never looked in a mirror and must rely totally on others' descriptions of his appearance. If and when he finally looks in a mirror, he will find he is better than he thought, worse than he thought, or simply much different than he thought. In any case, he cannot really grow until he is introduced to who he is.

Another common psychological filter is the *acquisition of roles*. All people have been assigned roles by society. Some people remain true to themselves despite their assignments, but others give up who they are and assume their role as their identity. For example, instead of being a person who is a physician, a woman may *become* a physician and equate her identity with this role. The role dictates that she must always be correct, gentle, and available to her patients.

The following are some of the problems that she experiences as a result of assuming the societally defined role of physician. If she must always be correct, she cannot admit mistakes to herself, her colleagues, or her patients. This will cause both interpersonal difficulties and a tendency to continue making the same mistakes. If she must be gentle, she must repress and deny feelings of an ungentle nature. The frustrations, confusions, and angers that normally occur in every occupation become submerged and fester within her. If she must always be available to her patients, she will deprive herself and her family of the important time they all need for personal growth and recreation.

Counseling can help people who have overidentified with their roles gradually peel them back and discover who they are. They will then be freed to define their roles according to who they are and not let their roles define them.

Confusion

Some people enter counseling *confused* as to who they are. As one person stated, "If you put me in a lineup, I couldn't pick myself out." These people may be genuinely confused because they see so many images when they look in the mirror that they don't know which one reflects their true identity. But more often these people know deep down who they are, what they want, and why they are upset, but they don't want to admit it to themselves. To help them keep this true identity at a distance, they *create* confusion. As long as they are confused and successfully confuse others, they don't have to experience the anxiety that would arise if they allowed their true self to emerge.

A woman may spend the majority of a counseling session listing all the things in her marriage she is unhappy about and how she envies the single women she knows. At the end of the session she states "Oh, I'm so confused, I don't know what is happening." In fact, she is not confused at all but avoids facing reality by artificially injecting confusion into the situation. She doesn't want to admit that she no longer loves her husband and wants to end the marriage.

If counseling is to be a new experience, it must introduce people to who they really are. People in counseling have been told over and over again how to live up to their images better. They have seldom been invited to reexamine their images to see if they are simply phantoms of a self that never existed or no longer exists. Counseling can introduce people to who they really are so they can begin to live their own lives and stop living the lives of people they are not.

BEGINNING A NEW RELATIONSHIP

Counseling offers people a new kind of relationship. An effective counselor is psychologically healthy, is altruistically concerned about the person in counseling, has a sound knowledge of human behavior, and has developed the skills to help people. It is unlikely that people entering counseling have someone with all these qualities with whom to relate on any meaningful level. Some people in their lives are concerned about them, but in a more passing, pragmatic way. Others are genuinely concerned, but don't possess much better psychological health than the person in counseling. Still others in the person's life have a genuine concern and may be psychologically healthy, but lack the knowledge of human behavior and/or the therapeutic skills to be of any real help to the person. Although counselors are not perfect, they should be better prepared to afford a healthy and helpful relationship than most of the others with whom the person relates. There are several qualities of a counseling relationship one does not often encounter in other relationships.

Counselor honesty

The counselor responds with benevolent honesty. Typically, people in counseling have received feedback that was honest but too harsh to accept or feedback that was benevolent but not sufficiently honest to be helpful.

The combination of honesty and kindness is powerful and productive, and the person in counseling may have experienced it rarely. Honesty means that the counselor reflects back to the person an accurate, untinted image of who the person is. Weaknesses as well as strengths are pointed out.

Counselors convey this honesty with a benevolence that flows from their basic liking of the individual and the wish to be helpful. The kindness is manifested by the counselor's warmth, carefully chosen vocabulary, and invitation to accept or reject the validity of their honest reflections. This is different from the "I'm hurting you for your own good" kind of honesty that the person is used to receiving and that is followed by a psychological assault.

Understanding

The counselor genuinely tries to understand in order to be helpful. The person in counseling probably has related with few genuinely understanding people. Many people don't want to understand because they would have to respond differently than they would prefer. Instead of understanding, people typically get advice, a lecture, a scolding, consternation, revulsion, a pep talk, impatience, moralizing, or rejection.

People in counseling are surprised when they begin to relate to the counselor and receive none of these responses. They begin to relate their problems either girded for battle or cowering in fear, waiting for the ax to fall. As they realize that the counselor is simply trying to understand what they are saying and is not judging or waiting to rush in and fix things, people can gradually relax and live an experience they have rarely encountered.

Person honesty

Counselors offer the person in counseling the opportunity to be honest. People in counseling have a need to be honest in two ways. First, they need to face the innermost thoughts, feelings, and experiences that they have buried because they were anxiety producing. In being completely honest with themselves, people feel a sense of relief and integrity they may have never before experienced.

Second, people in counseling also need to be honest with others. They need to share the positive and negative thoughts and feelings that have remained unexpressed. As people become stronger through counseling, honesty becomes a part of their daily repertoire of responses.

Risk taking

The counselor offers a relationship in which people can take risks and not suffer damaging consequences. There are very few relationships outside of counseling in which people can take risks, fail, and not have to pay a price, such as a lost job, a demotion, a poor grade, a fractured relationship, or a loss of self-esteem or reputation. In counseling, people can overshoot or undershoot their responses and the only price they pay is the honest reactions of the counselor couched in the counselor's continuing positive regard. When people in counseling eventually realize and trust the tremendous freedom that they have to experiment and take risks, growth becomes greatly accelerated. They learn that they can practice in counseling and increase their confidence to try their new behaviors outside of counseling.

New responses

The counselor offers new responses to the person in counseling. People who are in counseling have received the same advice, admonitions, and emotional responses over and over again. The people they have confided in have "helping cassettes" that play recorded messages. The following responses have been heard scores of times and now have little or no effect:

> You need to get your mind off yourself. Maybe you should do some volunteer work with people who have some *real* problems.
> You're too sensitive and take things too personally. You should learn to laugh more at life and not take yourself so seriously.
> I know you are grieving about your loved one's death. But he is suffering no longer. I'm sure he is happier than we are, and you will see him soon.
> Looks aren't everything, and being popular isn't the most important thing in life. You're beautiful inside, and that's all that counts.
> You should get your priorities straightened out because you're starting to lose touch with what's really important in life.
> Sex isn't everything.

Each of these "recorded messages" may be absolutely true. But such statements are seldom, if ever, helpful for at least three reasons. First, they do not touch the underlying causes of the person's problematic behavior. Second, words alone rarely have a healing effect but must be vehicles of empathy, warmth, strength, and hope in order to motivate people to change their behavior. Third, when people have repeatedly heard the same nostrums, they tune them out.

When counselors offer a new relationship, it need not include dramatic happenings. It could simply entail a smile that says "I know how you're feeling" or a demeanor that says "I'm not too busy to share part of my life with you," "I'm not so upset with my own problems that I can't be pleasant to you," "I'm not so insecure that you will be a threat to me," or "I'm not so needy as to expect something from you in return."

For many people entering counseling, any one of these expressions could be a new experience, and ten minutes of a new experience is worth more than ten hours of echoes.

INCREASING PSYCHOLOGICAL FREEDOMS

Counseling offers people a chance to increase their psychological freedoms. Most people who enter counseling lack psychological freedom in at least one significant area. It is possible that many of them did not possess a great deal of freedom to begin with, which contributed to their problems. Others may have had freedom at one time, but it decreased as their problems increased.

In counseling, they can discover the specific freedoms that they lack and work to increase them. The first step is for people to learn that they give themselves psychological freedom and take it away. This is an important insight because people tend to view their oppression as imposed by others. People who enter counseling often lack one or more of the following four basic psychological freedoms to one degree or another.

Freedom to acknowledge imperfection

Imperfections are weaknesses, faults, and mistakes. Many people have been taught that they should be perfect and that the shortest route to perfection is to deny imperfection. As a result they cannot say "I'm wrong," "I made a mistake," "I don't know the answer," "It's my fault," "I'm confused," or "I'm sorry."

Because they have trouble admitting imperfections to themselves and others, they create several problems.

1. They continue to make the same mistakes because they have given themselves no reasons to stop. The bunkers they construct to hide their imperfections also act as barriers to intimacy; consequently, the more hidden imperfections they have, the lonelier they will be.

2. They are always on guard lest someone penetrate their defenses and spot an imperfection. Their chronic vigilance prevents them from relaxing and enjoying life and consumes so much energy that little remains for more creative pursuits.

3. They have difficulty feeling empathy for others because they do not know what it is to feel imperfect. This lack of empathy will hinder their ability to relate with others in a mutually fulfilling way.

Counseling can give these people permission to be imperfect and help them understand that the path to growth is necessarily marbled with imperfection. As these people grow in their acceptance of their humanity, they are freer to enjoy life.

Freedom to assume responsibility for one's behavior

People who enter counseling often have not assumed sufficient responsibility for their behavior. Instead of accepting responsibility for what they think, they present their thoughts as if the thoughts were someone else's or as if they were just kidding. Rather than owning what they feel, they camouflage their feelings and allow them to leak out in anonymous ways. They do not accept the consequences of their behavior; instead, they blame others, their unhappy childhoods, or their "bad genes."

These people do not make their own decisions, but seek and take the advice of others; so if their decisions are poor, they don't have to assume responsibility for them. They do not keep the reins of their lives in their own hands, but hand over one or both reins to someone else and then complain that they are at the mercy of others.

The problem with not assuming total responsibility for one's behavior is that nothing will ever change. These people perennially wait for something good to happen to them or for someone to rescue them because the price for irresponsibility is helplessness. Counseling can demonstrate to these people that they are responsible for all their behavior and help them recognize that the advantages of assuming responsibility far outweigh the superficial disadvantages.

Freedom to disappoint others

People who enter counseling often have problems that were caused by their inability to disappoint someone. Usually they are able to disappoint casual acquaintances but become helpless when it comes to disappointing people they love and who love them. They have been "appointed" by significant others to behave in certain ways, and they lack the courage to "unappoint" themselves.

Two types of appointments are possible: major and minor. Minor appointments include being expected to spend a vacation at home, to share the personal parts of one's life with another, to help others when they request it, and to maintain friendships that have outlived their growth potential. Major appointments occur when a person is expected to go to college, to live at home until married, to live close by, to choose a specific career, to get married or marry a particular person, to practice the family's religion, to take a promotion, or to remain in a life commitment that has become destructive.

Many people feel helpless in the face of appointments. They abide by the situation despite their deeper needs, wishes, and values and eventually begin to suffocate. They begin to resent both the people who have appointed them and themselves for being so weak. Other people have grown accustomed to acquiescing to appointments and don't realize they are doing so. Acquiescence for them has become automatic.

Counseling can help these individuals recognize each appointment and give them an opportunity to reassess its appropriateness. If the appointment is contrary to their needs, counseling can help them develop the courage to disappoint others and reappoint themselves to a happier and more fulfilling life.

Freedom to allow contrary feelings to exist simultaneously

Many people in counseling lack the freedom to allow contrary feelings to coexist because the tension this creates appears to be unbearable. Consequently, they repress one of the contrary feelings in order to produce emotional unanimity.

Many people who enter counseling say they either love their spouses or hate them, are proud of their friends or jealous, have faith in God or do not believe in God, define themselves as brave or frightened. The truth is that feelings are almost never unanimous. The conscious anxiety people rid themselves of by repressing one of the contrary feelings only returns to haunt them in some other way. For example, the woman who "adores" her husband cannot understand why she is sexually uninterested, or the man who unequivocally believes in God cannot understand why he is terrified of death. If both these people could get in touch with their ambivalent and equivocal feelings, their behavior would be understandable to them, which would be an important step in solving the problem.

A second problem that arises with forced unanimity of feelings is that it erases conscious tension, which is necessary for growth. Much growth-producing tension stems from ambivalence of affect. For example, a man who "worships" his children is incapable of being a good father. Because he cannot entertain critical thoughts and feelings toward his children, he is ineligible to challenge, discipline, or present difficult reality to them or to allow them to suffer and to fail. If he had a more realistic attitude that entailed both negative and positive aspects, he could become an effective father.

CORRECTING MISCONCEPTIONS

Many people who enter counseling harbor misconceptions about their behavior, and these misconceptions often contribute significantly to their problems. Moreover, their misconceptions are frequently reinforced because they are shared by large segments of society. Counseling may be the first opportunity that people have to consider the validity of their misconceptions and to replace them with more accurate understandings. When this occurs, people are freed to make decisions that are more advantageous to them. There are several common misconceptions people bring to counseling.

Insoluble problems

People think their problems are insoluble for three reasons. They have honestly looked for solutions but lack the competencies either to see solutions or to do anything about the ones they see. Second, they do not *want* to see a solution because if they did, they would have to assume responsibility for making the appropriate changes in their lives. Third, others have agreed with these people's assessment of the situation because it appears accurate or because it is easier to agree than to disagree.

For example, a woman may come to counseling complaining that her husband is abusive but that she cannot leave him. She says that her religious beliefs forbid her to divorce, that her parents and friends would disown her, that she has four children who need a father, and that she has only a high school education and no marketable skills. She has constructed four airtight walls around herself and is dying from lack of oxygen. The way she has it set up, she *is* in an impossible situation, and all her friends agree that this is true. She approaches the counselor with the paradoxical attitude: "There's nothing that can be done about my problem, but I'm here for you to do something about it."

In fact, there are at least five steps she can take to solve her problem if she so desires. (1) She can try to get her husband to join her in counseling. (2) She can get counseling for herself. (3) She can discuss her problem with a clergyman, who may rectify her misgivings about separation or divorce being out of the question. (4) She can go to the appropriate social service agencies, where she can be directed to jobs, job training, child-care services, and other resources. (5) She can get group counseling or join a woman's group in order to obtain support and encouragement. Although she may methodically and reflexively thwart the counselor's attempts to help her see that her walls are movable, there are several solutions to her problem that she may eventually consider if she is suffering enough stress and can receive sufficient support.

Unbreakable promises

They believe they must abide by their promises, regardless of the damage they or others are experiencing because of them. Society tends to support this concept, especially when promises involve important areas such as work commitments, friendships, and marriage.

Of course, as a general principle, it is better to keep promises than to break them. But it is unhelpful for a promise to become more important than the reason for which it was made. A commitment should never be made to a promise, but rather to justice, growth, and love. For example, a marriage promise is made to aid the partners in their pursuit of growing in a sense of justice and love for each other. If justice is replaced by injustice, love turns to hate, and this situation is obviously irreversible despite honest efforts, then the marriage promise has outlived its purposefulness. To remain in the relationship simply to keep a promise signifies that the person lacks sufficient understanding of the purpose of promises or has a vested interest in remaining in a destructive situation.

There are other types of promises, such as family promises: a young man may promise to join his father's business after graduating from college. There are personal promises: a person may promise to tour Europe with a roommate. There are religious promises: a priest may promise to remain active as a clergyman for the rest of his life.

Although promises can be helpful, they can also be unhelpful in three ways: when a person views a promise as an end in itself rather than as a means to an end, when the person at the time of the promise did not have sufficient self-knowledge or sufficient awareness of the situation to make an authentic decision, and when a promise is used to lock a person in an objectively damaging situation.

Society tends to reward keeping promises. Even when people are seriously damaged by remaining in the commitments, they are likely to be viewed by a large segment of society as loyal and persevering; people who leave destructive situations are often viewed as weak and selfish. Consequently, people who are in a destructive commitment are caught in a double bind. If they keep their promise, they will continue to be damaged. If they break it, they risk being viewed with scorn by society, including many of their loved ones.

Counseling may be the first time a person is able to evaluate the reasonableness of keeping a promise that is causing significant damage. If one can place one's promises in a proper perspective and clearly view the psychological and moral damage that is being perpetrated, one may find the courage in counseling to move away from the promise to a more just and growth-producing alternative.

Victims

Many people present themselves in counseling as victims of a destructive situation or person. Under closer scrutiny, however, it may become clear that, while they are victims, they are consenting victims who allow themselves to be victimized because it permits them to fulfill some destructive need.

When consenting victims complain to others about their plight, they are likely to be met with sympathy, which serves to reinforce their perception of themselves as helpless victims. For example, a woman may complain to a friend that her husband comes home drunk almost every night and ruins the evening for the entire family. Her friend commiserates with her and offers a litany of suggestions, which are all dismissed as unworkable. It could be that the woman has a vested interest in her husband's coming home drunk. Deep down she may find sex repulsive and have a strong need to feel important to her children. As long as her husband comes home drunk, she is rescued from having sexual relations with him and is placed in a position of utmost importance to her children. She protects them from his drunken behavior and assumes the role and responsibilities of both parents, making her children reliant on her entirely.

In a real sense, she would rather have him arrive home drunk than sober; consequently, she makes no serious attempts to confront him with his destructive behavior. She views herself as an understanding wife who must make the best of a difficult situation. This is the concept she conveys to others and for which society rewards her.

Being a consenting victim can be a specific trait; for example, the woman whose husband comes home drunk may be a consenting victim only in her marriage. Or it can be a general trait in that she is a consenting victim in her relationship with her parents and her boss as well.

Unwilling victims could not foresee the damage they eventually suffered. They learn from the situation and take steps to see that it does not reoccur. Consenting victims tend to remain in situations of ongoing damage or tend to leave one damaging situation only to enter another.

While unwilling victims are likely to say "I learned one thing; I'll never get myself into a situation like that again," consenting victims are more likely to lament "Why do these things always happen to me?"

Counseling can help consenting victims realize what they are doing, why they are doing it, and how they can make some basic changes within themselves so that being a victim will never be the lesser evil.

Inaccuracies

People think their perceptions and interpretations are accurate. When they communicate their view of reality to others, it is commonly accepted as factual. For example, Mary complains to her mother about her husband: "Bill has become so irritable with me lately, and I can't understand why." Her mother is likely to spend a good deal of time trying to help her understand what Bill's problem is. By doing so, she directly reinforces her daughter's notion that her perception of Bill's behavior is accurate. But it may not be. Her perception or interpretation may be inaccurate in one of four ways.

First, Bill is not irritable. Mary is making unreasonable demands on him, and he is healthily declining to meet them. Mary would rather view his behavior as "irritable" than her demands as inordinate.

Second, Bill is irritable, not just with his wife, but with everyone. Mary ignores his irritability toward others or rationalizes that it is justified. She focuses on his irritability toward her and makes a personal issue of it. She asks "What's wrong with me? What's wrong with him? What's wrong with our relationship?" instead of seeing the problem as broader than that. Her attempts to answer these questions lead to frustration, which only complicates the situation.

Third, Bill is irritable and his wife knows why. She has been pressuring him lately to move to the suburbs, a move that will create significant financial and geographical burdens on the family. Mary fails to see that Bill's irritability increases with the pressure she exerts. Since she does not wish to view herself as the cause of his problem, she cannot see any cause and effect relationship between her behavior and Bill's irritability.

Fourth, Bill has always been irritable; it is nothing new. Bill has been irritable all his life, but Mary views it more clearly now. This is so because she is growing in psychological strength and is less inclined to deny the presence of his irritability, or she needs to scapegoat him as a means of explaining some problems that she has begun to experience.

Unfortunately, the few people Mary can confide in automatically assume that her perceptions and interpretations are accurate and inadvertently reinforce them. By the time she seeks professional help, she is more convinced than ever that her views are accurate. Perhaps for the first time in her life she will be afforded the opportunity to evaluate the accuracy of her perceptions and/or interpretations and learn how they have caused her many avoidable problems.

Self-deceptions

They are convinced that they know exactly what they are doing. Most people are unaware of how they are fooling themselves. They fail to realize that they have two hands and that sometimes the left hand does not know what the right hand is doing. This occurs because each hand is serving a different master. Many people do not understand this dynamic and view problems simply as having fallen into their lives as the result of bad fortune rather than bad decisions. The following are some common examples of one hand working at cross purposes with the other.

A man explains that he never remains with a job very long because he has yet to find one that really challenges him. He is aware that he is looking for challenge. He is unaware that he quits because he doubts his ability to do well once the honeymoon period on a job is over.

A woman complains that she has had a medley of unhappy love affairs and laments her bad fortune in finding the right man. She knows that she wants to be loved, but she does not know that she is currently incapable of giving love. While she beckons with one hand for men to come closer to her, she pushes them away with the other.

In these examples, the people are convinced that they know exactly what they want and what they are doing. It may not be until they enter counseling that they can discover that they are creating their own obstacles and frustrations because their needs and feelings are moving them in opposite directions at the same time. When people become aware of this, they are in a better position to make conscious, reasonable choices that will further their growth and sense of satisfaction in life.

SUMMARY

Although it is impossible for counseling to be a totally new experience, this should be its aim. Counselors may find it helpful to ask themselves questions such as the following:

If someone said to me what I am saying to him, would I find it helpful or would I whisper to myself "What else is new?"

How many times in this person's life has she heard what I am saying to her and felt what I am conveying?

Am I reacting as anyone else would to this person, or am I responding like a truly effective counselor?

The person in counseling's facial expression often indicates whether or not the counselor is echoing. A facial expression that says, "I'll listen politely to you, but I've heard what you've said a hundred times" tells the counselor that a different approach or response is required. When the person's face lights up and communicates, "I've never looked at it *that* way" or "I've never felt someone respond to me the way you are," the counselor can feel that counseling is taking place.

The remainder of this book deals directly or indirectly with how counselors can provide a new experience for people.

THOUGHT QUESTIONS

1. The text states that most psychological problems emanate from within, and the environment is merely the arena in which the battles are waged. How can this position be reconciled with that of many family counselors who hold that problems in family members are caused not so much by inner dynamics but by the interaction of family members?

2. Since most people possess at least one psychological imperative, what may be one that you possess that could negatively affect your work as a counselor?

3. The text states that in almost all human problems there is "contributing negligence," whereby the people involved are both perpetrators and victims. How could this concept be applied to a counseling relationship in which problems arise?

4. Anyone who has lived for 20 years has developed an assortment of "helping cassettes." What are some cassettes you have recorded and in what kinds of stressful situations are you likely to play them?

5. Regarding psychological freedom, how free are you to admit the mistakes you make as a counselor to yourself and to the person in counseling? How free are you to disappoint people in counseling by not living up to their expectations?

CHAPTER 3

The Person
in Counseling

People who seek counseling lack the psychological strength to solve their problems and, consequently, experience more dissatisfaction and distress in life than is necessary. For this reason, it is important that counselors understand the nature of psychological strength.

There are as many ways to define and describe psychological strength as there are theories of personality and counseling. The theoretical model described in this chapter is meant to be sufficiently broad that it can comfortably accommodate many, if not most, theoretical positions. In other words, while counselors of various theoretical positions may help people increase their psychological strengths in different ways, their goals are the same as those presented here.

The concept of psychological strength has three dimensions. The first dimension deals with *need fulfillment*. The more healthy needs people get met, the more psychological strength they possess. The more psychological strength they have, the more they handle stress constructively and behave in ways that ultimately bring them realistic degrees of satisfaction and happiness. The less psychological strength people possess, the more ineffectual they are in the face of stress and the more dissatisfaction and distress they experience.

The second dimension of psychological strength deals with *intrapersonal competencies*. The more effectively people deal with themselves, the more it is possible for them to relate to the environment in ways that are need fulfilling. The less effectively people deal with them-

33

selves, the more conflictual are their attempts to relate satisfactorily with the environment, which causes them distress.

The third dimension of psychological strength deals with *interpersonal competencies*. The more effectively people relate with others, the more likely they are to get their needs met. When people relate less effectively with others, they are likely to experience frustration and loneliness.

These dimensions interact with each other; that is, a change for the better or worse in one is likely to cause a similar change in the other. For example, a person who lacks self-direction (an intrapersonal competency) may tend to lack assertiveness (an interpersonal competency), which may reduce his chances of experiencing a satisfactory degree of freedom (a psychological need). By the same principle, the more freedom a person enjoys, the more it could increase her self-direction and, consequently, the more assertive she could become.

Intrapersonal and interpersonal competencies are not ordered hierarchically but interact on the same plane. In other words, the counselor would not necessarily help the person increase a sense of self-direction in the counseling session and *then* encourage him to be assertive inside or outside of counseling. As opportunities for self-direction arise, they are capitalized upon, and as opportunities for assertion arise, they are met. As one dimension of the psyche feeds the other, the person grows in strength. Figure 3–1 illustrates each of the dimensions in relation to the other.

Competencies	Need fulfillment	Psychological strength	Level of functioning
Very good ⟶	High ⟶	Good ⟶	Psychologically healthy
Average ⟶	Average ⟶	Average ⟶	Normal
Inadequate ⟶	Insufficient ⟶	Below average ⟶	Normal-distressed
Very poor ⟶	Low ⟶	Poor ⟶	Abnormal

Figure 3–1. Relationship between the dimensions of psychological strength.

The figure illustrates the following concepts:

1. As people increase their intrapersonal and interpersonal competencies, their need fulfillment increases. As they increase need fulfillment, they increase in psychological strength, which determines their level of psychological functioning.

2. People who seek counseling are likely to be functioning at the normal-distressed level or at the abnormal level. Normal-distressed people are within the outer limits of the normal range and experience

symptoms of distress—for example, discouragement, irritability, confusion, indecision, frustration, hurt, resentment, guilt, jealousy, interpersonal conflicts, employment difficulties, procrastination, or the inability to concentrate. People who are functioning on the abnormal level are experiencing more serious and impairing symptoms such as those seen in the transient stress disorders, personality disorders, psychoneuroses, addictions, somatoform disorders, sexual disorders, and psychoses.

3. The general goal of counseling is to help normal-distressed people increase their psychological strengths so that they can move in the direction of normal, nondistressed people and, ideally, in the direction of psychological health and to help people at the abnormal level progress to normal-distressed and normal nondistressed levels. How much people can be helped to improve their level of functioning depends upon the seriousness and duration of their symptoms and their potential to develop intrapersonal and interpersonal competencies.

NEED FULFILLMENT

The more psychological needs people get met, the stronger they become psychologically, just as the more nutritious food people eat, the stronger they become physically. People who get their needs met well enjoy good psychological health. Those who get their needs met adequately enjoy normal psychological functioning; that is, they are relatively free from distress but they are not psychologically robust. People who get their needs met to an inadequate degree experience symptoms of distress, within either the normal or the abnormal range. Few people who seek counseling are getting their needs met adequately.

Glasser indicates the importance of psychological needs when he writes:

> What is it that [counselors] attempt to treat? What is wrong with the man in a mental hospital who claims he is Jesus, with the boy in and out of reform schools who has stolen thirty-eight cars, the woman who has continual crippling migraine headaches, the child who refuses to learn in school and disrupts the class with temper outbursts, the man who must lose a promotion because he is afraid to fly? . . .
>
> Do these widely different behaviors indicate different [psychological] problems requiring a variety of explanations, or are they manifestations of one underlying difficulty? We believe that, regardless of how he expresses his problem, everyone who needs [counseling] suffers from one basic inadequacy: he is unable to fulfill his essential needs. The severity of the symptom reflects the degree to which the individual is unable to fulfill his needs.[1]

1Glasser (1965), p. 8.

There are many types of needs.[2] I chose the following for discussion because they represent some of the needs people who enter counseling seem to experience the most difficulty meeting. How strongly these needs are present differs from one person to another.

Giving and receiving affection

Giving and receiving affection are two separate behaviors and are not necessarily mutually inclusive. Most people are more familiar with the need to receive affection than with the need to give affection. Receiving affection is important because it allows a person to feel warm, accepted, and lovable. When people feel loved, they generally behave in loving ways. Some people have trouble receiving affection. They may give it but do not allow others to give it to them. A reason for this is that when people give affection, they have more control of the situation and thus feel less vulnerable than when they open themselves up to receive affection.

Giving affection is an underrated need; however, when people fail to express their love, they experience symptoms similar to those of people who hold in anger. When people give affection, they can enjoy its effects on others and can feel more loving toward themselves. People who do not give much affection tend to feel frustrated, useless, and emotionally arid. The reasons that people fail to give affection are that they do not possess sufficient affection to give, they feel their demonstrations of affection will be rebuffed, or the significant people in their lives are not capable of receiving affection.

Counselors can help people discover the primary impediment to getting one or both of these needs met. If the primary problem is within the person, the counselor can help him or her discover what assumptions or feelings are interfering with the adequate fulfillment of these needs. If the basic problem lies in the inability or unwillingness of significant others to meet these affectional needs, the counselor can help the person act on the available alternatives.

Counseling in the area of affectional needs can be especially anxiety producing because it may bring to light the possibility that the person does not feel lovable or that a relationship with a significant other is not founded on love but on some other need or emotion.

Counseling can be a situation in which a person's affectional needs can be met to a reasonable extent. As the person learns to accept the counselor's positive feelings as genuine and learns to share positive feelings toward the counselor, the person's affectional needs can be

[2]For a fuller discussion of the place of needs in psychological development, see Maslow (1968).

primed. The person can then be more confident and motivated to meet his or her affectional needs outside the counseling relationship.[3]

Being free

People need to have a reasonable amount of free choice in their lives. Free choice means that people make decisions on the basis of who they are and not on who they are supposed to be or on what other people want them to do. People need to experience a reasonable degree of freedom at work, in their families, and with their friends. They understand that certain responsibilities, though freely chosen, serve to inhibit freedom to a certain extent. However, they maintain sufficient overall freedom in their lives to remain psychologically solvent.

People who lack sufficient freedom tend to be robots at work, servants at home, and at the mercy of their friends. The less freedom they enjoy, the more automatic, mirthless, and resentful they become. Most people who lack adequate freedom have shackled themselves. They have discovered that certain benefits accrue from being a servant— namely, they do not have to assume responsibility for their lives or try to exact their freedom from others.

Some people lack sufficient freedom because they have erroneously assumed that a willingness to sacrifice personal freedom is a sign of love. The more they love a person, the more they are willing to sacrifice freedom. They have not learned that love and freedom are not mutually exclusive but mutually inclusive and are in direct proportion to each other. Some people lack freedom because they are in a relationship in which the other person makes demands that interfere with freedom. A parent, spouse, or friend has them imprisoned by their needs or values.

In counseling, people can be helped to understand the relationship between their lack of freedom and their unhappiness. Counselors can then help them recognize the causes of their lack of freedom and understand how it serves to protect them from greater anxieties. Counselors can help people understand that unfree people, except in rare circumstances, are consenting victims and that it is in their power to free themselves, even from what appear to be the most imprisoning situations and relationships.

Often when people begin to seek freedom, their behavior creates anxiety in others. For example, a man who is in an unfree relationship with his mother will find that she will suffer disequilibrium as he becomes more free. Counselors often have a dual role of helping the person deal with personal anxieties about becoming free and helping the person cope with the anxiety of the other person in the relationship.

[3]For a discussion of the importance and dynamics of affection, see Fromme (1972).

At first freedom can be very anxiety producing, just as are the first days out of a prison. But after the initial anxieties wear off, people can experience a sense of exhilaration that they may have never previously felt.

Counselors can also remember that freedom is an important part of a counseling relationship. Counselors who unduly pressure people to seek freedom in their lives may be defeating their purpose in that they are treating the person like a servant while admonishing him or her for not seeking freedom. Counselors can be careful not to lose sight of the importance of the person's free choice, even when that choice is contrary to the one the counselor would prefer.

Having fun

Fun is one of the most underrated needs. Children are acutely aware of the need for fun and give it a high priority. Many adults, however, think that fun is for children and should be inversely related to maturity. In fact, fun is an important part of psychological health. People who can look forward to a pleasurable event or fondly remember a joyful experience have a buoyancy that helps them ride above the drudgery and hurts that are part of daily life. Fun, leisure, and joy are lubricants that diminish the friction created by stress.

What constitutes fun varies from one person to another. Fun can be hiking, skiing, swimming, playing tennis, or bicycle riding. Fun can be writing, reading, painting, sculpting, or playing or listening to music. Fun can be relaxing with friends, experiencing the joy of an intimate relationship, playing with a child, or helping people who are less fortunate.

For some people who seek counseling, fun is mostly a memory. Their fears, angers, hurts, and guilts have expunged fun from their lives. They may be relating with people or be in situations that are devoid of joy. Their feeling about life is that it is all uphill, and they have begun to ask themselves if it is worth the struggle.

For other people, fun may never have been part of their lives; hence, they are unaware that they are missing anything. Other people miss having fun but lack the competencies to create fun and allow it into their lives. To compensate for this, they may attempt to substitute physical pleasure for psychological fun by eating, drinking, and having sexual experiences. Because physical pleasure does not stick to the psyche as well as psychological fun, these individuals find themselves compulsively seeking pleasure that does not touch them on a deep level and that creates its own set of problems.

Counselors can help people who lack adequate fun, leisure, and joy recognize their importance and understand why these qualities have been missing in their lives. They can also help people learn what kind of experiences would bring some joy into their lives and help them develop the competencies to make these situations happen.

While counseling could rarely be described as fun, it need not be so serious that it is devoid of mirth and laughter. For some people, counseling can be a much needed opportunity to enjoy a good relationship and have a good laugh once in a while, events that can be therapeutic in themselves.

Receiving stimulation

People need a healthy amount of variety and change in their lives. They need to experience invigorating relationships and new challenges in order to remain fully alive. While they are tied to necessary routines, they also consciously allot time for new experiences in their friendships, at work, and in leisure pursuits.

People who lack adequate stimulation become immersed in unvarying routines of work, socializing, and recreation that are dulling and suffocating. People who continually experience the same things tend to remain the same people; that is, they stagnate and fail to grow. They have no new things to think or feel, to challenge them to grow, or to talk about with others. They feel bored and boring. These people could range from the housewife who is locked into the same relentless routine of housework and mothering to the successful businesswoman who is locked into a rut of paperwork and meetings. Many people who seek counseling do not realize that their apathy, low morale, and general discontent stem from a lifestyle that, whatever merits it has, is unbearably the same. Unfortunately, boredom can be a sanctuary for some people because, while they do not enjoy being bored, it is less anxiety producing than beginning new behaviors that would ventilate their lives.

Counselors can introduce people to the importance of stimulation and help them relate at least some of their apathy and discontent to their suffocating lifestyle. Some people simply need to ventilate their lives in small ways; others need to make radical changes, such as going back to work or school or getting out of a relationship that has been dead for some time. In either case, people will need the insights, competencies, and courage to make the necessary changes in order to resuscitate their psyches.

Counselors can also realize that counseling should be a stimulating experience. Counselors who are so nondirective that they are sonorous or who continually rehash the same subject matter are doing little to whet the person's appetite for stimulation. While it is not the counselor's role to entertain, effective counselors relate in ways that are sufficiently varied and challenging that the person feels stimulated and alive.

Feeling a sense of accomplishment

People need to see the positive results of their efforts. The tasks they attempt can range from parenting to a project at work to playing golf. When people see the results of their labors, it creates a sense of satisfaction that strengthens them.

Some people rarely experience a sense of accomplishment. They may try very few things; so their sense of accomplishment is meager. Or they may try too many things, which results in each success being cancelled out by an equal number of failures. Some people attempt a reasonable number of tasks but lack the competencies to perform them satisfactorily or are in situations that do not allow success. Still other people do not accomplish things because it would make them feel responsible for accomplishing even more, which they are either incapable of or unwilling to do.

Many people who seek counseling say "Things just aren't going well. I seem to make a mess of everything. I'm beginning to feel 'What's the use of trying any more?' " Sometimes the feeling that they are gradually accomplishing something in counseling rekindles the possibility that they can begin accomplishing things in other areas.

People seek counseling because they do not feel effective at home, at work, with their friends, or in all three areas. Counselors can help these people pinpoint their specific areas of incompetence and begin to develop the competencies necessary to become more effective.

People should be able to meet some of their needs for accomplishment in counseling. Counselors can begin with a series of less difficult tasks, noting and reinforcing the successful completion of the steps. As the tasks become more difficult and the person's confidence increases, the person is able to carry his or her sense of accomplishment into tasks of graduated difficulty outside of counseling.

Having hope

People need to feel a sense of the possible, that it is possible to be freed of their depression, that they will be able to mend their marriage, or that they can make things better at work. When people experience hope, they are motivated to continue their efforts to make things better.

Even when the light at the end of the tunnel is dim, it can have a drawing power that generates movement in its direction.

However, when hope is lost or is so dim that it loses its power to motivate, people stop trying and experience despair. Losing hope can be a gradual and insidious process that has no clear beginning and no obvious end. People can imperceptibly slide into despair about themselves, their relationships, or their work. They surrender and are imprisoned by despair without ever realizing what happened.

Some people have never experienced much hope because they were taught they were hopeless. Others do not experience hope because they have tried so many things in so many different ways, all to no avail. And still others do not want to experience hope because they realize that if they do, they will have to move in directions that are frightening.

Counselors can realize that there is always hope. When people come to counseling in a state of near hopelessness, it is for one of two reasons: they are viewing a situation as hopeless when in fact it is not; or the *situation* they are in is hopeless, but *they* are not. People view situations as hopeless even though they are not because they lack the abilities to see the various ways the situation can be salvaged, or they need to see the situation as hopeless because then they do not have to assume responsibility for changing it. Some situations, however, *are* hopeless. For example, a woman's husband may be a hopeless alcoholic in the sense that he does not wish to stop drinking or abusing her. But *she* is not hopeless. She has the freedom to choose to remain in the destructive marriage or to leave it and make a better life for herself.

Counselors are in a unique position to offer people a realistic hope because they have often helped people with similar or worse problems and witnessed them grow through them and out of them. The counselor can meet the person's need for hope enough to engender a sense of the possible that will affect his or her behavior outside of counseling.

Having solitude

Most people do not recognize their need for solitude. They have become so distracted by everyday events that they view solitude as unnecessary, as wasting time, or as a luxury they cannot afford. Yet solitude—that is, being alone and quiet with oneself—is the basic way to keep track of who one is and sweep out the distractions that have cluttered one's system.

People who meet their need for solitude are conversant with their true selves and make sure that their needs and values do not become buried under the mountain of daily activities that seem important but are essentially irrelevant to their growth and happiness. People who

make time for solitude in their lives enjoy a sense of peace, purposefulness, and strength.

People who do not recognize their need for solitude or recognize it
but are too busy to meet it gradually become strangers to themselves.
They have lost touch with who they are and serve other masters, meeting the needs and upholding the values of other people and institutions,
rather than their own. Although they may be successful at work or
devoted parents, they are strangers to their own needs, feelings, and
values and thus behave in ways that are contrary to their best interests.
In general, people avoid solitude because they are frightened to become
reintroduced to themselves, since it may result in a radical revision of
the lifestyle in which they have invested too much to forsake.

Counselors can help people understand the importance of being
quiet and alone. At first people often do not realize how solitude will
help them with their financial worries or their problems with their
children. Once they have a glimmer of understanding, they are likely to
protest that they lack the time. Gradually, the counselor can help these
people work through their resistances, especially if the counselor provides time in counseling for quiet reflection. Counselors can invite
these people to take five or ten minutes out of a session to remain quiet
and focus on what is really going on within them. Frequently, these
people are surprised to discover that the more they get in touch with
their deepest thoughts and feelings, the less cloudy their picture becomes and the more relaxed they feel.

Having an existential purpose in life

Many people are not aware of their need for an existential purpose
in life. Some of them have no more purpose in life than to survive the
day. Others have compelling material purposes in life. They want to be
a bank manager by the time they are 30 and a vice-president by the time
they are 40. Or they want to acquire a certain amount of money or
material possessions.

People who are aware of their need for an existential purpose in life
look for a deeper sense of meaning. Instead of wanting to get something
from life, they want to give something to life. They want to make life
one degree better as a result of their short visit to it. Usually this entails
doing something directly or indirectly to make life a little easier, freer,
or happier for others.

People who are not aware of this need skim along on the surface of
life, taking what each day brings, but have no theme that ties their days
into a meaningful whole. Some people get so many material needs met
that they never give the existential vacuum within them a chance to

surface. Others, however, may gradually realize that what they are doing each day may have an importance of its own but does not make sense on any deep or lasting level. These people may experience a sense of existential frustration, although they may suffer its symptoms and not recognize its cause. They may complain: "There's something missing in my life, and every time I think I've found it, it evaporates, leaving me with a worse feeling."

Counselors can provide many people with their first opportunity to learn that life can be more than repeating endless cycles of working to pay bills and seeking excitement to diminish boredom. Of all the needs mentioned, this one requires the most growth, because it is primarily altruistic, and the most thought, because it is the most abstract.

When a person approaches counseling feeling that "something is missing," and the person is not experiencing depression or some other disorder, then he or she is likely ready to launch into meeting this need. Counselors can help these people discover what they want to give to life, what they would like written on their gravestone. When people recognize what they want to give, it may entail only minor revisions in their lifestyle or it may require them to make major changes. In either case, counseling can afford them the lights that they need and the courage that will be necessary to make a commitment to life.[4]

INTRAPERSONAL COMPETENCIES

People get their needs met according to how well they relate with themselves and others. Intrapersonal competencies are learned abilities that help people relate well with themselves. The purpose of intrapersonal competencies is to increase the quantity and quality of the person's need fulfillment.

People relate with others in much the same ways that they relate with themselves. When people relate with themselves comfortably, they tend to relate comfortably with others. When they relate with themselves in a conflictual way, they tend to relate with others in a similar manner.

People who seek counseling often lack the intrapersonal competencies to relate well with themselves. They are out of tune with themselves, if not in outright battle. The friction from their internal conflicts spills over into interpersonal relationships, causing tension. However, people who seek counseling often perceive their problem as stemming from something they are *doing* or something someone else is *doing*, and

---

[4]For a discussion of the place of purpose in life in psychological maturity, see Frankl (1963).

not from something they are *being*.

Intrapersonal relationships deal with three competencies: self-knowledge, self-direction, and self-esteem.[5] While there is some overlap in these areas, which are all part of the same self, they are separate competencies. Self-knowledge says "I know who I am"; self-direction says "I make my own decisions"; and self-esteem says "I am a worth-while person."

Self-knowledge

People who seek counseling often lack adequate self-knowledge, which consists of knowing their strengths, weaknesses, needs, feelings, and motives. The following are some examples of people who possess inadequate self-knowledge:

A man may hide his *strengths* from himself because this allows him to get his deep dependency needs met by having to rely on others. He prefers to be ineffectual and dependent rather than strong and autonomous. He comes to counseling complaining that he cannot seem to "take hold of life" when in fact his problem is that he cannot take hold of himself because he does not wish to know himself and act accordingly.

A woman may hide her *weaknesses* from herself while exaggerating her strengths. This permits her to feel effective, but the price she pays is a chronic sense of frustration that stems from entering situations in which she cannot succeed. She blames her failures and frustrations on the stupidity of others. She would rather think she is stronger than she is and fail than to admit her weaknesses and succeed at a more realistic level.

A man may hide *needs* from himself. He denies his need for prestige and exaggerates his need to help people less fortunate than he. He gets a job helping poor people but finds himself continually and increasingly frustrated with it. He blames his supervisor and takes a similar job, which activates the same frustrations. He would rather be frustrated and think he has a strong commitment to the poor than admit he needs a job that pays a decent salary and gives him some prestige and happiness.

A woman hides *feelings* from herself. She hides anger toward her husband and wonders why she has become sexually less responsive to him. She would rather be sexually unfulfilled for no apparent reason than have to admit her anger to herself, handle it constructively, and become sexually satisfied.

---

[5]For a discussion of the place of the self in the healthy personality, see Combs & Snygg (1959) and Jourard & Landsman (1980).

A man may hide *motives* from himself. A counselor, under the guise of being confrontive, actually uses counseling to vent his hostility on people who cannot hit back. He would rather have a dwindling practice, which he blames on the economy or on people's unwillingness to change, than admit his hostility, learn to handle it more appropriately, and have a psychologically and financially rewarding practice.

Causes.   People who possess inadequate or poor self-knowledge have learned to hide the more threatening parts of themselves to prevent and reduce anxiety. They were taught that they should have certain qualities, and any thoughts and feelings contrary to these qualities created anxiety. People with good psychological strength learned to handle the anxiety in constructive ways; those with less psychological strength employed defense mechanisms to hide the dissonant qualities and reduce anxiety.

Problems.   There are some common problems people experience when they lack adequate self-knowledge. One is self-alienation. People who lack adequate self-knowledge behave, in effect, like two or more people living within the same body. One part is a well-known friend and the other is a complete stranger. When the recognizable part of the person moves in one direction, the unrecognizable part or parts stay anchored in place or actually move in an opposite direction. These psychological tugs-of-war cause friction, which manifests itself in symptoms and/or interpersonal difficulties that are blamed on external situations.

Another problem is that their unrecognized parts significantly influence their behavior. Unrecognized parts of a personality do not disappear but manifest themselves in disguised ways, much to the confusion of the person and those around him. For example, a father may love his son but also have some deep but unrecognized feelings of resentment toward him. These feelings may appear in his relationship with his son in one of two ways. He may overcompensate for the resentment by being "too loving" toward his son. He spoils him and, in the process, ruins him. Or the father is perplexed by the fact that every time he makes a conscious attempt to get closer to his son, he only succeeds in pushing him away. The result of both dynamics is that he damages his son, all the while protesting that he has done everything possible to have a good relationship with him.

A third problem is they make poor decisions. A person's decisions can be only as good as the data on which they are based. People with inadequate self-knowledge make decisions on the basis of faulty or incomplete data; hence, their decisions cannot be in their best interests. A young woman decides to follow a very difficult course of study in college. Despite her modest intelligence, she "knows" she is smart enough to handle it well. After wasting great amounts of time and enduring many frustrations, she quits school, blaming the academic game playing of her professors.

Those who lack self-knowledge may find their unrecognized parts taint their perceptions. For example, a man hides his deep feelings of inadequacy. His boss tells him "Tom, I'd like you to help me with this new account—aw, no, skip it—I'll let Fred handle it." In reality, the boss said this because she wants Tom to work on a more important account. Tom, however, perceives that she thinks he is unable to handle the account successfully. Tom's hidden sense of inadequacy has led to a misperception of the boss's comment. As a result, Tom lapses into one of his frequent episodes of depression, which further increases his unrecognized sense of inadequacy.

A fifth problem is that they avoid situations that could introduce them to their unrecognized parts. For example, a woman thinks she is well adjusted emotionally and sexually. On a less than conscious level, she is frightened of intimacy and doubts her sexuality. Every time she begins to get close to a man, she discovers some flaw in him that she cannot tolerate and uses this as a reason to break off the relationship. She laments that there seem to be no decent, eligible men around anymore.

Sixth, they may manipulate people and be manipulated according to their unrecognized parts. For example, a student's unrecognized area is that he doubts his intelligence. He manipulates his girlfriend into writing his term papers for him because he is "too busy" or "too lazy." As long as he can avoid putting his intellect to the test by manipulating people and situations, he does not have to face his felt inadequacy. This student's girlfriend may have an unrecognized feeling that she is not very attractive or interesting. Hence, she allows herself to be manipulated by her boyfriend because she feels she has to give him *some* reason to continue to see her. The collusion that takes place in the relationship is seen in the contract. The boy says "If you allow me to think I'm intelligent by writing good papers that I pretend I could have written if I had the time, I'll allow you to feel attractive and interesting by continuing to see you."

A seventh possible problem is that they project unrecognized areas onto others in an effort to deny the presence of these areas in themselves. For example, a woman may have unrecognized needs to be successful at any price. She perceives her colleagues as backstabbers and criticizes them for their ruthlessness. By doing this, she successfully divests herself of the possibility that she possesses similar qualities. As a result, however, she is continually suspicious of others at work, which causes unhappiness in her and her co-workers.

Counseling implications.   Since it is likely that the many people who seek counseling lack adequate self-knowledge, it is helpful for counselors to recognize how this lack can manifest itself in the counseling situation.

People who experience difficulties due to their lack of self-knowledge rarely focus on the true cause of their difficulties—namely, themselves. They blame other people and situations and sometimes present a very convincing case. Counselors must realize that the first place to look for the cause of difficulty is the accuracy of the person's self-knowledge. If the person seems to lack self-knowledge, counseling can focus on this point. If it turns out that the person's self-knowledge is adequate, this frees the counselor to look to other areas of the self and then to the interpersonal area.

Unrecognized parts of a person are at the core of resistance in counseling. While the recognized part wishes to progress in counseling, the unrecognized parts remain stationary or move in opposite directions. Areas of resistance provide the counselor with clues as to where problematic, unrecognized areas lie.

Another indication of the presence and nature of unrecognized areas is that people who have inadequate self-knowledge taint their perception of the counselor and project their unrecognized parts onto the counselor. In a sense, the counselor can act as a blank tablet upon which the person draws his or her unrecognized areas. For example, when people read behaviors into the counselor that are not present or accuse the counselor of behaviors he or she is not participating in, these misperceived behaviors have had to come from *some place*, and usually their source is within the unrecognized areas of the person in counseling.

People may seek counseling for help in making an important decision—for example, whether to marry, continue their education, begin a particular career, or get a divorce. Often these individuals define their problem too narrowly. The problem may not be that they can't "make up their mind" but that they don't "know their mind." Counselors who fail to realize this and help people through a particular decision may be helping these people win a battle but lose a war.

Finally, counselors can be aware that people with inadequate self-knowledge tend to create situations in which the counselor will miss the presence of their unrecognized areas.

1. They do not introduce for discussion areas that may lead the counselor into an unrecognized area.
2. They attempt to manipulate the counselor away from these areas by discussing decoy issues or by focusing on the counselor.
3. They seek to enter into a contract of collusion that reads "I won't introduce you to your unrecognized areas if you do the same for me."
4. They "protest too much" as a way of covering up unrecognized areas and can, because they are so convinced, convince the counselor that he or she is wasting time probing a particular area.

Self-direction

Self-direction means that people direct their lives and assume full responsibility for the consequences of their behavior. The more people direct their own behavior, the more they live according to their nature and avoid situations in which their nature will be contorted. People who seek counseling are often lacking in adequate self-direction and may manifest it in one or more of the following behaviors.

They may *lack self-confidence*. Self-confidence is an integral part of self-direction because people must be capable of trusting themselves before they can actually direct their lives.

Causes.   People who seek counseling have often learned to distrust their abilities, perceptions, motives, and judgments. They learned self-distrust either because they were taught by their parents and others that they were wrong a good deal of the time or they were overprotected to the extent that they had few opportunities to test themselves and strengthen their self-confidence.

Problems.   People who lack self-confidence share one or more of the following characteristics. First, they may generally distrust themselves or distrust just one crucial area—for example, their ability to enter into intimate relationships. They may have good reason to doubt their abilities because they may never have developed them to a workable degree, or they may have good abilities but lack the confidence to test them. In either case, they suffer frustration because they often know what they want but lack the confidence to pursue it.

Second, they experience difficulties making decisions. Because they distrust themselves, they either decline or put off making decisions. In either case, important needs may not be getting met. Frustration and anxiety increase in both themselves and in others who are involved in the decisions.

Third, they may react poorly to failure. A failure is not simply a failure to them but a validation that their abilities and judgment are lacking. Instead of saying to themselves "I didn't do that well," they say "See how stupid I am."

A fourth characteristic is a reluctance to take risks. Because they distrust their abilities, perceptions, motives, and judgments, they fail to take the ordinary risks necessary to grow psychologically.

Fifth, people who lack self-confidence may behave in ways that make them psychologically invisible. This means that because of their meek and passive demeanor, they are passed over professionally and socially. They are passed over for promotion at work. When social invitations are extended, they are often left uninvited.

Sixth, they may attempt to undermine the self-confidence of others. It can be threatening for people with little self-confidence to relate professionally and socially with those who have good self-confidence. One way to reduce this threat is to attempt to undermine other people's self-confidence. This can be done by targeting their weak points and hitting them with sufficient accuracy and frequency so that they are left hurt and defending themselves. The problem with this is that, while the tactic may offer a certain amount of protection, it also serves to alienate people and reduce interpersonal need fulfillment.

Counseling implications.   In counseling, individuals who lack self-confidence need a fair amount of support before they feel ready to take risks both in and out of counseling. They will likely test the counseling atmosphere and the counselor a good deal before they risk any significant exposure. They may attempt to use the counselor as a manager under the auspices of "You know more about these things than I do; you tell me what to do." It may take a while for these people to realize the true purpose of counseling and to perceive accurately the role of the counselor.

These people are likely to view setbacks in counseling as proof that they cannot do anything correctly. Counselors can help these people understand that for every step forward in counseling, there is often one or more steps backward.

People who lack self-confidence may not trust the counselor or the counseling process as an outgrowth of their own lack of self-confidence. They may begin counseling by declaring that they do not believe in it but are there only to please a friend or loved one. Counselors can help these people articulate clearly the exact nature of their distrust and fears and help them associate them with their own lack of self-confidence.

Another tactic used by people who lack self-confidence is to attempt to undermine the counselor's confidence. These people may be astute at picking up the counselor's weak points and play them to distract the counselor from the person and the goals of counseling. When counselors feel off balance or on the defensive with a person, this is most likely occurring.

Counselors can also discern if the lack of self-confidence is appropriate. The counselor cannot blithely assume that a person's competencies, perceptions, and judgments are fine and all the person need do is recognize that they are. The person may be lacking in these areas, which accounts for the lack of self-confidence. When this is the case, the counselor's job will be to help the person strengthen these areas, thus realistically increasing self-confidence.

Once the counselor ascertains that the person is not weak in abilities, perceptions, and judgments but merely lacks confidence in them, two explanations for the low self-confidence are possible. The person may have unrealistically high self-expectations and may feel inadequate as a result. As the counselor helps the person reduce the unrealistic expectation, the person's self-confidence will increase. The other possible explanation is that the person may be consciously or unconsciously using poor self-confidence as an excuse for not living life fully. This could be passive-aggressive behavior aimed at disappointing loved ones, or it could be caused by unresolved guilt that will not allow the person to enjoy life. Whatever the cause, the counselor can help the person understand and overcome it.

Counselors can realize that pep talks do not help a person grow in self-confidence. People undoubtedly have heard many pep talks from those who know them better than the counselor does. In place of pep talks, the counselor can create an atmosphere in which people can freely and clearly articulate the specific areas in which they lack confidence. Then the people can explore the reasons for their lack of self-confidence and develop methods for solving the problem.

People with low self-confidence can learn to develop a healthy perspective on their mistakes and failures. When counselors help these people understand that even the most effective and psychologically healthy people make mistakes daily, they will develop a freedom to err that will allow them to take reasonable risks. Mistakes and failures can increase self-confidence when one learns something important from them and learns how to apply the learning to future situations.

People who seek counseling may *lack self-reliance*. Self-reliance is an important part of self-direction because the more people are able to create situations in which their needs are met, the more they will be able to direct their own behavior. On the other hand, the more people rely on others to meet their needs, the more likely it is that others will direct their lives.

Causes.   People failed to learn adequate self-reliance because they never learned to forage for their own psychological nourishment. This occurred because they were fed by others and hence never developed the competencies necessary to create situations in which their needs would be met.

Problems.   When people lack self-reliance, they may experience one or more of the following problems, which may lead them to seek counseling. They may experience a low-grade but ongoing sense of resentment. They resent themselves for being incapable of meeting their own needs. This self-resentment may show in feelings of self-depreciation, or it may be projected into resenting others. They may also resent others because they must rely on them for psychological nourishment and sustenance. Their deep need and deep resentment of others often causes them "to bite the hand that feeds them"; that is, they tend to drive away the very people they need so much.

Second, they find it difficult to attend fully to tasks because they are always on the lookout for sources of nourishment. Other things in life, such as school and work, are perceived as boring since their real focus is on receiving attention, support, and affection.

Third, they experience interpersonal problems. It is difficult for these people to truly love because their love is conditional. It is based on the principle "I'll nourish you as long as you nourish me." Checks and balances in the relationship are carefully monitored, and temporary shortages or stoppages of nourishment are met with anxiety and frantic renegotiations.

Because these people often depend on a relationship for survival, they are reluctant to be completely honest in the relationship. They would rather prostitute themselves psychologically than place the relationship in jeopardy. This contorting further weakens the person and makes him or her even less self-reliant; so leaving the relationship, even when it is abusive, becomes very difficult.

If a symbiotic relationship does terminate, they are likely to feel acutely depressed and helpless, as a person who has never learned to feed himself would feel when cast out on his own. At this time, these individuals are liable to latch onto another person simply for survival.

Counseling implications.   Because people who lack self-reliance tend to lean on others, counselors should not become a primary source of nourishment for them. A counselor may inadvertently assume this role and be pleased with how easily a person settles into a good relationship and cooperates with the counselor. However, when a counselor becomes a primary source of nourishment, the person is prevented from becoming self-reliant and from foraging on his or her own for psychological fulfillment.

Counselors can encourage the person to strengthen existing relationships that are heavily based on dependency needs. As the person attempts to become a full partner in the relationship, disequilibrium may result. The partner who was delicately balancing on the dependency need of the person in counseling may lose his or her balance. At this point the person in counseling may need to decide which is a higher value: becoming strong or keeping the partner. Sometimes these relationships can be transformed into strong ones, but more often they cannot, especially if the partner is not growing at the same rate as the person in counseling.

In this case, the person in counseling may go "cold turkey" and suffer through the symptoms of withdrawal from an emotional addiction. While counselors can help people through such periods, they should not offer to be a main supplier of need fulfillment for the person until another supplier can be found. This is a good time to help the person start becoming self-sufficient.

People who lack self-reliance can be helped to branch out emotionally. Instead of relying on a few sources of emotional nourishment, it is important for people to develop new friends, relationships, and interests. In other words, the more resources they have, the less reliant they will be on one or two sources of survival and happiness. When this occurs, people's overall welfare cannot be significantly damaged by the loss of any one relationship or job.

Counselors need not be fooled by people who lack self-sufficiency but overcompensate for it by assuming an "I don't need anybody" attitude. Deep down these people have strong dependency needs that are hidden beneath a facade of independence. These individuals may have an approach-avoidance relationship with the counselor. They may be tempted to become dependent on the counselor but will have equally strong needs to remain independent. Because both getting closer to the counselor and moving away create anxiety, constant tension may be present in the relationship for a period of time.

Those who seek counseling may *lack self-control*. Self-control is a necessary part of self-direction because it helps people channel their energies and allows them to guide their own lives. People with inadequate self-control behave in ways that interfere with their own need fulfillment and that of others.

Causes. People who lack adequate self-control failed to learn two important developmental tasks. They did not learn the ability to sacrifice short-range gratification for more important long-range goals, and they did not learn the importance of becoming their own masters rather than the servants of others or of alien parts of themselves.

Problems. People who lack adequate self-control may exhibit the following behaviors. First, they manifest poor self-discipline. These people are more interested in meeting their own needs than in meeting their work or social responsibilities. They expend time and energy unproductively or only on projects that interest them, ignoring those that may be equally or more important. They lack sufficient intrinsic motivation. Consequently, unless they are goaded by external pressures, they fail to attend to the more arduous tasks of daily living. Finally, undisciplined people seek immediate gratification. They have difficulty sacrificing the pleasure of the moment for long-range goals.

Second, they lack the ability to be self-governing. People who have difficulty governing their lives are controlled by internal or external pressures that cause the tail to wag the dog. As a result, they make decisions that seriously impair their need fulfillment and that they later regret.

These people may be controlled by irrational consciences. They conform to an inflexible moral code or set of stringent ideals that may cause them to make decisions contrary to their best interests. Sometimes their "shoulds" have so successfully taken over their consciences that they actually think it is they who are making the decisions rather than an irrational force that has taken their conscience hostage.

They may also be unhealthily governed by authority, which can include parents, bosses, older people, or the church. They follow the dictates of authority rather than their own well-thought-out and felt-out attitudes and beliefs.

These people may also be governed by what other people think. Before making any consequential decision, they may instinctively appeal to how others might judge them. They frequently lament "I really know what I need to do, but it would kill my parents" or "I know what I'd really like to do, but my friends would disown me or think I was crazy." This "what would the neighbors say" attitude confines them to a restricted and sometimes meager psychological diet.

Finally, they may be governed by raw needs and feelings. Their needs and feelings have not been sifted through a socialization process that allows them to work in the best interests of themselves and others. If they need something, they must have it now. If they feel something, it is as likely to be expressed destructively as constructively. Hence, they are not governing their behavior but their behavior is being governed by their needs and feelings. When needs for greed and sex and feelings of frustration and anger sidestep the socialization process, they are liable to cause behavior that is proximately or ultimately self-defeating.

Counseling implications. The counselor can first help people recognize how their undisciplined behavior is self-defeating. These people can gradually realize that while their behavior helps them skirt immediate anxieties, it deprives them of the orderliness and depth necessary for true happiness and fulfillment.

Because people with inadequate self-discipline often deceive themselves regarding the immaturity and unfairness of their behavior, counselors can confront them with the weakness of their rationalizations, excuses, and explanations. Since the person's poor self-discipline also is likely to manifest itself in the counseling relationship, the counselor will have ample opportunity to mirror back to the person clear reflections of the causes, dynamics, and results of his or her undisciplined behavior.

People who lack self-discipline must be dishonest a good deal of the time in order to avoid facing the consequences of their unorganized, disordered, or damaging behavior. As long as they can avoid facing these consequences, they have little motivation to change. Therefore, it is important for counselors to encourage people to be honest with others about their lack of self-discipline and to accept whatever consequences are appropriate.

Counselors can help people understand the causes of inadequate self-discipline. People can learn what fears have made it difficult for them to concentrate long enough to attend to important tasks; what angers cause them to disappoint, use, and damage people; what hurts foster the attitude "I've got to take care of me because no one else will"; and what guilts are causing the self-defeating nature of their behavior.

While working on the underlying causes of the lack of self-discipline, counselors can help people begin to take small, practical steps in strengthening this characteristic. People can be encouraged to be on time for appointments, to decline responsibilities they have little intention of fulfilling, to map out a few basic priorities and allot time for each, and to pick one or two projects that they will satisfactorily complete.

People who are governed by their irrational consciences often seek counseling to help them meet their "shoulds" even better. They tell the counselor that they should be a better spouse, parent, child, friend, or worker and seek help in contorting their personalities even further. Counselors can help these people realize the folly and destructiveness of their shoulds and focus on what they need to grow into fuller human beings.

People who are governed by authority tend to automatically cast the counselor into the role of authority and demand he or she assume the role. When the counselor declines, the person experiences the anxiety attendant to being on a rudderless ship. When the counselor asks the person "What do *you* want to do?" the person reacts with astonishment and often admits that no one has ever asked that question.

People who are governed by what other people think will resist behavioral change because they feel that their new behaviors will make waves that will drown them. Counselors can help demythologize the person's feeling that others care so much what they do and help them develop the strength necessary to act, even when the action will upset others.

People who are governed by their raw needs and feelings tend to flood the counselor with pressing needs that must be met immediately ("You've *got* to write a note to my teacher saying that I'm too upset to take the exam"). They also tend to splatter the counselor with whatever feelings of fear, anger, guilt, or hurt are brimming over at the time. Counselors can continually reflect back to these individuals the manipulative and destructive quality of their behavior and invite them to design more appropriate alternatives. Counselors can also assiduously avoid reinforcing these behaviors by not allowing them to work in counseling.

Self-esteem

Self-esteem means that people perceive themselves as generally worthwhile, capable, and benevolent. It develops from people behaving in ways that are consonant with their healthy values and reasonable expectations of themselves.

Self-esteem is mostly subconscious and taken for granted by people, just as sight and hearing are taken for granted. Self-esteem motivates people to get their fair share in life and to protect themselves from unnecessary demands and injustices. In other words, they treat themselves with the same care and respect as they would treat another person whom they esteem.

Causes.   People lack adequate self-esteem because they were taught that they were not competent or lovable by being made to feel ignored, unimportant, inadequate, unattractive, or burdensome. As people grow through adolescence and into adulthood, their feelings of unlovableness cause them to behave in unlovable ways, which increases their self-dislike.

Problems.   People who lack self-esteem exhibit one or more of the following behaviors. They perceive themselves with disrespect and disaffection and treat themselves accordingly. They may or may not recognize it, but they do not like themselves and would not choose themselves as friends or life partners. They view themselves as stupid, evil, weak, boring, or unattractive, and relate with themselves as they would to a person who possessed these qualities. Consequently, they ignore themselves; that is, they fail to take care of their own needs or attend to their basic values. As a result, they become weaker and more self-alienated, which only adds to their poor sense of esteem. They may also treat themselves poorly by making bad decisions, such as entering into or remaining in damaging living situations, relationships, or jobs. They settle for less in life because they feel they do not deserve more, or they invite destruction because it seems to be an appropriate fate. They may recognize the self-limiting and self-defeating aspects of their behavior and protest that they are unable to stop them. Or they may blame their unhappiness on other people or situations, such as work, society, religion, or fate.

Second, people who simply ignore or dislike themselves but do not hate themselves often attempt to get others to meet their esteem needs to compensate for their lack of self-esteem. They function on the principle "Since I don't respect or like myself very much, I *doubly* need you to respect and like me." In other words, they seek from others what they cannot give themselves. Like everyone, they have a self-esteem void and an other-esteem void, both of which need filling. However they attempt to fill *both* voids with the esteem of others, which cannot be done. Not realizing this, they compulsively seek others' esteem by an endless series of behaviors that drive them further from the behavior that will fill the self-esteem void.

A third behavior is attempting to fill the void left by inadequate self-esteem with synthetic substitutes. Because the emptiness of the void causes boredom, loneliness, or pain, they attempt to fill it with food, drink, or drugs. Or they may attempt to fill it with prestige, which is different from esteem in that it invites people to say "He is a successful person," which is quite different from "He is a good and lovable person." Other common fillers are material possessions, sex, excitement, adulation, and religion. All these can be healthy pursuits, but used as substitutes for self-esteem, they are as effective as filling a hole in the ground with quicksand.

Fourth, they may overidentify with a role. Because they do not view themselves as worthwhile, they overidentify with a role that they perceive as making them worthwhile. A man does not play professional sports; he *is* a professional athlete. A woman does not practice medicine; she *is* a physician. A man does not do religious work; he *is* a priest. A woman is not married to John Smith; she *is* the wife of Senator John Smith. These people do not possess a privately owned sense of self-worth; so they must rent it from a role. As long as they use a role for the purpose of self-esteem, they are unlikely to grow to any significant degree. And if the role discontinues, they are left with nothing.

Fifth, they cannot let others become psychologically intimate with them. Because they view themselves negatively, they cannot allow others to come close enough to share the same view. Consequently, they keep others at a distance through obvious or subtle tactics, or they place a pleasing facade between themselves and the people whom they invite to come closer. In either case, their deepest needs cannot be met. In the first situation, other people are too far away to meet their needs, and in the second instance, the facade receives the love and respect, not the person. Hence, the person is left whispering to himself or herself "If they only knew me as I do, they would never love me."

A sixth behavior is being capricious in their choice of friends and co-workers. They tend to choose friends on the basis of how people will meet their esteem needs. People who continually show respect, admiration, and liking are accepted as dear friends and valued co-workers. People who relate more matter-of-factly, even though they are good and enjoyable people, are discarded as deficient or poor company. Consequently, it does not take a great deal for these people to cross a friend off their list, leaving them with few if any lasting friends.

They do not tolerate well the loss of self-esteem. People with sound self-esteem have a reservoir of self-esteem; so if they lose some, it causes only temporary disequilibrium. People with superficial self-esteem have little or no reserve; hence, a sudden loss can cause acute anxiety or depression. Failure to receive a promotion becomes a catastrophe; rejection by a lover becomes devastating. These individuals tend to go to great and inappropriate lengths to win and keep jobs and friendships and relentlessly attempt to retrieve them after they are lost.

Another problem is their inability to forgive themselves. Just as one can forgive a person who is loved more easily than a person who is disliked, the person who does not have self-love ruminates and broods about transgressions. This occurs even when others have forgiven the person. These people use their guilt in a self-tormenting way that stubbornly withstands all attempts by others to help them return to the business of living. Sometimes these people permit the guilt to lie dormant until something nice happens to them. Then they stoke it up and allow it to spoil the pleasant experience.

Finally, people who dislike or hate themselves may get their esteem needs met in negative ways. Since they feel they can never be the best, they may set out to be the worst. They may be able to get some people to respect or admire them for the strength, cunning, callousness, or courage they manifest in antisocial behavior. This can be seen in the 10-year-old class bully or the 30-year-old prison inmate who likes prison life because he enjoys significantly more respect in prison than he does "on the street."

Counseling implications.   Lack of self-esteem can be obvious to the counselor. The way the person walks, stands, dresses, or talks may all give evidence of a lack of self-esteem. But sometimes people who feel low esteem do not present an obvious picture. They appear self-confident, buoyant, energetic, and attractive. Just as two people can appear to love each other when in fact they do not, a person can mask self-dislike. It may take a while for a counselor to see through the facade and discover behaviors that people with self-esteem do not display.

The counselor can remember that one of the ways people learn to feel unlovable is by being treated in unlovable ways. The first step for a counselor is to relate to the person in positive or at least nonrejecting ways. Sometimes this will be a challenge because people who dislike and loathe themselves often dislike and loathe others proportionately. Hence, the person in counseling may behave in unlovable ways, and it takes a perceptive counselor to see through the behavior and understand its causes. The counselor who chooses to see only likable people in counseling will not help many people who need the most help.

People who lack self-esteem are likely to be ambivalent toward counseling. The part of them that wants to learn to behave in ways more in keeping with their healthy values and realistic expectations wants to cooperate with counseling. However, the part of them that feels ugly or evil makes them feel they don't deserve esteem or happiness and may work to sabotage counseling. Often it is necessary to invite and allow the person to get in touch with the perceived ugliness, share it with the counselor, and place it in a more realistic, understanding, and forgiving light. Sometimes this can be done simultaneously with learning new behaviors; at other times it must be done prior to attempting any overt behavior changes.

These people may attempt to induce the counselor to meet their esteem needs. They may grow in counseling for the sake of earning praise from the counselor rather than growing for the sake of growth and self-acceptance. Counselors can be aware that, while some rewarding can be a necessary and important part of counseling, offering excessive rewards may simply give the person other-esteem rather than help him or her develop self-esteem.

People who lack self-esteem may also attempt to induce counselors to help them fill self-esteem voids with synthetic substitutes such as other-esteem, prestige, material acquisitions, or love relationships. While any of these goals could be a valid pursuit, none is an effective filler for self-esteem. This is often a difficult insight to help people attain because most people are convinced that if only they could "get" a desirable person to love them, they would have all the love and esteem they need, and their problems would be solved.

Counselors can be aware that people who lack self-esteem are not helped by being told they are actually better than they think they are. Psychological pep talks may create a temporary and superficial "positive self-concept," but it is likely to deflate at the first setback. While people may possess an inherent goodness by the fact of their existence, they must earn a sense of self-esteem. Counselors can help people pinpoint and change behaviors that detract from their esteem.

Finally, these people are likely to bring into counseling their reluctance to allow people to get close to them. Simply because a counselor is a counselor does not make him or her immune from being held at a distance or invited to relate intimately with a facade instead of a person. It may take time and a good deal of testing before the person will allow the counselor to get close enough to share the person's negative view of himself or herself. This takes delicacy and patience on the part of the counselor.

INTERPERSONAL COMPETENCIES

Interpersonal competencies are learned abilities that allow people to relate with others in mutually fulfilling ways. Interpersonal competencies complement intrapersonal competencies in that both are necessary for psychological growth. When people relate well with themselves and others, they will experience good need fulfillment. Difficulties in one or both sets of competencies will interfere with need fulfillment and may cause psychological symptoms.

Interpersonal competencies act as bridges that link the person with the external environment. The more bridges a person has and the stronger they are, the more needs will be met and the more psychological resources the person will have to share with others. People who seek counseling often lack one or more interpersonal competencies; hence, one of the goals of counseling is to help people unlearn their problematic ways of relating and learn new, more fulfilling ways. There are many interpersonal competencies. The following discussion describes some of the competencies with which people who seek counseling seem to experience the most difficulty.

Sensitivity to oneself and others

When people relate with others, it is important they be attuned to themselves as well as to the person with whom they are relating. Being sensitive to themselves means that as they talk and listen, they are keenly aware of their own thoughts and feelings and use them as data upon which to make appropriate responses.

Some people who seek counseling are poorly attuned to themselves. For example, as they listen to a person, their intellect may be responding to what the person is saying, but they are deaf to their own emotional reactions. After they leave the encounter, they may begin to experience the feelings of fear, anger, hurt, guilt, or love that were calling out at the time but fell on deaf ears.

Being sensitive to others means that people perceive the deeper thoughts and feelings that lie behind another's words and actions. For example, a man tells his wife that he will not be able to go away with her for the weekend as he had promised because he has to prepare a project for work. His wife assures him that she understands and that it is all right. However, he is unable to see the hurt look on her face that disappears in a flash and to hear the false buoyancy in her voice. He will be confused by her inattentive and passive-aggressive behavior over the weekend because she assured him that she understood his plight.

Being sensitive to others also means having a sense of empathy for them. People with empathy intuit others' sensitivities and vulnerabilities and bypass them unless there is a good reason to do otherwise. They don't tease people about sensitive areas, and they don't embarrass them. They recognize the right and the wrong times to say things. They also anticipate the needs of others; for example, they know without being told that a person needs to be given some affection or encouragement or to be left alone.

Lack of sensitivity to self and to others interferes with mutual need fulfillment because sensitivity acts as radar that detects thoughts, needs, and feelings in the person and those with whom the person relates. The less effective the radar is, the less deeply people will relate with others and, consequently, the less well people will know each other sufficiently to meet each other's needs.

In counseling, these people often experience difficulty concentrating on their and/or the counselor's reactions. For example, after offering some emotionally loaded feedback to the person, the counselor may ask, "Well, what have you been feeling?" The person may react with a dumbfounded look on her face and reply, "Oh, I was so busy listening to what you were saying that I wasn't thinking or feeling much of anything."

When appropriate, counselors can stop people and invite them to get in touch with the real thoughts and feelings that are underlying their words. After a while, people can learn to ask themselves, "Are my words communicating what I am really thinking and feeling or are they simply camouflaging my real reactions?"

Sensitivity can also be taught by direct example. Counselors can say, "What I am wondering now is whether I should let you continue with what you are saying or tell you that I think you are using your words to plow your feelings under." Here the counselor gives an on-view example of a person who is in touch with what he is currently feeling and is willing to share it with the other person so that the communication can become fuller and the relationship more satisfying.

Counselors can also help people learn how to become more sensitive to others. Counselors can ask questions such as "What do you think I'm really saying and feeling at this point?" More important, however, the counselor can help the person understand how and why he or she is insensitive and help the person recognize the problems that this insensitivity is causing.

Assertiveness

Being assertive means that people have learned to get from life what is rightfully theirs and to communicate in ways that are constructively honest. Assertive people do not permit others to block their paths to legitimate need fulfillment. They can comfortably go through each day saying, directly and indirectly, "This is what I need, and this is what I don't need."

Nonassertiveness.   At one extreme from assertiveness is nonasser-tiveness. Nonassertive people must rely on the beneficence of others to get their needs met. Either they passively wait to be nourished or they indulge in behaviors meant to earn donations from others. These people either try to exist on a meager psychological diet, or they latch onto a person who regularly meets their needs. In the latter case, the price the person pays for regular nourishment is often high. For example, the person may be asked to hand over personal freedom in payment for this service. When nonassertive people experience psychological hunger pains, they often ask the wrong questions. They ask "What's wrong with people that they won't meet my needs?" or "What's wrong with me that people won't meet my needs?" instead of the more helpful ques-tion "What's wrong with me that I don't go out and create situations in which I can meet my needs?"

Nonassertive behavior may stem from a person's lack of self-esteem. For example, a person may ask "Who am *I* to ask for what I need and say how I feel?" It could also originate from inadequate self-confidence in that the person feels that other people can take better care of him or her. Other nonassertive people may have lacked assertive models; hence, they have never had an opportunity to learn assertive behavior, even though their self-esteem is adequate.

Counselors can reflect to the person the disadvantages of being unassertive and indicate ample opportunities both in and out of coun-seling in which the person can begin a series of increasingly difficult assertive responses. The counselor can also act as an assertive model in the counseling sessions.

Aggressiveness.   At the other extreme of assertiveness is aggres-sion. Aggressive people take not only what is rightfully theirs but in-trude in the lives of others in unjust and inappropriate ways. They interrupt people, intimidate them, manipulate them, make inappropri-ate demands, criticize in destructive ways, and take over situations. They are generally loud, boisterous, and impervious to others' feelings. Because their aggressive behavior often gets them more than their fair share, they perceive no reason to discontinue it.

Aggressive people are often fearful of being ignored and overcom-pensate by making it impossible for people to ignore them. They may also be hostile people whose aggressive behavior is meant to vanquish others.

Although aggressive people often get short-term needs met by their behavior, they tend to alienate others, which prevents them from enter-ing into intimate, long-term relationships that would satisfy deeper and more meaningful needs. Hence, while these people may be surviving on a daily basis, their needs for intimacy, esteem, and acceptance remain largely unmet.

In counseling, these people are likely to behave aggressively toward the counselor, challenging his or her policies and personal qualities and making inappropriate demands. In these situations counselors can act as a model of assertiveness, standing by their policies yet not meeting force with force. Counselors can also gradually invite these people to recognize how their aggressive behavior, despite its short-term benefits, is to their overall disadvantage. As these people see the self-destructiveness of their behavior more clearly, they are in a better position to entertain more constructive options.

Being comfortable with oneself and others

Being comfortable with oneself and others means being transparent—that is, allowing oneself to be seen for who one is at any given moment. People who are transparent operate on the principle: Who you see is who I am. This allows them to be un-self-conscious and to invest themselves in the issues and in the people with whom they are communicating. They react spontaneously because they do not use censoring mechanisms to delay their reactions in order to erase parts of themselves that they do not wish others to see. In other words, they become part of the interpersonal process and not spectators observing it from a safe distance.

People who are uncomfortable with themselves are self-conscious to the point that they are a distraction to themselves. They reflexively sift their reactions, holding back those that may create anxiety and offering unauthentic responses to please others. They continually listen to an inner voice that says "How should I react now?" "What will make them accept me?" "What had I better not do or say?" They function on the principle "Who you see is not who I am but who I want you to think I am."

The basic cause of self-discomfort is fear. These people fear that if others see them as they really are, they will be thought less of or rejected or they may lack some power or control in the situation. Hence, they view many interpersonal encounters as contests to be won or lost rather than as opportunities for cooperation and enjoyment.

Their self-consciousness often causes them to act in ways that are tense, stilted, and guarded, which makes other people uncomfortable. In this milieu of mutual discomfort, few if any needs will be met by either person.

People bring their discomfort into the counseling situation and may create a state of contagion in which the counselor "catches" the discomfort. The counselor may begin to feel tense, distracted, or irritated. Counselors in this situation can "inoculate" themselves from the person's discomfort by separating themselves from the person's insecurities and by helping the person circumscribe anxieties so that they do not permeate the whole atmosphere. For example, a counselor may say "Let's see if you can put into one sentence what your major concern is right now." Often when people can isolate their greatest concern, they experience a certain peace, even if the concern itself is anxiety producing. This occurs because the person no longer needs to scamper about trying to camouflage the concern from himself or the counselor.

As the counselor continues to provide a warm and accepting atmosphere, the person becomes more willing to be transparent until he or she becomes an integral part of the session, and not a wary spectator.

Being freeing

People who are freeing allow others to be themselves. Their message is "Be who you are with me, and you are free to come and go as you please." This message invites others to relax and to get their needs met in ways that are most satisfying to them.

People who are not freeing post conditions others must meet before they will be permitted to relate with them in any meaningful way. Some common conditions people stipulate before allowing others to relate with them are:

You must be intelligent and logical.
You must be serious and correct.
You must agree with me.
You must not hurt my feelings.
You must be who I want you to be.
You must be as crazy as I am.

In other words, unfreeing people carry with them a psychological pillory into which others must squeeze their psyches if they wish to relate. The problem with this is that secure people will not wish to subject themselves to these conditions, and insecure people may accept them but demand more than they will give. In the first case, the unfreeing person is left with few, if any, need suppliers; in the second case, the unfree person must pay a high price for this basically damaging relationship. In neither case will mutual need fulfillment be adequate.

Freeing people allow others to meet their needs in the ways and places they choose. Unfreeing people have difficulty doing this. They often cast the gauntlet: "Either I meet the majority of your needs and you meet the majority of mine, or you'll be sorry." Although this ultimatum is rarely explicitly stated, it is readily felt when the other person attempts to get his or her needs met from other people and in other situations.

People who have failed to develop this competency are both frightened and needy. Their fear causes them to set up conditions for relationships that screen out secure people, whom they would perceive as threatening, and admit insecure people, who will meet their needs without being a threat. Some people are unfreeing because that is the way others treated them, and they have had no opportunity to learn any other way of relating with people.

Unfreeing people are likely to bring their conditions for relating into counseling. They commonly refuse to relate with the counselor unless the following conditions are met:

You share my religious and philosophical values.
You let me control the counseling situation.
You promise you will be able to help me.
You agree not to face me with realities I don't want to see.
You agree with my perception of my problem.

These conditions are usually presented immediately; so the counselor must be ready to react quickly to them. Obviously, counselors cannot agree to any conditions that would restrict their role. When the counselor communicates this fact, tension usually arises. The counselor can calmly explain that the basis of a counseling relationship is mutual freedom. During this period, which may last for one or a few sessions, the counselor is giving the person some important data upon which to make a decision about counseling. If the person is able to understand what the counselor is saying, he or she may decide to continue with the sessions with a much better appreciation for the nature of counseling. If the person chooses to continue, the counselor can gradually help the person recognize the fears and needs that are underwriting the conditions so that they can be dealt with and either reduced or expressed in more constructive ways.

If the person insists that the conditions are nonnegotiable, he or she may decide to terminate the sessions. If this occurs, it is a self-evident sign that the person was not a reasonable candidate for counseling at that time, although the person may need counseling. Nevertheless, if the counselor handled the situation in a firm yet understanding manner, the person may enter counseling at a time when he or she is more ready to use it.

Realistic expectations of self and others

People who have realistic expectations of themselves realize that they have imperfections. Consequently, they do not place pressure on themselves always to be correct, intelligent, benevolent, selfless, kind, mature, sensitive, firm, interesting, or attractive. Although they realize that each of these qualities may be a virtue, they also recognize that there will be times and situations in which they do not possess them and perhaps even fail miserably.

People with unrealistically high expectations of themselves generally react in one of two ways. They seriously expect to meet their unrealistically high expectations, which causes them to focus more on themselves than on the interpersonal event. They are so busy trying to earn high marks that the interpersonal encounter is simply a stage on which they are performing. Or they realize that they cannot meet their high expectations; hence, they avoid all but the most necessary and superficial interpersonal situations in order to protect their pride. In neither case can satisfactory mutual need fulfillment occur.

People who have unrealistic expectations of themselves were often taught that they had to be better than they were in order to earn praise and love. Others were taught that they had to be superior to everyone else; hence, they developed goals for themselves that in their mind would make them better than others. These individuals often say, "I can forgive others much easier than myself," as if to say, "I expect *others* to make mistakes, but I don't expect *me* to make mistakes."

In counseling, these people often present their self-ideals as their goals for counseling. They want counselors to help them reach their ideals rather than to help them face and accept their limitations. This often causes a point of tension because when the nature of counseling is explained to them, they often view it as a place where they must learn to become inferior. As the counselor helps these people understand the folly of their expectations, the fears and myths that created them, and their self-defeating nature, these people can gradually learn to relax with themselves and others.

Some people have unrealistic expectations of others. They experience frequent frustration and conflict in interpersonal relationships, which significantly reduces the potential for mutual need fulfillment. The following are some typical unrealistic expectations of others:

People must like me.

People must be reliable.

People must be fair.

People must not hurt me.

People must be there when I need them.
People must think of me first.
People must be honest with me.
People must not break promises.
People must not use me.
People must not talk about me behind my back.

Of course, most people cannot meet any one of these expectations, much less two or more. Consequently, those who harbor these unrealistic expectations either give up trying to relate with others in meaningful ways or they endure an endless series of hurts, frustrations, and fractured relationships.

People learned to have unrealistic expectations of others from having unreal expectations foisted on them. They naturally felt that if such expectations were made of them, it is logical that they should make them of others. Or the unreal expectations of others have been created to cover weaknesses in themselves; for example, a woman may demand that people love her because she lacks the ability to love herself.

Unrealistic expectations of people will likely be brought into the counseling situation. These people expect the counselor to be someone he or she can never be and likely *should* never be. The unrealistic expectations will be obvious when friction develops in the relationship. The friction often stems from the person's feeling double-crossed: "You're supposed to be kind all the time, and you're not being kind"; "You're supposed to be right all the time, and you were wrong." Counselors should be careful not to fall into the trap of trying to meet the unrealistic expectations of the person in counseling. Counselors who fall into this trap are tacitly agreeing that the expectations are reasonable. As counselors help these individuals discover the causes of their expectations and the problems they create, the person can begin the gradual process of dismantling them and replacing them with no expectations or expectations that are more firmly grounded in reality.

Self-protection in interpersonal situations

People who have learned this competency have faith in themselves that they will be able to handle whatever happens in a relationship. They have successfully learned the art of psychological self-defense; so they feel free to travel with confidence in any kind of interpersonal terrain. They have learned to spot potential dangers in interpersonal relationships and defuse them before damage occurs. If they do find themselves in a difficult situation, they also have the competencies to extricate themselves.

People who lack this competency fear that situations will arise in which they will be powerless to defend themselves. They may be frightened of any of the following:

They will be manipulated into being someone they don't wish to be or into doing what they don't want to do.

They will become trapped and imprisoned by the other person.

They will be deceived and ultimately rejected.

They will build hopes that will be dashed.

They will be used as a crutch, punching bag, crying towel, or sexual release.

They will experience feelings they cannot control—for example, feelings of dependency, sexuality, anger, or jealousy.

They will eventually do something that will seriously hurt the other person.

These people feel that the chances are at least reasonable if not good that any or all of these situations could occur, causing psychological damage. As a result, they either do not allow themselves to come close enough to people for these events to occur or they relate with only a very few people who, while tried and true, continually offer the same bland psychological diet.

These individuals never learned how to avoid interpersonal traps by anticipating them and taking appropriate action. For example, they never developed the permission or strength to convey "I'm sorry, but I can't do that or be that; so let's try a different way of relating." And if no constructive way of relating could be found, they never learned to say "I'm sorry; I have to leave this relationship now." They have not learned why feelings well up inside them as they get closer in a relationship and how to handle these feelings so that they do not control it. As a result, they either avoid relationships or tentatively approach them with an apprehension that dooms the relationship before it gets very far.

One reason people failed to learn this competency is that they were eyewitnesses to people being trapped, enslaved, and damaged in relationships. They assumed these events were an ordinary part of relating. They made a decision that they would never allow to happen to them what they saw happen to a mother, father, sibling, or other close relative.

They also may need to avoid close relationships or endure conflictual ones as a way of keeping themselves in a state of unhappiness they feel they deserve for one reason or another. Or they simply may not have had sufficient modeling in this behavior.

It is common for these people to bring their sense of interpersonal powerlessness into the counseling relationship. In fact, these fears may become more pronounced in counseling because people who lack the ability to protect themselves may view the counselor as a powerful person who can take control of them and their lives. As a result, they relate to the counselor from a distance and continually survey the area for possible traps. Counselors can allow themselves to be searched for weapons and assure the person that nothing will happen in counseling without mutual agreement. As counseling progresses, the counselor can help people find keys that will help them remain free in any relationship. Counselors can be careful not to debunk the person's fears because they could have some validity in the overall world of interpersonal relating. The best way to increase people's sense of security in interpersonal relationships is to afford them the skills to extricate themselves from stifling relationships and to develop competencies that will provide the basis for need-fulfilling interactions.

SUMMARY

With regard to need fulfillment, counseling has five goals:

1. Introduce people to their specific needs, since frequently people who enter counseling are experiencing psychological anemia but have no idea of the cause.

2. Help people acquire the courage and competencies to meet these needs. It is also important for these people to move away from significant others who refuse or are incapable of meeting these needs and to move toward those who are interested in a mutually fulfilling relationship.

3. Help people realize that it is their responsibility to get their needs met and not the responsibility of others. It is up to *them* to get freedom in their lives, to create a stimulating lifestyle, to give life meaning, to ignite a sense of hope in themselves, and to relate with people who are both willing and able to enter into a mutually need-fulfilling relationship and to refrain from relating with people who are not.

4. Meet some of these needs in the person in counseling, not to the extent that the person needs no one except the counselor, but in a way that encourages the person to get needs met with people outside of counseling.

5. Help people recognize that sometimes they are blocking their own need fulfillment. They may be clamping shut their own psycholog-

ical intravenous for several reasons: fear of getting close to people; anger at people, which prevents them from accepting concern or love; or unresolved guilt, which prevents them from enjoying life.

The majority of people who seek counseling experience difficulties with interpersonal or intrapersonal competencies. These difficulties are either a direct reflection of intrapersonal weaknesses or are a result of the person's lack of opportunity to learn interpersonal skills. In either case, the counselor's role is to introduce the person to the specific competency or competencies that are weak and to provide opportunities for the person to develop the competency both within and outside of counseling.

THOUGHT QUESTIONS

1. Of the eight psychological needs discussed in this chapter, which two do you get met the most, and how does getting them met increase your effectiveness as a counselor? Which two do you get met the least, and how does failing to meet them decrease your effectiveness as a counselor?
2. When can receiving affection from a person in counseling create a problem, and when can *not* accepting affection create a problem?
3. What cautions can counselors be mindful of when meeting the need for hope in the people they see in counseling?
4. A subtle yet destructive dynamic that can occur in counseling is that the person who lacks self-esteem grows in counseling to merit the counselor's esteem. How could you tell whether a person is progressing for the sake of growth or for the sake of winning your esteem?
5. No one is perfectly assertive in all situations. What stressful event could occur in counseling that would cause you to be aggressive? What event could arise that would cause you to be nonassertive?

CHAPTER 4

The Person of
the Counselor

Counselors and researchers tend to agree that the personality of the counselor is the most important factor in counseling. As Perez states, "What these research findings show is that experience, theoretical orientation and technique utilized are not the critical determinants for effectiveness as a therapist. The implication is strong in these studies that it is the counselor's personal qualities, not his education and training, which are a more promising criteria for evaluation of his effectiveness."[1]

The counselor's personality is the fulcrum on which are balanced knowledge of behavior dynamics and therapeutic skills. To the degree that the fulcrum is strong, knowledge and skills will work in a balanced way to effect positive behavioral change in counseling. To the extent that the fulcrum is weak—that is, the counselor's personality is not a helpful one—the counselor's knowledge and skills will not be effectively used or will be used in a damaging way.

The belief that a counselor's personality is the key influence in the counseling relationship calls forth two important questions.

1. Does this belief mean that a helpful personality compensates for inadequate knowledge of behavior and/or poor therapeutic skills? The answer is no. Human behavior is very complex, and while there is still a great deal that is unknown, there is also much that is known. Helpful

---

[1]Perez (1979), p. 80.

personal qualities, knowledge of behavior, and counseling skills cannot substitute for each other. A helpful personality that lacks knowledge and helping skills is like a good driver who operates an unsafe car. Despite the driver's qualities, a great deal of damage can be done.

2. Does it mean that personal qualities can be learned in the same ways and settings as knowledge of behavior and counseling skills? The answer is no, because people acquire personal qualities differently than they learn academic knowledge and skills. Personal qualities accrue from a complicated and continuing mixture of genetics, constitution, environmental influences, and the unique ways people tailor all these to fit their beings and/or shape their beings to fit these influences.

Advanced education and training are much more likely to influence growth quantitatively than qualitatively. In other words, they can help people become more of who they already are, but not different than they already are. For example, a series of lectures and readings can help counselors learn a good deal about the phenomenon of resistance in counseling. But academic knowledge cannot give people the self-awareness, patience, and strengths necessary to handle resistance. As Corey writes, "My main point is that I think it is misleading to dupe student counselors into the idea that counseling is a science that is separate and distinct from the behavior and personality of the counselor."[2]

This chapter discusses 12 more or less separate qualities a counselor should possess to a significant degree. These qualities are not ideals, but necessary requirements for effective functioning as a counselor. The ideal is to possess each of these qualities in its entirety, which, of course, is unattainable. For this reason, the concept of "becoming" is important. No matter to what degree counselors possess or lack a particular helpful quality, they can always become more than they are.[3]

COUNSELOR QUALITIES

The discussion of each quality cites specific reasons the quality is important in counseling, provides concrete descriptions of how the quality is manifested, and discusses how obstacles can interfere with these qualities.

[2]Corey (1977), p. 197.
[3]For other discussions of the characteristics of helpful counselors, see Brammer (1979), pp. 27-43, and Pietrofesa, Hoffman, Splete, & Pinto (1978), pp. 117-205.

Self-knowledge

Self-knowledge means that counselors know themselves well enough that they almost always know exactly what they are doing, why they are doing it, which problems are theirs, and which belong to the person in counseling.

Self-knowledge in a counselor is important for the following reasons. First, counselors who have an accurate perception of themselves will tend to have accurate perceptions of the people they see in counseling. Blind spots in self-perception can cause blind spots in the counselor's whole perceptual field. For example, if some counselors do not realize that they enjoy discussing sex more than any other topic, they may unconsciously angle people in counseling to speak at length about their sex lives. From this the counselor erroneously concludes that if people need to speak so much about their sex lives, sex must be the basis of their problems.

Second, the skills counselors use to know themselves are the same ones used to know others. Consequently, the more self-knowledge counselors have, the more chance they have to know others. For example, counselors who possess the skills to see through their own attempts at self-deception are in a better position to see through the ruses of the people they see in counseling.

Third, counselors who have acquired the skills used in self-knowledge are also in a good position to teach them to others. For example, counselors who have developed the ability to see beneath their subconscious motivations can teach these keys to the person in counseling.

Finally, self-knowledge permits counselors to feel and communicate genuine compassion to the person in counseling. When counselors are aware of and feel their weaknesses, they are in a much better position to feel with the person in counseling. These counselors are in touch with how it is to feel ashamed, stupid, frightened, hypocritical, weak, jealous, irrational, and guilty. When they tell a person, "I understand how you are feeling," their nonverbal behavior leaves no doubt that they truly do.

Counselors with a good degree of self-knowledge share the following qualities.

1. They are well aware of their needs. As counselors, they recognize that they must be especially careful with regard to the needs to achieve, to feel important, needed, superior, in control, powerful, and affirmed. While none of these needs is inherently damaging, the more

they mingle and compete with the need to be altruistically helpful, the less effective counselors will be.

2. They are well aware of their feelings. Feelings of hurt, fear, anger, guilt, love, or sex will be part of every counselor's responses. None of these feelings is problematic in itself and, in fact, can contribute much to the counseling relationship. Problems arise, however, when counselors are not aware exactly which feeling is operating. For example, counselors may be aware of their anger toward the person in counseling but may be unaware that the anger is simply an offshoot of hurt. Problems also arise when counselors are unaware of how a feeling is causing them to react in counseling. For example, they may be aware of sexual feelings toward the person but may see no connection between that and deciding that the person should attend counseling more frequently.

3. They are aware of what makes them anxious in counseling and what defenses they are inclined to use to reduce the anxiety. Questions regarding or attacks on their knowledge, sophistication, maturity, reasonableness, sexuality, strength, good intentions, common sense, attractiveness, openmindedness, or moral or therapeutic values may cause anxiety. They are aware of the defenses they could use to ward off the anxiety: becoming passive and dormant, hoping that the person will feel guilty and stop the assault; imperceptibly changing the topic; becoming suddenly nondirective and reflective; scolding, blaming, or threatening; using examples or analogies to distract ("I understand your frustration with me. It would be as if someone said to me . . ."); intellectualizing ("Let me try to help you understand your sexual feelings toward me"); teaching ("I think you are more hurt than angry at me. You see, what our psyche does when it is hurt is . . ."); daydreaming; using humor; giving pep talks; and tabling anxiety-producing issues until "a more appropriate time."

4. They recognize their strengths and weaknesses. A counselor whose strengths include a genuine affection for people can express this directly when a session is filled with confusion and despair, thus providing a source of support. This does not mean the counselor grabs for care as a surgeon grabs for a set of clamps. It simply reflects an awareness of an internal quality that has always been there but needs to be communicated directly at a particular time.

Effective counselors are also in touch with their weaknesses. Counselors who tend to blame others when things are not progressing well can use an awareness of this tendency to slow down their reflexive response to blame long enough to provide another option. These counselors realize that because they are always growing, they will continue to develop new skills and acquire new weaknesses. Consequently, they are constantly reassessing their abilities and liabilities because no tally is ever final.

One of the main obstacles to continuing self-knowledge is that counselors use the same defenses as everyone else to protect themselves from an accurate view of themselves and their work. They tend to congratulate themselves when things are going well in counseling and to blame a lack of progress on the resistance or poor motivation of the person in counseling.

Competence

Competence means that a counselor possesses the physical, intellectual, emotional, social, and moral qualities necessary to be a helpful person. Competence in a counselor is important because people enter counseling to learn and develop the competencies needed to live more effectively and happily. The counselor's role is to teach these competencies. Consequently, the more competencies counselors possess, the more they will be able to teach them, both directly and indirectly. Counselors who lack physical stamina, intellectual acuteness, emotional sensitivity, social awareness, or sound moral values will be in a poor position to teach these competencies.

One of the main differences between a friendship and a counseling relationship is the competency of the helper. Effective counselors have a combination of academic knowledge, personal qualities, and helping skills. It would be rare to find a friend with this combination. If a counselor does not possess strengths in all three areas, the counseling relationship is no different, and therefore no more helpful, than any other relationship.

Competence in a counselor also generates confidence in the person in counseling. Confidence is what gives the person the momentum to take risks in counseling that have never been taken but are necessary for personality growth. People in counseling make intuitive judgments about their counselor's competencies. For example, a person may tell a friend "My counselor seems to be brilliant, but he is difficult to relate with" or "My counselor is a very caring person, but she doesn't seem to know what to do with me." It takes only a few sessions for a person in counseling to develop abiding confidence in a counselor or a nagging doubt that threads its way through each session.

Competence in a counselor also is important for the efficient use of time in counseling. The more competent the counselor, the more counseling will have specific goals and concrete methods of achieving them. The counselor and person in counseling share an ongoing sense of direction that enables them to evaluate progress and make appropriate changes to ensure continuing growth. The less competent the counselor, the more time is spent on "fishing expeditions," unproductive discussions, and hit-and-miss stratagems.

Counselors who continually strive to become more competent share the following qualities.

1. They continually increase their knowledge of behavior and counseling by reading relevant professional periodicals and books, attending conferences, and discussing their cases with colleagues. To these pools of public knowledge they add a private wisdom that stems from their personal experiences in life and counseling.

2. They seek new life experiences that will help them hone existing competencies to a sharper edge and develop new skills. They do this by accepting risks, responsibilities, and challenges that cause them a certain amount of anxiety. They then use this anxiety to actualize previously untapped potential.

3. They try new ideas and approaches in counseling. From their study and experiences evolve new frontiers that they are willing to explore and implement in their counseling. While confident in their competencies, they are always willing to add a new one to their repertoire. New theories and approaches are considered and old ones reconsidered with a new and deeper understanding. They are always looking for one more way to be more helpful to the next person they see in counseling.

4. They evaluate their effectiveness by scrutinizing each session with an eye to how it could have been more productive and by inviting ongoing, final, and follow-up evaluation from the people they see in counseling.

One of the main obstacles to developing new competencies is the myth that an academic degree and a fair amount of experience automatically and irrevocably qualify a person as an effective counselor. The fact that some states must force counselors to continue their education if they wish to be relicensed points to the fact that the myth is a powerful one.

Good psychological health

Counselors need not be paragons of psychological health, but they should possess at least sound psychological health. They also should be more psychologically healthy than the people they see in counseling. The counselor should possess the qualities the person in counseling would like to develop.

Good psychological health in a counselor is important because personal psychological health must underlie the counselor's understanding of behavior and skills. When understanding and knowledge are built on sound psychological health, they form a very positive force in counseling. When they rest on a base of inadequate psychological health, they become forces that lead to confusion and damage.

Counselors are models of behavior, whether or not they choose to be. Every counseling session is a period of intense tutoring in adaptive behavior. When counselors lack psychological health, their frame of reference will be defective, causing even more anxiety in the person. When this occurs, the counselor has become part of the problem rather than part of the solution.

The better a counselor's psychological health, the more helpful the counseling relationship is likely to be. Counselors in poor psychological health can become contaminated by their overdriven needs, idiosyncratic perceptions, and distorted values, creating conflict, confusion, and iatrogenic (doctor-induced) symptoms.

When counselors lack adequate psychological health, one of two things will occur with regard to the person in counseling. Either the person will possess enough psychological strength to sense the problem and therefore terminate counseling, or the person and the counselor will enter into a relationship based on neurotic collusion in which the problems of one feed on the problems of the other. This allows both to maintain their problems while sharing the illusion that they are making progress.

Psychologically healthy counselors share the following qualities.

1. They get their needs for security, love, nurturance, power, sex, and affirmation met primarily outside of the counseling relationship. As a result, the need to be helpful in the altruistic sense is their most powerful need in the counseling relationship.

2. They keep their past and current personal problems out of counseling. They do not approach each session weighted down with the unfinished business of their lives, such as unresolved childhood fantasies of heroism, romance, and sex; conflicts regarding members of the same sex, opposite sex, or authority figures; or biases against certain socially disapproved behaviors, values, or personality types. They also do not allow their current personal problems to interfere with their work. Counselors can learn to focus on a person in counseling with the

same intensity and freedom from distraction that a biologist enjoys while peering through his or her microscope. Counselors cannot afford to have many days in which their personal concerns impair their concentration or create the attitude "You think *you've* got problems!"

3. They are aware of personal biases and weak spots, which helps them recognize situations that may activate these problem areas. They can separate what *they* would like for the person in counseling from what the *person* would like.

4. They are not only surviving in life but living it quite well. Their lives outside of counseling are stimulating and enjoyable. They read, write, travel, play, and enjoy the company of diverse friends and the privacy of being alone. They oxygenate their psyches outside of counseling so that they resuscitate people in counseling without becoming burned out. They do not ordinarily find counseling burdensome because they bring to it a buoyancy created by their personal lives.

One of the main obstacles to counselors' functioning in a psychologically healthy way is that they allow the fears and dissatisfactions of their personal lives to drive them into establishing a pseudocommunity made up of counseling and people in counseling. In this community they feel a sense of security, importance, and satisfaction. A vicious cycle begins: the more they get needs met in this pseudocommunity, the less they need their family, friends, and avocations. And the less they need them, the more they psychologically feed off the people they are supposed to be helping and withdraw from the people who can help them the most.

Trustworthiness

Trustworthy means that the counselor is not a threat to the person in counseling. Trust in a counselor is important for the following reasons.

First, one of the essential goals of counseling is to encourage people to reveal their innermost selves. In order to do this, the person must be able to feel that the counselor will understand and accept the revelations without shock or disapproval. If the person cannot feel this sense of trust, revelations will be superficial or nonexistent, thus frustrating the purpose of most counseling.

Trust includes confidentiality. People must believe with absolute certitude that both the fact that they are in counseling and the nature of what they reveal will be kept absolutely confidential unless they release the counselor from confidentiality. What people reveal in counseling is often very difficult for them to hear, and it is doubly difficult to have a counselor hear it. But to have an outsider know it can be devastating to the person and destroy the counseling relationship.

People in counseling need to trust the counselor's motivations and character. They need to rest assured that the counselor's main motive is to help them and that no motives are contrary to or more pressing than this. They should not be distracted by the possibility of being used as an experimental subject, surrogate need gratifier, or primarily as a source of revenue.

Finally, when people experience the consistency, acceptance, and confidentiality of the counselor, it helps them develop a deeper sense of trust in themselves. As they better understand their needs, feelings, impulses, motivations, defenses, weaknesses, and strengths, they can accept them more fully. When this occurs, people no longer fear, but can recognize and control their behavior. Once people can trust themselves, they are capable of trusting others, which is the first step in establishing meaningful and satisfying relationships.

Counselors who inspire trust share the following qualities.

1. They are reliable and consistent. They arrive on time for appointments and finish on time. They keep their promises and live by their agreements. There are no surprises. While they have their good and bad days, they are not temperamental or moody. They are not happy one time and depressed another; they do not exert maximum energy at one session and coast the next; they are not wildly confrontative at one visit and passively spectatoring at the next. They do not make haphazard shifts in orientation or procedure from one stage of counseling to another. The people they see in counseling are confident who is going to be awaiting them at the next session and are not forced to make adjustments to fit the vicissitudes of the counselor.

2. They verbally and nonverbally assure the person that confidentiality is absolute. They do not assume that the person in counseling realizes this. They do not mention, directly or indirectly, any other people they see in counseling. For all the person knows, he or she is the only one the counselor sees. Moreover, all phone conversations, correspondence, and reports dealing with the person are openly discussed and shared. These counselors' behavior makes it virtually impossible to doubt their professionalism.

3. They never make a person regret having made a revelation. They listen nonjudgmentally and accept revelations with understanding and kindness. The counselor who is confused by what is shared makes certain that the person understands that the confusion is not disapproval. The counselor may bring up a revelation later in counseling, but it is done so the person doesn't feel haunted by it.

4. They are responsible, in the literal sense of the word. They are able to respond to the person totally so that the person feels confident that the counselor will not miss much and certainly nothing of value. They respond with keen awareness of who the person is by remembering all pertinent information and keeping records straight. They respond by answering phone calls, by not forgetting appointments or suggestions, and by filling out forms before the deadline. They respond in an ethical and professional way that ensures the person the counselor has provided a growth environment with maximum potential. They respond by seeking consultations when necessary, making intelligent referrals, and terminating counseling at the appropriate time.

One of the main obstacles to trustworthiness is the counselor's distraction with other matters. These distractions cause counselors to be careless: They forget relevant material; they are late for appointments and dismiss people early; they are preoccupied during the sessions with "more pressing" business. Counselors who are "busy people" with "hectic schedules" and "many commitments" must be especially careful that these pressures do not interfere with their trustworthiness.

Honesty

Absolute honesty means that the counselor is transparent, authentic, and genuine. These characteristics are important in counseling for the following reasons. First, transparency allows the counselor and the person in counseling to get as close to each other as is helpful. Counselors who protect or hide parts of themselves from the person in counseling create a buffer zone that hinders intimacy. Psychological intimacy is important in counseling because it enables both the counselor and the person to relate directly and openly. To the degree that there are bunkers between a counselor and the person in counseling, growth will be impeded.

Second, honesty permits the counselor to give unvarnished feedback to the person in counseling. Most people receive very little personal feedback from others, and when they do, it is often dishonest and inaccurate because it is tinted by the overly positive or negative attitudes of the person giving it. Honest feedback is a precious commodity and one that requires absolute honesty in a counselor.

Also, honesty in a counselor is a genuine invitation for the person to be honest in return. It is one thing for counselors verbally to invite a person in counseling to be honest; it is another for counselors effectively to invite a person to be honest by being honest about themselves and the person in counseling. When counselors "jump into the water" first, the person is brought a step closer to the possibility that counseling is a safe place to be honest.

The counselor can be a model of how to be honest in constructive ways. People often undershoot or overshoot the target when they first attempt to be absolutely honest. A counselor who is honest communicates "Here is a way you can be truly honest without unduly hurting other people." When people in counseling can witness the constructive expression of honesty and experience its salutary effects, they will be more inclined to be honest with themselves and the people in their lives.

Counselors who are absolutely honest share the following qualities.

1. They are congruent; that is, their real self (who they are) is identical to their public self (who they allow others to think they are). They realize that honesty with people in counseling means much more than simply refraining from lying to them. Their behavior says to a person "Who you see is who I am."

2. They realize that absolute honesty creates anxiety in the person toward whom it is directed, and they are prepared to deal with it. They do their best to prevent avoidable anxiety but recognize that both the nature of the message and the way the person perceives it can create anxiety. They also realize that the person will attempt to reduce the anxiety by denying the validity of the message, by attacking or withdrawing from the counselor, or by becoming emotionally upset. However, honest counselors do not allow these reactions to deter them from conveying information that ultimately could be helpful.

3. They have a clear and reasonable understanding of what absolute honesty means. They realize that they cannot share everything they think and feel during a counseling session. They know that they must be selective but refuse to use this as a loophole through which honesty escapes. They operate according to four principles: (a) Every significant emotional reaction that deals with the person is shared within the same session that it occurs. This allows the reaction to remain fresh and prevents it from becoming intellectualized, forgotten, or submerged so as to haunt or sabotage future sessions. (b) If these counselors are distracted to a significant degree by something outside of counseling, they share this fact (though not necessarily its cause) so that the person will not think he or she caused the distraction. (c) When asked personal questions, effective counselors either answer them directly or directly decline to answer them, then deal with the implication for counseling. They do not deflect the question with the hope that the person will

eventually forget it. (d) Counselors who have questions or thoughts (in contrast to emotional reactions) regarding the person can express them at a later time if current expression would be an unnecessary intrusion into the flow of counseling at that point. In other words, they give the person in counseling the same degree of honesty that they would appreciate receiving.

4. They recognize the importance of conveying both "positive" and "negative" honesty. Positive honesty means that good feelings about the person in counseling are expressed forthrightly and un-self-consciously. People in counseling need to know what about them makes others feel good as well as what makes them feel anxious. Effective counselors also communicate problematic feelings about people in counseling. However, they do this with a spirit of kindness and optimism.

One main obstacle to absolute honesty in counseling is a need to be liked and/or to remain as stress-free as possible. These needs allow counselors to grant themselves "therapeutic dispensation" from honesty. They may decide that a certain honesty would not be "facilitative," would be "too much, too soon," or is simply a "countertransference reaction." This allows them to avoid honesty except when it poses little or no threat to them.

Strength

Counselors have the courage to do what their deepest selves say is the helpful and just thing to do in counseling. Strength is the midpoint between intimidation and weakness. Strength in a counselor is important because it allows the person in counseling to feel safe. The person sees the counselor as one who can remain steadfast in the face of manipulation, who can support the person despite the excess weight of his or her problems, who can handle personal needs and problems so they do not interfere with counseling, and who can accept criticism without falling apart or attacking in return.

The counselor also needs strength to withstand the psychological assaults and manipulations of the person in counseling. The "weaknesses" that a person brings into counseling can be very powerful. At times the person will attempt to overpower the counselor with sheer force. At other times, the person will try to seduce the counselor with pseudocooperation, compliments, and gratitude. It takes a strong counselor to withstand these attempts and to accept and help the person in spite of them.

Strength also removes the counselor as a source of distraction to the person in counseling. Some people in counseling are forced to worry as much about the counselor as they do about themselves. This may occur when a counselor lacks the strength to keep himself or herself separate from the person in counseling, to refrain from injecting personal needs into the relationship, to allow the person to leave counseling, or to adhere to professional ethics.

Finally, strength is important because it can be contagious. People often enter counseling because they lack the strength to be assertive, to resist the manipulations of others, and to enter into intimate relationships without losing their selfhood. The counselor's strengths can be gradually transfused to the person, who can then grow in self-protection, self-sufficiency, and self-sharing.

Strong counselors share the following qualities.

1. They set reasonable limits and adhere to them. Limits in counseling are important because they help define the nature of the relationship, encourage the best use of time and energy, and clarify both parties' responsibilities. Counselors must set limits with regard to the length and number of sessions, the counselor's availability between sessions, the extent to which a counselor is willing to intervene in the person's life outside of counseling, and the amount of fees and method of payment. Counselors not only set clear and reasonable limits, but adhere to them, despite pressure to make exceptions.

2. They can say difficult things and make unpopular decisions. There are times when a counselor must say things that will evoke hurt and anger in the person, no matter how kindly they are said. At other times, counselors must make decisions that will upset the person—for example, to increase or decrease the number of sessions, to refuse to intercede for the person outside of counseling, or to discontinue a counseling relationship. Although it may be difficult, effective counselors act according to their best judgments because their need to be helpful is stronger than their need to be liked.

3. They are flexible. Their strength allows them to approach both counseling and the person in counseling with an openness that invites new ideas, procedures, and challenges. They are willing to listen to and seriously consider the ideas and suggestions of the person in counseling. They are able to try new approaches to facilitate the counseling process and to redefine the limits of counseling in the face of new developments. They can tailor their philosophy of counseling to keep up with their professional and personal growth.

4. They are able to remain separate from the person in counseling. Their self-identity is clear, which allows them to become involved in both the person in counseling and the counseling process while remaining separate enough to be of help. They empathize with, but do not

overidentify with, the person in counseling, so they do not *become* the person. When the counselor overidentifies with the person, there is no longer a counselor in the room but simply two people immersed in the same subjectivity. Effective counselors are involved in the process of counseling, but not immersed in it. Their separateness allows them to resist being swept along by whatever maelstrom of emotions is operative at the time.

One of the main obstacles to a counselor being strong is the need to be an agreeable person—one who does not create anxiety in another. Effective counselors possess a "kind strength." Kindness without strength nurtures weakness; strength without kindness breeds resentment. A judicious combination of the two invites growth.

Warmth

Warmth means being kind, caring, and compassionate. Warmth is communicated mostly nonverbally—through tone of voice, expression of eyes, posture, and gestures. Warmth is important in counseling because it melts defenses. People bring into counseling the same defenses that caused them problems before counseling. In fact, they may reinforce their defenses upon entering counseling in order to handle this new and unfamiliar stress. Neither verbal support nor the mere fact that they are in the sanctuary of counseling is enough to melt defenses. Only the counselor's warmth will gradually allow people to relate with themselves and the counselor in ways that are free from distortion.

Warmth also invites sharing on an emotional level. There is an important difference between sharing personal data with the counselor and sharing the emotionally laden deeper parts of oneself. The professional role of the counselor is enough to call forth information from people; but only the counselor's warmth will invite people to share their being. Intellectual insights without warmth are like seeds without sunshine—their potential will never be actualized. Warmth creates a nurturing environment in which insights, feelings, and hopes unfold and can become part of the person's life outside of counseling. This is possible because warmth appeals directly to the heart, and until the heart is involved, no changes of any substance will occur. For example, a person may leave a counseling session *knowing* the counselor cares because the counselor *said* so. A second person leaves counseling *feeling* that the counselor cares because he or she *showed* it. The second person is likely to do more with that session than the first.

When people receive warmth, it eventually allows them to be warm toward themselves. One problem with many people in counseling is that they have run out of warmth; consequently, they have lost the ability to be kind, caring, and compassionate with themselves. As they regain this ability, they can share warmth with others. This allows them to experience the good feeling that sharing warmth brings, and it also elicits warmth from other people, which is essential in a good relationship.

Warm counselors share the following qualities.

1. They receive at least adequate warmth in their personal lives and therefore can afford to share it with others. When counselors fail to receive adequate warmth in their lives, they become businesslike and distant. Counselors who receive warmth deeply appreciate its preciousness and wish to share it with others.

2. They distinguish between warmth and humidity. Warmth is prudent, melts defenses, and unfolds potential. Humidity is omnipresent, sticky, and oppressive. It heightens defenses and suffocates potential. The warm counselor is caring and freeing; the humid counselor is needy and possessive.

3. They are nonthreatening. They allow people to feel comfortable and reasonably relaxed in their presence. Their message is "I will do nothing to make you feel less a person." They do not send messages that declare "To be accepted by me, you will have to be intelligent . . . interesting . . . docile . . . tough . . . reasonable . . . mature . . . moral." They accept people where they are and work from that point.

4. They are deeply in touch with their own humanity. They are like "old shoes"—they are not perfect and may not always look attractive, but they make people very comfortable. For them, caring, kindness, and compassion are not academic tools with which to prod and seduce people into growth. These qualities have become a natural part of their being and have evolved from dealing with their own insecurities, frailties, mistakes, and shortcomings. Their attitude is "Let's see how we two imperfect people can help each other get where you want to be."

One of the main obstacles to warmth is an intellectualized approach to life. Intellectualized counselors specialize in figuring out people rather than feeling with them. These counselors sometimes misunderstand the meaning of the concept of "professional distance" and include in it the necessity of keeping an emotional distance between themselves and the person in counseling.

Active responsiveness

The counselor is dynamically involved in the process of counseling. Active responsivity is the midpoint between being hyperactive to the point of distraction and stuporously passive to the point of being somnolent. Active responsivity in a counselor is important because it communicates personal caring. When a counselor is obviously alert, asks the right questions, gives helpful feedback, reacts emotionally, and shares responsibility for the helping process, the person cannot help but feel the counselor's genuine enthusiasm, caring, and liking. People may feel that an inordinately passive counselor is professionally, but not personally, concerned. The feeling of professional concern tends to wear thin, especially when the person is putting a great deal of time, energy, and sacrifice into counseling. One common complaint heard about counselors is "He just sat there and listened, nodded a few times, repeated what I said, and told me when my time was up." While this could be a distortion manufactured by the person's resistance, the complaint seems to be so common that one is led to believe there must be some truth in it.

Active responsivity also stimulates and encourages the person to react spontaneously to the counselor. This gives the counselor eyewitness information as to how the person relates with others. Prudent "mixing it up" with the person will render a storehouse of fresh information that the counselor has no other way of attaining.

When counselors are actively responsive to people in counseling, they engage in situational teaching. By their responsiveness, they are saying "Watch me relate with you. Watch how I assert myself without demeaning you. Watch how I express my feelings, articulate my confusion, and admit my mistakes." By observing the counselor in action, people receive guidelines and permissions that will help them relate more effectively both within and outside of counseling.

Finally, people in counseling need new ideas. Most people are in counseling because they have tried their own solutions to problems with little or no success. Although solutions lie within the person, people can get help from others' ideas and reactions. People in counseling often need to understand how to make better decisions, how to delve into themselves to discover answers to their questions, how to learn from mistakes, and how to evaluate the effectiveness of their behavior and predict the consequences of their decisions. They do not need to be given answers. They simply need some ideas to use as stimuli for further growth.

Counselors who are actively responsive share the following qualities.

1. They relate *with* people and not merely *to* them. They exchange ideas, feelings, and confusion and don't simply reflect them. They realize that they can be verbally or nonverbally actively responsive and

that their responsivity should be a help and not a hindrance to the process. They perceive themselves as an equal partner in the relationship.

2. They challenge the person in counseling in helpful ways. They challenge people to get more in touch with their feelings, to become more honest and assertive, to take more risks, to become more committed, to admit their mistakes, to be more careful in their interpretations, and to try new approaches to problems. They challenge, not by intimidating, but by instilling a sense of the possible and a vision of a more fulfilling life.

3. They react to people in ways that elicit meaningful responses. They are willing to evoke responses that run the gamut from tentative, intellectualized ones to forceful, emotionally charged confrontations. In either case, the counselor invites people to be who they are so that they can become who they want to be.

4. They are willing to share equal responsibility with the person in counseling. They are responsible *to* the person; that is, they actively try to help the person achieve the goals that he or she set for counseling. This is in contrast to being responsible *for* the person, which means the counselor assumes ownership of the person. It is also in contrast to accepting little or no responsibility for the progress of counseling.

One of the main obstacles to active responsivity is the counselor's fear of getting involved, which means getting close, being vulnerable, making mistakes, and being held partially responsible for the progress of counseling. Beneath a misguided notion of what professionalism means, these counselors remain distant, aloof, and passive, not so much as a part of their philosophy but as a part of their self-protection.

Patience

The counselor can allow situations to develop naturally, without prematurely injecting personal ideas, feelings, or values. Patience allows the person in counseling to develop and progress at a natural pace. Counselors cannot force or accelerate psychological growth any more than a person can make a tree grow faster by continually watering it and stretching its limbs. Premature insights, revelations, and decisions reinforce fears and resentment and prolong rather than shorten the duration of counseling.

Patience in a counselor connotes more interest in the person than in the results. This may sound like a fine distinction, but it's one many people in counseling recognize. As a person in group counseling told the counselor, "I think you are more interested in the finish line than in those of us who are running the race." Impatience in a counselor implies more interest in a successful termination than in the struggling person.

In an atmosphere devoid of inordinate pressure to perform and produce, people are free to plumb their depths and unravel the needs, dreams, feelings, abilities, and values that have never seen the light of day. They then can use them to chart life along lines that call forth who they can become rather than who they were supposed to be. The restless counselor rushes in with ideas, interpretations, and solutions and deflects people from an inward focus on themselves to an outward focus on the counselor. The impatient counselor is like a tour guide who takes people to all the places *he* wants to visit. This results only in smoldering resentment.

Patient counselors share the following qualities.

1. They tolerate ambiguity. Because human behavior is so complex, there is a good deal of ambiguity in counseling relationships. It is not uncommon for effective counselors to whisper to themselves "What in the world is happening now?" The counselor allows this question to surface and uses it as an invitation to the person to trudge with him or her through the ambiguity, searching for some clarity and meaning. Impatient counselors perceive ambiguity as a threat and an obstacle rather than as a challenge and an opportunity. They grab the first handy set of keys and attempt to pry open the lock of ambiguity, prematurely and erroneously assigning meanings to it that only confuse the person.

2. They can sit back and allow people to follow their own lights, even when the lights look more assuring to the people in counseling than to the counselor. Effective counselors may feel that they know a shortcut, but they also understand the importance of a person making a personal decision after discussing it with the counselor, living out the decision, and learning from the consequences. A person in counseling who uses the counselor's shortcuts quickly gets to where the counselor wants to go, but this only increases the distance to where the person wants to go. The point is not so much *where* the person goes, but *how* he or she gets there.

3. They are not afraid to "waste time" in the interest of growth. They recognize the person in counseling needs rest periods, digressions, and some coasting. Most people work very hard in counseling. Because of the nature of the relationship, the person in counseling works much harder than the counselor because the counselor's work is limited to a few minutes each week, which catapult the person into six and a half days of difficult work. The impatient counselor is like the

football coach who sits resting on the sidelines for the first half of the game, then exhorts his players to give 120% in the second half. Because the coach is not playing the game himself, he lacks empathy for those who are, thus becoming incredible and a source of resentment.

4. They can retain insights and questions that would interrupt the flow of a session and use them later. The impatient counselor brims over with insights, questions, and hypotheses that will help the person "use time better" and "get down to brass tacks." While "tightening up" a session is sometimes necessary, patient counselors realize that messages that read "You're not doing this well—here, let me help you" are more inclined to impede than to accelerate progress.

One of the greatest obstacles to patience in a counselor is the need to be successful. These counselors focus not on the person in counseling, but on themselves; the person is simply a means to an end. The message to the person in counseling is "I don't care who you are—only what you can do for my ego." Accelerating the counseling process in order to bring success closer has the same effect as driving one's car at a high rate of speed to get to a service station before the car runs out of gas.

Sensitivity

Sensitivity means counselors are aware of the subtle dynamics and vulnerabilities present both in the person in counseling and in themselves. Sensitivity in a counselor is important because it communicates safety. When people feel the counselor's sensitivity, they are free to spend less time and energy protecting themselves and more effort discovering who they are and who they wish to become. These people realize that whatever "psychological incisions" the counselor must make will be done carefully and in a way that prevents unnecessary pain.

Sensitivity also communicates sensibleness. People in counseling who feel the counselor's sensitivity are confident he or she will not ask them to do things beyond their capability. Moreover, these people are confident that the counselor's plan for them is tailored to their unique personality and not fashioned from ill-fitting, off-the-rack nostrums.

Most people who enter counseling are unaware of their real problems. While they present symptoms as problems, their true problems are buried beneath layers of defenses and pseudoproblems. The sensitive counselor takes stethoscopic readings of the deeper parts of the person and draws the real problems to the surface. Without this sensitivity, counseling will remain on a superficial, symptom-oriented level that will bring about only short-term effects.

As people increasingly experience the counselor's sensitivity, they become more in tune with themselves. They learn to ask themselves the right questions and to recognize the telltale signs of denying and contorting their deeper parts. As they develop these abilities, they become more sensitive to others and receive more sensitivity in return.

Counselors who are sensitive share the following qualities.

1. They are sensitive to their own reactions in counseling, reading them as reflexively, skillfully, and attentively as they read those of the person. Because of this inner sensitivity, they are the first to know when they are becoming frightened, angry, bored, fooled, distracted, satisfied, sexually aroused, or confused. This knowledge is immediately utilized to help them understand and clarify what is occurring in the relationship.

2. They know when, where, and how long to probe a person. Sensitive counselors use the person's almost imperceptible verbal and nonverbal cues as guides through defenses, resistances, and vulnerabilities. This is in contrast to counselors who never probe because they lack confidence in their probing skills or those who probe according to their own charts and not those of the person in counseling.

3. They ask questions and convey information the person perceives as threatening in ways that take the person's specific vulnerabilities into account. They recognize the difference between being brutally frank and helpfully honest. They cushion what they say in ways that avoid unnecessary pain without diluting the honesty of the message.

4. They are sensitive to their own vulnerabilities. They realize that they, like all human beings, possess tender spots. They know exactly where these sore spots are located and recognize how they tend to protect them. This enables them to understand and accept the nature of their vulnerabilities and to overcome them when possible. In so doing, they are free to use their energy and concentration more productively.

A chief obstacle to sensitivity is self-consciousness. Counselors who focus on their own needs for success, who continually plan their next move, and who habitually protect themselves against threat cannot be attuned to the subtle emotional nuances emanating from the person in counseling.

Freeing

A freeing counselor is able to be a significant influence in the person's life while leaving the person free to reject that influence. Until persons are entirely free to be themselves, counselors don't know whom they are working with in counseling. The less free a person feels, the more it is the public self, rather than the real self, that relates with the counselor. Consequently, many of the clues that the counselor picks up from the person and acts upon are false ones because they are not flowing from the real self. Only when the person can speak any thought, express any feeling, ask any question, or consider any decision does the counselor truly know the person in counseling. While a counselor may offer the person complete freedom, the person may accept it in gradual steps.

Freedom also brings people in counseling closer to who they really are. Many people in counseling (as well as those not in counseling) live according to someone else's plan, often without realizing it. Typically, parents' plans are adhered to until they are traded in or added to by spouses or friends. Freedom allows people to see, perhaps for the first time, the marked discrepancies between who they are and who the plan says they should be. As they trade in the needs, dreams, and values rented from others for their privately owned ones, they can begin to shape a more fulfilling life.

Freedom reduces the need to rebel. People who do not feel free from others often rebel to establish independence. A young woman may refuse to attend college mostly because her parents are pressuring her to do so. A young man may marry a woman primarily because his mother is doing all she can to prevent the marriage. Unfortunately, some people bury themselves in a deep hole in order to buy a little freedom and control over their lives. They unnecessarily become martyrs for their freedom. When people in counseling can develop a true sense of freedom, they become eligible to make choices that are good for them, regardless of the approval or disapproval of the significant people in their lives.

The more freedom people are allowed in counseling, the more freedom they can allow themselves. Most of the unnecessary restraints that people bring into counseling are self-imposed. They use other people as an excuse for not acting freely. Once they can develop the confidence to make free choices, they can allow others to act more freely. As they unshackle the people with whom they relate, all become free agents rather than fellow inmates in a relationship.

Freeing counselors share the following qualities.

1. They place a high value on freedom in their own lives. They make their own decisions and act according to their own expectations and values. They recognize that all freedom is relative and are willing to make compromises and sacrifices based on free choice and not on weakness. Because they experience the positive and sometimes

exhilarating results of freedom in their own lives, they are ardent advocates of freedom in counseling.

2. They recognize the difference between manipulation and education in counseling. Manipulation means that the counselor pushes a person into making decisions that the counselor wants more than the person does. It may look like a personal decision because the person dutifully makes it, but the only decision the person made was to please the counselor. So this person, who appears to be "making better decisions," is actually getting worse.

The manipulating counselor confuses *acting* better with *getting* better. Education means that the counselor helps people clearly realize the options at their disposal and the possible consequences of each. The counselor then sits back and lets the person make the choice.

3. They understand the difference between superficial and true freedom and help people in counseling appreciate this important difference. Superficial freedom means that people can act any way they choose. True freedom means two things: first, that a person has the same capacity to choose to act or to choose not to act—that is, the choice is not controlled by overdriven needs, compulsions, or unbridled emotions—and second, that the results of the choice will not unnecessarily damage someone else. The freedom a counselor gives is not a license to behave selfishly and imperviously; it is an invitation for people to assume complete responsibility for their behavior, enjoying the rewards and accepting the consequences.

4. They exercise and value true freedom in the context of the counseling relationship. They understand that in a counseling relationship, as in any other, freedom is restricted by the nature of the relationship. The nature of counseling is to help the person become more psychologically healthy. Both the counselor and the person in counseling are free to behave in ways that directly or indirectly achieve this result. To the degree that one or the other behaves in ways that significantly violate this goal, the other is free to terminate the relationship. This understanding of true freedom allows both the counselor and the person maximum latitude in working toward the goals they have agreed upon, but it still protects each from being used by the other in a destructive manner.

One of the main obstacles to being a freeing counselor is the skewed logic "I know what's best for this person; this person wants to know what is best for him; therefore, it is my responsibility to prod him along the paths that I feel he needs to take."

Holistic awareness

A holistic approach in counseling means that the counselor is aware of the whole person and does not approach him or her with tunnel vision. This does not mean that a counselor is an expert in all areas; it simply indicates an awareness of the several dimensions of a person and of how one dimension may affect others.

A holistic approach in counseling is necessary because a person has several dimensions. To focus on one could seriously limit the effectiveness of counseling. The following dimensions of personality interrelate but are separate enough to consider individually: physical, emotional, social, sexual, and moral-religious. The importance of understanding the nature and dynamics of these dimensions is seen in the following example. A college student seeks help because he is underachieving. After discussing the problem for a while, the counselor discovers that the student has poor study habits. However, the counselor realizes that few problems are that simple. After further sessions, he realizes that the poor study habits stem from the student's depression. In trying to understand the depression, the counselor discovers that the student is harboring a great deal of repressed anger toward his father and has discontinued taking his thyroid pills since returning to school. This student's problems covered the intellectual, emotional, and physical dimensions and all must be dealt with in order to help the young man.

A holistic approach is also important because it is not uncommon for a problem in one dimension to get referred to a different one. A person's emotional conflict (anger) may manifest itself in the physical dimension (ulcerative colitis); a physical problem (diagnosed or undiagnosed diabetes) may manifest itself in the sexual area (impotence); or an emotional conflict (guilt) may manifest itself in the intellectual area (inability to concentrate). It is important to deal with the primary problem and not to waste time on the referred dimension.

By being holistically aware, the counselor can reduce the effects of an insoluble problem in one area by expanding growth in a different dimension. For example, a young woman's fiancé has died, and she brings her inconsolable grief into counseling. After a few supportive sessions, however, the counselor becomes aware that she is actually mourning more for herself than for her fiancé. She had been a shy, withdrawn person with a good deal of self-doubt. Her fiancé protected her, made her feel worthwhile, and gave her a purpose in life. His death symbolized the demise of her hope for a happy and meaningful life. While counseling cannot bring back the woman's fiancé, it can resurrect her. Through counseling she can not only regain her feelings of self-worth and purpose but assume private ownership of them so that their existence no longer depends upon the presence of another person.

Counselors who respond holistically share the following qualities.

1. They are acutely aware of the dimensions of personality and their complex interplay. They do not artificially reduce a person's problem into the one, two, or three dimensions with which they feel the most comfortable. Nor do they assume that a dimension is conflict free until it is adequately evaluated.

2. They seek appropriate consultation and make intelligent referrals. While it would be unrealistic to refer a person to five specialists, counselors should not diagnose and treat dimensions for which they are not qualified. For example, a nonmedical counselor should not assume that a person's depression is nonmedical; a medical counselor should not assume that a person's depression can best be treated with medication. And no counselor should assume all religious conflicts are neurotic simply because he or she is not qualified to understand or treat them.

3. They are familiar with and open to many theories of behavior and may even have some theories of their own. While they may feel more confident in a particular theory, they recognize that there is no one theory or combination of theories that adequately explains all behavior. They attempt to fit their skills and theories to the person in counseling rather than sculpting the person's behavior to fit their skills and theories.

An obstacle to a holistic approach is counselors' insecurity and lack of humility, which do not allow them to admit that there are dimensions of a person that they are unqualified, either by academic degree or experience, to treat.

BEGINNING COUNSELORS' CONCERNS

People who have not yet done counseling or who have done relatively little counseling often share several concerns. The following discussion focuses on some questions that beginning counselors ask themselves or their teachers and supervisors. The answers are not meant to be dogmatic. They best fit the overall philosophy expressed in this text.

Psychological health

Do I have to be a paragon of psychological health before I can effectively help people? The answer to this question is no. It is a reasonable assumption that, all other factors remaining the same, the better a counselor's psychological health, the more effective he or she will be. While counselors seek to progress toward their ideals, the majority of them seem to be ordinary people who have a special interest in helping others. Their interest does not make them immune to the types of problems that the population in general experiences. Sometimes counselors are impatient, defensive, and arrogant. At other times they are irritable, distracted, depressed, unreasonable, and uncaring. They can misperceive situations, introduce their prejudices into counseling, and like some people in counseling better than others and treat them accordingly.

While counselors can work to modify these behaviors, they can also use them as a learning experience for the person in counseling. As people in counseling see the counselor handle his or her imperfections and as they learn to deal with the counselor's humanity, real growth can take place.

However, counselors whose psychological health significantly interferes with self-knowledge and self-esteem, or with their abilities to relate smoothly and honestly with people, are unlikely to be generally effective.

Harming people

Can I do irreparable harm to someone in a counseling session? The answer to this question is a qualified no. Fortunately, psyches are generally more resilient than bodies in the face of stress. One mistake in surgery could cause a person to die, but a mistake in counseling is unlikely to result in a comparable effect. This is not to say that people cannot be seriously damaged in counseling, but this kind of damage usually is the result of ongoing mistakes over a period of time.

It is unlikely that a counselor could "say the wrong thing" in a session or miss a communication that, in itself, would cause dire consequences. The stronger the counseling relationship, the more mistakes it will absorb. The stories that are told about a counselor saying the wrong thing or not saying the right thing, which caused a person to decompensate into an acute psychotic episode or to commit suicide, are largely untrue. When such episodes occur, it is likely that they would have happened no matter what the counselor did or even whether or not the person was in counseling.

By the time beginning counselors are allowed to do counseling, they should have sufficient sensitivity and common sense, regardless of their level of skills, to preclude creating a traumatic situation for a person.

Counselor responsibility

How much responsibility do I have for the people I see in counseling? It is helpful for beginning counselors to keep in mind a number of points when considering this question. The counselor did not cause whatever problems the person has. Moreover, the problems were present for weeks, months, and most likely years before the counselor came into the person's life. Therefore, the counselor cannot reasonably assume responsibility for either the cause of the person's problems or their cure.

Nor can the counselor ordinarily assume responsibility for the person's behavior outside of counseling. If a person leaves the session and gets drunk, beats his wife, or takes an overdose of sleeping pills, it would be inappropriate for the counselor to hold himself or herself responsible any more than cardiologists should hold themselves responsible when their patients have heart attacks hours after a consultation.

To assume such responsibility is grandiose, naive, and self-punitive. It is grandiose because it assumes that the counselor has supernatural powers to change behavior that the person is incapable of or unwilling to change. It is naive because it reflects a lack of understanding of behavioral dynamics, especially how people can use even the most salutary situations as instruments of self-destruction. It is self-punitive because the counselor berates himself or herself for something beyond his or her control.

Counselors are not responsible *for* the people they see in counseling, but they are responsible *to* the people seen in counseling. This means that counselors do all that is reasonable and appropriate to help the person during the counseling relationship. This is the only valid contract with regard to responsibility. The counselor agrees to give his or her care, knowledge, skills, energy, honesty, strength, and hope. To promise and assume more responsibility than this is unreasonable and, in all likelihood, countertherapeutic.

Caring and accepting

How much can I or should I really care about and unconditionally accept the people I see in counseling? Caring and unconditional acceptance are terms used so much in the counseling literature that they may cause beginning counselors to create these sentiments artificially in themselves or to become discouraged because they do not feel them. Caring is directly related to knowing and liking. The more a person knows and likes another, the more he or she will care about the other. The less a person knows another, or if a person knows but does not like another, the less genuine care can be present. Therefore, it is unrealistic to expect a counselor to care deeply and genuinely about a person during the first sessions of counseling. Genuine care is not a commodity that counselors possess by the very fact that they are counselors. They may have a humanistic concern for people, but a personal and deep feeling can grow only gradually as the counselor increases his or her knowledge and liking of the person.

Some beginning counselors wonder if it is possible to care *too much*. Without getting lost in semantics, it seems that it *is* possible to care too much about a person in counseling. Caring too much is less likely to be grounded in a genuine, healthy caring and more likely to stem from a counselor's overdriven need to be a rescuer or a success.

It is not unusual that a counselor would care somewhat more about the person than the person does. The hope is that the counselor's care will gradually become contagious and that people will begin to care about themselves. However, when the counselor cares significantly more than the person, the counselor assumes responsibility not only for what happens in the counseling session but for the overall outcome of counseling. This type of counseling relationship is likely to end unsatisfactorily.

The concept of being unconditionally accepting is more complex. Does "unconditionally accepting" mean that *whatever* the person does, the counselor's acceptance will remain unwavering? Does it mean that the person can abuse the counselor by missing appointments, by not paying bills, and by using him or her in ways that are self-destructive or destructive to the counselor? This kind of acceptance is countertherapeutic since it injures both the counselor and the person in counseling. It seems more reasonable and honest to set some limits on acceptance. These limits can be much broader than those offered by society in general and by the person's friends and relatives, but they should be tailored to the goals of counseling, which can be articulated as follows: "As long as your behavior is at least broadly consonant with the agreed upon goals of counseling, you can expect that I will do my utmost to accept your behavior. However, if your behavior continues to be dissonant with the agreed upon goals of counseling, I can still accept you as a human being but I cannot continue to accept you as someone I feel that I can help in counseling."

The basic value of counseling, one that takes priority over caring and acceptance, is justice. When the counseling relationship becomes unjust to either or both of the people in it, it has outlived its purpose. Ethical principles underscore this point; for example, the ethical standards of the American Psychological Association state, "The psychologist attempts to terminate a clinical or consulting relationship when it is reasonably clear that the consumer is not benefitting from it."[4]

Lack of experience

Won't people in counseling know I am just a beginning counselor, and won't that create some difficulties? While this concern is understandable, there is rarely any basis for it in reality. Few beginning counselors are challenged regarding their age or experience. People tend to assume that if the counselor has been placed by authorities in a position of trust, the counselor must be capable of handling the situation. Hence, the counselor is likely to be more concerned than the person in counseling. The person who challenges the counselor with regard to his or her experience can be assured in a matter-of-fact way that the counselor meets the professional requirements of the agency. Usually this gentle yet straightforward approach will suffice. People who continue to make the counselor's age or experience an issue are likely using it as a decoy away from their real concerns, and their reaction can be dealt with as any other form of transference and resistance. If the person pushes the point, and especially if it appears to have some validity, most agencies have a policy to guide the beginning counselor in this situation.

Failure

What if I fail with a person I'm seeing in counseling? There are three general ways counselors can be unsuccessful. The first is that the counselor can make a large mistake or a sufficient number of small mistakes that cause the person to terminate counseling prematurely. Second, the counselor can be competent and the person in counseling can be cooperating fully, but a "goodness of fit" is lacking; that is, the two people seem to be operating on different wavelengths. Third, the counselor may be working effectively, but the person wishes to sabotage counseling for some reason. Counselors who tend to be self-blaming will blame themselves for all three types of "failure." Counselors who tend to blame others will blame the person in counseling for all three types of "failure." The realistic counselor will attempt to judge accurately the cause for the discontinuance of counseling and react appropriately.

If the first cause seems likely, the counselor can learn from his or her mistake and use the memory of it to avoid making it again. He or she can remember that all counselors make mistakes and that even the best counselors have made significant mistakes but learned from them.

[4]American Psychological Association (1977), p. 5.

If the counselor accurately judges that the premature termination is attributable to the second cause, he or she need not view it as a failure but simply as a case of "wrong chemistry" that can occur in any relationship.

In the third cause, the counselor can realistically view it as a situation that was likely to be unavoidable and that comes with the territory of counseling.

All professional people fail at times; failure is a price both counselors and people in counseling may have to pay for taking risks and being human. As Corey states, "We can't realistically expect to succeed with every client. Even experienced therapists at times become glum and begin to doubt their value when they are forced to admit that there are clients whom they are not able to touch, much less reach in a significant way."[5]

Pitfalls

What are some pitfalls of which I can be aware as a beginning counselor? There are several pitfalls in counseling of which *all* counselors can be aware; however, beginning counselors may be particularly susceptible to six of them.

Trying to do too much too soon.   Beginning counselors are often impatient to put their years of learning and practice to work. They also may not be secure in their skills as a counselor; hence, they push for early successes to buttress their confidence.

Unfortunately, the counseling relationship and process, like most relationships and processes, cannot be rushed. Counselors who attempt to accelerate the process tend to be overly active and place undue pressure on people to make positive changes in their behavior. The result is that people will firmly resist the process or will superficially comply with the counselor's teachings and exhortations and then suddenly terminate by either disappearing or by becoming suddenly "cured."

Teaching instead of relating.   New counselors have recently finished a college and graduate academic curriculum of from six to ten years. They have been lectured at continually during this time. A natural consequence of this experience is to reduce anxiety in counseling by lecturing. The counselor may present a seminar on anger at one counseling session, a class on communication at the next, and a workshop on sexuality at the third. This reduces the counselor's anxiety

[5]Corey (1977), p. 243.

because it allows the counselor to think that he or she is *doing* something, and it reduces the person in counseling's anxiety because it is easier to be a student than to be a client or a patient.

Unfortunately, the more lecturing that occurs, the less counseling will take place. Beginning counselors can use their academic knowledge in counseling to help them understand the person and to help them make the most appropriate responses. But simply passing on one's class notes to the person will impede the counseling process and relationship.

Being overly accommodating.   It is helpful for counselors to be reasonably accommodating as far as scheduling appointments, allowing the person to select the issues to be discussed at a particular session, and allowing access to the counselor. Sometimes, however, beginning counselors, consciously or unconsciously, feel inadequate as counselors and seek to compensate for this by bending over backwards for the person, even though it may be detrimental in the long run.

Inexperienced counselors may set limits that are too broad or too changeable. They allow people to control the session with extraneous content or by putting the counselor in the "hot seat." They allow people in counseling to let their bill or agency fee slide without payment. They "gladly" schedule special sessions, take phone calls between sessions, and reschedule people even when it is inconvenient to do so. It is as if these counselors were saying "I know I'm not a very good counselor yet, but I'll make it up to you in other ways." The problem is that the "making up" behavior may be countertherapeutic.

Attributing counseling problems to inexperience.   Certainly some problems arise in counseling because the counselor is a novice. However, many problems with which the beginning counselor must deal would arise with any counselor. The following are some typical examples.

A person prematurely terminates after only a few sessions and the counselor blames it on the fact that he mishandled the situation because of his inexperience. However, studies indicate that 37 to 45% of people who seek counseling in urban mental health centers prematurely terminate after the first or second interview.[6] It is unlikely that all these people were seen by beginning counselors.

A person may tell a beginning counselor "Well, it looks like neither one of us knows what to do right now." The counselor inter-

---

[6]Garfield (1980), p. 4.

prets this as a reference to her youth or inexperience, whereas the person would have made the same statement to any counselor at that point.

A person is very resistant to change and continually treads water or backslides in counseling. The beginning counselor is convinced that if he had only a few more years experience, he could help the person through the impasse. In fact, the person may be objectively very difficult to work with in counseling and would present the same challenge to the most experienced counselor.

It is understandable and perhaps appropriate that beginning counselors feel somewhat insecure as they begin their career. However, it is important that they separate the problems they may create due to their inexperience from problems and behaviors that would be present no matter how skilled and experienced they were. Failure to do this causes novice counselors to misperceive situations in ways that cause them to feel inadequate, which can create a self-fulfilling prophecy.

Assuming a "counseling personality." Possibly because there is so much written about what a counselor should be, beginning counselors have a tendency to change dramatically when they walk into the counseling room. The young man who was smiling and laughing minutes before enters the counseling room with a ponderous, empathetic look plastered on his face. The young woman who was actively and totally involved in a discussion at the water cooler becomes passive and reflective as she settles into the counseling session. The previously mentioned young man is afraid to smile in counseling because he learned that counseling is not a social but a professional relationship. The young woman is passive and reflective because she learned that counselors should not intrude their personalities into the counseling situation. The result is that both counselors become caricatures of some phantom being called "The Effective Counselor."

Counselors who overidentify with the role of counselor lose contact with the best counseling resource they have: themselves. Instead of asking themselves what they can do at this point in counseling, they ask what Jung would do at this point or what their supervisor would do or what the textbook said should be done.

It is important that beginning counselors distinguish between *becoming* an effective counselor and *acting* like an effective counselor. The person who acts like a counselor is like a child who acts like a fire fighter—he says and does all the right things, but he never extinguishes any fires. The qualities of an effective counselor are not meant to be worn in counseling as a surgeon wears "greens" into the operating room. They are meant to be assimilated into the counselor's unique personality and to become a part of it, just as a coat of paint becomes a part of a building. Only the uniqueness of the counselor's personality gives meaning to the qualities of an effective counselor.

Ruminating after difficult sessions.   There is a difference between evaluating a session in order to learn from it and ruminating about it for hours afterward, which creates more self-torment than learning. Sometimes beginning counselors spend time second guessing themselves after a difficult session. They ask themselves or fellow students or counselors "Should I have said what I did, or would it have been better not to say it?" "If it was good to say it, should I have said it when I did or later in the session?" "Should I have agreed to see him twice next week, or did I get hooked into something I shouldn't have?"

Such questions can go on endlessly because the dynamics of difficult sessions can go on endlessly. Counselors who tend to spend much time in post mortems can realize that whatever mistakes were made in the session, they will not be rehabilitated by brooding over them. Since they will be likely to discuss the session with a supervisor, they can limit their own postsession evaluations to 15 minutes, focusing on the one or two major areas of concern. They can scrutinize these areas and make a tentative plan for dealing with them in the next session. After 15 minutes, they can stop and do something far more important than counseling; they can continue with the business and joy of living.

SUMMARY

Each quality discussed in this chapter is a necessary part of a helpful person and an effective counselor. Like vital signs in medicine, it is not good enough that *most* of the qualities are present. The absence or negligible presence of even one of the qualities could significantly interfere with the progress of counseling and could even cause counseling to be a damaging experience. As Weiner says, counseling "is not a benign procedure. Ample evidence indicates that it can be harmful as well as helpful to patients and that the major factors influencing good and bad outcomes reside in the therapist and how he conducts treatment."[7]

It is also important to understand that these qualities do not operate in a vacuum. The personality of the person in counseling can influence the actualization of these qualities in a counselor. A very gentle, kind person may elicit great sensitivity on the part of a counselor while a boisterous, intimidating person may diminish the counselor's ability to be sensitive. This is not to say that a counselor's qualities depend on the

[7]Weiner (1975), p. 22.

attributes of the people seen in counseling, but it would be unrealistic for a counselor to expect to function at maximum potential with every person in counseling.

For practical reasons, the qualities are listed separately. In practice, however, they interrelate, and one quality either helps or hinders the others, depending upon its strength or weakness. Beginning counselors will find themselves applying these qualities in counseling "by the numbers"—that is, they will be aware of how present each quality was in a particular session and strive to increase its presence in the next session. This is an important and necessary part of counseling, as long as it does not become distracting or compulsive. After some years of experience, however, counselors find that these personal qualities meld with their knowledge of behavior and counseling skills to form one growth-producing force. As Bugental writes:

> Just as an accomplished pianist (or any artist) is one who has thoroughly mastered the fundamentals of the craft in order to be free to be truly creative in expression, so the master therapist has incorporated the mechanics of the processes to the point that they are invisible. The pianist no longer "plays the piano" but only draws music forth from the instrument which has become integral to the artist. The therapist no longer "does therapy" but relates so authentically with the client because the skills are integrated completely into the professional's way of being.[8]

THOUGHT QUESTIONS

1. In terms of self-knowledge, what are two of your greater strengths that would help you as a counselor? What are two of your greater weaknesses that could interfere with your effectiveness as a counselor?
2. Of the 12 qualities of an effective counselor discussed in this chapter, which 2 do you feel you most possess and which 2 do you feel you need to work on the most?
3. The text states that every significant emotional reaction that deals with the person in counseling should be shared within the session in which it occurs. What is your reaction to this concept? Could you imagine a situation that would represent an exception to this principle?
4. The text states that absolute honesty is necessary for a counselor to be effective. What are some situations that could arise in counseling in which you would find it very difficult to be absolutely honest?
5. Of the 7 concerns typical of beginning counselors, which one do you feel reflects your greatest concern? Do you have a concern that was not mentioned in the text?

[8]Bugental (1978), p. 44.

CHAPTER 5

Stages of Counseling

Like any other developmental process, counseling follows a sequence. It is important for counselors to recognize a sequence so that they will have a framework within which to function and a means to evaluate where in the process they are. As in human development, these stages tend to be somewhat flexible and overlapping, and each stage must be passed through successfully if counseling is to be effective. There is more than one way to view the stages of helping. The format presented here best fits the philosophy of counseling reflected in this text.[1]

The helping process can be divided into six stages: (1) information gathering, (2) evaluation, (3) feedback, (4) the counseling agreement, (5) changing behavior, and (6) termination. Figure 5-1 reflects this process. It demonstrates an important concept—namely, that both the person seeking help and the counselor have two major choice points with regard to beginning the counseling relationship. The first point occurs when the person seeking help and the counselor initially meet. The person has made an uninformed decision to get help, and the counselor has made an uninformed decision to see the person; that is, the counselor does not know whether or not the person is a reasonable candidate for counseling.

The second choice point occurs after the first three stages, when both the person in counseling and the counselor have gained sufficient knowledge upon which to make an informed decision. The decision is

---

[1]Other formats can be found in Brammer (1979), Carkhuff & Anthony (1979), Weiner (1975), and Egan (1982).

Uninformed decision			Informed decision		
Stage 1	Stage 2	Stage 3	Stage 4	Stage 5	Stage 6
Information gathering	Evaluation	Feedback	Counseling agreement	Changing behavior	Termination

Figure 5–1. Counseling stages.

whether to continue counseling or to seek an alternative that would be more appropriate and helpful.

The six stages can be telescoped so that they fit both short-term and long-term counseling, just as basic surgical procedures are the same whether an operation lasts a half-hour or ten hours.[2] Counseling meant to last only five or ten sessions would pass through each of the stages in an abbreviated manner. Long-term counseling could spend 5 sessions on the first three stages and 50 to 150 sessions on the last three. However, it is doubtful that any kind of counseling could be effective without spending at least some time in each stage. If a counselor skipped the information-gathering stage, there would be no foundation for counseling; if the evaluation stage is skipped, the counselor would not know what the person's problems are; if the feedback stage is eliminated, the person could not make an informed decision; if there is no counseling agreement, there would be no course to follow; if behaviors are not changed, there is no counseling; and if the termination stage is ignored, the person will be left with no sense of closure.

This does not imply that counseling does not actually begin until the fourth stage. Counseling begins the moment the counselor and the person in counseling meet. The first three stages can be therapeutic in themselves in that to progress through them, the person and counselor are relating on levels that deal with cognition, emotions, needs, values, and conflicts. As the counselor listens, probes, reflects, understands, and clarifies, the person can be growing in insight, confidence, and hope. The main difference between the first three stages and the last three is that the focus of the first three is on sharing important information, which can be therapeutic in itself. The focus of the last three stages is on helping the person change behavior so that he or she can live more effectively.

STAGE 1: INFORMATION GATHERING

The more information counselors have, the more valid their evaluations, the more accurate their feedback, and the more sound their rec-

[2]For counseling stages tailored for crisis intervention, see Chapter 13.

ommendations. Therefore, it is helpful for counselors to recognize the various areas of information that must be tapped. The information index in Figure 5–2 represents the main sources of information for the counselor.

Continuum A–B represents the time dimension. Information about the person's past helps the counselor understand how the person got where he or she is. Information about the present indicates how well the person is functioning currently, and information about the future tells the counselor who the person wishes to become. As these pieces of information are brought together, they can give a reasonably good picture of who the person is and why the person is seeking help.

Continuum C–D reflects the importance of getting both intrapsychic and interpersonal information. Intrapsychic information consists of learning about the person's perceptions of reality; his inner conflicts and how they are handled; the relationship between who the person is, thinks he is, and wants others to think he is; as well as the person's beliefs, values, and hopes. Interpersonal information comprises the dynamics involved in how the person relates with others, whether these relationships are satisfying or dissatisfying to the person or to the people with whom he or she relates.

Continuum E–F denotes what the person thinks and feels about herself, others, and relevant events. It is not only important to know the content of the person's thoughts and feelings, but to recognize how they interact and perhaps conflict. For example, when asked how she viewed her father, a woman responds "I have nothing but the utmost respect for him." When she is asked how she *feels* about her father, she replies "I resent him more than words can say."

The information index highlights cautions in information gathering. Typically, people seeking help lure counselors into talking about the past, discussing interpersonal relationships, and focusing on ideas. The counselor who is successfully lured will have a fragmented and inaccurate picture upon which to make a clinical evaluation.

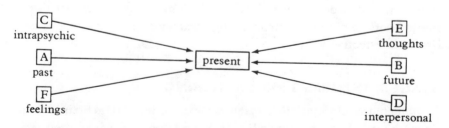

Figure 5–2. An information index.

Questions

In addition to being aware of the various dimensions of information, it is helpful for counselors to have a clear idea of what specific information they want. The information must be relevant and gathered in a relatively short time. The following format of questions can be helpful in accomplishing this goal. Whether one asks specific questions or gathers the information indirectly depends on the counselor and the situation.

1. "Why do you feel it would be a good idea to talk with me?" This question is meant to ascertain the person's motives for seeking counseling and his or her view of the problem. A person may reply "I didn't think it would be a good idea—my mother did." A person may present the problem as feeling depressed, worried, insecure, confused, or scared. The counselor can then help the person describe the nature of his or her problem more specifically.

2. "How long have you felt this way?" The answer to this question gives the counselor some idea as to whether the problem is long-standing or of short duration. Counselors can be aware that people sometimes describe their problem as short-lived, but further probing indicates that it was present for a long time and only recently became activated.

3. "What do you think is causing these problems?" This question is meant to disclose how much insight the person has and how much responsibility he or she is taking for the problem. A person may answer "I don't have the slightest idea" or "My boss is the cause of the problem" or "I've always been insecure, and this new job is hitting every insecurity I have."

4. "How have you been dealing with the problem up to this point?" The answer to this question will give the counselor some idea of the person's defenses, adaptive responses, and use of environmental supports. The person may answer "I don't think it's a problem; my husband does" or "I've been distracting myself with work and probably eating and drinking too much" or "I have tried several alternatives that I thought a good deal about, and I've discussed it with my family, but I still need a little more help."

5. "How do you expect counseling will help you?" The question is meant to elicit the person's expectations of counseling. One person may answer "I don't have the slightest idea." Another person may respond "I think you can tell me what I should do." A third person may react "I hope you will be able to help me see what I'm doing wrong, so I can stop it."

6. "How much time and effort are you willing to invest in working on your problem?" Answers to this question will tell the counselor how accurately the person assesses the seriousness of the problem and how much personal motivation he or she has to solve it.

7. "Can you tell me some things about your past that you think may be helpful to my understanding of who you are today?" This question is meant to get a psychological snapshot of the person. A detailed case history is rarely necessary as part of the information-gathering stage and may only serve to distract from current issues and affects.

8. "What are some of your strong points?" This question is meant to give the counselor some idea of the person's strengths and also gives the person an opportunity to bolster his or her self-esteem, which may have been diminished in talking about the problem.[3]

Interaction and reaction

In addition to having the person tell the counselor about himself or herself, the counselor must have an opportunity to see the person in action. The information the person has given is hearsay; that is, its validity depends upon the person's willingness and ability to perceive and communicate accurately. Counselors who restrict themselves to hearsay information are likely to get an inaccurate picture of the person, which will negatively affect the evaluation and feedback. Two ways counselors can become eyewitnesses to the person's dynamics are through interaction and reaction.

Interaction means two things: challenging and relating warmly with the person. *Challenging* means probing the person in a gentle, tentative way. Challenging differs from confronting, which is ordinarily inappropriate at this stage (see Stage 5 for a definition and description of confronting). When a counselor challenges the person's perceptions, motives, insights, defenses, expectations, and values, he or she invites the person to entertain the possibility that his or her way of perceiving reality and reacting to it may not be entirely accurate or helpful.

For example, a counselor may ask "Bill, you say your mom is pretty unreasonable. Is it possible that sometimes she is being reasonable but you don't want to see it that way?" The counselor creates some natural stress to see how the person reacts to it. Does he handle the stress differently than he *says* he handles stress? On being challenged, does he show some behavior that he has successfully covered up until now?

---

[3]For self-evaluation questions that counselors can ask themselves regarding the effectiveness of their information gathering, see Benjamin (1974), pp. 20–24. He discusses questioning by the counselor on pp. 65–90.

Does he respond by attacking, withdrawing, or deftly avoiding the challenge? Does he respond well, seeing the challenge as an opportunity to learn something about himself or to clarify a situation?

Counselors who are reluctant to challenge a person at this stage are taking the same risks as a physician who declines to thump a person's sensitive abdomen. Sometimes the best way to see where it hurts is to probe, even when it causes some pain.

Warmth is another part of interacting. Relating warmly means that the counselor naturally and genuinely communicates positive feelings toward the person by smiling, encouraging, and complimenting the person when it is appropriate. This affords the counselor a chance to see firsthand how the person responds to positive feelings, whether he or she accepts them naturally. Does she freeze and become suspicious? Does he ignore them? Does she seek them and cling to them? Does he respond well only when positive feelings are forthcoming? The answers to these questions will give the counselor some important information as to how the person handles warmth: whether the person accepts it and grows from it or rejects it and deprives himself or herself of valuable psychological fuel.

A second way to elicit firsthand information is by *reacting*. This means that the counselor is finely attuned to his or her own reactions to the person. The counselor is like a harp. When a chord is struck, the counselor knows *somebody* struck it. And, if the counselor knows he or she did not strike it, then it must have been the person. The counselor can reasonably assume that the ways the person "plays" him or her are similar to the ways the person "plays" other people. Some typical chords that are struck are feelings of threat, anger, sympathy, tenderness, affection, sexuality, frustration, confusion, distrust, repulsion, curiosity, and caution.

This information can tell the counselor how the person tends to "make" other people feel, at least under certain circumstances. This material can give the counselor otherwise unobtainable information as to how the person "gets" others to treat him or her.

The information gained from interaction and reaction affords counselors material that they could not obtain simply by asking questions and letting the person tell a consciously or unconsciously edited story.[4]

---

[4]Information counselors should communicate to people considering counseling is discussed in Chapter 14. Some counselors find that psychological testing gives them an added source of information. For a summary and evaluation of tests that can be used for this purpose, see Osipow et al. (1980). For a discussion of what clients should look for in counselors, see Goldberg (1977), pp 237–249.

STAGE 2: EVALUATION

As information gathering nears an end, the counselor begins to evaluate it. This evaluation evolves around five issues.

Symptoms

Symptoms are signs indicating that a person is overloaded with stress. Academically, there are two kinds of symptoms: those included in the formal diagnostic categories—for example, those presented in the *Diagnostic and Statistical Manual* of the American Psychiatric Association (DSM III)—and those not included in any formal diagnostic classifications. Some examples of symptoms presented as diagnostic categories are depression, anxiety states, phobias, obsessions, compulsions, personality disorders (such as antisocial and passive-aggressive), sexual dysfunctioning (such as impotence and frigidity), and sexual disorders (such as child molesting and rape). Some examples of symptoms that do not fit the traditional diagnostic categories are: inordinate fear, anger, guilt, confusion, frustration, procrastination; feelings of inadequacy, hypersensitivity, fatigue, jealousy, distractibility; interpersonal conflicts; job inefficiency; and religious desolation. Many people who seek counseling refer to their symptoms as their problem. For example, a person may tell a counselor "My problem is that I'm depressed . . . or can't sleep . . . or am tense all the time."

It is important for counselors to assess the nature and severity of the symptoms. Some symptoms need immediate and direct intervention. For example, people who are deeply depressed, severely anxious, have such acute psychosomatic symptoms as severe headaches and insomnia, are currently addicted to alcohol or drugs, or are an imminent danger to themselves or others need immediate symptomatic relief because their symptoms are seriously damaging and preclude the effective use of counseling.

Other symptoms are less damaging and either do not significantly interfere with counseling or actually create sufficient distress in the person that they facilitate it. These symptoms can be monitored and may be used to gauge the progress of counseling. As the person grows in counseling, the symptoms should diminish.

Cause of symptoms

There is one generic cause of symptoms; namely, something is significantly interfering with, or threatening to interfere with, a basic psychological need. Some of these basic needs are the need to experience a reasonable degree of security, love, esteem, accomplishment, stimulation, freedom, joy, and purpose. When an important need is interfered with, stress results. And when stress is left unmitigated, it will immediately or eventually cause symptoms, depending upon the intensity of the stress and the coping skills of the person. Basic needs can be significantly interfered with in four ways:

1. An objectively psychologically damaging event occurs (loss of a loved one, divorce, termination of a love relationship, imprisonment).
2. The person seeking help is in an important relationship with someone who is behaving in ways that significantly interfere with the person's basic needs (a woman is married to a man who treats her destructively).
3. The person seeking counseling behaves interpersonally in ways that discourage others from meeting his or her needs. For example, a man acts abrasively with women and gets rejected; a woman behaves seductively with men and gets used.
4. The person seeking counseling has intrapersonal dynamics that ultimately interfere with need fulfillment. For example, a man feels inadequate and therefore does not allow others to get close enough to meet his needs; a woman has unrealistically high expectations of herself, which she pursues to the detriment of getting her basic needs met.

These causes may not be mutually exclusive. A man may behave abrasively with women (interpersonal maladaptive behavior) because he perceives himself as inadequate and fears rejection (intrapersonal maladaptive behavior). Hence, he rejects women before they can reject him. There also may be more than one cause underlying a symptom, and two or more causes may interact. The more skilled a counselor becomes, the better he or she can see the interrelating of causes and symptoms and causes with causes. Figure 5–3 shows the interaction between symptoms, stress, and the causes of stress. It is important that counselors assess the cause(s) of the symptoms accurately because they will dictate the methods of resolution. If the cause is misdiagnosed, the method of resolution will be ineffective.[5]

Relief of symptoms

What can be done to modify the behavior that is causing the symptoms depends upon the nature of the cause. If the cause is an objectively stressful event, then cognitive restructuring, ventilation,

---

[5]See Chapter 3 for a fuller discussion of the relationship between need fulfillment and intrapersonal and interpersonal dynamics.

SYMPTOM

↑

OVERLOADING OF STRESS

↑

SIGNIFICANT INTERFERENCE WITH NEEDS

- Psychologically damaging event
- Significant other interferes with needs
- Person relates maladaptively with others
- Person relates maladaptively with self

Figure 5-3. Interaction between symptoms, stress, and causes of stress.

and reassurance may gradually allow the person to feel more secure, loved, or competent. This in turn reduces the stress, which diminishes the symptoms. If the cause is a significant other interfering with the person's need fulfillment, then the person can be helped to perceive and handle the situation more constructively or to withdraw from it. If the person's maladaptive behavior in interpersonal situations is causing the symptoms, then the counselor can help the person develop better social competencies or a better sense of self, depending on the basic problem. If the cause is the person's intrapsychic conflicts, they can be isolated and the person can be taught how to deal with them more creatively. The specific steps taken and the time they require depend upon the nature of the behavior, its duration and severity.

Readiness for counseling

Not everyone who seeks counseling is a reasonable candidate; that is, not all people will be able to use counseling to their advantage. The following are some factors counselors may consider when assessing the person's readiness for counseling. Each of these factors is on a long continuum. Obviously, if a person were to be at the positive end of the continuum on all these factors, it is likely that he or she would not need counseling.

1. People who accept responsibility for their problems are likely to be better candidates than those who blame others. People who express some variation of "I need to learn how to handle things better" are likely to be better candidates than those who say "If only my husband ... wife ... boss ... friends ... treated me better, everything would be all right."

2. People who are willing to work to earn feeling better are likely to be better candidates than those who want to feel better without changing their maladaptive behavior. Perls said "Very few people go in therapy to be cured, but rather to improve their neurosis."[6] Although Perls may be overgeneralizing, there is sufficient truth in his sentiment to evoke caution.

3. People with strong, intrinsic motivation to change are likely to be better candidates than those with weak intrinsic or primarily extrinsic motivation.

4. People who are psychologically minded are more likely to be good candidates than those who are not. Psychologically minded people are insightful and able and willing to appreciate the cause and effect dynamics of their behavior. For example, a person who can recognize that when she gets angry at a person she denies it but later subtly punishes the person who made her angry is likely to be a better candidate than someone who absolutely denies anger and can see no connection between her anger and her passive-aggressive behavior.

5. People who have good environmental supports that reward growth are likely to be better candidates that those who lack such supports.

6. People whose fears cause significant distress will likely be better candidates than those whose symptomatic behavior greatly reduces anxiety or provides pleasure. People who are addicted to alcohol, drugs, or food; those who compulsively gamble, steal, or sexually act out; and those whose symptoms act as effective tools to get much needed attention or as weapons with which to punish others are less promising candidates for counseling.

7. People who are capable of communicating in ways that can be understood and of listening in ways that allow them to assimilate information are likely to be better candidates than those whose symptoms significantly interfere with their ability to communicate. For example, people with severe depression, agitation, withdrawal; those with cognitive disturbances such as hallucinations, delusions, disorientation, or memory impairment; and people with speech disorders such as mutism, verbigeration, or echolalia are not good candidates for counseling.

Great caution must be exercised in deciding who is a reasonable and who is a poor candidate for counseling. Persons who are not good candidates at present can be referred by the counselor to a more appropriate type of intervention (detoxification, chemotherapy, weight-control programs, behavior modification, hospitalization), which may

[6]Perls (1969), p. 39.

enable them to become reasonable candidates in the future. It is possible for a counselor to accept a poor candidate into counseling. This can be done as long as the counselor does not give the person false hope regarding the effects of counseling.[7]

Person/counselor fit

Not all counselors can help all people who seek their help, and it is a destructive expectation for counselors to think otherwise. Counseling relationships are similar to marriages: when serious, ongoing problems arise, it is often a consequence of two people trying to stay together who never should have started together. Counselors who feel that they can help and should agree to help anyone who makes an appointment are deluding themselves. The main medium through which a counselor works is the therapeutic relationship. Ordinary relationships are delicate and tenuous; counseling relationships are much more so.

Counselors are human beings with weaknesses, biases, fears, angers, and values. They can learn to recognize what their delicate areas are and work to strengthen them. However, they can also recognize that once in a while a person in counseling rubs one or all of these delicate areas the wrong way. When this occurs, it is better to refer the person to someone else. One counselor may have a difficult time relating with very hostile, powerful, demanding people. Another counselor may experience inordinate stress relating with very passive, docile, clinging people. A third counselor may have difficulty accepting the person's presenting problem: homosexuality, child molesting, child beating, alcoholism, drug addiction, abortion, sexual promiscuity, rape. The more counselors are in touch with their humanity, the more sensitive they will be to the kinds of people and problems they are more likely to be able to help.

It is both a professional and ethical responsibility to screen people for counseling. Ordinarily, a counselor who agrees to see someone in counseling is communicating that he or she has *good reason* to expect that counseling will be *reasonably successful*, that the *counselor can work effectively* with the person, and that the *time, energy, hardship, and financial investment will be worthwhile*. If any one of the four italicized factors is absent, a serious professional and ethical issue arises.

One factor that greatly contributes to tarnishing the reputation of counseling is the counselor who agrees to work with people who cannot be adequately helped through counseling. This leads to the conclusion that "counseling doesn't work" instead of "counseling doesn't work

---

[7]For further discussion of the selection of candidates for counseling, see Garfield (1980), pp. 41–68.

with certain people," who should have been referred to a more appropriate source of intervention. Counselors who are intelligently selective are providing a positive service to people who are seeking help and to the counseling profession.[8]

It is unlikely that an evaluation will be made with absolute confidence and certainty. Human behavior is usually too complex for that. However, counselors can develop working hypotheses with a reasonable amount of confidence. When they do, they are ready for Stage 3.

STAGE 3: FEEDBACK

Feedback consists of the counselor sharing relevant information with the person seeking help. The purpose of the feedback is to provide sufficient information to enable the person to make an informed decision with regard to beginning a counseling program. Four principles can help counselors provide feedback that is meaningful and helpful.

Characteristics of the information

The information can be given as clearly, succinctly, concretely, and prudently as possible. "Clear" means simple, jargon-free language. "Succinct" means short, without drawn-out descriptions and analogies. Feedback, even with the most psychologically disturbed people, can be given in one session. "Concretely" indicates down-to-earth, easily grasped concepts. Sometimes a simple diagram helps. "Prudently" means that the counselor instills a sense of concern (when it is appropriate) without creating a state of alarm. A helpful attitude is "You've got some problems that do need attention, but there is something you can do about each of them."

Strengths and weaknesses

The feedback can include both strengths and weaknesses. Usually it is better to begin with strengths and finish with weaknesses. When the procedure is reversed, the person may become so defensive or demoralized that he or she may not hear some important part of the discussion of the problem. Another option is to intersperse strengths and weaknesses.

Inviting questions

The person can be invited to ask questions both during and after the feedback. Questions can be answered in a straightforward yet supportive way. Sometimes people ask a litany of questions in order to forestall the

---

[8]A different discussion of evaluation can be found in Weiner (1975), pp. 51–72.

feedback process. When this is the case, the person can be invited to hold his or her questions until the end of the session.

Recommendations

After communicating the feedback to the person, the counselor makes recommendations. The counselor can explain that recommendations are not orders but serious, well-thought-out suggestions. The following are some common recommendations:

Continue counseling on a weekly basis or more or less frequently as the seriousness of the problem dictates.

Continue individual counseling; or begin group, marital, or family counseling; or combine individual counseling with one of the other types.

Continue counseling, but with another counselor. This would occur when the counselor feels that someone else would be significantly more helpful, either because of a personality conflict or because the person's problem requires help outside of the counselor's area of expertise. When this recommendation is made, it should be done prudently and without communicating to the person that he or she is being rejected.

Recommend a more suitable type of intervention—for example, substance abuse counseling, a weight-control program, readings or a course in psychological health, a support group, or religious direction.

Recommend no further intervention because the person's difficulties are quite normal and are simply a part of the person's development and growth.

Recommend no further intervention because, as a result of the sessions up to this point, the person has gained sufficient insight and courage to handle the problems without further professional help.

Recommend no further intervention because, although the person has problems that merit counseling, he or she is not psychologically ready for counseling. The person may not be experiencing sufficient stress or is experiencing stress, but it is controlled by defenses that are currently impenetrable. In either case, the person's motivation and accessibility are less than those necessary for effective counseling. Counselors can exercise care not to convey that the situation is hopeless. The difference between "not being ready" and "hopeless" can be explained, accompanied by an open invitation to return at some time in the future if the person so chooses. On the other hand, these people should not be led to believe that they do not need counseling.

If the sessions preceding the feedback progressed the way they should, neither the feedback nor the recommendations will be a surprise. Counselors need not feel that the feedback should consist of dramatic insights and discoveries. Consciously and unconsciously, the counselor has been preparing the person for the feedback and recommendations as the evaluation progressed.

No matter what the recommendation, it is unhelpful for the person to make a decision on the day of the feedback. The person can be invited to think about the feedback, assimilate and discuss it with others if he or she chooses. The counselor is careful not to convey the attitude that the person would be foolish not to accept the recommendation or that the counselor does not care if the person follows the recommendation. A more helpful attitude is one that conveys "I think the recommendation is a sound one, but what is more important is that it is *your* decision."

At this point, the person in counseling has a second choice point as to whether or not to begin counseling. This time the choice is an informed one. The person understands much more about himself or herself, about the nature of counseling, and about the personality of the counselor. If the person chooses to continue counseling, he or she will be a much stronger candidate and counseling will continue with good momentum. If the person chooses not to continue counseling, this decision may save the person and the counselor a great deal of time, energy, and frustration.

STAGE 4: COUNSELING AGREEMENT

Although counseling has been taking place during the first three stages, both the counselor and the person in counseling possess much more information than they did when they began. Using this information as a frame of reference, the counselor and the person in counseling can come to an agreement on four issues: the practical aspects of counseling, roles, expectations, and the goals of counseling.

Practical aspects

Practical aspects include how often the person and counselor will meet, the length of the sessions, the policy regarding canceled and failed appointments, and the billing procedures. If there is no need to modify these based on the information gained from the first three stages, it is helpful to restate them in order to underline their importance. However, sometimes the counselor has learned information that causes him or her to adjust some of the practical aspects to fit a particular person and situation. When this is the case, the counselor can explain the modifications and the reasons for them.

Roles

The second part of the agreement deals with role expectations. The specific roles depend on the counselor, the person in counseling, and the situation. For example, the counselor may explain that his or her role will be the same as it was during the first three stages or more passive, reflective, varied, confrontative, direct, ambiguous, questioning, silent, active, or listening. It is helpful for the counselor to offer a brief explanation why he or she feels the nature of the role will facilitate growth.

It is important to remember that *assuming* a role is not the same as *playing* a role. When a man returns from work, he assumes the role of father, which is helpful and appropriate. Hopefully, he does not play the role, which means that he is acting a part that is not he. A counselor may legitimately assume a role in a counseling situation that would be inappropriate to assume in other circumstances, but the role should be a part of him or her and not simply an ill-fitting cloak.

The role of the person in counseling is also discussed. A counselor may feel it is more helpful for the person to bring to each session whatever is on his or her mind or may suggest that the person's past needs more attention and should be the area of focus for a time. Another counselor may wish to concentrate mostly on the present and on feelings, or a counselor may want to focus mostly on what goes on inside the counseling room. One counselor may invite the person to relate personally as well as professionally, asking questions and getting to know the counselor, while another counselor may wish to remain more impersonal.

When both the counselor and person in counseling clearly understand and agree that their roles feel comfortable and will facilitate growth, they are in a better position to work as a synchronized team rather than stumbling over each other at every turn.

Expectations

Expectations can become more explicit than they were during the first three stages because each person has a better grasp of the situation. The counselor shares his or her expectations that involve the responsibilities of the person in counseling. These issues might deal with honesty, making concerted efforts to reach the goals of counseling, placing a high priority on counseling, doing homework assignments, discussing counseling with others, and viewing counseling as a seven-day-a-week experience rather than a 50-minute-a-week visit.

The person in counseling can also share his or her expectations of the counselor. The person can tell the counselor what he or she would find helpful and unhelpful. Often in this early stage of counseling people are not in a position to articulate clearly how the counselor can be of more help. Consequently, the counselor can help the person along these lines and invite the person to keep the counselor apprised of growing and changing expectations as counseling progresses.

Goals

As a result of the first three stages, both the person in counseling and the counselor have a clearer picture of the problems and the possible solutions. Goal setting in counseling is perhaps the most important part because it ties the whole process together. For this reason it requires a certain amount of time and care. The goals of counseling should have certain characteristics.

First, they are specific and measurable. For example, an agreed upon goal is that a person overcome his or her fear of getting a job. This goal is specific in that it zeros in on a clear target. It is measurable because the steps toward the goal can be readily charted, and it is relatively easy to tell how much progress has been made toward accomplishing the goal.

In contrast, a person may have as a goal to be more happy, less anxious or depressed, to become a better husband or mother, or to get to know him- or herself better. These goals are so general, abstract, and difficult to measure that they are unworkable. This counselor and the person in counseling need to target in on what specifically does "more happy" mean? Why exactly does the person feel tense? Why specifically does the person think he is not a good husband? The more vague and abstract the goals, the less chance counseling has to approximate them.

Second, they are realistic. The goals of counseling are always restricted by the potential of the person in counseling and the limitations in the person's environment. For example, two 38-year-old women wish to enter law school. They seek counseling to help them make the psychological changes necessary to bring this about. For one of these women, this may be a realistic goal and for another it may not be. One woman is divorced, intelligent, and energetic. She worked as a court clerk and feels that she has the motivation, skills, and understanding of what it means to be a lawyer. She seeks counseling because she is not sure if she wants to leave the security of her present job, whether she wants to make the sacrifices that both law school and a career as an attorney demand, and whether it will deprive her two adolescent children of the parenting they still need. She knows what she wants, but she is not sure that pursuing it would be a wise choice.

The second woman is married to a man who does not want her to go to law school. He wants her home with the four school-age children, and he would have to get another job to secure a loan to finance law school. The woman is of modest intelligence and has been depressed. The thought of going to law school has served to raise her from her depression. She has no knowledge of law or law as a career but came upon the idea when she read about another woman whose life was changed when she became a lawyer. She seeks counseling because she wants to learn how she can go to law school and keep her husband happy and children healthy. It is unlikely that the second woman's goal is one that can be attained in counseling, even though it is essentially the same goal as that of the first woman.

A second aspect of realistic goals is that few of them are of an all-or-nothing nature. For example, a man seeks counseling to help him relate more effectively at work. "More effectively" for this particular man may mean increasing his effectiveness by 20, 50, or 70%. It would be unrealistic to expect counseling to allow him to function with complete effectiveness.

Third, the goals are psychologically healthy. Some people's proposed goals are consonant with psychological growth. They want to become more assertive, autonomous, and confident; less angry, fearful, and confused. Other people, however, may seek counseling to maintain equilibrium through means that are not psychologically healthy. For example, a person may want to learn to survive in a work situation that is intractably damaging, to leave a family situation in ways that would be injurious to self and others, or to begin a project for which he is not prepared and that is doomed to fail. While it is the prerogative of those in counseling to choose their own goals, it is the counselor's responsibility not to become a collaborator in destructive behavior.

Fourth, they are often hierarchical. Some people have only one goal in counseling. The previously mentioned woman who wishes to go to law school could be an example of this. Many people, however, have several goals. For example, a man may list the following goals: to be more comfortable sexually, to change jobs, to have a less conflictual relationship with his parents, to recapture religious fervor, to relate more comfortably with women on dates, and to lose 30 pounds.

The items on this list do not automatically lend themselves to a hierarchical arrangement. Once the counselor knows the man better, it may become clear that the goals cannot be arranged in alphabetical order and pursued. It may be that the inordinate pressures at work are causing ongoing damage, and until they are alleviated, the man is in no position to work on any of the other goals. Once that pressure is alleviated, the next step may be to refer the person to a medically supervised weight-control program through which he can lose weight and feel more presentable. While he is losing weight, the next step may be to explore the reasons for feeling sexually confused or uncomfortable about himself. When this issue is on its way to resolution, the next step may be to examine what makes dating an anxiety-producing experience and then to date. When the dating anxiety gets under control, the next step may be to understand and work on his conflict with his parents. When all these are reasonably under control, he may be at peace enough to be able to work on his religious doubts and conflicts.

Sometimes when the first two or three goals in the hierarchy are attained, the rest take care of themselves. For example, in the case above, the man's conflicts with his parents and his religious conflicts may be resolved as side effects of achieving the previous goals.

There are two points of caution with regard to placing counseling goals in a hierarchy. One is that the counselor must walk the middle path between excluding all material in the counseling session except that dealing directly with the current target goal and allowing the person to dabble in one target after another, which results in no consistent movement toward any goal.

The second caution is that agreed upon hierarchical goals must not be set in cement. When the counselor understands more about the person, it may become imperative to rearrange the hierarchy. In the case of the man, the counselor may discover that until his religious conflicts are resolved, there will be no movement toward any of the other goals. A shift in the hierarchy may be necessary when the person and the counselor work hard at attaining a subgoal with no meaningful results. This could indicate that another goal in the hierarchy or a hitherto unrecognized goal must be dealt with first.

Fifth, the goals belong to the person in counseling. Sometimes, especially when people bring general, abstract, or vague goals to counseling, the counselor gets trapped into making them more concrete and manageable. For example, a woman may say she is depressed but doesn't know why because she has a beautiful husband, children, and home—all any woman could ever want. After several unsuccessful attempts to help the woman articulate the cause of her distress, the counselor may decide why she is depressed: she is denying her disappointment with a marriage that has become drab; she resents the fact that her husband won't let her go back to work; she feels guilty about having recently placed her father in a convalescent hospital; and she is repressing sexual feelings because she has no place to get them met.

On the basis of these hypotheses with which the person reluctantly and tentatively agrees ("You're the doctor—I expect you know more about these things that I do"), they launch into trying to reach the counselor's goals. Of course, nothing good is likely to result from this counseling relationship because the goals are the counselor's and not those of the person in counseling. Even if the counselor is correct on all the hypotheses, the woman has never claimed the goals for herself.

It is essential that the counseling goals be clearly owned by the person and that counseling not continue until this occurs. To spend a few sessions trying to clarify goals could be appropriate. But when the goal of counseling is to discuss the goals of counseling, this usually results in unproductive expeditions in which both the counselor and the person continually meet themselves exactly where they began.

Sixth, goals are frequently evaluated. Aiming at goals in counseling is similar to aiming at any kind of target. After attempting to hit the target a few times, it is sensible to examine it to see how successful the efforts have been.

Since goals are specific and measurable, it should not be too difficult to gauge progress toward them. When the counselor and the person agree that they are progressing in the right direction and on schedule, it provides a mutual sense of confidence and accomplishment that can add momentum to their quest. If, after a reasonable time, it becomes clear that the counselor and the person have gradually strayed from the target or that they are on target but progressing too slowly, they can consider questions like the following: Is there a condition that must be met first? For example, the person may need more time to trust the counselor before becoming committed to the goal. Is there some deep ambivalence developing toward the goal as it gets closer to realization? Maybe a man is becoming less confident that divorce is the best thing for him at this point. In any case, it is much better to look at the target early and at short intervals to see the path counseling is taking than to assume counseling is squarely on track, only to discover later that it has been spiraling out of control.

Developing a counseling agreement may take one session or three or four. If the counselor and the person are still struggling and negotiating over an agreement after five sessions, it is likely that the person is not sufficiently motivated to use counseling, there is a problem in the counselor-person relationship, or else the counselor is not sufficiently skilled to develop the agreement.[9]

STAGE 5: CHANGING BEHAVIOR

Exactly what occurs during this stage depends upon the person and his or her problem. However, there are some common experiences that occur during this stage with which counselors can be familiar. These issues may arise before this stage, but they arise more obviously and regularly at this time. The following are ten situations with which counselors frequently must deal while helping the person change behavior.

Focusing on responsibility

This crucial issue often arises, despite the counselor's previous efforts. People in counseling frequently view counselors as psychological architects whose role is to provide a blueprint telling the person who he is, what his problem is, how he should solve his problem, and when he should take each step in the process. Even the most experienced counselor can be insidiously trapped into assuming this role. When this occurs, the counselor is taking responsibility not only for the person's changing behavior but for the person's life.

Counselors can resist the manipulations and temptations to become managers for people in counseling. If persons in counseling need someone to take the reins of their life, they likely need more intensive treatment than traditional outpatient counseling can afford. The counselor's stance toward the person in counseling should always be:

You tell me who you are today.
You tell me what your problem is today.
You tell me how you wish to solve it.
You tell me when you are going to try what strategies.

Obviously, a person could respond "If I could tell you all these things, I wouldn't be in counseling in the first place." And in one sense this retort is valid, but in a deeper sense it is not. The assumption

[9]A thorough discussion of the importance of counseling agreements can be found in Goldberg (1977), pp. 31–61.

underlying counseling is that the answers to these questions can lie only within the individual. The counselor's role is not to answer these questions, but to provide an environment and a relationship conducive to helping the person grow in the insight and courage necessary to answer the questions and translate the answers into practice. In other words, one of the general goals of counseling is to help a person become his or her own counselor.

Inward searching

People who are in counseling, like most people, operate almost solely on an external level. Their approach to life is "I've got a problem here, and I have to figure out a way to solve it." The focus is almost entirely on the *problem outside* of them and not on the *person inside*. As a result, they are likely to experience the same types of problems continually.

For example, a 30-year-old woman comes to counseling because she is depressed that she cannot find a marriageable man. The more frantic and depressed she becomes, the more she sabotages her relationships with men. After several sessions of internal searching, she makes the following discoveries:

> She has a void within her that is comprised of feeling unimportant, unlovable, and purposeless, and she believes only a man can fill that void.
>
> She looks upon marriage as a psychological and social validation of herself. As long as she is unmarried, she and society look upon her as psychologically lame; as soon as she gets married, she will be seen as psychologically healthy. A good deal of the pressure she feels is not to get married but to feel good about herself.
>
> She thinks the best way to get a man is to be sexually active and has not realized that this is not going to get her the man that meets her qualifications. In other words, she is attracting exactly the kind of man that she dislikes.
>
> She is very ambivalent about marriage. On one hand she wants to get married, but on the other she resents men because she needs them to make her happy. She fears her deep need for a man will enslave her just as her mother became enslaved to her father. She is fearful that if she does marry, she may find herself disillusioned, which would rule out her last hope for happiness on this earth. Her deep ambivalence is reflected in her behavior with men, causing her unnecessary conflicts.

As she works through these insights, which until now had been unconscious, she feels far less pressure to get married. She has begun to fill her void intrapsychically with a clear appreciation for her worth and goodness, to which counseling introduces her. Extrapsychically, she fills the void with new friends, a more fulfilling job, and hobbies she always enjoyed until she began her "manhunt."

When she does date, she is more selective, acts in keeping with her deeper values, and relates more comfortably. Dates are no longer examinations that she can pass or fail, but evenings to enjoy in themselves. She still would *like* to marry, but she does not *have* to marry.

People in counseling often resist inward exploration because they are fearful of what they will discover. Therefore, it is necessary for counselors to develop skills that allow them to help people work through the resistance and a sense of timing that helps them judge the right time to explore a given insight.[10]

Utilizing insights

There are two points of view about the insights gleaned from inward searching. One is that the insights alone may bring about the psychological equilibrium necessary to reduce symptoms and create growth. The person's problem may remain, but the person has outgrown it; so it is less or no longer a nuisance.

A second point of view is that inward searching provides the blueprint for external behavioral changes and that both are necessary for maximum personality growth. This view recognizes that not all human problems are solvable, but as long as one is in counseling, one might as well try to solve the ones that are. This view combines the benefits of inward searching and problem solving into a two-part process.

The woman in the previous example did not simply rest with her inner reflections and discoveries, but used them to chart some concrete, observable changes in her daily life. She finished college, changed jobs, broadened her circle of friends and interests, changed her way of relating with men, returned to her religion, and used the psychological dividends of this change to fill her void and strengthen her being. As a result, she has not only solved the problem she brought to counseling, but has grown as a person.

Mirroring

Counselors act as mirrors in which people can see themselves. There are two ways of mirroring: intrapsychically and interpersonally. "Intrapsychically" means that counselors reflect back to people who they are so that they can make appropriate changes in their behavior. Often there is steam on the mirror that people look into daily, and it

---

[10]For a fuller discussion of inward searching, see Bugental (1978).

hides the parts they don't want to see. In mirroring, the counselor says, in effect, "This is the way you look to me now. If you agree that's who you are, what changes, if any, would you like to make? If you don't agree that's who you are, let's figure out why we have different perceptions." This is important because most people in counseling don't have a clear and complete picture of themselves, which leads them to behave in inappropriate and unhelpful ways. It is also important because very few, if any, people in the person's life would have the skills, concern, benevolence, and courage to reflect back to the person how he or she appears. When a person gets a clear, unbiased picture, he or she is in a position to make some meaningful changes.

Equally important is interpersonal mirroring. This means that the counselor reflects back to the person how he or she "comes on" with people and what responses this behavior elicits. The counselor might say "I'm starting to feel angry (manipulated, anxious, confused, distracted, sympathetic, bored, frightened, stupid, guilty, hurt; or warm, relaxed, comfortable, happy, empathetic, interested)." The message that the counselor is conveying is "When you act the way you are, this is the response you are likely to elicit from people. If you want that response, it's okay; but if you don't want it, let's see how and why you elicit it."

As long as counselors are affectively neutral about the issue at hand, they can trust that their reactions to the person are similar to those that other people would have. This is priceless information for people in counseling because they may be oblivious to the effects of their verbal and nonverbal communication on others. People may wonder why others "always" manipulate, reject, seduce, misunderstand, or avoid them when all they ever do is behave in friendly and reasonable ways.

Both intrapsychic and interpersonal reflection must be done as nonthreateningly as possible. It is likely to be threatening to some extent because people generally become anxious when they hear something about themselves that they didn't know, even when the feedback is positive. The only purpose of mirroring is to be helpful; it is never to put a person "in his place."

Confronting

A counselor may point out significant discrepancies in the person's behavior or lifestyle. This is different from mirroring, which simply reflects back to people who they appear to be. It also differs from challenging in that challenging is more gentle and invites people to reexamine the accuracy of their perceptions; confrontation is more assertive and focuses on people's deeper motives and contradictory behavior.

Confronting is one method of interpretation. The message in confrontation is "You say you are this, but is it possible that you are something different?" For example, a counselor may say "Bill, you keep saying you want to save your marriage, but the way you've been acting makes me wonder if there is a part of you that does not want to save it" or "Nancy, you tell me that you want to use counseling, but you consistently forget what we talk about from one session to another and seldom work on anything between sessions."

Some cautions must be exercised regarding confrontation. It is important that the relationship between the person and the counselor is strong enough to support the confrontation. In other words, although people may not enjoy confrontation, they realize it is being done in their best interests. In addition, counselors must have reasonable certitude that any confrontation has a sound basis in reality.

Timing is also important. The confrontation should take place at an appropriate time; that is, not be introduced "out of the blue" or when the person is not sufficiently strong or insightful to learn from it.

Finally, counselors can be sensitive to the nature of their motives. Is the confrontation actually a personal attack disguised as a helpful strategy, or does it stem from a counselor whose sole interest is helping the person learn something important? If it is an attack, the tone will be "Tim, who do you think you're kidding." If it's a valid response, the tenor will be "Tim, I'd like to share some perceptions with you and see what you think about them."[11]

Giving support

Counselors offer reassurance and positive reinforcement and reduce people's anxiety by showing them the positive and hopeful aspects of a situation and by rewarding positive behavior with genuine and spontaneous smiles, encouragement, and support. Giving support can be a very effective aid to the counseling process. On the other hand, it can also be an area for caution.

When reassuring the person, it is important that such support is justified by reality and is not a hollow pep talk that will backfire. Statements such as "I'm sure things will turn out fine" or "I have faith in you that you'll do well" are usually ill advised. A better type of reassurance is reflected in "Let's do our best, and, whatever happens, we'll work very hard together to handle it well." This communicates a more

[11]For a thorough discussion of confrontation, see Adler & Myerson (1973).

reality-based reassurance that focuses on the counseling relationship as a source of support and not on the success or failure of a particular event.

Positive reinforcement also has areas of caution. Counselors can be careful about what they reward. A man may tell a counselor that he was *finally* able to assert himself at work. He proudly relates the incident to the counselor, who congratulates him for his willingness to take a risk and for successfully asserting himself. However, if the counselor had delved more deeply into the matter, he would have seen that the "assertiveness" was a ploy to escape some rightful responsibility at work. In effect, the counselor rewarded the person for being manipulative and shirking responsibility.

It is often difficult for counselors to delve into situations that the person proudly presents as evidence of progress. There is a pressure for the counselor to allow the person to bask in the feelings of accomplishment. For the counselor to examine the situation appears distrustful and rude. However, in keeping with the axiom "All that glitters is not gold," counselors could do well to gently examine situations lest they reward a problematic behavior.

A second caution regarding positive reinforcement is that it can create a situation in which the person in counseling is growing to earn the praise of the counselor. This counseling relationship can never end because, as soon as talk of termination begins, the person regresses as he or she realizes that growth without the praise of the counselor is meaningless. Ideally, growth should be its own reward, and, as people progress in counseling, there should be less need for counselors to reward their efforts. However, in the first phases of counseling, when people's efforts are not yet sufficiently effective to merit rewarding results, it is necessary for counselors to reward their efforts. Under most circumstances, positive reinforcement should be given judiciously and probably more sparingly than it ordinarily is.

Reverse shaping

The counselor helps shape the behavior of the person in counseling. By a judicious use of reward, expectation, insight, and confrontation, the counselor helps the person modify behavior. Reverse shaping is when the person does the same thing to the counselor. Because conscious and unconscious shaping is almost continually operative in all human beings, the shaping attempts of the person in counseling probably equal those of the counselor. People in counseling can subtly and not so subtly reward and punish counselors. Counselors who behave in ways that please people may be rewarded either by people showing new evidence of growth or by people complimenting them. When a counselor displeases a person in counseling, the person is apt to regress or attack the counselor.

When people's shaping efforts are obvious, they can be dealt with easily. But people who are "cooperative" and whose only wish is "to get strong enough to handle my own problems" can adroitly shape the counselor without the counselor being even slightly aware of it.

Some people bring a script to counseling that has a bad ending. They hire the counselor as an actor who will help them bring about the desired destructive ending in the most "officially approved" way possible. The ending of the story may be suicide, getting fired, getting rejected by loved ones, remaining in a destructive relationship, proving that one is hopeless, getting hospitalized, or making the counselor a failure. Each progressive act is an escalated attempt to shape the counselor's behavior so that he or she will help the person bring about the desired end of the story.

Counselors can react constructively to shaping behavior in two ways. The first is that, every time the person creates a situation in which the counselor feels quite pleased or quite displeased, the counselor can ask: Why is this person telling me this (doing this)? How does he (or she) expect me to respond? Will my response be feeding into the person's strengths or weaknesses?

Second, it is helpful for counselors to focus on the agreed upon goals of counseling, despite the person's pressures to ignore them. This will eventually either spotlight the destructive ending of the script and allow the counselor to invite the person to change the ending or cause the person to terminate when he or she sees that the counselor is not willing to be shaped. If the latter happens, it is better to have it occur early than to have the counselor continue as a co-conspirator in the person's destructive behavior.

Transference

This means that a person displaces onto a counselor feelings, attitudes, or impulses that were part of a previous relationship. The counselor who represents an authority figure likely will be reacted to in the same ways the person has reacted to authority in the past—for example, with attitudes that are defensive, hostile, or ingratiating. The person may react to the counselor's personal qualities with positive or negative transference. The way the counselor looks, speaks, sits, thinks, emotes, and values may trigger a transference reaction. A person may say "I hate it (you) when you get that god-almighty expression on your face (because you are my father when you do that)" or "I like coming here (I like you) because I feel comfortable and understood (the way my mother always made me feel)."

Sometimes the transference is direct ("I don't like you"); at other times, it is indirect—that is, directed at the counselor's profession ("I always felt people went into psychology to solve their own problems") or directed at the domain of the counselor ("Why is this room always so cold?").

Counselors can be aware that not all of a person's reactions in counseling stem from transference. People can relate to counselors directly, without transferring any residuals of past relationships. For example, the fact that a person is angry at a counselor does not mean he is manifesting negative transference. The person's anger may be present and appropriate, and to deal with it as transference would be uninsightful of the counselor and demeaning to the person in counseling. Moreover, all conflicts between the counselor and the person in counseling need not be transference. A person with a devout religious faith may not agree with some of the values of a counselor who views religion as neurotic. To label this person's value conflicts with the counselor as transference misses an important reality conflict that needs resolving.

Counselors can also be aware that all transference reactions have a quality of resistance. As long as people are spending time and energy loving or hating the counselor, they are not progressing toward the mutually agreed upon goals.

How much resistance the transference creates determines whether the counselor should interpret it or let it slide. In general, indirect expressions of mildly positive transference should receive the least attention, and direct manifestation of intensely negative transference should receive the most.

Another point of view on transference reactions is that they can be dealt with in a direct, interpersonal manner rather than in an analytical, working-through fashion. For example, a counselor may reply to a woman who challenges him on being sexist: "I agree that a sexist counselor would not be helpful to you. However, why don't we refocus on our goals, and if you see any concrete data to substantiate your concern as we go along, we can deal with it at that time." This type of response respects the woman's concern yet does not allow it to distract her and the counselor from the main purpose of counseling.

Countertransference

Countertransference consists of inappropriate reactions by the counselor to the behavior of the person in counseling. It can be positive; that is, the counselor has caring and affectionate feelings of a kind and degree that are not merited by the reality of who the person is. Counter-transference also can be negative; that is, the counselor feels angry or bored with a person who has done nothing to merit these reactions. As with transference, not all pleasant or unpleasant feelings toward a person in counseling are necessarily countertransference. A counselor may have reason to like or to be upset with a person, and these reactions should not be stifled or worked through as countertransference, but dealt with appropriately.

Countertransference can be both an advantage and a hindrance to counselors. It can be an advantage when it teaches counselors something about themselves. For example, a person may have a habit of responding that angers the counselor. The counselor can then scrutinize himself or herself as to what vulnerability was tapped by the person's behavior. Countertransference can be a hindrance to counseling because strong, inappropriate feelings of liking or disliking a person can sufficiently interfere with the counselor's clinical judgment and helpful responses, causing progress in counseling to be seriously impeded. When this occurs, the counselor must assume responsibility for working through the feelings or, if necessary, refer the person to another counselor.

Interpretation

Interpretation introduces to people in counseling previously unknown information about themselves. In other words, the counselor pulls back the blinds and permits the person to see behaviors that were relegated to the subconscious or unconscious layers of personality. The goal of interpretation is increasing self-knowledge. The more self-knowledge people have, the more able they are to change their behavior.

Most interpretation centers on self-deceit. People do not wish to acknowledge parts of themselves and so repress and deny them. However, these hidden behaviors (thoughts, feelings, defenses, motives, conflicts, or values) do not disappear but influence people's actions in ways of which they are unaware. This allows people to vent these less than conscious behaviors without having to accept responsibility for them. For example, a man has unconscious, negative feelings toward his family. He thinks he comes home quite late every night because he is too busy at work. His late arrival allows him to shorten his time in an unpleasant situation and to upset the people who are upsetting him without having to face exactly what he is doing and why. In the meantime, both he and his family are unhappy, and they feel there is nothing that can be done about it.

Interpretation ordinarily poses a threat to the person in counseling because the repressed material being introduced is not pleasant or it would not have been repressed in the first place. Also, the new information that stems from interpretation means that the person will have to let go of old behaviors and adjust current behaviors to the new information. For example, once the man who gets home late discovers what he is doing and why, he will feel more anxious and have to use the anxiety to change the situation in one direction or another. Therefore, it is not unusual for people to resist interpretation.

Because interpretation in counseling is a delicate operation, counselors can be familiar with the important issues involved. Counselors need to know *what* to interpret. Generally, it is more helpful to interpret the person's defenses before the person's conflicts so that the interpretation doesn't get intercepted and defused by the defenses. It is also generally more helpful to interpret process (how and why the person is doing or not doing something in the counseling session) than content (what the person is saying). Interpretation should be selective in that only behaviors that are significantly affecting the person need to be considered.

Counselors should also know *when* to interpret. Interpretations are more likely to fall on fertile ground when the person in counseling is close to the level of awareness required to grasp the interpretation, when the person is sufficiently relaxed and comfortable with the counselor, and when the counselor has reasonable certainty that the interpretive hypothesis is correct.

The counselor also needs to know *how* to interpret. Counselors can explain the nature of interpretation to the person and begin gradually by offering less threatening interpretations. Interpretations should be phrased tentatively ("Could it be that . . . ?") and concisely since unnecessary words serve only to distract.

Interpretation plays less of a role in crisis intervention and short-term counseling than it does in counseling that is of longer duration and addresses deeper problems.[12]

STAGE 6: TERMINATION

It is helpful to remember that termination is a *stage* of counseling and not simply the last few sessions. This stage could encompass the last quarter of counseling. During it, the counselor begins preparing the person to leave counseling. The counselor increasingly points out the

_____

[12]For further discussion of transference, countertransference, and interpretation, see Singer (1965).

success the person is achieving. The message is "You seem to be doing more and more on your own and doing it well." This helps the person see that the distance traveled in counseling is a good deal longer than the distance that remains.

The counselor also begins pulling back as a source of support, feedback, and guidance. This does not mean he or she diminishes interest in the person; it only means that the counselor demonstrates the interest in a different way, much as parents show their concern for a child differently as the child matures.

Counseling becomes a place to check in. The sessions consist more of the person saying "I've got a problem that came up last week. Let me tell you what I'm going to do about it, and if you've got any thoughts you can let me know." This level of autonomy is later elevated to the final level: "Let me tell you how I solved a problem this week. I purposely didn't tell you about it because I wanted to handle it on my own. If you've got any thoughts when I'm through, I'd be glad to hear them."

Usually at about this time someone introduces the topic of termination. While it is sometimes said that it is better for people in counseling to initiate the subject of termination, this does not appear to be necessarily true. Sometimes the fact that the counselor brings it up first is supportive because people view it as a validation of their own thoughts and a compliment to their progress. Also, some people assume that bringing up termination is the rightful role of the counselor.

When initiating the topic, the counselor might say "You seem to be doing so well that I'm wondering if you have given any thought to tapering off our sessions?" Of course, the counselor would ask this question only when the person has had good momentum for a reasonable period of time. The person may respond "It's funny you ask that. We must be on the same wavelength because I have been thinking about it, too." Other responses might be "I haven't given it much thought, but I suppose it is something we should start planning for" or "No, I haven't. Why? Do *you* think I'm ready to stop?" The counselor must deal with the dynamics underlying the responses. This final response likely indicates that the person and counselor are viewing things differently or the person is dependent on counseling and resistant to even the thought of terminating.

The person in counseling who initiates the topic of termination might say "You know, I've been thinking that I may not need to come here as often because I'm handling things pretty well." The counselor may respond "Why don't you tell me what you've been thinking about it?" and react appropriately to the person's explanations.

After there is agreement that counseling has progressed to a point where terminating is an issue, the next step is usually to taper off the number of sessions. Generally, the longer the counseling relationship, the longer the tapering-off period. Tapering off usually means reducing the number of sessions from four each month to two. Sometimes that is sufficient but, with some people, it is helpful to continue tapering off to once each month and then to a "come in as the need arises" basis. Tapering off is meant to avoid the shock of autonomy that can cause separation anxiety and regressive behavior.

It is helpful to recall at this stage the nature of a goal; that is, it is something to be aimed at that may not be totally achieved. Hence, counseling does not necessarily continue until the goals are ultimately and irrevocably attained. More often, counseling helps people to approximate more closely their goals and to live more effectively with what distance remains between where they are and where they would like to be.

An adjacent concept is that a person's growth toward goals does not terminate with the end of counseling. By the time people terminate counseling, they should have built up a momentum that will continue to carry them in the direction of their goals.

The clinical judgment regarding termination considers the relationship between how far a person has progressed in counseling and how much more counseling can or should do for the person. When people have a clear picture of their ultimate goals and good momentum in the right direction, they are ready to finish the job on their own.[13]

Finally, people do not always terminate counseling with profuse feelings of gratitude toward the counselor. Although this can be discouraging or confusing to the counselor, it is understandable. When counseling has been a difficult experience for a person and has cost a great deal of time, energy, tension, hard work, and money, the person may feel like a football player after a grueling victory. He truly enjoys the victory but he feels that he put at least as much into the victory as the coach, and the coach is getting paid. Consequently, he feels no special need to express appreciation. He's happy he's won; he feels it was worth it; he's glad it's over; and he wants to go home.

Some people still have not completely resolved the fact that they needed help or needed to depend on another person. Therefore, to thank the counselor would be admitting that they needed him or her. Obviously, it would be nice for people to resolve these feelings before the

[13]Termination, like any other stage of counseling, can have its unique difficulties. For a discussion of the difficulties, see Chapter 11.

termination of counseling, but what is "nice" and what is "real" are sometimes two different things.

Some people have not been good at showing gratitude and saying goodbye for the 20 or 40 years they've been on earth; so counseling may not have changed that. It doesn't mean these people did not receive a great deal from counseling; it simply means they cannot adequately express their gratitude.

On the other hand, the fact that some people show profuse gratitude does not necessarily indicate they received a great deal from counseling. They may just be thankful that counseling is finished or that they escaped from counseling without having to face their deepest, most dreaded problem.

Counselors can take satisfaction from the fact that they helped people and that these people's lives will be better, even though some people's lives will never be more than marginally fulfilling. If a counselor expects to receive greater satisfaction than that, he or she may have to find it outside of the counseling room.

SUMMARY

It is important that counselors recognize the developmental dimension of the counseling relationship. When counselors possess a general theoretical and practical frame of reference, it lends both direction and order to what otherwise could be a chaotic and frustrating experience.

An understanding of the stages of helping is beneficial to both counselors and people in counseling. It is helpful to counselors because the stages act as directional markers that help counselors steer a steady course toward growth. It is also helpful to people in counseling because, once the sequence of stages is explained to them, they can feel a sense of security and purpose.

THOUGHT QUESTIONS

1. If you were limited to only *one* question in the information-gathering stage, what would you ask? Why would you ask it?
2. With regard to selecting candidates you would see in counseling, what is one type of person and one type of problem that you think would be best referred to another counselor? Why do you feel this way?
3. After a few sessions, your antagonism toward the person you are seeing reaches such a peak that it is obvious you can no longer be of help to him. When you recommend that he see another counselor, he

retorts "You just don't like me. That's why you want to get rid of me." What do you respond?

4. When you experience negative countertransference toward a person in counseling, how are you likely to show it? When you experience positive countertransference toward a person, how are you likely to show it?

5. What specifically would you like to hear from a person in counseling after the successful termination of a counseling relationship? What will it mean to you if you don't hear it?

CHAPTER 6

Cognition
in Counseling

Cognition is a property of the intellect. It refers to perceiving, interpreting, thinking, remembering, imagining, deciding, and reasoning. Cognitive theorists hold that cognition significantly influences behavior. How people perceive events often determines their emotional reactions, and the combination of cognition and emotion results in a behavioral response.[1] Consequently, although two people may experience the same event, their reactions may be quite different.

For example, two men experience the death of their wives. One man perceives the loss as the end of his world. He feels that, without his wife, life has no meaning and that he is unable to function. This perception causes him to feel devastated. As a result, he takes an overdose of tranquilizers so he can "join her." The other man perceives the death of his wife as a great loss, but he does not equate his wife or his marriage with life itself. He feels great sadness and pain, but he is not devastated. After a reasonable period of grieving, he lives a productive and fulfilling life.

The belief that thoughts significantly affect behavior is as old as recorded history. Epictetus, in the first century, wrote: "Men are disturbed not by things but by the view they take of them." George Kelly states: "Events do not tell us what to do, nor do they carry their mean-

---

[1]For further discussions of the role of cognition in counseling, see Beck (1976), Ellis (1973), and Vaimy (1975).

ings engraved on their backs for us to discover. For better or worse, we ourselves create the only meanings they will ever convey during our lifetime."[2]

Because cognition exerts a significant influence on behavior, it is helpful to understand some of its basic dynamics. Like all theorists, cognitive theorists differ from one another and sometimes differ from themselves at various points in their development. Hence, this chapter does not present *the* cognitive viewpoint but a reflection and elaboration on several cognitive theorists. It is meant to show a spirit and whet the appetite for further study in this area.

FAULTY ASSUMPTIONS

Cognitive assumptions (hypotheses, beliefs, constructs) are created by people to help them control and make sense out of their lives. In 1924, the philosopher Hans Vaihinger wrote: "It must be remembered that the object of the world of ideas as a whole is not the portrayal of reality—this would be an utterly impossible task—but rather to provide us with an instrument for finding our way about more easily in the world."[3] Without cognitive assumptions, each new person and event that enters our awareness would be an unknown quantity and create great anxiety. Cognitive assumptions can be true or false; that is, they may fit reality or distort it.

Development

Faulty assumptions seem to be mostly learned, although some theorists believe there is some biological predisposition underlying them. This learning can occur in any of five ways. It can occur by direct experience. A girl's first date turns out poorly. Rather than viewing the boy as insensitive, scared, or inept, she generalizes that *men* are insensitive and cruel.

It can occur by vicarious experience. A boy observes how his father is manipulated and emasculated by his mother and generalizes that women are treacherous. A third way is by direct instruction. A girl is told by her mother that sex is "not nice" and is given reading material by the mother that "proves" this assumption.

It can also occur by symbolic logic. A boy sees anger destroy his parents' marriage and concludes that anger is bad and to be avoided at all costs. Unfortunately, he fails to distinguish between destructive and

---

[2]Kelly (1970), p. 3.
[3]Vaihinger (1924), p. 15.

constructive anger. Because his major premise is false, his conclusion is erroneous.

Fifth, misconstruing cause and effect relationships can cause faulty assumptions. A child may interpret being held back in the second grade as meaning he is stupid when, in fact, he was young to be in that grade and his parents wanted him to socialize with children his own age.

These five methods of learning may be referred to as "natural learning." However, another kind of learning is motivated by the need to reduce anxiety. A high school student lacks the psychosocial competencies to relate well with his peers. He must either accept this fact or "learn" that his problems are not his fault. He withdraws from his classmates, and the classmates leave him alone. The fact becomes contorted into a faulty assumption: "My classmates don't like me. I know this because they ignore me." He decides that it's not his problem because he has never done a thing to harm his classmates. This young man has successfully created a learning to help balance his disturbed dynamics. In other words, he has taught himself that he is "OK" and his classmates are "not OK," thus reducing his anxiety about his real or perceived inadequacies.

Errors in thinking. The following are some typical errors in thinking that lead people to form faulty assumptions.

1. *Overgeneralizations.* Women are manipulative. Men are exploitive. Life is absurd. You can't trust people. People at work don't like me.

2. *All-or-nothing concepts.* Either I get accepted in graduate school or my life is over. Either you love me unconditionally or you don't really love me. Either you will help me or there is no more hope.

3. *Absolute statements.* I must obey my parents. I should keep promises. I must be nice. I should be right.

4. *Semantic inaccuracies.* I failed versus I made a mistake. This is the end versus this is a setback. I must get the promotion versus it would be better if I got the promotion. I can't do it versus I won't do it. I know so versus I think so. I hate him versus I dislike him. I love him versus I really like him. I feel devastated versus I feel bad. She is hostile toward me versus she is angry at me. I am panicked versus I am frightened.

5. *Time discernment.* What was valid in the past is not necessarily valid in the present. What is valid in the present will not necessarily be valid in the future. For example, a person may state "Counseling doesn't work for me because I tried it a few years ago with no results."

Or another person may say "They're not thinking of giving me a promotion now; so I don't think I'll ever get one."

When people fail to sharpen their discriminations and to avoid these errors in thinking, they will allow the heart of the faulty assumption to remain untouched and unaltered.

Characteristics

Time dimensions. Faulty assumptions may deal with the person's past, present, or future. One person may have a faulty assumption related to the past: "My parents didn't love me." This assumption allows her to avoid getting close to people because she reasons that if her parents didn't love her, who else could find her lovable?

Another person may have a faulty assumption related to the present: "I don't have any marketable skills." This causes him to seek jobs significantly below his capabilities and outside his areas of interest.

A third person's assumption is related to the future. He has the catastrophic expectation that if he gets married, it will never work out because his mother was divorced three times.

Each of these faulty assumptions can create significant, but unnecessary, anxiety and unhappiness in the lives of those who harbor them. It is also possible for the same person to have all three faulty assumptions, which would cause near paralysis.

Only current faulty assumptions are influential in behavior, even though they may have been learned in the past. Analogously, people smoke today not because they began smoking 20 years ago but because smoking reduces their anxiety today. People experience problems currently because they are presently harboring faulty assumptions. When a person says "I know my parents wished they'd never had me," it freezes her into a helpless position. What can she do about this now? But if a counselor examines her closely, an update of this faulty assumption will likely surface: "If people don't like me, I'm worthless." When she can get rid of this faulty assumption, whether or not her parents wanted her will be irrelevant for all practical purposes.

Patterns of faulty assumptions. People who enter counseling may have one very influential faulty assumption that significantly hinders life or a series of minor faulty assumptions that, taken together, cause severe limitations.

Faulty assumptions often fall into clusters in which there is a hierarchy. For example, a student may believe she must be a great success if she is to be a worthwhile person. From this general faulty assumption evolve the following specific faulty assumptions in descending order of influence:

1. The best way to be a great success is to be a surgeon.
2. The best way to get into medical school is to get accepted at a particular university.
3. The best way to get into a particular university is to spend every free second studying.
4. The best way to avoid temptations not to study is not to have friends, dates, or get involved in activities that will waste time.

It is not surprising that in October of her senior year of high school, this student is suffering severe anxiety attacks. She has gotten almost no ongoing psychosocial needs met since elementary school and is scheduled to take college board exams in two weeks. She thinks they will determine her fate for the rest of her life. Since it's too late for a counselor to work with faulty assumptions 3 and 4, counseling would begin by focusing on faulty assumption 2, at least to effect some short-term relief. However, to save this young woman needless anxiety over the rest of her life, the counselor will want to dismantle the highest faulty assumption. If someone had done this during her freshman year, high school would have been a growing and joyful experience.

When people don't understand the faulty assumptions that goad others into inappropriate and self-defeating behaviors, they are likely to be of little help. For example, the young woman's mother kept telling her not to worry, and her father told her not to study so hard. Her high school counselor told her that he was confident she would do well, and if she didn't, it wouldn't be the end of the world. But the young woman is asking herself "How can I *not* worry; my entire happiness hinges on this test. How can I *not* work so hard—that's like telling a man whose house is on fire to take his time getting water! And my counselor says 'It's not the end of the world' if I don't get into the right school. It's not the end of the world for *him*!"

Underlying deficiency.   Faulty assumptions can always be traced back to an actual or perceived deficiency within the individual. For this reason, faulty assumptions are not only important indicators of a person's problems but also indicators of what the person lacks to be reasonably well adjusted and happy. The following are some faulty assumptions and the personal lack that each could spotlight.

1. *Faulty assumption:* "I can't talk in front of a group of people."
   Translation: "I'm a phony and can fool people individually, but a whole group will see through me and see my shallowness."

2. *Faulty assumption:* "I must get accepted into college or I'll die."
   Translation: "I feel stupid, but if I get into college, I won't feel stupid anymore."
3. *Faulty assumption:* "I'm oversexed."
   Translation: "I am very uninteresting, but if I flaunt my body in front of people, they will find me interesting."
4. *Faulty assumption:* "It's not nice to hurt people."
   Translation: "I am very vulnerable, and if I hurt other people, they will likely hurt me back, and I'll be annihilated."

The translation of a faulty assumption is frequently another faulty assumption; for example, "If people hurt me, I will be annihilated." It is important to demythologize this belief, but it is even more important to see the weakness from which it stems.

Malignant and benign assumptions.   All faulty assumptions need not result in psychological disturbance. Malignant ones often do, but benign ones don't. A malignant faulty assumption might be "Everyone I care about must love me." A benign one might be "I married the best person I could have ever possibly married." Sometimes benign faulty assumptions can even be functional. For example, a man may falsely assume he is an important person. This generates "important behavior" of a nonintimidating, friendly type. He impresses people with his "importance" and many doors open that would not if he had seen himself realistically. Of course, ideally, a person should harbor *no* faulty assumptions, but, just as a surgeon doesn't repair every organ that could use a little strengthening, the counselor must be reasonably selective in the effort to save time and expense.

Resistance to change

The biggest problem confronting a counselor with regard to faulty assumptions is that they are often resistant to change. It is naive to think that merely using logic, argumentation, and teaching will lead a person to surrender a faulty assumption that has been harbored for many years. The word *harbored* connotes protection and sanctuary. When faulty assumptions are basic to the person's functioning, people may not only cling to them, but may fight to the death to preserve them. Undoubtedly, many people have become martyrs in the process of protecting their faulty assumptions. Some people even have allowed themselves to be killed ("I deserve to die") rather than to reassess or let go of a faulty assumption. Tampering with a person's faulty assumptions can be a hazardous pursuit, regardless of the apparent cooperation.

Faulty assumptions can be difficult to change for several reasons. One reason change is difficult is that faulty assumptions are often kept private. They may be hidden even from the person who owns them. This is the reason it takes time and patience to learn what specific faulty assumptions people have and then help the people themselves learn what they are.

The second reason is that some of the more critical faulty assumptions have been present since childhood. A child may have erroneously learned in early childhood that she is unlovable. She assumes this to be true and adapts and compensates for it, just as if she had been born with one leg shorter than the other. By adulthood, her equilibrium depends upon maintaining her handicap. To lose it suddenly would cause psychological disequilibrium.

Third, the faulty assumption may be an integral part of a person's personality structure, just like the seventh story of a 14-story building. For example, a man may be in a destructive marital relationship but believes divorce is out of the question because it would be completely unacceptable to his family and friends and devastating to his wife and children. Being unhappily married is at the core of his life. If he were suddenly to correct his faulty assumption, it would cause earthquakelike tremors throughout his being. He would have to make dramatic shifts in his self-concept, think about changing his occupation, or leave the area. He would have to face his problems squarely or discover a new excuse for his problems because the bad marriage would no longer fill that role. He would tarnish his image with his family and friends, which he feels would lead them to reject him. When all is considered, he would have to learn how to live alone and take care of himself. It is easier for this man to maintain and nourish his faulty assumption that he must remain married.

A fourth reason for the difficulty in changing faulty assumptions is that a person who spends a quarter of a century or more hoarding evidence to prove a faulty assumption is unlikely to surrender it easily. To do so would mean he or she would be faced with the insight that years of psychological conflict were unnecessary and avoidable. Some people would rather be "right" than happy.

Maintenance

Faulty assumptions remain entrenched and resist change because they are "proven" correct almost daily. People can reinforce their own faulty assumptions in various ways. For example, a woman has a faulty assumption that she is superior to other people. She "proves" this assumption to be "true" every day by using the following methods:

1. *Selective inattention.* When people surpass her in ability, she doesn't notice it or ascribes it to something else.
2. *Selective attention.* When she occasionally does something superior, she focuses on it for a long time so that it seems as if she is consistently doing superior things.
3. *Fictitious rewards.* She is appointed office manager because no one else wants the job but assumes it is because she is special.
4. *Solicited feedback.* She asks people for "honest feedback" in a way that manipulates them into reinforcing the faulty assumption.
5. *Intermittent reinforcement.* Just as her faulty assumption begins to falter for lack of evidence, someone tells her she is superior, which revives the faulty assumption.
6. *Cognitive dissonance.* When information that contradicts her faulty assumption is presented—for example, she doesn't receive a promotion—she reduces her anxiety by assuring herself that the company is saving her for something better.

Together with all the classic defense mechanisms, these methods protect this woman from having any reason to question the faulty assumption. People who have faulty assumptions that reflect a *negative* attitude toward themselves have an additional method to "prove" their faulty assumptions: self-fulfilling prophecy. For example, a boy whose faulty assumption is that he is uninteresting anticipates that his first date will be a disaster. The tension the faulty assumption creates makes him tense and almost mute on the date. In a very real way, he has prophesied what would happen on the date and made it come true. The unpleasant experience simply proves what he always has felt about himself.

When people have faulty assumptions of others, especially those with whom they work or relate closely, they can force the other to fit the faulty assumption, thus proving it beyond a reasonable doubt. A man assumes, on faulty evidence, that his wife is a flirt. At the next party they attend, he spends the major portion of the night discussing politics and sports with his male friends. After a lengthy time, he notices that his wife is dancing with another man. This is all the proof he needs. Sometimes in a marriage the wife will have the faulty assumption "He wishes he didn't marry me." Because she feels rejected or resentful, she begins to act negatively in the relationship. When her husband finally loses his temper and says something, the response easily evoked is "See, now it's finally coming out."

A person can also help maintain a faulty assumption by finding other people with essentially the same faulty assumption and entering into relationships with them. The result is that each reinforces the other's faulty assumption in a *folie à deux* fashion. A man and woman who both have the faulty assumption that you can't trust anybody may successfully exclude most other people from their lives; so the only trustworthy people left are each other. They may fall in love and get married. Each brings home horror stories that reinforce their faulty assumptions. After a while, they become so emotionally isolated, even from each other, that one or both develop psychological symptoms and can't figure out why. The mutual faulty assumption may be so subtle and ingrained in the relationship that a counselor may have great difficulty discovering it.

It is also easy for a person to set up situations in which faulty assumptions will be directly rewarded. For example, a woman believes that all men want is sex—they're not interested in her as a person. However, she frequents bars that are known to be body shops; she wears seductive clothes and perfume; and, sure enough, almost every man she meets propositions her. What more proof does she need?

Significant others can inadvertently and indirectly reinforce a person's faulty assumption out of good intentions. A teenager has the faulty assumption that she must get a certain boy to take her to the senior prom or the year will end with depression and despair. Rather than pointing out the faultiness of the girl's assumption, the mother gladly helps the girl plan the best way to fulfill her wish.

People can also directly reinforce another's faulty assumption. For example, a wife has the faulty assumption that her worth depends upon her performance. When she performs well around the house, everyone loves her and tells her what a great person she is. When she burns the dinner, loses the car keys, or forgets to change the linen, everyone tells her what a dolt she is. All these stratagems help maintain and nourish faulty assumptions.

Examples

Faulty assumptions fall into four areas: those regarding oneself ("I'm uninteresting"), others ("My wife doesn't respect me"), life ("Life is cruel"), and God ("God doesn't like me"). Since faulty assumptions regarding oneself are often at the core of those in the other three areas (although the other areas are also important), the following ten examples represent some of the more typical faulty assumptions people bring into counseling.

I must be loved by everyone I love.   These people don't want to be loved by everybody, just the people they are attracted to, respect deeply, or love. This could be a parent's assumption regarding his or her older children or older children regarding their parents. It could be people dating each other or people married to each other. When the love is not reciprocated or not returned in the specific ways these people desire, they are "crushed," "devastated," or "heartbroken" and behave accordingly. In fact, of course, they are none of these. They are hurt, perhaps deeply hurt, but this is a long way from devastation.

The catastrophic expectation that these disasters could occur virtually holds an ax over these people's psyches. If they make the wrong move, they are dead.

Like many faulty assumptions, this presents a no-win situation. If the person "gets" the other person to love him, he accomplished it through psychological prostitution, thus losing self-esteem. If he is unsuccessful and is rejected, he has lost the other person, which causes the "devastation." In either case, serious damage is done.

People learn this faulty assumption from their parents and society, or they learn it to protect themselves from knowing and taking responsibility for themselves. As long as they are distracted by whether or not others love them, they are rescued from getting to know themselves and taking personal responsibility for their lives and happiness. They have it set up so that if they are happy, it is because someone loves them; if they are sad, it's because they are not loved. Their well-being is contingent on others. Counselors can help these people understand the damage they are doing to themselves by attaching their psychological lifelines to others.

People must treat me fairly.   Some people work on the assumption "I treat people fairly; so others should treat me fairly." This assumption is usually a double myth. Although the person believes she treats others fairly, a close examination of her behavior generally reveals that she is capable of treating others unfairly, as is anyone else. In the second part of the assumption, she fails to discriminate between what people should do and what they actually do. People should treat each other fairly, but in reality they sometimes or often do not.

Deep down, these people realize they can't always be treated fairly because people are imperfect. But they pretend that they don't know this and can respond to injustice by saying "Well, if this is the way things are, I quit." This dynamic is similar to that used by a child when he sees his team is headed for certain defeat. He takes his ball and goes home, thus rescuing himself from defeat while enjoying a sense of righteousness.

People with this faulty assumption may have learned it from their parents and society and simply need some reeducation so that their naivete doesn't spoil their lives. More often, however, this faulty assumption was learned to hide the fear of failure. These people delude themselves into thinking they are willing to take the risks necessary to attain success and happiness. On a deeper level, however, they are frightened to take the required risks. Therefore, they use real or perceived injustices as excuses for withdrawing from difficult situations. Counselors can help these individuals see the dynamic supporting the faulty assumption and help them change it.

Happiness is THE goal in life. People who harbor this faulty assumption generally believe one or all of three things: (1) that happiness resides outside themselves (hence, they are always looking for it as one does for a lost child); (2) that once they find happiness, it will be theirs forever; and (3) that there is only one path to happiness.

Because this faulty assumption is constructed on one or more of these three myths, these individuals will experience far less happiness than they would had they possessed a valid assumption regarding happiness.

If the person directly learned this assumption from significant others, counselors can help by demythologizing its foundations. Happiness does not lie outside of people, but is a by-product of facing reality and handling it well. And there are as many paths to happiness as there are paths in reality. People who harbor a faulty assumption regarding happiness usually have one main happiness target: They must be a physician, attorney, or engineer. They must get married. They must have children. They must be financially and socially comfortable. They must be more successful than their friends. They must live in a certain area.

Sometimes this faulty assumption is not learned naturally but is learned to balance the person's dynamics. These people are, on a deep level, fearful of success and happiness (see Chapter 7). They realize that if they narrowly target happiness, they will never hit it. This creates a certain equilibrium for them. They are deluding themselves into thinking they can handle success and happiness but never have to put themselves to the test. Counselors can help these individuals understand the service that this faulty assumption provides and give them a better option.

I'm at the mercy of my environment. Some people have learned this assumption from their parents and society, but others have a vested interest in seeing people and situations as unchangeable. This view permits them to avoid stress and the risks that would be entailed in changing the situation. A wife sees her husband's reluctance to relate on a "meaningful level" as intransigent. As long as she does, she doesn't have to confront him seriously, which may evoke responses she doesn't want to hear.

People also may see events as causing automatic, prescribed reactions. A man may react to his wife's death with the belief that life is also over for him. He believes this because this is how he was taught to react, or he instigated his own learning as a defense against living out the rest of his life in a full, loving, and satisfying fashion. When people have directly learned this assumption, counselors can help reeducate them. When the learning has been motivated by the person's fears, counselors can help these people learn the role that the faulty assumption plays in their lives and help them understand that they can develop the psychosocial competencies to master their environments.

Other people know better than I what's good for me. Those who believe this fail to discriminate between being an expert on things and being an expert on a particular individual. Lawyers are experts on the law; physicians, on medicine; counselors, on mental health; and members of the clergy, on religion. But none of these experts is an expert on any particular person, with the possible exception of himself or herself.

People with this faulty assumption would not walk into a store and tell the salesperson "Pick out a suit that you think I will look good in and I'll take it." Yet, they go to experts for advice (even next-door neighbors can be experts), and implement the suggestions into the most important areas of their lives.

These people have learned from their parents and society that everyone has better ideas than they, or they have created this learning as a defense against taking responsibility for their own lives. If another's suggestion works well, they delight in this and learn to consult the same person when advice is needed in the future. If the advice doesn't work, they blame the giver and learn not to return to the same person for future help. In neither case have these people assumed responsibility for their behavior or learned a thing about themselves or the people or situation that was creating the concern.

Counselors must be especially careful not to get seduced into becoming another advice giver, which would further perpetuate the destructive dynamic. Individuals with this faulty assumption often preface their remarks to the counselor with "I know you don't give advice and I don't want your advice, but. . . ." They then proceed to ask for advice.

I must get what I want.   Some people work on the assumption "If I want it, it is critically important to my well-being that I get it; if I don't get it, I will be miserable." These people have been conditioned, or have conditioned themselves, to believe that they have voids that only specific people and things can fill—like a specific virus that can be cured only by a specific serum.

A professor wants a promotion. If she doesn't get it, she either disintegrates or girds herself for a battle to the death.

A young man wants a specific woman to love him. If she doesn't, he seriously contemplates killing himself.

It is interesting that as people approach middle life, they have forgotten most of the things they didn't get and "couldn't live without." People with this faulty assumption confuse wanting something, which means desiring it, and needing it, which implies it is necessary for survival and happiness.

People learn this assumption naturally or construct it for their own devices. They discover that when they communicate that they *must have* something, the chances of getting it significantly increase. For example, a college student learns that when he tells a professor he *must* get at least a "B" in a course or he won't graduate, or get into graduate school, or maintain his scholarship, he is likely to get a "B." If he doesn't get the grade, he can focus all his energy and wrath on the professor instead of himself. This is an example of a faulty assumption that creates, at least on a superficial level, a "no-lose" situation.

Counselors can help these individuals recognize the difference between needing and wanting something. They can help them understand that while it would be nice to get what they want, it is not a disaster if they don't. Counselors can also point out that to the degree people *must* have something outside themselves—a promotion, for example— they lack something within themselves—a sense of personal worth, for example. Since inner gaps cannot be adequately filled by external factors, the counselor can help these individuals develop the inner resources that will diminish the overbearing strength of their needs for psychological and material acquisitions.

I am controlled by my past.   Some people believe their lives could be significantly better if they had a different history. They frequently assure themselves and others: "If it weren't for the fact that

my father was an alcoholic, I could relate to men better."

my mother was divorced three times, I wouldn't be fearful of marriage."

I was put back in the fourth grade, I would have more confidence in my intelligence."

I lost a leg in the war, I would be doing great things now."

People with this faulty assumption fail to understand that their problem is not the past, but their *attitude* toward the past. Some people have had objectively terrible pasts and become self-actualized; others with objectively good backgrounds have become psychologically disturbed people.

Counselors can help these individuals understand that a person's past is never a sufficient cause for happiness or sadness. Many people harbor this faulty assumption as an integral part of their dynamics. As long as they use their past as an excuse to live ineffectively, they can avoid current responsibility for their problematic behavior. Their attitude is that they have been dealt a "bad hand" in life and are simply playing it out and trying to cut their losses. Counselors can help these individuals recognize the destructiveness of their assumptions and invite them to develop new competencies to handle the present.

I have to be special.   Although they would deny it, most people with this faulty assumption feel that being "special" means being superior to others. People with this need will often strive to be special at any cost to themselves or family. If they can't be special in a positive direction, they will be special in a negative one. As one person said, "Either I'm going to be the best person in the world or the worst. In either case, I'll be different from everyone else."

Many people learn this faulty assumption because it has strong environmental supports. Others cultivate this learning to compensate for feeling very "unspecial." If they succeed in feeling special, they do not have to address their deep inadequacies or at least feelings of inadequacy. If they are unsuccessful, they can give up ("If nobody is going to appreciate my specialness, to hell with them"). They assume the life position of the unwelcome hero, retire from life, and live off the meager psychological pension that their faulty assumption provides for them.

Counselors can reeducate people with this assumption to understand that the opposite of "special" is not being "mediocre" or "ordinary," but simply *being*. Being means giving and getting the most out of each day without being distracted by society's grading system.

There is a "worst thing" that can happen to me.   Some "worst things" are to be wrong, to fail, to appear foolish, to be rejected, to be deeply hurt, and to be alone. People who harbor this faulty assumption live their lives giving wide berth to even the slightest possibility of any of these events occurring. This is analogous to a boat captain steering a course miles distant from beautiful islands because of the possibility of becoming grounded on one. For example, people may avoid rejection by not allowing themselves to get emotionally close to anyone or by making a person so reliant on them that they cannot possibly be rejected.

Individuals with this faulty assumption trade happiness for safety. They are seldom happy, because the closer they get to a good relationship or situation, the more their worst-thing anxiety increases. They avoid worst things by not getting too close to the possibility that they could occur. This prevents catastrophe on the one hand and the realization that they lack, or feel they lack, the psychosocial competencies to get what they want on the other. They remain frozen at a point of safety between discovering their inadequacies and experiencing catastrophe.

Counselors can help these people learn that no external event can ever be a worst thing. Not only have people survived, but many have grown through all the worst things. Worst things can only develop internally when people believe that a person or situation can devastate them.

It's too late for me to change.   Superficially, the feeling that this faulty assumption generates is despair. People who harbor this faulty assumption feel that they have grown too old to make any substantial changes in their lives. "Too old" may be any age from 20 to 70. On a deeper level, however, these people often feel a sense of relief. They are like the soldier who surrenders and feels resentment and despair. However, on a more honest and deep level, he is relieved. He realizes he can live out the duration of the war within the safe confines of a prison camp.

Like all faulty assumptions, one of the largest problems is that a person can make the assumption true by firmly believing that it is. These people react to efforts to help them change with amusement, then disbelief, and finally resentment.

There is sufficient evidence to indicate that middle-aged and older people can make substantial changes in their lives, but these data are seldom persuasive to these people. The rejoinder is often "Well, that's nice for them, but they aren't me."

This faulty assumption can be naturally learned from society. Most often, however, it is a self-taught assumption carefully constructed to permit the person to surrender to people, circumstances, and life in general before he or she gets killed.

Counselors can help these individuals understand that they have a choice between surrender and a remobilization of psychosocial forces that will enable them to return to the battle and negotiate a better peace.

CONSIDERATIONS FOR COUNSELORS

The following points may be helpful for a counselor to keep in mind when dealing with faulty assumptions.

Patience

It often takes time for faulty assumptions to surface. A person will not walk into the counseling room and say "Here are four faulty assumptions I'm trying to change." As people feel relaxed in the counseling relationship, they will gradually allow the counselor to see their faulty assumptions. Although some cognitive theorists downplay the importance of warmth and empathy in counseling, it seems that these qualities can facilitate the emergence of faulty assumptions. Just as a surgeon prepares a patient before removing an appendix, a counselor can prepare the person in counseling through the medium of a sound relationship before attempting to extract faulty assumptions.

It is generally unhelpful for a counselor to grab for faulty assumptions as a child would grab for fish in a pond, because the result is likely to be the same. The more the counselor flays about in search of faulty assumptions, the more they will disappear, leaving decoys or nothing in their place.

Unhelpful reactions

Counselors can be careful not to *reinforce* faulty assumptions. A man matter-of-factly tells the counselor that his wife has made it clear she is going to leave him. She left a note and has gone to live with her mother. This launches the person and counselor into a long discussion on how to react to the situation, a discussion punctuated with signs of genuine warmth and empathy from the counselor. The problem is that the man's wife has *not* made it perfectly clear that she plans to leave him. The man's wishful thinking or catastrophic expectation was produced by an angry exchange with his wife that ended with her visiting her mother for the weekend to cool off.

Counselors can be careful not to *induce* faulty assumptions. A counselor may view the person's request to taper off in counseling as a sign of resistance. The suggestible person accepts the counselor's faulty assumption, and a half-dozen sessions are spent attempting to uncover the source of the assumed resistance. In fact, the person was making good progress and had made a reasonable request.

Counselors can inadvertently *reward* false assumptions by encouraging ventilation of the accompanying emotions. Sometimes the catharsis that accompanies the affective results of a faulty assumption actually reinforces it. In a real sense, the counselor who allows deep catharsis under these circumstances is saying "I agree with you. You have good reason to be upset." In fact, the person does not.

Emotions

Counselors can understand that even though they are dealing primarily with problems in cognition, emotions are equally important. For example, emotional intensity can often provide a clue that the counselor is getting close to a faulty assumption. It is also important for counselors to understand that emotions flowing from a faulty assumption are no less powerful and potentially damaging than those based on a valid one. Therefore, counselors must also help people deal with emotions.

Unconscious assumptions

The most damaging faulty assumptions are often the less conscious ones. Since the person is highly confident that the assumption is true, this confidence shows in his or her behavior and can fool the counselor. For example, a woman may unconsciously be dissatisfied with her marriage, but tells the counselor "Thank God for my marriage. That's the only thing keeping me sane." Because the person relates this with genuine confidence and honesty and the counselor wants to believe the marriage is good, he gladly joins her in the faulty assumption. As a result, the woman's basic reason for seeking counseling is left unattended.

The process of surrendering a faulty assumption is often unpleasant for the person in counseling. The increased distress the person experiences as the faulty assumption is challenged will often be interpreted by the person as "getting worse." For example, the woman who eventually uncovers her dissatisfaction with her marriage may lapse into a state of depression.

Validity

Counselors can realize that not *all* assumptions are faulty. Counselors who tend to define their main role as detectives hired to find faulty assumptions see them everywhere. A man may have the assumption

"I'm not very intelligent" and may have mapped out his life to accommodate it. His assumption may be valid and tampering with it and his life plans may be a destructive pursuit. It is important that a counselor have a preponderance of evidence that an assumption is false before assuming that it is. Otherwise, the *counselor's* faulty assumption is trying to change the person's valid one.

Shared faulty assumptions

Counselors and people in counseling can share the same faulty assumption. For example, the counselor and the person may have had negative experiences with marriage. When the counselor hears the person say "I'll never try marriage again—what a neurotic institution it is!" the counselor "empathizes completely." The counselor misses the point that institutions are only as healthy as the people that comprise them.

Hiding assumptions

The best way to protect a faulty assumption from the scrutiny of a counselor is never to mention it. However, the person may be manifesting the pernicious effects of the faulty assumption. Counselors should be alert to this possibility, consider separately each clue conveyed by the person, and try to look for the "wires" that connect it to the originating faulty assumption.

Dispelling assumptions

Counselors cannot reason, argue, or talk a person out of faulty assumptions. They must present evidence, not once, but over and over again until it becomes irrefutable. Counselors themselves can be a source of evidence when they don't live up to the faulty assumptions of the person in counseling; for example, when they are not shocked by "shocking" revelations and when they do not reject the person when he or she becomes angry with them.

Insight, with regard to faulty assumptions, means that the counselor has helped the person in counseling recognize not only the faulty assumption, but how he or she suffers from it and causes others to suffer from it. Hence, insight is not only intellectual ("Now I understand") but emotional ("Now I *feel* what I've been doing"). Insight is rarely a specific event. It is typically a gradual, graduated, and undramatic process. Also, the fact that a person gained insight during one session does not mean he or she will remember it at the next one. Gaining an insight and keeping it are two parts of an ongoing process often separated by many sessions.

Entangling the counselor

Counselors can become an integral part of the person's faulty assumptions in one of two ways. First, the counselor can become a target for the faulty assumptions of the person in counseling. A person may harbor the assumption "People don't like me unless they can use me to get something they want." It is clear that the counselor likes the person; so the obvious question is "What does the counselor think I can do for him?" The counselor will sense a wariness in the relationship that conveys "What do *you* get out of this?" but may not realize its source.

Second, people in counseling can project their faulty assumptions onto the counselor. A woman may have the faulty assumption "I'm not very smart" and be convinced that the counselor shares it. The woman's reaction is either relief brought on by the idea that the counselor won't challenge her assumption or anger—"It's all right for me to think I'm stupid, but I don't want my own counselor to think I'm stupid."

Proving faulty assumptions

People in counseling can manipulate counselors into "proving" that a faulty assumption is valid. One week a person tells the counselor "I'm not as intelligent as you think. You expect too much of me." The counselor replies that she is certainly as intelligent as the counselor thinks. At the next session, the woman announces she is quitting counseling because she's "much better." In essence the counselor responds "How can you be so stupid as to think that? We haven't begun yet." The counselor has just proven to the woman that her faulty assumption was correct—namely, that she is not very smart.

One of the main problems with faulty assumptions is that a person can make them "come true." For example, people may believe that if their spouse leaves them, it will be the end of the world. The spouse does leave and the person does make it the end of the world (by committing suicide) or the end of the spouse's world (by committing homicide). Counselors must be careful not to inadvertently dare a person to make a faulty assumption come true. The counselor's role is to teach the person that no event inevitably causes psychological disaster and that the person does have constructive alternatives for responding to even the most traumatic situations.

New realities

Changing from a faulty to a valid assumption does not necessarily and automatically bring with it the psychosocial competencies to deal with the new reality. It is important, therefore, that the counselor who wishes to challenge faulty assumptions be willing to help the person go through the debriefing process and begin the rebuilding process. To assume that simply puncturing faulty assumptions is the sole purpose of counseling is to create a potentially dangerous situation.

SUMMARY

Understanding the causes, nature, dynamics, and effects of faulty assumptions is a good place for a counselor to begin, but it is a poor place for a counselor to finish. Most often, diagnosing a faulty assumption is only the beginning of a lengthy process that often includes several other stages.

THOUGHT QUESTIONS

1. One faulty assumption many counselors harbor is that if people in counseling cooperate, counseling will be a successful enterprise. What are at least two damaging side effects of this assumption?
2. Many people enter counseling with the faulty assumption "Other people know better than I what's good for me." How can even experienced counselors get led into reinforcing this assumption, and what steps could be taken to prevent this from happening?
3. What is one faulty assumption you may have about people who need and seek counseling? How could it interfere with counseling?
4. What cautions can counselors keep in mind when they allow and encourage people to release their emotions?
5. What do you think are two common faulty assumptions people have regarding counseling? How would you help them articulate them? How would you deal with them?

CHAPTER 7

Emotions in
Counseling

Whether emotional reactions stem from an accurate or inaccurate interpretation of reality, they must be understood and dealt with adaptively if personality growth is to occur in counseling. The interaction between cognitions, emotions, and actions reflects a system of reciprocal causality. As Albert Ellis writes: "Just as cognitions importantly contribute to emotions and actions, emotions also significantly contribute to or 'cause' cognitions and actions, and actions contribute to or 'cause' cognitions and emotions. When people change one of these three modalities of behaving they concomitantly tend to change the other two."[1]

Although there are many definitions of emotion, the one given by Arnold is a clear and useful one; she defines emotion as "the felt tendency toward anything intuitively appraised as good (beneficial), or away from anything intuitively appraised as bad (harmful). This attraction or aversion is accompanied by a pattern of physiological changes organized toward approach or withdrawal. The patterns differ for different emotions."[2]

The word *emotion* is a derivative of the Latin word *emovere*, which means to move out. The purpose of any emotion is to move a person toward safety and need fulfillment and away from harm and need deprivation. It has been said that human beings wither and die without love.

[1]Corsini & contributors (1979), p. 194.
[2]Arnold (1960), p. 182.

Yet all the basic emotions are necessary for survival because each has a specific contribution to make to the stability of a person's overall functioning. For example, people need love, but they also need hurt, which teaches which situations are damaging; fear, which anticipates threat and warns of impending danger; anger, which removes obstacles to need fulfillment; and guilt, which helps them avoid hurting themselves and others.

When emotions function properly—that is, according to their purposes—they energize and give direction. For example, if a man is angry at his wife, his anger may move him (energize) toward his wife (direction) in order to resolve the problem.

There are several places, however, where the process can break down. A person can repress the emotion so it neither energizes nor gives direction. For example, a man may repress his anger at his wife. In this case, the anger festers and spills over into symptomatic behavior, such as depression or passive-aggressive behavior toward his wife. A person may lack adequate control over an emotion; so it permeates him and/or causes him to explode. The man who is angry at his wife may physically assault her. A person may be energized by the emotion but have no direction. For example, a man may feel intense anger, but can find no reason or target for it. A person may be energized by the emotion, but it may have a false direction. The man who is angry at his wife may displace it on his children or himself. Most people in counseling tend to fall into one or more of these four situations.

Because emotions energize and give direction, it is important to label them correctly, just as medicines must be labeled correctly. Unfortunately, both counselors and people in counseling tend to use generic words to describe emotions. Common generic words used to describe problematic emotions are feeling anxious, nervous, tense, and stressful. Although the use of generic terms may be appropriate in research and theory, they are generally unhelpful in counseling. These terms are so nonspecific that they have little practical value. It is important that counselors help people get in touch with the specific emotion, or combination of emotions, that is causing them distress. This process greatly facilitates resolving the problem. Specifying emotions is important because it makes the cause of the emotion and the direction much clearer.

Specifying emotions is a four-step process. The person must first discover what specific emotion is causing the generic feelings. For example, a counselor can help a woman discover that she may be anxious because she is frightened or tense because she is angry or that a stressful situation may really be a hurtful situation. Then the counselor can help her arrive at directionality—that is, *"Who* are you angry at?" or *"Who* is hurting you?" Next, the counselor can help the woman discover the reason for the specific emotion: *"What* is causing you to feel guilty?" or *"What* is causing you to be fearful?" The final step entails asking *"How* have you typically handled this emotion in the past and with what results?" and *"What* can you do to resolve this feeling constructively?"

Although there are many emotions, most problematic emotions stem from four basic ones. The four emotions that seem most frequently to motivate people to seek counseling are hurt, fear, anger, and guilt. It is unlikely that a counselor sees many people whose emotional problems and symptoms do not stem from one of these emotions or a combination, variation, or disguise of them. Emotions such as sadness, jealousy, shame, shyness, depression, grief, loneliness, discouragement, as well as problems with sex and love, often can be traced to hurt, fear, anger, and guilt or a combination of them.

These four basic emotions are not problematic in themselves; they are not "negative emotions." Emotions are two-edged swords that, when used according to their purposes, cut in the direction of growth and happiness but when used contrary to their purposes, cause conflict and damage.

The following discussion of four emotions and their relationship to counseling does not reflect the complexity of emotions and the great problems in researching them. As Strongman writes, "Specific human emotions are extraordinarily complex; the names used to describe them cover a multitude of behaviors and experiences. This complexity makes them virtually impossible to study with precision and agreement between researchers."[3] However, emotions play an important role in counseling and need to be discussed, even though the discussion must necessarily be oversimplified.[4] The more counselors understand the dynamics underlying each of these emotions, both in the person in counseling and in themselves, the more they can help people understand and use emotions in a growth-producing way. This chapter deals with hurt, fear, anger, and guilt.

---

[3]Strongman (1974), p. 148.
[4]For a more thorough discussion of the theoretical aspects of emotions, see Arnold (1960, 1970); Candland, Fell, Keen, Leshner, Tarpy, & Plutchik (1977); Izard (1977); Plutchik (1962).

HURT

Hurt is the feeling of pain people experience when they are psychologically injured. This emotion is grossly underestimated in the field of mental health. While anger and sex receive the most attention, hurt may cause at least as many conflicts and, in fact, is at the heart of many problems with anger and sex.

Causes

A person can be injured psychologically and suffer pain in three ways. The first is through the normal course of everyday interaction. Someone says or does or fails to do or say something that injures the person. For example, a man may spend a good deal of time and talent on a successful project, but his boss gets the accolades. The man is hurt as part of participating in life.

A second cause of hurt is naivete. A person who harbors an unrealistic expectation may feel hurt when it is not met. For example, a college student tells her roommate of two weeks that she is fearful of boys. She is terribly hurt when she discovers that her roommate shared this information with six other students at supper that evening. This type of hurt is preventable.

Third, people can want to be hurt. One dynamic may be that the individual can then feel justified in behaving in some destructive way. For example, a man desires to have extramarital sex but his conscience and self-concept won't permit him to experience it. So, on less than a conscious level, he sets up a situation whereby his wife will hurt him. When this occurs, he assures himself that he now has a justifiable reason to seek extramarital sex ("If that's all she thinks of me, I'll find someone who really cares about me").

A second dynamic is that a person may create situations in which he or she will be hurt in order to atone for unconscious guilt. A man may have treated his deceased father poorly and never dealt with the resultant guilt. Consequently, he unconsciously allows himself to be hurt as a way of assuaging his guilt feelings.

A third dynamic can be seen in people who allow themselves to be hurt in order to manipulate others. For example, a woman allows her husband to abuse her psychologically or physically so that she can then manipulate him by using his guilt as a lever.

Fourth, people can be hurt by standing in the path of other people's growth. For example, an overprotective mother exhorts her adult son to remain at home rather than pursue a career opportunity in another city. Despite her pleadings, he decides to move out on his own. Consequently, she feels terribly hurt.

Fifth, a person can be hurt by misinterpreting another's behavior. A woman may be told by her roommate that she plans to move out soon. She interprets this as meaning her roommate no longer likes her. In fact, the roommate likes her a great deal and fears becoming too dependent on her.

There are three counseling implications of these causes of hurt. First, the counselor's initial response to a person's feelings of hurt can be to help the person drain the wound as completely as possible. The more the person can see the entire wound, feel it, and share it, the more healing can take place. The deeper the wound, the more time and counseling sessions it will take to deal with it.

Second, a counselor can help people perceive hurt more realistically. Living life fully makes people vulnerable to everyday scratches and bruises. Also, the closer people become in a relationship, the greater the chances of getting hurt. People can be helped to understand that these types of hurt are badges of growth, so they will no longer need to ask "What's *wrong* with *me* that I get hurt like this?" A counselor can also help people realize some hurts can be brushed off. When a hurt stuns and knocks people down, they can learn to perceive it in a way that allows them to recuperate and return to the business and joy of living. Even the deepest psychological hurt never destroyed anyone who did not wish to be destroyed.

Third, counselors can help people realize that they may have been hurt in retaliation for a hurt they perpetrated. For example, a woman embarrasses her boss in front of several customers. Later in the day, she is very hurt when her boss criticizes her in front of her co-workers. With the counselor's help, she comes to see the relationship between the two events which at first had eluded her.

A fourth implication is that both the person and counselor can get hurt in counseling because an open and honest relationship will inevitably cause hurt. Honesty will cause hurt and so will misperceptions, misunderstandings, mistakes, and conflicting needs, motives, and values. The best way for a person in counseling and a counselor not to hurt each other is to relate superficially. But part of growth in counseling entails being hurt and learning how to react well to it in order to transfer this learning to comparable situations outside counseling.

Constructive reactions

When people react to hurt in a growth-producing way, they admit the hurt and handle it constructively. Handling hurt well—that is, in a way conducive to healing and growth—entails four steps. The first is to admit the hurt. The second is to examine what the hurt means. When people are hurt, they can ask some important questions: Am I being too sensitive? Did I have an unrealistic expectation? What does the hurt mean in the context of our relationship? Did I misperceive the hurt? Did I deserve to get hurt? Is there a vulnerability within me that needs strengthening?

The third step, when it is appropriate, is to check out the possible meaning of the hurt with the person causing it. This dialogue may help heal the hurt so that the relationship can continue, perhaps stronger than ever. Or the dialogue will deepen the hurt, thus focusing the nature of the problem more clearly. When dialogue is not possible, people remain stuck with the hurt but can realize they have control over how much they allow it to interfere with their lives. The final step is to learn a lesson from the hurt that will help prevent a similar situation in the future.

A counselor can teach these steps directly and indirectly. Directly, a counselor can lead the person through each of these steps and explain the reason for them and their importance. If a person is not used to reacting to hurt well, this process may have to be taught dozens of times, over dozens of hurts. The deeper the hurt, the more difficult it will be to help the person focus on the process. The counselor need not be distracted by the amount of hurt any more than a surgeon is distracted by the amount of blood. The procedures remain the same for small wounds or massive trauma.

Counselors can also teach these steps indirectly and, perhaps, more effectively by the way they react to being hurt by the person in counseling. The counselor can communicate some variation of "Ouch! That hurt" and deal with it constructively.

Destructive reactions

People react destructively to hurt in seven ways.

Denying the hurt.   People deny feeling hurt because they view it as an admission of weakness. They state: "Don't be silly. I'm stronger than to be hurt by something like that." Others deny hurt because they view its admission as a criticism of the person who hurt them. They feel: "How can I be hurt when she did it out of love?" Still others deny hurt because they don't want to give the offender the satisfaction of knowing that he "got to them." A fourth way to deny hurt is to intellectualize: "I'm so used to being hurt that I'm beyond the point of hurting." Counselors can help these individuals understand that when hurt is denied, it simply incubates. This causes a gnawing, unconscious pain that affects their happiness and that of those around them.

Hurting back. Some people react to hurt by hurting back. They may do so reflexively, without thinking, or they may save the hurt and cash it in at a more opportune moment. Sometimes people hurt back by hurting someone other than the offender. A man may have been hurt by his wife but hurt the children as a way of getting back at her.

Counselors can help people realize that when they hurt another in retaliation, the hurt in the relationship becomes compounded. Moreover, retaliatory hurt often causes guilt, which adds to the stress of the situation. The original hurt becomes only one-third of the overall dynamics.

Disguising hurt. Some people disguise their hurt by covering it over with another emotion that is easier to admit and communicate. A person may claim "I'm not hurt; I'm just angry," "I'm not hurt; I'm just disappointed," or "I'm not hurt; I'm just depressed." The problem with disguising hurt is the same as the difficulty that develops when people try to hide a fire. Sooner or later the hurt will burn through the defense and permeate the person.

Counselors can help people recognize that hurt is often a significant part of their fear, anger, and depression and that the sooner they can get in touch with hurt, the sooner the secondary emotion will disappear.

Wallowing in hurt. A person may admit hurt, savor it, and splatter it onto others. The underlying dynamics of wallowing in hurt are that the person needs to suffer in order to atone for unresolved guilt, to get attention, and to manipulate others by causing them to feel sympathetic and guilty.

Counselors will find these people especially challenging because they have a vested interest in hanging onto their hurts. The counselor's efforts to help them will be met with significant resistance. However, it is incumbent on the counselor to demonstrate to this person how self-destructive the behavior is and to show the person the secondary gains involved in the hurt. As long as people nourish their hurt and lick their wounds, they will not be happy and others will not wish to relate with them.

Anesthetizing hurt. Instead of dealing directly with hurt, some people spray the wound with psychological analgesics: food, drink, sex, sleep, drugs, and work. Counselors can help people understand that the problem with psychological painkillers is that they compound the original problem. While they deaden the conscious hurt, the deeper hurt remains to cause symptomatic behavior. Moreover, these psychological analgesics often cause guilt, which significantly increases the original anxiety the hurt caused.

Hiding from futu.. hurt. Having been hurt, these people, consciously or unconsciously, decide never to place themselves in a similarly vulnerable position. This is the "burned child" reaction to hurt; that is, the child who is burned on a stove may decide never to go near a stove again. This child was not taught how to remain around stoves without getting burned.

The counselor can demonstrate to these people that they are paying an enormous price for safety. People then can be helped to reenter situations of risk, to prevent hurt, and to handle hurt constructively when it does occur.

Hurting oneself. Paradoxically, when some people are hurt, they respond by hurting themselves further. For example, a child may be scolded at supper and refuse to eat his dessert even though he wants it. An adolescent is hurt by her parents and reacts by not studying for a test, which she fails. A man is hurt by his wife and refuses to have sex that evening, even though he looked forward to it all day.

The dynamics of self-hurting behavior are twofold. The first dynamic is to make the offending party feel guilty. The message is "Look what you've done to me. You've hurt me so much I don't even care about myself anymore." The second dynamic is to punish oneself for being vulnerable. This dynamic is generally seen in people who define themselves as "tough" and/or "perfect" and who feel ashamed that they have succumbed to hurt. They feel "If I'm so stupid as to be hurt by this person, I *deserve* to suffer even more."

Counselors can help these individuals recognize that self-hurt is a very destructive dynamic that breeds resentment, weakens the person, and discourages others from getting close.

Counselors can also realize that they are vulnerable to hurt. It is helpful for them to recognize the strategies they knowingly and unknowingly use to avoid hurt. While these stratagems may protect the counselor, they may also create unhelpful buffers in the counseling relationship.

FEAR

Fear stems from anticipation of a specific physical or psychological threat. Since psychological threat comprises the vast majority of the fears of people in counseling, this dimension of fear will be discussed.

Fear, like hurt, is a word few people entering counseling use because people, especially adults, aren't supposed to have fears. Consequently, people entering counseling use words that reflect fear but are distant enough to be more acceptable, such as tense, worried, anxious, upset, confused, indecisive, insecure, miserable, nervous, restless, and bored.

When a counselor can help the person in counseling translate these inadequate synonyms into the word *fear,* the causes of and the paths to resolution of the fears will become clearer.

Fear's favorite disguise is anger. Fear evokes a fight or flight response. When people respond with fight, they reflexively feel anger and mistake the anger for the basic feeling when, in fact, it is simply coating fear. It is helpful for counselors to realize that most angry people are really frightened people and most angry responses aimed at counselors are actually fear responses. Recognizing this, counselors can cut through the decoy of anger and introduce people to their fears.

Because the psyche has a wide flank to defend, human beings are open to many threats and, consequently, experience many fears. The following four fears are common ones that people bring to counseling. Each has a protective quality that can help people avoid harm. However, when fears are too numerous or intense, they either paralyze people into inactivity or energize them to attack needlessly.

Fear of intimacy

People with an inordinate fear of intimacy react to it in one of three ways.

1. They construct a psychological moat, creating a safe distance between themselves and others. The moat may be obvious, so that others perceive the person as "emotionally distant," or it may be covered by a false bridge of extroversion and friendliness.
2. They manufacture pseudoconflicts to avoid intimacy. As they grow closer to other people, they consciously or unconsciously pick a fight or concoct a problem that creates distance and brings welcome relief.
3. They develop a counterphobic reaction. These people *push* for intimacy in a relationship in a way that is "too much, too soon." This approach invariably scares off the very people with whom the individual wishes to become intimate.

There are four counseling implications of the fear of intimacy. The first is that counselors can expect these people to handle the fear of intimacy in the counseling relationship in the same ways they do outside of counseling. If the counselor recognizes this and points it out in helpful ways, it can provide an important, on-the-spot learning experience.

Second, counselors can help people develop the psychological competencies needed to approach intimacy with confidence. For many people "intimate" is simply a synonym for "trapped" or "foolishly vulnerable." Counselors can help these people learn to approach intimacy with prudence and assertiveness, which allows them to enjoy its beauty while significantly diminishing the risks.

Third, if the person in counseling is eventually able to enter into an emotionally intimate relationship with the counselor, it is important for it to end as a positive experience. If the person terminates feeling "burned" (that is, used or fooled), then counseling succeeded only in substantially reinforcing the individual's original fear of intimacy.

Finally, counselors will spend a good deal of time dealing with fears. One of the basic elements of counseling is that the counselor and the person in counseling become emotionally intimate. Frequently, fear of intimacy causes an "intimacy dance" in which the counselor takes a step toward the person and the person takes a step back or to the side. Then, as the person takes a step toward the counselor, the counselor steps sideways or backward. This is natural and to be expected. It is important for both persons, however, to recognize the dance steps.

Fear of rejection

People with an inordinate fear of rejection can react to it by emotionally, if not socially, withdrawing from situations in which rejection is possible. These people feign disinterest in whether they are accepted by others in order to soften the blow if rejection occurs. Typically, they may relate with those who are not likely to reject them—for example, with children and other psychologically needy people or with animals or things, such as work, hobbies, or cars.

They may react by being anonymous. These people do not allow themselves to be known beyond the outer, most superficial layer of their personalities. This is a protection against being known, which to them means possible or likely rejection.

Third, people who fear rejection may try to preclude the possibility of being rejected. This is attempted in one or all of three ways. First, these people may attempt to buy guarantees of nonrejection by being nice, ingratiating, and overly helpful. Second, these people may become weak and helpless, which plays on the sympathy of others. Third, they may anticipate rejection and reject first in order to save themselves some anguish.

Four implications for counseling can be discussed with regard to the fear of rejection. The first is that most, if not all, people who fear rejection reject themselves. They fear others will see the parts they see as objectionable, evoking further rejection. Counselors can help people discover that many of their perceived negative traits are not really negative, but simply human or, in some cases, positive. This will help people become more self-accepting and lessen their inordinate fear of rejection.

Second, many people who fear rejection have acceptance as their highest priority. Counselors can help these individuals rank their priorities. They can be encouraged to place the highest priority on being healthily transparent and honest and not on striving to gain the acceptance of others. This approach places the focus on the person and who he or she wants to become and not on others and who they want him or her to be.

Third, it is helpful for counselors to realize that some people who inordinately fear rejection *want* to be rejected. For them, being rejected is painful, but less so than being accepted and becoming symbiotically dependent. As one person said, "I'd rather feel rejected and free than accepted and trapped." Obviously, being accepted is not really synonymous with being trapped, but it is to people with strong dependency needs.

Finally, both the counselor and the person in counseling will have a fear of rejection. The person's fear often will create marked ambivalence toward the counselor. On the one hand, the person wants to open up; on the other hand, he or she has been rejected in the past for opening up far less with more trusted people. Counselors have both personal and professional needs to be accepted by the person in counseling. Without this acceptance, the counselor is neutralized. Hence, the counselor has to walk a narrow line between being honest with the person and not rejecting him or her.

Fear of failure

People can react to the fear of failure by refusing to take risks. These individuals operate on the principle "If you don't try something, you can't fail." Or they may belittle success. This strategy entails diminishing everything so that nothing has much importance. Getting into college or graduate school is "not important." A particular boyfriend or girlfriend is "no big thing." Examinations and interviews are "stupid." They may react by overpreparing for endeavors. These people overprepare for projects and social engagements in an effort to prevent failure.

This time and effort spent on overpreparation simply increases anxiety and does not guarantee that failure will be prevented.

There are four counseling implications for the fear of failure. First, people who fear failure will perceive counseling as an endeavor in which they will succeed or fail; consequently, they will react to the fear of failing in counseling as they would to other similar situations. The counselor can be aware of the presence and meaning of these behaviors and reflect them back to help these people see the destructiveness of their responses.

Second, most people with an inordinate fear of failure underestimate their strengths and overplay their weaknesses. Counselors can help these people develop a realistic picture of strengths and weaknesses and help them begin making decisions that maximize the former and avoid the latter.

A third implication is that most people with an inordinate fear of failure operate on an all-or-nothing principle: they want *big* success or *no* success. These people then convince themselves that they are not in a position to be immensely successful; so they don't have to try anything. Counselors can help these people recognize the self-protective nature of this principle and learn that the road to success is paved with dozens of small, sometimes imperceptible triumphs.

Fourth, both the counselor and the person in counseling want to be successful. Hopefully, both fear failure. Their fears of failing will cause each to move too quickly at times, in an effort to bring success closer, and each will move too hesitantly at times, in attempts to avoid failure. This situation becomes a problem only when the fear of failure is equally strong in both partners, so that fear is controlling the relationship.

Fear of happiness

As paradoxical as it sounds, some people experience a deep fear of being happy. Of the fears already mentioned, this one is perhaps the least conscious. Generally, the fear of happiness is seen in such claims as "I *do* want to be happy, *but* . . . ." What follows the *but* is a disclaimer.

Three types of people fear happiness. The first type wants happiness but is afraid to take the steps necessary to become happy. These people don't want to change problematic parts of their personalities or terminate their conflictual relationships because it would cause an acute stress while being unhappy produces only a dull ache.

The second kind of person feels happiness is not deserved. Because of unatoned guilt, these people can avoid happiness despite their achievements in life.

A third type of person does not want to be happy and views the suggested steps toward happiness with only token interest. Happiness would raise many problems for these people.

1. Happiness would mean becoming successful, but success would mean they would have to keep working and risking to remain successful, and they really don't want to do that.
2. Happiness means they would have significantly more freedom to carve out their own existence. This creates anxiety in people who have always been forced into choices, either by others or by their own dynamics.
3. Happiness means they would be open to love. Love requires honesty, transparency, vulnerability, and intimacy—all of which are too frightening for these people.

Five counseling implications are present with regard to the fear of happiness. First, the beginning of counseling can be spent helping people decide if, indeed, they want to become happier or want to remain the same. Until this decision is made and evidenced by observable efforts to change, little counseling will occur. When pinned down, some people must admit they don't want to be happy. This at least helps them face their motives more honestly and will prevent much wasted time in counseling.

Second, counselors can realize that people who have a deep fear of happiness are very challenging. Since every step in counseling is a step toward greater happiness, each will be met with resistance. Counselors can be especially understanding and patient with these people, although not to the extent that no counseling is taking place.

Third, people balk at happiness because their fears, angers, and guilts shackle them into boredom, misery, or both. Counselors can help these people chip away and gradually loosen these constraints.

Fourth, counselors can help people prepare for increasing happiness just as a prison inmate must be gradually prepared to live outside prison walls. Each step toward happiness will bring a new set of anxieties the person must learn to handle.

Counselors ordinarily do not have a fear of happiness. However, the fear of happiness is not unusual in a person in counseling. This creates a special challenge to the counselor, since becoming more successful, free, and loving are basic counseling goals. People who balk at happiness have an uncanny way of drawing people into a partnership of unhappiness. They offer a powerful temptation to others to respond "Look, if you really want to be unhappy, I'll be glad to help you out." Counselors are only slightly less susceptible than others to this temptation and must be watchful for it.

ANGER

Many people have been taught that anger is a negative emotion; therefore, they attempt to expunge it from their repertoire of emotional responses. As a result, they deny being angry or use less-threatening synonyms, such as upset, frustrated, disappointed, confused, annoyed, or hurt. The counselor's first job is to help angry people realize and articulate their anger in ways that can lead to positive action.

Causes and purposes

Anger has two causes. The first occurs when an obstacle is placed in the way of need fulfillment. The intensity of the anger is contingent on the strength of the need. A person who wants to have the weekend off will be angry when he is told he must work on Saturday. But he will be less angry than if he were denied a promotion that he feels he deserves. When another person creates the obstacle to need fulfillment, the anger is directed toward the other person; that is, it is *other-anger*.

The second cause of anger occurs when people interfere with their own need fulfillment. For example, a college student needs to get a "B" in a course, works hard at the start, but inadequately prepares for the mid-term examination, thus earning a "C." Whether or not she admits it, she is angry at herself. This is *self-anger*.

The general purpose of both other-anger and self-anger is to energize the person to bring about eventual need fulfillment in the frustrated area. The target of each anger, however, is different.

The purpose of other-anger is to energize behavior that will either remove the obstacle to need fulfillment or remove the person from a situation where an important need is consistently unmet. In the example of other-anger, the employee denied the promotion can use his anger to appeal the decision and, if the appeal is unsuccessful, can use the energy to decide whether or not he wants to remain in this particular work situation.

The purpose of self-anger is to energize the individual to change behavior that is interfering with his or her need fulfillment. In the example of self-anger, the student can channel the anger into understanding why she slacked off and how she can increase her efforts so she can raise her final grade.

It is important for counselors to recognize the difference between self-anger and other-anger. To confuse the two causes and targets of anger and/or to lump them into one amorphous concept of anger is tantamount to confusing two different kinds of precision instruments or melting two precision instruments into one useless or damaging one. The more that people can learn to distinguish between the two kinds of anger and use them according to their purposes, the more need fulfillment and growth they will enjoy.

When anger is not handled constructively, problems can arise in four ways. First, people who are responsible for frustrating their own needs blame others. In this situation, self-anger is replaced by other-anger, which will cause the anger to be directed at the wrong target. The person or persons who constitute the wrong targets (the scapegoats) will retaliate directly or indirectly for the unjust anger they receive.

Second, people whose needs are being interfered with by another person or persons feel anger but turn it toward themselves (self-anger). Because the anger is aimed at the wrong target (the self), the need will continue to be frustrated. The more that inappropriate self-anger is generated, the less people like themselves, and this in turn leads to behavior that will not be need-fulfilling.

Third, other-anger may be channeled in the appropriate direction (outwardly), but may be expressed destructively. For example, a wife may be angry at her husband but may express it in disguised, veiled ways or in displaced ways, such as becoming angry with the children instead of her husband. These destructive expressions will only create more conflict, and the cause of the need frustration will remain.

Fourth, self-anger may also be channeled in the appropriate direction (inwardly), but may be expressed destructively. Instead of using self-anger to change some problematic behavior, people simply use the anger to scourge themselves, just as a parent may beat a child with no thought of helping the child learn from the offense.

Counselors can help people aim self-anger and other anger at the appropriate target and express it constructively.

Manifestations of self-anger

There are several common manifestations of self-anger that is handled destructively. However, a note of caution can be kept in mind. It is impossible to attribute a specific dynamic to a particular behavior. For example, to say that crying is a manifestation of sadness is naive. Crying could also indicate fear, anger, hurt, guilt, joy, or an allergy.

The following behaviors are commonly associated with people who turn anger against themselves in destructive ways.

Depression. People who experience depression can punish themselves by successfully avoiding happiness in their lives. The key to relieving this type of depression is to identify and understand the self-hatred.

Addictions. Included in addictions are alcoholism, drug dependency, compulsive gambling, and compulsive work. The self-anger may not be seen in the actual behavior, but in the inevitable self-defeating effects.

Wrong people and places. This is choosing as friends or associates people who are insecure or disturbed or choosing to live and work in situations that cause needless stress and unhappiness.

Reckless behavior. This behavior is seen in a person who takes needless and careless risks—psychological, physical, or financial.

Martyrdom. Martyrdom implies unnecessary suffering under the guise of love, charity, fate, or religious fervor.

Bumbling. Through this behavior people cause unnecessary problems for themselves by acting in typically foolish or inept ways when they are capable of behaving better.

Physical manifestations. People with self-anger sometimes manifest it by an unkempt or bizarre appearance, by being excessively heavy or thin, which can unknowingly set up rejection, or by exhibiting psychogenic physical disorders such as ulcers, headaches, stomach problems, sexual problems, and hysterical symptoms such as fainting, seizures, numbness, deafness, or blindness.

Degrading behavior. This comprises any behavior that makes a person feel ashamed. It could include allowing oneself to be abused emotionally, physically, or sexually or initiating behavior that is self-degrading, such as stealing, sexual misconduct, cheating, lying, or causing oneself public embarrassment.

Counseling implications of self-anger

Counselors can be conversant with the manifestations and dynamics of self-anger. It is fruitless for counselors to attack the behavior directly—for example, to tell a person he should choose better people with whom to associate, that she is becoming an alcoholic, that he should lose weight, or that she is being masochistic. It is likely that the person already knows that the behavior is not helpful and is in counseling to learn how to change it. Efforts to help the person change the behavior must be accompanied by excursions into the possibility of self-anger as the underlying cause.

If the self-anger is appropriate—that is, people are behaving in ways that are damaging to themselves—the counselors can help these people channel the anger into changing the offending behavior. For example, if a student cheats in school, the self-anger may be used to discover and remedy the causes of the cheating.

The self-anger may be inappropriate. For example, an unmarried young man may despise himself because he masturbates once a week. The self-anger and self-rejection that stem from masturbating cause him to behave in self-defeating ways—to lose interest in school, to withdraw from friends, and to pick fights with virtual strangers. Counselors can help people develop more realistic expectations and a self-accepting attitude.

The self-anger also may be inappropriate if it is being mischanneled toward the self when it should be directed toward others. For example, a young woman may actually be angry at her mother, who has manipulated her to remain at home. Instead of feeling the anger toward her mother and directing it toward a solution, she bends the anger inward because it is safer to feel depressed than to be angry with her mother. Counselors can help these people recognize the true target of their anger and utilize the anger to call forth a growth-producing change in the situation.

Counselors can also be aware that people who indulge in these behaviors are very likely to bring them into the counseling relationship. Sometimes these behaviors can be very subtle. For example, people in counseling may too easily accept the counselor's interpretation that reflects negatively on them. The counselor states "I think you're using your depression as a weapon against your husband." The person replies "I never looked at it that way, but I think you're right. How awful of me!" The counselor congratulates himself both on the accuracy of the insight and the obviously palatable way he communicated it. In fact, however, the person in counseling is simply accepting another hammer with which to hit herself over the head as part of her self-anger.

Counselors can also look for traces of self-anger in themselves. Under the guise of being "honest," "liberating," "tough," or "cautious," counselors may be setting up a failure experience for themselves and the person in counseling.

Manifestations of other-anger

Following are some common examples of destructive other-anger—that is, anger channeled toward others, whether or not it should be. The same caution should be exercised here as when examples of self-anger were discussed. Other-anger is a frequent dynamic underlying these behaviors, but it may not be the *only* dynamic and, in some cases, may not be present at all.

Moralism. This term denotes perverting morality to demean other people. The theme of moralism is either "You are a bad (weak, sinful, selfish) person and you'd better face up to it and mend your ways" or a more "compassionate" version: "It's not your fault that you are not as good (strong, moral, religious) as you should be. Let me help you become like me."

Hostile talk. This includes ridiculing, acerbic comments, odious comparisons, sarcasm, tantrums, complaining, destructive criticism, gossiping, and being hostile under the guise of honesty.

Shutting down. A person may shut off emotions in the presence of the person toward whom anger is directed. The person is saying "I'll share my mind with you and maybe even my body, but I won't share my heart with you. This is your punishment for making me angry."

Purposeful ineptness. Deep down, a person may choose to be inept because the results will punish the people toward whom anger is directed. Examples of purposeful ineptness are motivated forgetting ("Oh, I forgot to pick up your dress at the cleaners for the party tonight") and nonthinking behavior ("Oh, I didn't mean to embarrass you in front of your boyfriend")

Victimizing. The angry person may cause others to be wrong or to fail by placing expectations on them they can't possibly meet, by making people dependent, then using or rejecting them; by competing with people with the primary motive of *beating* them rather than simply winning; and by placing people in double bind, "damned if you do, damned if you don't" situations, leaving them with the appropriate feeling "I can't win."

Ambushing. The person will find some reason, sooner or later, to attack or reject someone. It may be done obviously ("You'd better not cross me, or you're going to be sorry") or by a much more subtle attitude that says with a smile "I'm going to give you enough rope until you hang yourself."

Passivity. An angry person may refuse to budge in a direction that would be helpful to the person toward whom the anger is directed. A wife wants to buy a new house, which the couple can afford, but her husband has to "think some more about it." A husband wants to take his wife out for an evening, but she is always "too tired."

Getting sick. Obviously, people can get sick unavoidably. But if they become sick when others are most counting on them, it raises the possibility that the sickness is caused more by anger than by germs. For example, a woman who is angry with her boss may work hard to set up a complicated project but call in sick the day it must go into effect.

Counseling implications of other-anger

Manifestations of other-anger may be directed at the particular person or people toward whom the person feels angry, or they could be part of a generalized, diffuse anger that includes all people as targets. The common element in all of them is that the person does not connect the behavior with anger and, in fact, may vehemently deny the possibility ("After all my parents have given me, how could I be angry?"). The challenge for the counselor is to help people see at least the possibility of a connection between the behavior and anger, without arguing the point.

As with self-anger, it is important for people to recognize when other-anger is appropriate and inappropriate. Making this distinction will help people deal with it constructively. Similarly, counselors can be aware that people who indulge in other-anger behaviors outside of counseling will bring them into the counseling relationship.

Counselors can also realize when they are behaving with destructive other-anger. Counselors can be moralistic ("You're being kind of neurotic about this"), engage in hostile talk ("I wish I were taping this session so you could hear how phony you sound"), shut down ("Why is it so necessary that you see me emote?"), be purposefully inept ("I'm sorry I'm late again—I went overtime with my last patient"), or ambush ("I didn't say anything, but I knew if you kept missing our appointments you'd eventually fall off the wagon"). There are several thoughts about anger a counselor can keep in mind. It is true that a counselor cannot call "time out" at every turn to examine whether a piece of behavior is motivated by self-anger or other-anger; by necessity, some behavior must be allowed to pass. But when one of the previously mentioned behaviors occurs enough to suggest a pattern, or if it occurs only once but in a very dramatic way, the counselor can focus on it and examine it with the person.

Everyone indulges at times in destructive self-anger or destructive other-anger. Usually, the overall psychological health of the person and/or the relationship can absorb these mistakes. Problems arise, however, when people have so much anger that the results of it are interfering significantly with their own need fulfillment or that of those closest to them.

GUILT

Guilt is the feeling of discomfort or shame that people experience when they think, feel, or act in ways they consider wrong, bad, or immoral. Guilt plays an important role in psychological growth and happiness. When guilt is appropriate, it helps people refrain from behavior that damages their sense of self-esteem and that places a distance between them and others. Guilt can motivate a person who has participated in guilt-producing behavior to rectify its damaging effects and to change future behavior. Appropriate guilt is a preserver and restorer of self-esteem.

Guilt is appropriate when people behave in ways that legitimately reduce their self-esteem. The word *legitimately* is an important qualifier for three reasons. One is that people may have unrealistically positive expectations of themselves and may feel self-hatred when they fail to meet them. For example, a young man feels appropriate anger toward his parents because of the inordinate pressures they place on him. He inappropriately berates himself for having these feelings.

Second, a person's sense of lovableness may depend on another person's evaluation. For example, a young woman who recently graduated from college wishes to move out of her parents' home, but when she broaches the subject, the parents send her some variation of the message "How could you be so ungrateful as to leave us by ourselves?" The daughter finally manages to gain enough strength to move out, but she is flooded with guilt because her sense of self-esteem is largely interwoven with what her parents think of her.

Third, a person's sense of self-esteem can be tied to unreasonable moral absolutes. When people are unable to behave according to these absolutes, their self-esteem is diminished. Some common moral absolutes are anger is bad, sex is sinful, self-fulfillment is selfish, obedience is good, hurting another is wrong, promises should be kept, and loyalty is a virtue. What makes these moral injunctions absolute is that they tolerate no exceptions. In reality, anger can be destructive, but it also can be constructive and, in fact, in certain situations it would be immoral *not* to express anger. The same kinds of qualifications can be made with the other moral absolutes.

Counselors can help people recognize when they feel guilty and help them discern whether the guilt is appropriate or inappropriate. The results of this discernment will suggest the next step.

Types

It is important for counselors to understand that there is not one monolithic dynamic called *guilt*. In reality, there are three kinds of guilt: psychological, social, and religious. This distinction is not merely theoretical because the specific kind of guilt will dictate the particular path to resolution.

Psychological guilt occurs when people behave in a way that contradicts their self-concept. Unlike social guilt, which is interpersonal, psychological guilt is intrapersonal; that is, it deals with individuals' relationships with themselves.

Social guilt stems from being psychologically or materially unjust to another person. The social dimension of a value system tells a person that there are certain ways to behave in order to help others, and there are certain ways not to behave because such behaviors would damage others.

Religious guilt occurs only in religious people who feel that their behavior can hurt God or can at least place a wedge between themselves and God.

Sometimes the three types of guilt are mutually exclusive; that is, a person feels psychological guilt but not social or religious guilt. At other times, one act can cause all three guilts in the same or varying intensities.

It is important that counselors understand the difference between the three kinds of guilt because resolving one does not resolve any of the others. A person may confess his sins to a minister and be relieved. However, after the good feeling wears away, he begins to feel troubled again. He feels forgiven by God but does not feel forgiven by himself or by the people he has damaged. The self-punitive feelings that stem from this realization could cause him to misbehave again, thus repeating the cycle. In counseling, a person may resolve the psychological guilt that accompanied a particular behavior but be left with the social and religious guilt unresolved. Until each guilt can be resolved and used for growth, it may imperceptibly increase in size—like a tumor—and cause destructive behavior.

Guilt can be either *conscious* or *unconscious*. If an individual lacks the psychological strength to deal with guilt, defense mechanisms will intercept it and relegate it to unawareness. This allows a person who may be permeated with guilt to state "I've never done a thing that I've felt guilty about in my life."

When guilt is unconscious, it cannot be used as an instrument of growth because, for all practical purposes, it does not exist. Furthermore, unconscious guilt causes self-punitive behavior as a way of atoning for the guilt. While this self-punishment relieves some of the anxiety caused by guilt, it causes its own set of problems. First, because the self-punishing behavior is motivated by unconscious guilt, there is no control over it, so it can invade the important and precious areas of the person's life—for example, work performance and love relationships. Second, self-punishing behavior almost always damages loved ones, which adds even more guilt as fuel for the destructive process.

Third, because the person is not aware of what behavior caused, or is still causing, the unconscious guilt, it is likely to continue, causing a relentless cycle of self-punishing behavior. Finally, the more self-punishing behavior the person indulges in, the more he or she is filled with self-dislike or self-hate. This causes its own vicious circle with a downward spiral.

Manifestations

It is difficult to distinguish clearly self-punishing behaviors from self-anger behaviors because there is often a good deal of overlap. However, some behaviors are likely to be motivated more by unconscious guilt than by pure self-hate.

The conviction that there is something wrong with oneself. Despite repeated reassurances to the contrary, people may believe there is something physically or emotionally wrong with them.

Indecisiveness. As long as people allow themselves to remain on the horns of a dilemma, two things are happening. First, they experience a good deal of tension, and, second, they are unable to get needs met in the particular situation.

Creating disappointment. This is the "Is that all there is?" syndrome. These individuals are always looking forward to some happiness, and when they reach it, they are disappointed.

Psychosomatic or hypochondriacal symptoms. Psychosomatic symptoms are real physical symptoms that are caused as much by psychological factors as by physical ones. Hypochondriacal symptoms are physical complaints that are imagined or are real but magnified. When such symptoms are caused by unconscious guilt, pain is very frequently part of the symptomology. It is interesting to note that these symptoms often get worse just prior to some event that a person is looking forward to enjoying.

Overdriven needs. One overdriven need is to be perfect. The perfectionist sets unattainable goals for himself and others. Consequently, he is continually disappointed. Another is to assume inordinate obligations. This person manages to assume obligations of a type or variety that effectively prevent enjoyment of life. A third is to worry. These people move from one crisis to another. The solution of each problem only opens the way for two more.

Habitually embarking on doomed ventures. This behavior occurs in friendships, marriage, business ventures, and political causes. It is the "signing up for failure" syndrome. Each failure is met with surprise, even though close friends and relatives saw the "hand-writing on the wall" from the start.

Snatching defeat from the jaws of victory. This type of individual does well until the very end and then manages to self-destruct. The student who has an "A" going into the final examination does not show up for the test.

Religiosity. The relevant characteristic is that religion is used as an excuse to suffer and to be unhappy. This is motivated not by a positive attitude toward God but by a negative, guilt-ridden attitude toward oneself.

Counselors can help people recognize the possibility that some of their self-created problems are meant to be self-punishing. When the person in counseling can entertain this as a possibility, the counselor may be able to help the person trace the self-punishing behavior back to its possible causes. These guilts may be appropriate or inappropriate or of long or short duration. In any case, the guilts can be uncovered so that the person can resolve them constructively.

Atonement

Conscious guilt provides an opportunity for constructive resolution through the process of *atonement,* which means that the person uses the guilt constructively to become more at one with himself and with the people who were damaged by the misbehavior. Unlike the resolution of guilt through self-punishment, the main goal of atonement is not simply to reduce anxiety but to heal as many wounds as possible and to make changes in order to decrease the likelihood of the same behavior occurring again. Counselors can help people in counseling learn a process of atonement.

Acknowledging the guilt feeling.   This entails a person admitting "I feel guilty." The counselor can help a person become aware that guilt can camouflage itself with other emotions and help the person ferret it out.

Discovering the true source and magnitude of the guilt.   Guilt can be displaced from one behavior onto another. A woman who is actually guilty that she is not as loving as she could be toward her children may displace this guilt. She may think that her guilt stems from not visiting her own mother more often. She finds it easier to feel guilty for not being a good daughter than to feel guilty for not being a good mother.

Guilt can also be inordinately intense. A college student may cheat on an exam and feel great and prolonged guilt, totally out of proportion to the situation. In reality, the student has an added source of guilt—a deeper, hidden guilt because he is treating his girlfriend in abusive ways. The counselor can help this man separate the two guilts and atone for each separately.

Atoning for appropriate guilt.   Once appropriate guilt is isolated, it must be atoned for or it will continue to cause unconscious self-punishing behavior, which is always destructive, not only to the guilty person but often to innocent bystanders. Atonement must be gauged to the specific kind of guilt the person is experiencing.

Psychological guilt—that is, guilt that stems from violating one's self-concept—must be atoned for differently than social guilt. The counselor can first help people discern whether or not their self-concept in this particular area is appropriate. If a person's self-concept is inappropriate and based on ideals rather than on reality or if the self-concept is inappropriately negative, the basic problem is the self-concept and not the guilt that flows from violating it. The counselor can help the person align the self-concept with reality, and this will diminish the amount of inappropriate guilt the person feels.

If the self-concept is appropriate, then the counselor can help people discover why they behaved in a way that violated it. For example, if part of a person's self-concept is that he is honest, but during a confrontation with his wife, he lied to her, the counselor can help the man understand why this occurred. What needs, motives, fears, and angers prompted him to lie rather than to tell the truth? If telling the truth would have caused significantly more problems, what is going on in the overall relationship that is manifesting itself in this no-win situation? The answer to these and similar questions will give the person information that, if acted upon, will decrease the potential for similar behavior in the future.

Social guilt (guilt that stems from damaging another, directly or indirectly) can include attempts to undo the harm. The counselor can help the person understand that merely apologizing to another ordinarily does not constitute atonement. How atonement is accomplished depends upon the kind of damage. If a person's reputation is damaged, attempts can be made to undo the harm. If the person cheated another out of monies or goods, they can be returned. If the person damaged another's sense of lovableness, attempts can be made to heal the wound.

Sometimes direct atonement may be impossible—for example, if the damaged person is deceased. Atonement in this or similar situations can be indirect. This may be done by taking a special interest in the welfare of one's own family or friends or by volunteering to work with people who need someone's care and warmth. In other situations, it may not be possible to rectify the damage. In these cases, counselors can help people accept this reality and learn from it so they can avoid similar mistakes in the future.

Religious guilt (guilt for behaving in ways that place a distance between oneself and God) stems largely from one's view of God. People who view God as one who can be vengeful, hurt, disappointed, authoritarian, or jealous will experience guilt when they fail to achieve the level of perfection this view of God requires.

This is an especially difficult situation for two reasons. The counselor who attempts to help the person modify his or her negative image of God will be met with resistance and anger. The counselor who attempts to raise the person to a level of perfection that surpasses human nature is attempting the impossible. A second problem deals with the counselor's religious persuasion. The counselor who is not religious may be unable to empathize with the person in this situation. The counselor who shares the person's negative view of God may simply compound the guilt.

Counselors can help people understand that harsh views of God often are projections of their views of their parents and/or teachers. People who relate to an authoritarian or neurotic God frequently had authoritarian or neurotic parents and teachers. As people's psychological health and self-esteem increase, they will relate to a God who is psychologically healthy and loving. In fact, for religious people, progress in counseling often can be measured by how their image of God changes from a frightening, angry, and authoritarian one to one that is comforting, loving, and freeing.

In an age that tends to view guilt as a neurotic and unnecessarily bothersome emotion, it is important for counselors to recognize that guilt can be a very appropriate emotion that generates adaptive behavior. One role of a counselor is to help people separate their appropriate from their inappropriate guilt so that they can grow in the self-worth produced by constructively handling guilt and be freed of the self-disparagement caused by inappropriate guilt. Another counselor role is to help people with overly stringent consciences develop a more realistic attitude toward themselves and people with slack consciences more fully appreciate the hurt that their behavior causes others.

SUMMARY

Dealing with emotions is an important part of counseling. When emotions are appropriate in nature and strength, they energize the person to behave adaptively. When they are inappropriate, they further distort the person's perceptions and consequently cause maladaptive behavior.

It is impossible for counselors to help people always deal with emotions effectively. Sometimes people will overshoot and undershoot the targets of their emotions. At other times, even though their emotional reactions are appropriate, it may be disadvantageous for people to express them. All these situations are a normal part of everyday behavior. However, it is necessary to keep these imperfect situations within workable limits—that is, short of becoming typical. Only when people mishandle their emotions a significant amount of the time do problems and symptoms occur.

THOUGHT QUESTIONS

1. What could a person do or say in counseling that would hurt you the most? How would you deal with it?
2. It has been said that people become counselors because they fear intimacy in their own lives; hence, they enjoy the intimacy of a counseling relationship while still remaining at a safe distance. How would you respond to this sentiment, and do you see any truth in it for you?
3. Most people have a fear of failure. How could your fear of failure affect the way you do counseling?
4. A counselor says "The people I see in counseling seldom become angry with me, and I seldom become angry with them. We both know we're there for a purpose and work together and get the job done." What is your response to this statement?
5. It would seem that if counselors have deep insight into themselves, they would feel a certain guilt about their role as counselors for at least a few reasons. What could some of these reasons be? How might a counselor handle the guilt in constructive and destructive ways?

CHAPTER 8

Communication in Counseling

Communication bridges the psychological space between the person in counseling and the counselor. As soon as the person enters the counseling room, communication begins, and it continues until the person leaves the room. There is never a moment during a counseling session when communication is not occurring. And there is not a moment when both the counselor and the person are not sending and receiving messages at exactly the same time. This chapter deals with seven elements of communication that are particularly relevant to counseling.[1]

THE THREE DIMENSIONS OF COMMUNICATION

All communication is three dimensional; it involves a personal, a contextual, and a relational dimension. These dimensions deal with the question "What is the *real* message that the person is sending the counselor?"

Personal dimension

The personal dimension consists of messages that people in counseling send the counselor regarding themselves. There are three levels of personal messages.

Level III messages. Level III consists of the message "This is who I want *you* to *think* I am." For example, a person may communi-

[1]For further discussions of communication in counseling, see Beier (1966) and Ruesch (1973).

cate with his behavior "I want you to think that I am a very cooperative person." If the message is accurate (that is, the person is truly cooperative), no problem will arise. But if the message is false, the less perceptive counselor may be lulled into a sense of complacency while the person is actually resisting the process of counseling. The less psychological strength people possess, the more likely they are to send false Level III messages, not only in counseling but in the other parts of their lives. Because false Level III messages are not backed by actual behavior, conflicts arise both for the person and for those who believe or believed the false message.

Counselors can ask themselves during a session "This person obviously wants me to view him as cooperative (or intelligent, stupid, benevolent, strong, weak). Does he want me to believe this because it is true or because this is how he skirts reality?"

Level III messages, like all messages, can be sent consciously or unconsciously and obviously or subtly. When the false message is communicated unconsciously and subtly, it takes a very vigilant counselor to see through it. When counselors eventually discover that they have been fooled by a person in counseling, it is usually because they believed a false Level III message.

Level II messages.   The Level II personal message is "This is who *I think* I am." It reflects the image that people in counseling have of themselves, whether or not it is accurate. If it is accurate, no problems will arise. If it is inaccurate, problems can occur both inside and outside of counseling. Examples of Level II messages are "I have superior intelligence," "I am a kind person," "I am boring," and "I am neurotic."

People in counseling often have inaccurate self-images that help them further some destructive need. For example, a person may think she is intelligent, not because she is but because she *needs* to think she is. As long as she thinks she is intelligent, she can blame her problems on the stupidity of others. By the same principle, as long as a person views herself as helpless, she need not move in any direction with her life.

Counselors can be careful not to automatically accept Level II messages as valid. The person who communicates "I think I am kind" may need to feel kind because he is hostile. However, when counselors believe the false message, the person's hostility may escape the counselor or be labeled as something different, since it is obvious that kind people do not behave in hostile ways.

Level I messages. The Level I message is "This is who *I am*." It reflects the true nature of the person at that time. In other words, if a person is fearful, he or she communicates "I'm scared." The person with modest intelligence communicates "I had better lower my aspirations." The person who is angry communicates "I'm furious. Maybe I'm not supposed to be, but I am."

Consonant and dissonant messages. In psychologically healthy people, all three message levels are consonant. They can be diagrammed as follows:

Level III	A	I want you to think that I am frightened.
Level II	A	I think I am frightened.
Level I	A	I am frightened.

The letter A signifies that all three messages match.

People with less psychological health are inclined to send dissonant messages. The following diagrams reflect some of the combinations that can occur. The letters signify the difference in messages.

Level III	B	I want you to think that I am reasonably happy.
Level II	B	I think I'm reasonably happy.
Level I	A	I'm depressed.

Level III	B	I want you to think that I'm not angry with you.
Level II	A	I think I am angry at you.
Level I	A	I am angry at you.

Level III	C	I want you to think I have no sexual concerns.
Level II	B	I think I'm sexually confused.
Level I	A	I have homosexual tendencies.

No matter how much or how little psychological health people have, they are likely to communicate in a consonant way when dealing with innocuous issues. However, the less psychological strength a person has and the more threatening the issue, the greater the likelihood of dissonant messages.

The implications for counseling are twofold. First, counselors can be aware that there are three levels on which people can communicate who they are. As counselors grow in skills and experience, they become more adroit at sensing cues that support or negate Level II and Level III messages. Second, most people who seek counseling send dissonant messages when communicating in areas of threat. Hence, one of the goals of counseling is to reduce the number of dissonant messages in any particular area and, ideally, to extinguish them.

Contextual dimension

Contextual messages deal with the content of the message. There are three levels of contextual messages.

Level III messages. Level III contextual messages follow the theme "This is what *I want* to discuss." This reflects a topic with which the person feels familiar and safe, even though it may be painful. But these people have rehearsed the topic so well with themselves and others that, in effect, they are reading a script rather than genuinely communicating. The psychological area that the script covers may be important. In this case, the counselor can help the person discard the script and communicate about the area in a spontaneous, nondefensive way. If the area that the script covers is of little current importance, the counselor can help the person shift attention to more relevant, albeit more threatening, areas.

Level II messages. Level II contextual messages communicate "This is what I know you want me to discuss." After a few sessions people in counseling can become astute at picking up the counselor's favorite topics. These topics generally stem from the counselor's theories as to what causes problematic behavior. Different counselors may focus on anger, sex, childhood, dreams, cognitive assumptions, or communication. People consciously or unconsciously tune to the channel that the counselor likes, because they know that it holds little promise and because the counselor "must know what he's doing."

Level I messages. Level I contextual messages communicate "This is what *I should* talk about." These topics deal with the deepest layers of hurt, fear, anger, guilt, confusion, and despair and must be dealt with eventually if people are going to effect any significant change in their behavior.

Counselors can be aware that the first stages of counseling are often replete with Level III and Level II contextual messages, whether or not they are conscious.

Counseling is likely to begin with Level III communications because the person has been preparing well for the first sessions. The person's "story" is clearly delineated in his or her mind, and the person usually experiences little real difficulty relating it. The person's presenting story is rarely the real story. In fact, it is not uncommon that, once people progress into the heart of counseling, they forget what their presenting story was. This does not imply, however, that counselors should discard Level III communications as superficial, because the person's presenting story is usually pregnant with clues as to what the real story is.

As counseling progresses, the person may drop from Level III to Level II contextual communication. As people begin to know the counselor, they gradually slip into the same wavelength. This is a particularly challenging stage for the counselor because it can erroneously signify that easy communication and good rapport have been established. However, if the person seems to enjoy this level of communication and experiences little or no anxiety, it is likely that while the person and the counselor are on the same wavelength, it is the wrong wavelength.

If the counselor suddenly changes frequencies into an area that seems important but has been conspicuously absent in the sessions, the person may react with agitation, which could be a clear indication that Level I communication has been broached.

Level I communication becomes most frequent during the latter parts of counseling. The person no longer speaks in the smooth, easy voice of a news reporter. Because the material is meaningful and threatening, the person's voice is often tight, hesitant, and affectively laden.

Relational dimension

The relational dimension deals with the messages that people in counseling send regarding their views of the counselor. This dimension has two levels.

Level II messages.   Level II is "This is who I want you to think that I think you are." An example of this message is "I want you to think that I think you are a very competent counselor and that I am very lucky to be seeing you." The supporting dynamics of this message could be to curry the counselor's favor so he or she will treat the person kindly and gently and not cause any significant degree of anxiety.

Another example is "I want you to think that I think you are an arrogant, uncaring person who helps people because it makes you feel superior and affords you a nice income." The underlying dynamic here could be to keep the counselor at a distance so that the counselor cannot get close enough to the person to touch vulnerable areas.

The first stages of counseling are often comprised of Level II relational messages, even though such messages may be unconscious. Since most social relating is done on Level II, it is only to be expected that this would carry into counseling. Consequently, it is important that counselors not get fooled by these communications.

One clue that a Level II response might be operating is that the sentiment the person expresses toward the counselor has no basis in reality. For example, a woman may tell her counselor after only four sessions "I can't tell you how much better I am feeling about myself already because of your help." Or a man may say after a few sessions "I'd like to bring up some religious conflicts I'm having, but I can tell you're not a person who puts much stock in religion." As the person grows in psychological strength and in trust in the counseling relationship, he or she will gradually gravitate to Level I relational messages.

Level I messages.   A Level I relational message is "This is who I *really* think you are." This message comprises the true ideas and feelings that the person in counseling has regarding the counselor. The ideas and feelings may be positive, negative, or ambivalent, but they are genuine and are offered to the counselor as possible aids in the growth process.

PROBLEMATIC COMMUNICATION

Controlling

People in counseling often send messages to modify the counseling environment or relationship. The more vulnerable people are, the less they can allow others the freedom to respond as they desire. Vulnerable people handcuff others so that they can respond only in certain constricted and prescribed ways. Evoking the responses they want allows these people to relate with others, yet, at the same time, remain safe from threat and damage. It is important for counselors to recognize the control value of verbal and nonverbal messages so that they do not become unknowing victims. When counselors' responses are controlled by the person in counseling, the counseling relationship becomes no different than any other unhelpful relationship that the person has experienced.

The emotional climate.   People in counseling can control the counseling situation in two ways. The first is to create an emotional climate that is comfortable for them. It may be a positive climate of friendliness and kindness that is created to prevent intrusion into vulnerable areas. The warmth of the climate is fostered to render the counselor's tools useless. Once this friendly climate becomes established, it successfully restrains the counselor from acting in unfriendly (anxiety-producing) ways.

The person can also create a negative emotional climate filled with skepticism and antagonism. This negative climate keeps the counselor distant and may grow so dense that the only "reasonable" option left is for each or both to terminate counseling.

People in counseling may send unclear, self-canceling, and double messages that serve to confuse the counselor. This confusion may successfully confound the counselor to the point that he or she is only marginally effective.

As long as counselors feel constrained from making certain responses and forced to make others, or if they experience inordinate confusion, it is likely that they are being enveloped in a mist meant to disengage them as effective helpers.

The counselor's responses. A second way people can control the counseling experience is by evoking from the counselor specific responses that allow people to maintain their current level of maladjustment. The evoked responses either widely miss or reinforce the person's faulty assumptions. For example, a person in counseling may cause the counselor to miss the target by inviting the counselor to discuss sexuality a great deal of the time when the person's true vulnerability lies in other areas. People may elicit responses that reinforce faulty assumptions by evoking angry and rejecting responses from the counselor. These reactions underscore these people's assumption that no one likes them. They have a vested interest in maintaining this assumption because it allows them to continue to withdraw or behave in a hostile manner.

Lack of awareness. People are often unaware of how they control their environment through communication. They have been doing it since early childhood, and it has become automatic. It is not uncommon for people to think they are not communicating anything significant when, in fact, they are, that they are communicating one message when they are actually communicating a contrary one, or that they are inviting one kind of feedback when they are really inviting a different type.

Skilled manipulation. People also learn that both verbal and nonverbal messages have different degrees of probability of response. For example, if a person tells a counselor "I'm so fortunate to have you as my counselor," the probability of a positive response is great. If a person tells a counselor "If you were more interested in helping me than seeing as many patients as you can, I would be doing a lot better," a negative response will likely result.

The more vulnerable people are, the more likely they are to be skilled in eliciting constricted, highly predictable responses from the counselor. These people's survival depends upon their ability to avoid or reinforce their faulty assumptions.

With regard to this principle, it is helpful for counselors to be mindful of the following points.

1. People in counseling often attempt, through the messages they send, to sculpt the counselor into a familiar likeness. They evoke responses that quickly or gradually sculpt the counselor into an old friend or an old enemy. They do this so that they will be able to predict the counselor's responses and deflect the counselor from the areas of vulnerability.

2. Counselors can be aware of their vulnerabilities because it is their vulnerabilities that are hooked by the person's evoking messages. For example, if a counselor needs to be esteemed, the person may send the message "I know some people who don't like you," the counselor may bite, and the rest of the session is spent discussing the counselor and the message rather than the person, the person's problems, and the person's avoidance behavior.

3. When the counselor successfully avoids responding in prescribed ways to evoking messages, tension will be created in the counseling relationship. It is as if the counselor has shredded the script that the person wrote, forcing the person to relate to an unencumbered counselor. This may cause great consternation in the person and a feeling that the counselor is not playing fair. When this occurs, it is important for counselors to handle the situation gently but firmly, clearly explaining what is happening.

4. Counselors must detect evoking messages if they are going to handle them successfully. Since the person in counseling has lifelong experience in camouflaging evoking messages, it is quite possible that a counselor will be hooked, especially in the initial stages of counseling. When this occurs, counselors can disengage themselves from the evoking messages and help people discover what vulnerabilities are being protected. If counseling becomes conflict ridden or stagnant, it often means that the counselor has been successfully hooked and is either being torn apart or frozen in a state of confusion or inactivity. When this occurs, it is often necessary to consult with a supervisor or colleague who has the benefit of an outside view.

5. Counselors can determine if their responses are being evoked by the messages of the person in counseling. One way is for the counselor to have a reasonably firm grasp on the proximate and long-range goals

of counseling. When counselors have a clear view of where they want to go, they will be more sensitive to attempts meant to lure them in other directions. When counselors lack this grasp, they are more open to unproductive excursions chartered by the fears and vulnerabilities of the person in counseling.

A second method counselors can use to help them discern whether their responses are free or evoked by the person in counseling is to ask themselves some questions:

> Do I feel completely comfortable with the way I am responding right now, or is my response stronger, weaker, or more vague than I really feel?
>
> Am I responding in a way a "nice person" should or in the way a courageous, helpful person would?
>
> How does the person react when I respond in a nonevoked manner? For example, how does the person react when the message invites me closer and I remain in place, when he pushes me away and I move closer, or when she attacks me and I step aside?

If the person reacts with anxiety and anger, it could be that the counselor didn't move into the assigned square. If the person easily assimilates the counselor's move, it could be that no evoking message was sent.

Third, counselors can examine their ongoing attitude and approach toward people in counseling. If counselors feel that they must react to one person delicately, another harshly, one sympathetically, and another good naturedly, their behavior possibly is being evoked. Counselors who are genuinely free (that is, unevoked) react to the reality that is present in each session. In other words, the reality may call for empathy one day and confrontation the next. Counselors who have one continuing approach to a person may well be playing by some subliminal ground rule laid down by the person in the very first session. These are the same ground rules the person lays down for everyone because they best protect him or her from reality. However, this attitude may also cause the majority of the person's problems.

6. It is helpful for counselors to know what cognitions and emotions are likely to be evoked in them. Obviously, no one can declare that a particular cognition or emotion is automatically an evoked one. All cognitions and feelings can be either evoked or unevoked. However, some seem more likely to be evoked than others.

With regard to cognitions, people in counseling sometimes evoke ideas in the counselor that the person needs extra support, attention, gentleness, toughness, guidance, protection, consolation, or warmth. Common evoked emotions are anger (meant to prove some negative quality about the person), eroticism (to distract the counselor from dealing with the real issues), confusion (to create a smokescreen that brings counseling to a standstill), guilt (meant to induce the counselor to be less demanding), fear (meant to keep the counselor at a safe distance or to work harder and show more concern), and helplessness (to discourage the counselor from making further efforts).

Counselors who typically experience any of these cognitions and emotions with regard to a particular person in counseling may need to examine the source of the cognition or emotion.

Communicating through symptoms

Psychological symptoms are codified messages. These messages are codified because the people who send them do not wish to accept ownership for the real messages. If they were to take responsibility for the real messages, their inadequate psychological strength could not absorb the anxiety that would be created.

Types of messages. Typically, there are four message combinations. The person in counseling sends a codified message to himself about himself. For example, a man may develop a phobia that prohibits him from going to work. The true message he is sending himself is "You are beginning to have sexual feelings toward another man at work, and this could mean that you have homosexual tendencies." Since this man would define homosexuality as the worst thing that could befall him, he cannot possibly send this unmitigated message to himself. Consequently, he codifies the message into abnormal symptoms: "You're afraid to leave home, but you don't have the slightest idea why." This message has great facilitative value because it accomplishes two things: it rescues him from the anxiety-producing situation at work, and it does so while protecting him from the true message, which would also produce anxiety. His phobia causes less distress than if he had gone to work and been faced with the specific possibility of homosexual inclinations.

The person in counseling sends a codified message to herself about a significant other. For example, a woman's true message to herself is "I deeply resent my husband because he is more interested in everybody and everything than he is in me." She cannot tolerate owning this message because it would mean facing her own feelings of inadequacy, reappraising her idealized image of her husband, and confronting him with the real message, which she is loath to do. To avoid the severe anxiety that would be created by these eventualities, she develops symptoms and sends herself the codified message "I feel very depressed, and there is absolutely no reason because I have a good life and a lovely family." She cannot understand why she is depressed ("Maybe it's early menopause") because she doesn't want to. By encoding her real communication, she trades a specific anxiety for an anonymous depression.

The person sends a codified message to a significant person other than the counselor. For example, an adolescent feels a good deal of at least subconscious, if not conscious, resentment toward his parents. He lacks the psychological skills and strengths to communicate this message in its original form. Consequently, he telegraphs it through the medium of delinquent behavior: "You make me feel inadequate as a son; so I'm going to make you feel inadequate as parents." His delinquent behavior allows him to deliver his message with great impact without having to assume responsibility for it. Unfortunately, he encodes the message so cleverly that the parents miss the point. They blame his behavior on the influence of his "no-good friends" and fail to recognize the real dynamics.

The person in counseling sends encoded messages to the counselor. A woman may tell her counselor: "I'm so depressed I don't think anyone can help me." The counselor must decipher the possible true message hidden in this woman's depression and reflected in her statement. There are at least three possible true communications masked by the woman's symptoms:

> Assure me that there is hope because I'm bordering on despair and that panics me.
>
> I don't intend to help myself; so you and my husband better start giving me what I want if you want me to get better.
>
> I want you to tell me I will get better so that I can prove you wrong, since proving people wrong is my only source of satisfaction these days.

Implications for the counselor. It is important for counselors to read the verbal and nonverbal communications of the people they see in counseling, in order to discover the true message that lies beneath their disturbance. Much of counseling is spent deciphering messages secreted in the person's symptoms. Until the real message is discovered, superficial progress can be made, but no reason exists for the disturbance to stop because neither the counselor nor the person really knows why the person is in counseling until the key messages inherent in the symptoms are discovered. Up to this point, the person thought he was in counseling because he was discomforted by his symptoms. He now realizes that the discomfort was only a side effect of some very powerful messages being sent to himself and others. Only at this point can the person make an authentic decision for or against counseling, because only at this point does the person actually know—for the first time— why he is there.

Discovering the message hidden by the person's symptoms does not ensure progress. The person must first decide whether to accept or reject ownership of the decoded messages. If the messages are owned, the person must then decide whether he or she wants to strengthen the areas of weakness reflected in the communication or whether he or she wishes to terminate counseling and look for some other solution to the problem.

LISTENING

Listening is the basis of a counselor's effectiveness. The one behavior that effective counselors do most is listen. Without listening, counselors cannot know who the person in counseling really is and, without this knowledge, cannot help him or her. Unfortunately, listening is one of the most difficult behaviors in which human beings participate. The following are some considerations with regard to listening in counseling.

Listening and hearing

It is important to distinguish between hearing and listening. A counselor could hear everything a person says in a session and not listen to a single word. *Hearing* is the physiological reception of sound. A person hears the rain, the laughter of children, the sound of a train. *Listening* is the physiological reception of sound plus its psychological interpretation. Hearing is a relatively simple process; listening can be very complex. People seldom create barriers to hearing, but they often construct barriers to listening.

The following is an example of the difference between hearing and listening. A woman begins a counseling session with the statement "Boy, I'm glad to be here." The counselor responds "Well, that's good. What shall we talk about today?" The woman begins to relate an incident that she wants to share with the counselor. The counselor's response indicates that he has heard what the woman has said. But he has not listened. If he had, he would have asked himself the following questions:

> Is she trying to convince herself that she is glad to be here? Why wasn't she just glad to be here? Why did she have to go to the trouble of announcing it?
>
> If she is glad to be *here*, where isn't she glad to be—with her husband, her children, her work, herself?
>
> Did she say this as a response to my statement last session that she seemed to be losing interest in counseling?
>
> Is she finally settling into counseling and loosening up her resistance?
>
> Is she softening me up for something she wants some feedback on later in the session?
>
> Is she simply genuinely glad to be here?

A simple, declarative statement by the person in counseling was chosen to demonstrate the kinds of questions that a listening counselor entertains. Most statements in counseling are grammatically and psychologically more complex.

Obviously, counselors cannot listen with equal intensity to every statement the person makes, or they would miss every other sentence in the session. However, as counselors become more experienced, they become selective, listening more fully to one statement than another, but always listening. For example, if this woman starts each session with a similar comment, it would call less attention to it. If, however, she seldom or never begins a session in this way, the counselor may well entertain all the possibilities mentioned. The counselor can then select which questions to follow up, either by immediately responding to the woman or by using the questions to make more sense out of the forthcoming session.

Since most messages that a person sends to a counselor in the initial stages of counseling often have several layers of meaning, it is important for counselors to realize that one simple statement may house many different meanings.

Functions

Listening has several functions in counseling. People in counseling need not only to be heard but to be listened to. It is likely that these people have talked about their problems with many others, but few or none actually listened to them. The reason for this is that few people really listen to others, and when they do, they prefer to listen to something pleasant rather than somebody's problems. Hence, it is possible that by the time people seek counseling, they have burned out their few listeners.

Listening is also important because people need to listen to themselves talk out loud rather than simply talk to themselves. Thoughts and feelings become reified and concretized when spoken aloud. People can then get a handle on their thoughts and feelings and choose to do something constructive with them or to reject them as invalid and search for more valid ones. As people speak aloud and know they are not only heard but listened to, they become introduced to themselves. It is not unusual in counseling for a person to say "I never knew I felt that way, but now that I say it, I guess I do." After the person shares many words with the counselor, feelings begin to trickle and finally flow into the communication. When counselors listen, they invite people to become who they are.

Finally, listening to a person in counseling is important because it can teach people how to listen. One of the problems that bring people into counseling is that they don't listen very well to themselves or others. In the first stages of counseling, people typically talk a good deal but listen very little. Counselors who invite people in counseling to repeat the counselor's messages are likely to hear themselves misconstrued in important ways. These people probably react similarly to the messages of the significant others in their lives. Listening can be taught both indirectly through modeling and directly by tutoring people in how to develop alternate interpretations for messages and then how to validate them. When people in counseling learn to do this effectively, they will prevent many avoidable problems in their lives.

Barriers

Some common barriers interfere with listening. The largest barrier is that people don't want to listen. They can't help hearing a message, but they can control whether or not they choose to listen to it. Both the counselor and the person in counseling may realize that if they truly listen to a message or become aware of its different levels and possibilities of meaning, it could be anxiety producing. For example, if a person in counseling hears the counselor say "I will be going away for a month in July, but I will have a colleague cover my calls," the person responds "Oh, that's good that you'll get a chance to get away." This woman hears the message but doesn't want to listen to it because she would have to get in touch with what it possibly means to her:

> Does the counselor really care about me if he so easily leaves me for a month?
> What if I really need him? Will I be able to get in touch with him?
> I resent him palming me off on some colleague whose name I don't even know and don't want to know.
> Will I be able to function four weeks without counseling?
> I really feel hatred for him right now for being so cavalier about our relationship.
> Have I become *this* dependent on him?

On some level of awareness, this woman realizes that if she listens, she will feel the accompanying anxiety and will need to decide whether to keep it to herself or share her thoughts and feelings with her counselor, neither of which she wants to do. She removes herself from this dilemma by not really listening to the counselor and will be shocked two months later when the counselor reminds her that this will be the last session for a month.

Another barrier to listening is that a person has too much inner noise and static. For example, counselors may hear the person in counseling but listen to themselves. They may be thinking about the research paper they are in the midst of writing, what they will say to their spouse that evening, or where they will have lunch and with whom. Hearing the person but listening to oneself will naturally occur off and on throughout a counseling session. But if it is a typical occurrence, the counselor must examine the reason for this and do something to solve the problem.

A third barrier to listening is that a person is thinking back or ahead. For example, a counselor may think back to what a person has just said—"What did *that* mean?"—and spend 30 seconds trying to figure it out. Or the counselor may be thinking ahead: "What am I going to say that will be the most prudent and helpful when he is through talking?" Again the counselor loses 30 seconds of listening time. The average person speaks over 200 words in one minute, and this doesn't count the amount of nonverbal communication, which may be even more meaningful. Losing "only" a couple of minutes in a session can be a costly experience. To prevent lost listening time, counselors can stop the communication instead of thinking back. They can say "Could we stop a minute? I'm still back on what you just said and need to understand it better before we go on." In terms of thinking ahead, the counselor can listen to each word and, when the person is finished, say "Well, you've said some important things. Let me take a minute to assess and clarify them and then maybe I can give you some feedback." In both cases, the counselor is freed to listen to every word.

NONVERBAL COMMUNICATION

It is important for counselors to be keenly aware of the presence and meaning of nonverbal communication. The following are some of the basic concepts regarding nonverbal communication in counseling.

Relationship to verbal communication

Nonverbal communication is an extremely important factor in counseling because it qualifies the verbal communication. The messages that a person's body sends may be congruent with what is being said verbally. On the other hand, nonverbal behavior may amplify, dilute, deny, or give a completely separate message from that expressed verbally.

Congruent nonverbal communication means that the person's nonverbal behavior substantiates the verbal communication. For example, a person in counseling may state "I'm really glad to be here today," and the person's face and body language indicate this is true. She is genuinely smiling; her face is bright; her eyes "look glad"; and her body is relaxed.

Amplified nonverbal messages communicate even louder and stronger than the verbal message. For example, a man may tell a counselor in a rather casual, matter-of-fact tone of voice "I'm not feeling so hot this week, Doc." He says this in the same manner as he would say "By the way, I won't be able to come next week." His benign tone of voice and colloquial phrasing give the impression that he is slightly disconcerted. But his face shows agony. His eyes are dark and foreboding; his mouth is wincing and dry; he holds his head down and stares at the floor; his hands are strangling each other; and his legs are crossed at the ankles in a very awkward, taut manner. The counselor translates "not feeling so hot" as "I'm very anxious and depressed, and I'm scared!" The counselor will try to help the person put this nonverbal message into words and get more in touch with exactly how he feels, why he feels it, and what he can do to get some relief.

Diluted nonverbal messages subtract from the verbal message. A woman in counseling says "Yes, I think I'm making pretty good progress." The tone of her voice is that used by a child who says "Yes, I guess this spinach tastes good, sort of." The tone of voice is much more tentative than the verbal message. Her eyes are saying "I think this is what you want to hear; so here it is." Her face has a frozen smile, her hands are fiddling with her purse, and her back is at a 30-degree angle from the back of the chair. The counselor translates her nonverbal behavior: "I think I'm making a *little* progress, but it's not much of a help so far."

Nonverbal behavior can *deny* verbal messages. For example, a man says to a counselor "I think this is going to be the last time I come in, because we don't seem to be getting anywhere." But the tone of his voice is not convincing. His voice has a pleading quality that says "What I really need is for you to care enough about me to give me some reasons to stay." His eyes say "Please don't believe what I'm saying," and he lingers in much the same way as a child who announces to his parents that he is going to run away from home in five minutes.

Nonverbal communication also can convey a message completely *disconnected* from the verbal one. A woman may say to her counselor "I'm so worried about my mother moving in with us that I can't think straight. I know she will be hard to live with and. . . . " The counselor, watching and listening intently, sees and hears two separate topics. The verbal topic is the woman's mother. The nonverbal topic is the counselor. In barely perceivable ways, this woman is communicating anger toward the counselor. She is glaring at him in a way that does not fit the topic. Her voice has an angry edge; her mouth is tight; and her words are clipped. She introjects little asides such as "I can see you're amused by all this." So while the woman is discussing her mother, she is throwing darts at the counselor, and her affect is much more congruent with dart throwing than with her concerns about her mother. The counselor can now help the woman separate the two distinct topics, which are so tightly intertwined that she is probably unaware that she is communicating anger toward the counselor.

Counselors must "listen" to two stimuli: the words from the mouth and the sounds and mannerisms from the soul.

Categories of nonverbal behavior

There are four general categories of nonverbal communication: anatomy, movement, sounds, and dress. Certain *parts of the body* communicate. The eyes can send messages that one is happy, sad, alert, dull, distracted, frightened, angry, loving, confused, relaxed, guilty, seductive, mischievous, playful, or ashamed. The mouth can communicate that the person is happy, sad, cocky, angry, cynical, frustrated, disbelieving, perplexed, mocking, seductive, bored, tense, or relaxed. The contours of the hands, legs, and feet give only general messages of being relaxed or tense. One's overall posture communicates relaxation, seductiveness, withdrawal, defensiveness, aggression, anxiety, or uninvolvement.

Movement denotes how one moves one's anatomy. Eyes can stare into space, flit frantically around the room, avoid contact with the counselor's eyes, and glare. Arms, hands, or fingers can remain at ease, gesticulate wildly, cling tightly to each other or the arms of the chair, fiddle with objects (such as purses, pencils, and note pads), point menacingly, gesture in seductive or loving ways, or protect like a shield. Legs or feet can shift frequently, spread seductively, kick menacingly, tap nervously, twist tensely, or rest peacefully.

Sounds are nonwords that come from a person and often elaborate on word communication: sighs, groans, whines, laughs, snorts, wheezes, gasps, coughs, sniffles, belches, and stomach rumblings. Included in sounds are tones of voice, which can be high, low, seductive, harsh, unsure, tight, happy, sad, frightened, angry, surprised, powerful, or weak.

Dress often communicates what people feel about themselves and what kind of interaction they would like with others. Clothes can be used to camouflage the body, to tell people to go to hell, to enhance appearance, to declare independence, to reflect casualness, to get attention, to seduce others, to invite ridicule, to appear interesting, or to communicate despair or apathy. Included in dress are personal hygiene, hair, makeup, jewelry, and perfume.

All the elements listed under anatomy, movement, sound, and dress communicate something about the person, who may be aware or unaware of what he or she is communicating. Effective counselors perceive so much nonverbal communication in almost every session that they need to decide which communications to comment upon and which to let pass.

Translating nonverbal communication

No verbal or nonverbal behavior has a universal meaning; that is, no specific communication has the same meaning for everyone or always has the same meaning for a particular person. A man who folds his arms across his chest may at one time find it the most relaxing way to sit. At another time he may be protecting himself from what his counselor is saying to him, covering his stomach that he recently noticed was getting larger, trying to muffle the sounds that his stomach is making, or attempting to avoid hitting or hugging the counselor.

A woman who is fiddling with the bottom of her dress may be nervous and unaware of what she is doing. At another time she may be trying to cover more of her legs because she is sitting in a soft chair and her dress is sliding up, seductively calling the counselor's attention to her thighs, or trying to keep her legs warm because she feels cold.

The hasty and confident translation of nonverbal behavior into "obvious" messages can cause problems in counseling. Verbal and nonverbal messages are kaleidoscopic; that is, they often take on different shapes, colors, and configurations, depending upon the situation. The skilled counselor may say "I've noticed that your words are saying one thing but your face seems to be saying something different." The counselor then invites the person to clarify the situation. The less skilled counselor may say "Your mouth is saying some very nice things to me, but your eyes are saying that you're angry. What are you angry about?" It is obvious that the counselor's interpretation is "signed, sealed, and delivered." All the person can do is admit the counselor is correct or be seen as resistant, lacking in trust or insight.

Counselors can also communicate nonverbally in all the same ways as people in counseling. It is important for counselors to realize that people in general are fairly astute at picking up nonverbal messages, since psychological survival during the early years of life depends largely on how accurately one perceives nonverbal communication.

Some counselors tend to think that they have more control over their nonverbal behavior than do the people they see in counseling. A counselor may be listening to a person and say to himself or herself "Who does this guy think he's kidding?" The counselor is completely oblivious to the barely perceptible sneer at the corner of the mouth and the look that says "I hope you don't think I'm so stupid that I'm buying what you're saying." Instead of verbally communicating these thoughts and feelings, the counselor says "Good. Well, I think I'm getting a clear picture of your relationship with your wife. Let's meet next week at the same time." The person leaves the session aware of the deception. On a deeper level, the person may register a sense of distrust that may not even be conscious, a distrust that may significantly interfere with several future sessions, much to the confusion and consternation of the person and the counselor.

The best protection against this type of situation is for the counselor to communicate inner thoughts and feelings verbally, even if they are apt to increase the tension level between the counselor and the person. For example, the previously mentioned counselor could have said "You say you had sex with your secretary to help you become a feeling person again so that you could bring that warmth into your marriage. Is it possible that, in addition to that reason, there were other motives less easy to think or talk about?" Here the counselor's reservations are put to a potentially helpful purpose, not concealed and not communicated nonverbally in a way that is damaging to the counseling relationship.

Generally, if the counselor is thinking or feeling something about the person in counseling, he or she *is* communicating it. It's up to the counselor whether the message will be communicated verbally, which may create growth, or nonverbally, which may cause damage.

SILENCE AS COMMUNICATION

Silence in counseling is an important communication in itself and can be understood and handled effectively by counselors. Silence may be golden for parents with a houseful of noisy children, but in counseling, silence can be threatening and confusing. For this reason, it is helpful to distinguish between three types of silence: creative, neutral, and conflictual.

Creative silence

A creative silence is one during which the person in counseling is reflecting on what has just been said or felt. A woman may have just said "I've never thought about it in this way, but I think I've always resented my son because my husband enjoyed being with him more than he enjoyed being with me." The woman stops and stares at a spot in space. She is obviously contemplating what this insight means. Various thoughts are passing through her mind, and she is experiencing a wide range of emotions. She may remain silent for a minute or five minutes, relating solely with herself. This is a creative silence because something new is happening that may evoke pleasant or unpleasant feelings, or a mixture of the two.

One key indicator of creative silence is the "staring at a spot in space." This signifies intense concentration. During this time, the counselor can "sit on his hands"—that is, do nothing but watch and wait. The counselor allows the person to stroll through his or her inner space and nonverbally invites the person to take all the time needed. This could be a very productive moment.

It would be obtrusive for a counselor to interrupt this silence with inquiries such as "What are you thinking about?" This is a sure way of causing the person to lose a train of thought. Nor is it helpful for the counselor to interrupt with statements such as "It seems that you are on to something." People can be allowed to come out of these silences on their own. Sometimes a person is not ready to share the thoughts and feelings that comprised the silence. The person may need time to assimilate the insights and become more comfortable with them before communicating them to the counselor. When such is the case, the counselor can be sensitive to the person's hesitation or reluctance and suggest that the situation be discussed at the next session. While it is true that some of the spontaneity of the insight may be lost in sharing it later, it is a smaller price to pay than that for manipulating the person to share things against his or her will.

Neutral silence

Neutral silences flow from not knowing what to say. Initial counseling sessions sometimes have neutral silences when the person is at a loss as to what to say next. People don't know what they want to say. They don't know what is important and what is not, what the counselor wants to hear and what the counselor doesn't want to hear. Unlike the "staring at a spot in space" indicator in creative silence, the eyes nervously flit from one place to another and intermittently stop to look imploringly at the counselor and ask "What am I supposed to do now?"

The longer the counselor allows this silence to continue, the more tension will build up inside the person, further short-circuiting his or her ability to focus on a particular area of importance. The counselor can wait until it is clear that the silence is not a creative one, then step in. The counselor may say "Can you tell me what you're feeling right now?" Counselors who wait out such silences with the expectation that the person should be allowed to find his or her own way out of the silence may be expecting too much in the early stages of counseling. Once the person has gotten used to the counselor, such waiting out could be more appropriate, as long as it is benevolent and patient.

Conflictual silence

Conflictual silences may be caused by fear, anger or guilt. People may be frightened to talk either because they were hurt the last time they did or because the next matter that should be discussed is threatening. They may be angry at the counselor and be using the silence as a passive-aggressive way of communicating the anger without taking much of a risk.

Generally, when people are frightened, their nonverbal behavior says "I really don't want to be here." When they are angry at the counselor, their behavior says "I'm not going to help you out one bit." The guilty person avoids the counselor's eyes and squirms.

When it is at least somewhat clear that the silence is caused by fear, gentle questions and reassurances can reduce the fears. Often, once the person can see that the counselor is attuned to the fear, this is enough to free the person to begin speaking. Advising people that it may be good to talk about their fear, but that the choice is theirs, assures them of freedom and control in the situation. If the fear is causing strong reluctance to talk, it may be better to drop that particular topic and go on to less threatening ones so that the person doesn't become immersed in tension and frustration.

When the silence is motivated by anger, it may evoke anger in the counselor, who then nonverbally communicates "I'm not going to talk until you do." In this situation, the passive-aggressive behaviors of both parties inextricably lock horns. Once the presence of anger is obvious, it may be better for the counselor to confront the dynamics directly: "You seem to be communicating something to me by your silence. Can you tell me what you're feeling more directly?" This may immediately generate an open and honest dialogue. Even if it doesn't, it's a healthy response on the part of the counselor, which lays some groundwork for a good exchange later in the session.

When faced with conflictual silence, a counselor can communicate with his or her attitude "We have a problem here, and this is my way of trying to solve it as quickly and easily as possible." If the person refuses to cooperate, the counselor can patiently wait until the person is ready. Time is not being wasted because every minute of silence signifies the intensity of the emotion and the extent of the person's inability to handle it well. This information will be helpful later when dealing with the significance of the situation.

Silences in counseling need not be feared or avoided, but can be used as very helpful instruments. While silences are viewed socially as undesirable, they can be viewed therapeutically as opportunities for growth.

STAGES OF COMMUNICATION

Communication reflects the degree of psychological closeness between the person in counseling and the counselor. Most counselors today feel that it is important for people in counseling and counselors to work closely together. The more psychologically intimate they become, the more they can know each other and relate in growth-producing ways. The more distance between the counselor and the person, the less counseling is a relationship and the more it may be a seminar in psychotherapy.

Figure 8–1 illustrates the progressive stages of communication be-

Person in counseling →								Counselor →							
8	7	6	5	4	3	2	1	1	2	3	4	5	6	7	8
You talk to me.	Let's talk about it.	I'll talk about them.	I'll feel about them.	I'll talk about me.	I'll feel about me.	I'll talk to you about you.	I'll share my feelings about you with you.	I'll share my feelings about you with you.	I'll talk to you about you.	I'll feel about me.	I'll talk about me.	I'll feel about them.	I'll talk about them.	Let's talk about it.	You talk to me.

Figure 8–1. Stages of communication in counseling.

tween the counselor and the person as they develop within the counseling relationship. Each stage represents an area between movable barriers that both protect the individual from hurt and deprive the individual of deeper need fulfillment. Beginning with the most distant form of communication, the following discussion shows how these levels can develop in counseling.

Stage 8: "You talk to me"

This is the most distant area of communication. The person sits across from the counselor with the nonverbal message "It's your move." This could occur as the person walks into the counselor's room for the first time, or it could be the fiftieth counseling session. The message is "I don't know what to say" or "I won't say anything."

Stage 7: "Let's talk about it"

"It" means inanimate subjects like the weather, which team won the game last night, the office decor, the scheduling of appointments, or the fee. Although every session includes some "it" talk, the more it invades the session, the less psychological closeness develops between the person and the counselor.

Stage 6: "I'll talk about them"

"Them" is anyone but the person in counseling and the counselor. "Them" can be parents, spouse, children, roommates, dates, fellow employees, and employers. A person in counseling may discuss others in a manner dissociated from himself or herself (for example, "My roommate is going to quit school after this semester" or "I think my boss is heading for a nervous breakdown").

The person in counseling may also discuss others whose actions affect him or her directly or indirectly (For example, "My parents are talking about getting a divorce" or "My boyfriend is thinking of going away to college"). In either case, the information is shared in an impersonal, matter-of-fact way.

"They" talk is relatively safe because "they" are not present and because it ordinarily places a distance between the person and the counselor.

Stage 5: "I'll feel about them"

This stage adds feelings to Stage 6, and this is an important addition. A person may say "My parents are thinking about getting a divorce, and I'm torn between feeling sorry for them and being furious at them" or "When my boyfriend told me he was going away to college, I almost panicked." With the addition of feelings, the focus shifts from "them" to the person in counseling and gives the counselor more material with which to help the person.

Stage 4: "I'll talk about me"

The focus here is on the person in counseling, but is limited to factual information. The person may say "I flunked my English exam yesterday." The counselor may respond "How do you *feel* about it?" And the person may reply "Well, it means I'm going to have to study a lot harder." The person declines to answer the counselor's question and merely adds more factual information.

Many people never have progressed past this stage and become confused and frustrated when the counselor says "You are telling me about what you *thought*, but you are not telling me about what you *felt*."

Stage 3: "I'll feel about me"

This stage adds feelings to the information given at Stage 4. A person may say "I didn't get the promotion, and I was really surprised and disturbed by my reaction. I always felt I wasn't a competitive guy or a person who was interested in material things. But I guess I've been fooling myself, because I'm more depressed than I've ever been before."

Stage 2: "I'll talk to you about you"

The "you" in this stage is the counselor. This person feels secure enough to share thoughts about the counselor directly with him or her. For example, a person might say "I haven't told you this before, but I think you are really a fine person," "Sometimes you really distract me," "I think you were half asleep today," or "I think you're disappointed in me." Stage 2 responses don't *always* reflect a growing confidence in oneself and the relationship. For example, an aggressive person may communicate Stage 2 messages in the first session: "You sound just like my father, and he's the cause of my problems." But, ordinarily, Stage 2 responses are a sign of good progress.

Stage 1: "I'll share my feelings about you with you"

In this last stage, the person is adding feelings to Stage 2. For example, a person may say "I feel very good being with you now," "I really hate you when you pin me down like that," or "I'm frightened that I'm becoming too dependent on you."

Ordinarily, Stage 1 communications are a sign that a person has developed a good deal of self-confidence, confidence in other people, and confidence in the counseling relationship. Often, some of the most productive and rewarding work in counseling is done at this stage. However, a cautionary note should be added. If counseling begins to focus on Stage 1, so that large amounts of time and energy are spent on the relationship between the person in counseling and the counselor, this could be regressive and damaging. The reason is that the counseling relationship can be used as a paradigm of a psychologically healthy relationship, but should not become an end in itself, reducing the need and dampening the motivation of the person to focus on relationships outside of counseling.

Practical implications

There are several practical implications that flow from the schema in Figure 8-1.

Quality of communication. It's important for the person in counseling, as well as the counselor, to realize that quantity of communication in counseling is not nearly as important as quality. People in counseling and counselors can talk up a storm at each session with very little being accomplished. It is important for at least the counselor to be aware of the relative closeness of the communication so that progress can take place within the counseling relationship.

The counselor's role. It is important for counselors to realize that they also move on the continuum from Stage 8 to Stage 1—"You talk to me" to "I'll share my feelings about you with you." A counselor is unrealistic to be relating primarily on Stage 8 or Stage 4 and expect a person in counseling to relate on Stages 3, 2, or 1.

The best invitation to "come down a number" is to be at the number oneself. This concept is opposite to early ideas of the role of the counselor, which placed the counselor at Stage 8 and viewed the other stages as unprofessional. Again, a note of caution is necessary. When attention is focused on the counselor and his or her thoughts and feelings rather than on those of the person in counseling, then the counseling has become that of the counselor and not that of the person. The counselor goes to Stages 4, 3, 2, and 1 to facilitate the person's progress toward these stages, and not as ends in themselves. For example, the counselor may say "I was so angry with my students today, I almost walked out of the class," to which the person in counseling may re-

COMMUNICATION IN COUNSELING 209

spond "That's just how I felt when my kids met me at the door last night full of complaints."

Shifts in stages. In general, progress in counseling can be measured by the person's growth through the various stages. Typically, the early part of counseling finds the person at Stages 8, 7, and 6; the middle part, at Stages 5, 4, and 3; and the final parts, at Stages 2 and 1.

After people are in counseling for a while, they may develop a range. In the middle phase of counseling, they may start a session at Stage 7, go to Stage 3, and finish the session at Stage 5. The same is true for counselors, thus giving an accordion effect of two people moving closer at times and further apart at other times. Also, one person may move closer while the other moves further apart.

Shifts in stages often appear within a single session. Counselors can use these shifts as barometers to measure atmospheric changes in the relationship and to trace them to their source. For example, a person may begin the session at Stage 2 and suddenly regress to Stage 8. This obviously signals that something dramatic has occurred, and it is incumbent on the counselor to help the person discover what it is.

Progression through the stages. It is not helpful to force a person through the stages. It is often frustrating for a counselor to terminate counseling successfully with a person who relates easily at Stages 2 and 1 and start anew with the next person, who may well be back at Stages 8, 7, and 6. Sometimes there is a tendency to try to pull people through the stages prematurely rather than to allow them to move at their own pace. On the other hand, sometimes it is necessary to nudge people toward a less distant stage or they will remain at distant stages throughout counseling.

Progress to less distant stages of communication in counseling usually precedes progress outside of counseling. Often people who have progressed to Stage 4 in counseling may be communicating at Stage 5 outside of counseling. Progress outside often lags by one or two stages until the end of counseling.

Individual differences. It is important for a counselor to know how much progress to expect realistically from a person. One person may have fairly good psychological strength and enters counseling at Stage 3. All other factors being equal, this should be short-term counseling. Another person may enter at Stage 8 and stay there for the first three or four sessions. Perhaps a reasonable goal for this person is reaching Stage 4 or 3. Counselors need not feel they must help a person progress to Stage 1 for counseling to be successful. While that is the ideal, the combination of a particular counselor with a particular person in counseling may make termination at Stage 3 or 4 more realistic. A third person may enter counseling at Stage 3 and, because of deep psychological blocks, take two years in counseling to reach Stage 2 or Stage 1.

Applying the schema.   This is a theoretical schema and is meant to demonstrate one phenomenon of communication in counseling. Trying to use it in a concrete, absolute way will lead only to confusion and frustration.

SUMMARY

Communication between the counselor and the person in counseling is the heart of the counseling relationship. As long as the communication conduits are open, ideas and feelings can flow freely between the two people. The trouble with open conduits is that both pleasant and unpleasant ideas and feelings can flow through them. The counselor must invite all communication, even that which is difficult to receive. By the same token, the counselor can create a trusting relationship so he or she can also share anxiety-producing communication with the person in counseling. Once the communication lines are open, they will not automatically stay open forever. The counselor and the person in counseling must continually unclog the conduits and reinforce them. This is a full-time job.

THOUGHT QUESTIONS

1. This chapter states that some commonly evoked emotions are anger, eroticism, confusion, guilt, fear, and helplessness. Every counselor has at least one area of vulnerability. Which of these six reactions would you be most vulnerable to? Why?
2. What is your strongest asset as a communicator and what quality do you need to improve in order to be an effective communicator as a counselor?
3. Regarding listening to messages, a person says to you after three sessions "I'm really lucky I got you for a counselor. You seem to really care about me and understand where I'm coming from." What are at least four dynamics that could be occurring here?

4. The most common barrier to listening is that people simply don't want to listen. What kind of content in a counseling session would you find difficult to listen to?

5. Some counselors purposely sit in certain ways, talk in measured tones, and look chronically empathetic. They do this in an effort to communicate care, warmth, and acceptance. They don't know it, but what are they *really* communicating?

CHAPTER 9

Avoiding Reality in Counseling

People hide parts of who they are from themselves and others. The fact that people do not view themselves objectively is one of the greater obstacles to personality growth both in and out of counseling. The more people know themselves—that is, their deepest needs, feelings, and motives—the more accurate their psychological map will be, enabling them to navigate a clearer path through life. The more there are hidden, unexplored parts, the more confused and lost people become.

The hidden territory is comprised of needs, feelings, and motives that, if recognized, would create significant anxiety. One of the main goals of counseling is to reduce the area of uncharted self so that a person's psychological map will be more accurate and helpful.

The behaviors used to avoid threatening parts of reality are defense mechanisms and defense tactics. This chapter discusses those defense mechanisms and defense tactics that are likely to be encountered in the counseling relationship.

DEFENSE MECHANISMS

A *defense mechanism* is unconscious or subconscious behavior designed to help people perceive something they strongly need to perceive, even though it is not present in reality. Defense mechanisms also allow people not to perceive something they don't want to perceive, even though it is present in reality.

An underrated dynamic

Defense mechanisms may be the most underrated dynamic in human behavior because people do not like to admit that they are capable of fooling themselves in important matters. People don't like to recognize that they *need* somebody more than they love him or her; that someone is not as fond of them as they think; that they hurt people, and not always for their own good; that they are freer in a particular situation than they pretend, or less free than they'd like to think; that they are less competent in some areas than they think; that their altruism sometimes is a camouflage for self-serving behavior.

Even psychologically healthy people can, at times, unknowingly hide parts of themselves from awareness so that they will experience less anxiety about themselves and life. Therefore, it is important that counselors have a sound knowledge of defense mechanisms so that they and the people they see in counseling will remain, as much as possible, on paths that lead to growth.

Early learning

Defense mechanisms are learned very early in life. Three-year-olds typically use denial ("I didn't spill my milk"—even though there is milk all over the table and no one else has been in the room); projection (*"You* made me spill my milk"—even though there was no one within 15 feet); and somatization ("I don't want to go to school today—my stomach aches").

As people develop intellectually, they may discard primitive defenses for more sophisticated ones. For example, a college student may no longer use denial ("I didn't cheat on the exam") but may have graduated to rationalization ("Sure I cheated. I'm not going to let some neurotic professor's unfair exam keep me from getting into law school, where I can learn to help thousands of poor people"). By the use of rationalization, the student has turned cheating not only into acceptable behavior but into virtuous behavior.

Many families have a favorite defense mechanism that the whole family employs. Projection as a family defense can be seen in the following dialogue in a family counseling session:

> *Husband to counselor:* My wife's problems are beginning to interfere with my whole life. I'm even starting to get in trouble at work.
>
> *Wife to husband:* If you'd take a stronger stand with the kids and not let them run the house, it would reduce *my* problems by 90%.
>
> *Teenage daughter to parents:* I don't think things were that bad until

we started this stupid counseling. Now the doctor has us *all* upset.

This interchange gives a good clue as to why the family's problems are not getting solved; no one is assuming any responsibility for them.

People in counseling can be helped to unlearn their defenses and to learn to face reality squarely. Ideally, a person can be taught to become allergic to the inordinate use of defense mechanisms so that reality creates less anxiety than does the thought of hiding from it. The more a person has used defense mechanisms and the larger the repertoire of defenses, the longer it will take to unlearn them.

Anxiety-producing situations

People with good psychological strength are capable of allowing a great deal of threatening material into awareness without feeling inordinately anxious. People who lack psychological strength frequently use defense mechanisms to avoid threatening reality. For example, a young man views himself as a good student but receives a grade of "C" as a final mark in a course. The dissonance between the concept he has of himself and the reality of receiving a "C" causes anxiety. To reduce the anxiety, the young man uses the defense of projection ("The professor is incompetent; that's why I got a 'C' ") or rationalization ("My roommate had serious psychological problems that affected me all semester"). By employing these defenses, the young man can continue to perceive himself as a good student when, in fact, he is simply an average one.

It would seem that people would tend to hide the negative parts of their personality and welcome the positive ones. But this isn't always true. Some people hide the positive parts of themselves and welcome the negative. For instance, a young woman perceives herself as unattractive and uninteresting. Although she doesn't especially like feeling this way, she uses these feelings as excuses to withdraw from people. In other words, her negative self-concept provides her with protection against becoming close to people and risking hurt and rejection. One day a young man asks her on a date, which creates cognitive dissonance between her negative self-concept and the positive reality. To reduce the anxiety, she assures herself that he must have been dared by his fraternity brothers to ask her out or that he has some nefarious motives.

This young woman has a vested interest in tilting a positive reality into a negative one because she can then continue to withdraw. If she allowed herself to entertain the possibility that she is more attractive and interesting than she thinks, she would have to relate more with people and take more risks, which would present a great threat. In other words, she'd rather feel unattractive and be safe than attractive and risk hurt. She would rather *think* that she is uninteresting than begin relating with people and risk *knowing* it.

It is important for counselors to realize that, for people with negative self-concepts, positive reality can be as threatening as negative reality is for people with positive self-concepts. Counselors can be careful not to enter into a tug-of-war with these people, insisting that the person has some very positive points while the individual insists that he or she does not. If this occurs, the counselor is likely to become frustrated and eventually communicate the sentiment "How could you be so stupid as not to see how attractive you are!" With this thrust, the person wins the tug-of-war. It may be more productive for the counselor to help these people recognize the defensive quality of their negative self-concept and develop the psychosocial competencies to deal effectively with the threatening reality.

Problems with defenses

One problem with defense mechanisms is that hidden parts of the personality do not disappear. Uncharted psychological territory affects a person's psychological atmosphere in a very real way. A man may deny that he is angry at his wife, but the anger still affects their relationship. Hiding material from awareness is tantamount to hiding a fiery wastebasket in a closet. Although the fire is "out of sight, out of mind," the basket will smolder in the closet and eventually will cause more damage than had it been found and dealt with immediately.

The second problem is that hiding parts of the personality is analogous to navigating with an inaccurate map. The map tells people where all the smooth roads are located, but it fails to apprise them of the dead-end roads and cliffs. The navigator will run a confusing and sometimes dangerous course, often repeating the same mistakes and arriving at the wrong places with the wrong people.

A third problem with defense mechanisms is that they usurp energy that could be used for growth. The more defenses people employ, the more energy they allocate to their "defense budget." People who use many defenses are often fatigued, apathetic, and susceptible to illness because of their depleted energy and resistance.

Counseling implications

Responding to defense mechanisms. Defense mechanisms are analogous to crutches. It is better for healthy people not to use crutches because they impede progress. But if someone has a sore foot or a broken leg, crutches become a lesser of evils; that is, it is better to use crutches and remain mobile than to refuse them and come to a standstill or fall.

Defense mechanisms can be helpful at times. For example, in crisis situations, they buffer a pain that would, in its raw form, cause great anguish. In these cases, defense mechanisms allow a person to retreat, recoup, and return to the painful reality and deal with it effectively. But when a person typically uses defense mechanisms to avoid stress, they are cumbersome, energy depleting, and weakening. In this situation, the counselor can help *melt* defense mechanisms in counseling so that the person can let go of the crutches they provide. The main way is to strengthen people as a whole so that they no longer need the crutches of defense mechanisms and gradually discard most of them.

The second way is to *nudge* the defense mechanism directly, explain to people how they are using it, and extend an invitation to let go of it. In other words, the counselor gently nudges the crutch to see if the person can walk without it.

For example, a person in counseling may say "My wife's drinking is causing our family to disintegrate." A counselor may respond at the right time "I'm sure her drinking is creating some real problems at home. Could it be that if you could learn how to handle her drinking more effectively, things could get a little better?" The counselor is nudging the person's crutch of projection. If the husband is ready to discard it, he might reply "I see what you mean. Maybe I'm contributing to some of the tension because I don't *want* to deal with the problem well. In fact, I wonder if I don't use her drinking sometimes as an excuse to misbehave."

If the husband is not ready to discard the defense, he will reply "Well, we had a happy family before she began to drink. If she would stop drinking, we could be the same happy family again." The counselor may want to nudge further: "I understand what you're saying. It's only that sometimes how we handle a problem can make things easier or harder, and I'm wondering if it's possible that you could be handling the problem a little better." The person may reply "Well, it could be I'm not handling it very well. I'm sure open to suggestions." Or the person may respond "Hey, I *told* you; it's *her* problem. I don't need anyone putting another trip on me—I get enough 'trips' right now, thanks." This is a door-closing response. For the counselor to pursue the point any further will only entrench the defense, thereby increasing the length of time it will take to melt it.

Defense nudging is different from *defense shoving,* which can be damaging. In defense nudging, the counselor gently tests the defense to see how much support it is to the person. In defense shoving, the counselor pushes the defense. This results in the person falling off balance or pushing back equally hard to maintain equilibrium. The following is an example of defense shoving.

A man may tell the counselor, "I love my wife so much; I don't know why I hurt her this way." A counselor may shove this man's defenses by stating "Well, I think you *need* to feel that you love your wife so much. But it sounds to me like you may have strongly mixed feelings toward her, and that's what's causing the behavior you're concerned about."

The counselor's interpretation may be correct, but because he or she grabbed rather than reached for an insight, the person's defense system may have inadvertently been reinforced. This kind of "too much too soon" response is a major cause of people terminating counseling as the ultimate defense against a shoving counselor.

Defenses can also be *ripped away*. Ripping away defenses is never helpful. Defense mechanisms are like scabs on a wound; they cover a sore until the organism has time to heal. In a counselor's impatience to heal a wound, he or she may rip away the scab, but this is often countertherapeutic for three reasons: It is unnecessarily hurtful; it only causes another, thicker scab to grow; and it prolongs the healing process.

Counselors who are inclined to rip away defense mechanisms generally exhibit one of the following characteristics. They may have difficulty creating a nurturing atmosphere that will gradually strengthen the person so that the defenses fall off naturally. They may be impatient and want to "cut through the garbage and get the job done." This may be a good axiom in business or politics, but it is ordinarily a damaging one in counseling. They may be hostile and attack the person in counseling under the guise of being helpful ("I'm hitting you for your own good"). The following is an example of defense ripping.

A man may tell a counselor "I didn't go for any job interviews again this week. I had a bad cold during the first part of the week, and my car broke down after that."

The counselor may reply "Bullshit. You didn't go for job interviews because you are petrified of getting a job. You are scared that you'll fail the interview or that you'll get the job and bug everybody so much like you always do that you'll have to 'resign' your third job this year."

Although this type of counselor reaction could be helpful to a particular person at a particular point in counseling, ordinarily it would not be a therapeutic response. The counselor may receive a grade of "A" for insight but a grade of "F" in being helpful. The only time that defense ripping "works" is when the person's defenses are about to fall away anyway. The question then arises: Why set up a state of antagonism when warmth would work just as well? The adversary system may work well in a court of law, but it rarely works well in counseling.

Defense mechanisms can remain untouched by the counselor—that is, allowed to remain and function. Since one of the main goals of counseling is to introduce people to themselves, allowing defense mechanisms to remain unchanged would be atypical. But there are two situations in which a counselor may not wish to melt defenses at a particular time.

The first situation occurs when the counselor and the person make a deal. The counselor implicitly communicates "If you will admit that you really want a divorce, I'll let you feel that you still love your husband very much and that you've done everything possible to keep the marriage together." Although "dealing" in counseling may not be the best way to help people grow, it may be necessary at times. In this example, it could be that progress in counseling has come to a standstill for some time because the woman cannot admit to herself that she really wants to divorce her husband. If the obstacle can be removed by the woman admitting she wants a divorce, then this will open the door to examining the whole situation more clearly and helpfully. The counselor may later confront the woman with her role and responsibility in the deteriorating marriage.

The second situation in which a counselor may not want to touch a person's defense system is in a crisis situation. For example, a man may come to a counselor in a state of panic. He tells the counselor that his wife just left him and took the children with no warning. He is acutely agitated and torn between killing himself and killing her. He relates a litany of wrongs that his wife has perpetrated on him and the children and clearly sees himself as the victim and his wife as the villain.

This would not be the time for defense nudging, defense shoving, or defense ripping. The first goal in this situation is to reduce the man's anxiety and to clear his thinking so that he can take some appropriate action. It is not the time to increase his agitation by confronting him with all the inconsistencies of his story and his obvious use of projection as a defense.

Allowing defenses to remain does not mean that a counselor agrees with or reinforces the defenses, since this would be dishonest and cause significant problems later in the relationship. Counselors can listen to the defenses and respond that they understand how the person must feel, but to agree with the defenses is harmful. In the previous example, the counselor could respond "You feel very angry, frightened, and confused. If your wife did all the things you say, I certainly can understand it." The person in counseling may be so agitated that he may not even hear this response but may feel the support. Or the person may respond "Well, she *did* do them—there's no doubt about that," to which the counselor nods in understanding. Or the person may respond "Hey, don't you *believe* me that she did all those things?" The counselor may answer "It's very hard for me to know, because I wasn't there. But I think we have a problem here that needs solving, no matter who or what caused it."

To agree with the person's defense system—that is, for the counselor to respond "Your wife sounds like a very disturbed person"—would be burning bridges that may be useful later in counseling. For example, it will be harder to get the husband to accept his responsibility in the situation. He will undoubtedly tell his wife what the counselor said, thus creating a great obstacle to her joining them in counseling. Deep down, the man himself may have lost some confidence in a counselor who was induced to choose sides so easily.

Person's use of defenses.   A person entering counseling often brings an overworked defense system that is causing one of two problems. It may have been successful in helping the person evade difficult parts of reality, but the price for such evasion is what brings the person into counseling. Second, the overworked defense system may have worn thin, and previously hidden thoughts, motives, and feelings are seeping or flooding into awareness.

In either case, the person has a strong need to repair and strengthen the defense system. This is the reason most people enter counseling— to continue to dodge reality but without paying the price that they are presently paying. Even when people protest that they want to face reality and learn to deal with it effectively, this is often (but not always) a ruse to lull both them and the counselor into a false sense of confidence.

It is important for counselors to realize that people bring into counseling the same defense system that has often worked very well for them, and the unwary counselor can easily fall victim to it, just as many others have. It is a humbling thought but a true one that even the best counselors can be deceived.

Naive counselors will be deceived often and never know it. Wary counselors will seldom be deceived, but their suspiciousness will do more harm than good. Vigilant counselors are neither naive nor wary. They know that what sounds good isn't necessarily good and are able to help the person appreciate the difference. The following is an example of how people in counseling can attempt to deceive counselors by using defense mechanisms. In this and other examples throughout this chapter, keep in mind that people can make similar statements and not be deceiving themselves or the counselor. However, in the following examples, assume that the person's statements and the counselor's interpretations are determined more by defense mechanisms than by reality.

The person may come into counseling and tell the counselor "I didn't feel like coming today, but I knew it would be good for me. I'm trying not to give in to my scared self—so here I am." The counselor may be deceived by this defense mechanism and reply "Well, that's a good sign! It sounds as if your healthy self is beginning to gain some control."

But if the hidden part of the person could have spoken, it might have said "I don't think I'm getting anywhere in counseling. But if I didn't come today, it would have made me face that realization more squarely, and then I would have to do something about it. I would either have to decide to terminate counseling or to talk about my feelings of discouragement. I'm not ready to do either; so it's easier for me to keep the appointment and pretend that things are progressing nicely."

Counselor's use of defenses. Counselors also employ defense mechanisms, both in their personal lives and in counseling. A counselor's knowledge of behavior is not an automatic safeguard against using defenses. In fact, knowledge of behavior can be used to hone a rather ordinary defense system into a very sophisticated one. Knowledge of behavior can be used to justify actions that would have been unjustifiable in the person's "unwashed" state. For example, a person may have been rather timid about expressing anger before studying counseling. But now that he or she understands that "a counselor must be confrontive" to help people face themselves, the person feels justified in insulting and lambasting people in counseling. The counselor's pent-up frustrations and anger have, through the magic of rationalization, become a "therapeutic tool."

The following example shows how counselors can use defense mechanisms to deceive themselves and, consequently, deceive the person in counseling. A counselor may tell a person in counseling "I think I've been getting lenient with you and letting you drag your feet in counseling. I'm going to have to get a little tough with you, but it's for your own good." The person responds "Well, maybe that's what I need. I usually function better if someone gives me a kick once in a while to keep me honest."

Although neither the counselor nor the person may be aware of it, the hidden part of the counselor is saying "This guy's passivity reminds me so much of my father's, which I hated. I can't do anything about my father now, but I can 'beat up' this guy under the guise of 'toughening him up,' and that will make me feel better."

Counselors must always recognize the possibility that they could be deceiving themselves and the people they see in counseling at any given time. One safeguard is for counselors to discuss their cases with supervisors or colleagues.

The common factor in all these examples is that each person heard what he or she wanted to hear and consequently was reluctant to entertain any other possibility. When both the counselor and the person can approach each other with "This is what I *think* I feel, but we'd better see if that's what I *really* feel," counseling will progress more effectively.

Counselor and person negotiations. The defense mechanisms of the person in counseling can negotiate with those of the counselor and vice versa. This dynamic is as powerful as it is subtle. The hidden agreement between the counselor and the person evolves from the basic theme "I won't unearth your most hidden parts if you don't unearth mine." The covertness of this agreement cannot be overstressed. The following is an example of defense negotiations between a person in counseling and a counselor.

A woman in counseling has two deeply hidden parts: one is that she would like to leave her husband and find a more affectionate, healthy mate; the second is that she has deep religious doubts hidden beneath religious fervor. The counselor also has two deeply hidden parts: he doubts his skills as a counselor, and he feels guilty for charging a large fee.

The specific agreement between the defense systems of the counselor and the person may read as follows. Person to counselor: "If you don't make me look at my desire to leave my husband and at my serious religious doubts, I won't make you face your inadequacy as a counselor or your guilt for charging more than most other counselors." The "No Trespassing" areas are clearly posted. These two people could meet for a hundred or three hundred hours and discuss every conceivable topic and problem without either one trespassing. And in so doing, both could feel that progress has been made, pointing to what, in reality, are only superficial changes in behavior. Both terminate counseling feeling that it was a successful endeavor. And according to their hidden parts, it *was* successful. Both people paid their respects to mental health without having to face themselves and make any significant changes. The good feeling that accompanies the termination of counseling stems from the relief that the hidden parts were not unveiled.

Warning shots are often fired in counseling to enforce the negotiated agreement between the defense system of the person and that of the counselor. The counselor may inadvertently approach the "No Trespassing" sign of the person in counseling: "You say you love your husband, but do you ever feel, deep down, it would be nice to relate with someone different for a change?" or "You tell me frequently how thankful you are for a strong religious faith, but sometimes I wonder if, deep down, you have some doubts that aren't easy to look at?"

The person may now fire some warning shots. To the latter question, she replies "Where in the world did you ever get such an idea? The one thing I have to cling to is my faith, and you're trying to take that away from me! I thought you were supposed to be *helping* me, not *destroying* me. I'd be better off talking to a priest. At least *he* would appreciate my values and have the skills to help me live them out. And he'd be an awful lot cheaper, too."

The message is clear: "You'd better back off or you'll get hurt." The counselor receives the message and responds "I didn't mean to upset you. The question just passed through my mind. If you feel comfortable with your religious beliefs, I guess that's all that's important." The counselor realizes that he has touched upon one area that is surrounded by thick defenses, but comforts himself with the idea that she is not ready to deal with the situation; so he tags it for a later time. After the counselor backs off and the woman feels safe, she apologizes for her outburst and assures him that she is fortunate to be seeing him. The counselor tells her there is no need to apologize, that it was a healthy exchange, and they both move on to less threatening and less important topics.

Some people have an uncanny ability to detect the deepest fears in others. Good counselors possess this ability. But counselors can remember that many people in counseling also have this ability. The more hidden or unaccepted fears counselors have, the more they are vulnerable to psychological blackmail. In the previous example, if the counselor felt reasonably confident in his skills and felt justified in charging his fee, he might have responded to the woman's outburst in one of the following ways:

Could you tell me more about why you are upset with me?
Could we talk more about the idea that your faith is all you have to cling to?

You seem to feel that sometimes I don't know what I'm doing or that I say some pretty foolish things.

Let's talk about my fee for a few minutes since that seems to be concerning you.

The counselor demonstrates both his self-confidence and his genuine concern for the person by gently remaining steadfast and helping the woman gingerly explore some frightening territory. He may or may not get far at this time, but he is teaching the woman something that is very important—namely, that she has a strong and caring counselor and that, sooner or later, she will have to confront her deeper fears.

Common defense mechanisms

People who study or practice counseling know what defense mechanisms are. They know their names and definitions. But an academic knowledge of defenses and a working knowledge of them are very different. Counselors can be intellectually familiar with defense mechanisms; yet their counseling sessions may be replete with them, although the counselors are unaware of it. Counselors frequently encounter the following defense mechanisms, both in the people they see in counseling and in themselves.

Repression.   Repression means that a thought or feeling is intercepted before it reaches awareness. A person in counseling may assure the counselor "I'm not upset that you canceled our appointment last week. You need a day off just like anyone else." This statement alone could be an indicator of repression or it could be accurate. The nonverbal communication that accompanies the statement often gives telltale signs that repression is operative. If the person says it a little too jovially, defensively, or casually, it could indicate that some resentment is being repressed.

Depending on the circumstances, a counselor may wish to deal with the discrepancy between the statement and the accompanying nonverbal communication or just tag it and come back to it later. If the counselor deals with it immediately, he or she may start with a general approach and narrow it to a particular one. For example, the counselor may state "A lot of people feel upset when their counselor cancels an appointment. Is there a part of you that feels a *little* upset?" The person may answer "Well, I hadn't thought about it, but now that you mention it, I was a little irked." With gentle encouragement, the person may get in touch with some anger and be able to communicate it.

On the other hand, the person may respond "No. As I said, I can understand why you'd need a day off. If anything, I felt relieved that I didn't have to come in." Again, depending on the circumstances, the counselor may drop it there or may continue "The reason I asked is that you seemed to be trying to convince me that you had no upset feelings; so I was wondering if you felt that maybe you shouldn't have those feelings."

The person may respond "Well, you've done so much for me, I guess I feel that I don't have the right to feel angry with you, just because you miss one session." This statement presents a clear possibility that, with a little permission from the counselor, the person will be able to release some feelings. Or the person may reply "As I told you *twice*, I wasn't angry. It sounds as if you would like me to have been angry, but I assure you I wasn't!"

This statement is a door-closing one; hence, the counselor probably would be better off dropping the topic but remaining alert to unconscious leakage that would indicate that the person was upset. For example, the person may go on to state "You'd think with a two-week interval, I'd be brimming over with things to talk about, but I really have nothing to say. Why don't *you* talk today for a change?"

On the other hand, there may be no observable leakage, which indicates the person is either too frightened to loosen the repression or is not repressing any feelings.

Obviously, counselors cannot stop people at every turn and search them for defense mechanisms; however, counselors can realize that people get themselves into trouble by repressing just a little thought here and a little feeling there. As they allow dust to accumulate under the rug, they begin tripping over it, hurting themselves and those closest to them. If a counselor can teach a person in "here-and-now" circumstances to bring up particles of dust and deal with them, there can be much transfer of learning to situations outside of counseling. So when the woman goes home and her husband says "I'm sorry I'm home late for dinner; I hope you're not upset," she may now say "Well, I am upset, and here are the reasons."

Counselors can also use repression to screen out threatening ideas, feelings, and motives. For example, a counselor may have sexual feelings toward a woman he is seeing in counseling. Instead of admitting them and dealing with them constructively, he represses them. This causes him to avoid sexual topics, to take an unnecessarily confrontive approach to keep her at a distance, or to create a situation that leads him to suggest that she see another counselor. So while conscious sexual feelings may have caused him some anxiety, which he could have dealt with constructively, his repressed sexual feelings sabotage the counseling relationship.

Denial.   Denial is the inability to acknowledge threatening aspects of reality. The following is an example of denial in a person in counseling.

> *Person:* You always see me so late in the afternoon, you must be pretty tired by the time you have to listen to me.
> *Counselor:* Does it seem to you that I'm tired when we meet?
> *Person:* Oh, no! No, I didn't mean that. No, I meant only that it must be hard to listen to someone's problems after a long day.
> *Counselor:* You feel that maybe my concentration may be running a little thin by this time?
> *Person:* No. I only mean that it must be hard for you.
> *Counselor:* Could it be that you feel I'm not as interested or energetic when we meet?
> *Person:* No. I don't want to make a big deal about it. Let me tell you about what happened to me this morning.

Depending on the situation, the counselor can continue dealing with the denial. For example, she may say "Well, why don't we spend just a few more minutes on this because I'm picking up some concern from you that may be legitimate. If you had a choice, would you choose an earlier time?" Or the counselor may drop the issue, either because it is relatively unimportant compared to the issues she knows will be dealt with in the session or because she feels it will be fruitless to pursue the matter at this time.

A counselor may also use denial. A person may say "Why does counseling cost so much? You must admit that you guys charge outrageous fees. What if I didn't have the money? Would you see me anyway?" Anger surges within the counselor, who responds with a tight voice, reddened face, and forced smile "You are concerned about the cost of counseling?" The person responds "Are you *angry* that I asked that?" The counselor responds too quickly "Of course not! It's a very reasonable question. Don't worry. If I were angry, I would tell you." The problem is that the person *does* know it, and the counselor *doesn't*. The counselor is teaching the person, firsthand, how to use denial to avoid unpleasant reality.

Projection.   The defense of projection has two functions. First, it transfers the blame for a person's shortcomings, mistakes, and misdeeds onto others. Second, projection allows people to attribute their unacceptable impulses, thoughts, and desires to others.

A married woman tells her counselor that she is seriously considering termination because she "knows" that the counselor thinks she should leave her husband, and she feels she never wants to do that. In fact, the counselor is not leaning in one direction or the other. The woman is projecting onto the counselor her unconscious wishes to leave her husband. In projecting these feelings onto the counselor, she can terminate counseling before she need acknowledge and accept her wishes to leave her husband.

Projection is a defense available to counselors as well. For example, counselors can easily blame the person in counseling for any lack of progress. Counselors can assure themselves that if only the person were "more motivated," "less passive," "more mature," or "less resistant," counseling would progress nicely. But the first question the counselor can ask is "What could I be doing differently to help untrack this person?"

Counselors also use projection when they attribute their own motives or feelings to the person in counseling. For example, a counselor may tell a person "I've noticed in the past few sessions that you seem to be placing an emotional distance between us." In fact, it is the counselor who is withdrawing emotionally because he is beginning to feel personally attracted to the person and fears it.

Rationalization.   Rationalization allows a person to present logical and socially approved reasons to justify behavior and also to soften disappointments or failures. The following is an example of how people in counseling may rationalize.

A woman may say to her counselor "I canceled our appointment last week because my mother was sick, and I didn't feel I should leave her alone. And then I was having trouble with my car and felt if my car broke down, it would really create problems for me. And I had to study for a final exam that I had to take that night."

The counselor is aware that none of these excuses sounds particularly valid, and the sheer number of them underscores the feeling that there is more to the canceled appointment than the woman is letting on to the counselor and possibly to herself.

The counselor may respond "It seems that last Tuesday was a very tough day. But I wonder if there was something about coming to counseling last week that didn't feel just right to you, even if none of the other things had happened." If the real reason for the canceled appointment is barely out of consciousness, this response could invite it into awareness. If the real reason is further from awareness, more work will be necessary.

Counselors can also use rationalization in counseling. For instance, a counselor may receive a note from someone in counseling stating that he is terminating because he thinks he is getting worse instead of better. To soften the disappointment and the possibility that she made some mistake with this person, the counselor assures herself that the man's motivation for counseling was poor and that it's better that he terminates now instead of wasting more time. This allows the counselor to avoid considering the situation any further. If the counselor had looked at reality squarely, she could have understood the reason for the note and contacted the man. They possibly could have met one more time to discuss the situation and attempt to resolve the problem. Whatever the man's final decision, the counselor would have learned something and felt better about the situation.

Intellectualization. People use intellectualization to interfere with or cut off such normal emotional responses as anger, hurt, fear, or guilt from the event that caused them. The following example shows the intellectualization of a person in counseling: "I was deeply upset when my fiancée broke up with me last week, but now I'm seeing the situation much more clearly. She is a 'daddy's girl' who is used to getting her own way with men and having them fall all over her. She was attracted to me when I was still in the dependency stage of our love; so I was into being her slave. Her wish was my command. Of course, the more I babied her, the more she worshipped me. But being in graduate school really accelerated my maturity. I'm no longer a starry-eyed adolescent. I want a mature woman who wants a husband to relate with and not a daddy to play with. She obviously couldn't handle this change in me; so she is off trying to find someone else to order around. I can't tell you how lucky I feel that this happened *before* we were married."

This young man has used his intellect to sever his feelings from awareness. He is deeply hurt that his fiancée broke off with him. He feels confused, inadequate, lost, and revengeful. His counselor will have to do some psychological suturing—that is, find the severed feelings and sew them back to the corresponding event. This will enable the young man to get in touch with his feelings so that he can deal with them more constructively.

Counselors also can intellectualize in the counseling relationship. A person in counseling states "I'm really depressed today, and I don't know why. But this is the first time I've ever felt that it would be nice to have a fatal disease and die." The intellectualizing counselor responds "Well, by now you should know why you're depressed. Remember we talked before about how repressed anger causes depression. You are furious at your husband but felt if you told him, he would go out and get drunk again. You allow him to manipulate you covertly with his drinking problem. As long as you do that, you will be depressed."

In reality, the counselor may be alarmed at the woman's increasing depression. But instead of being in touch with these fears and sharing personal concern, the counselor gives her a lecture and effectively squelches his feelings rather than using them to help the woman.

Reaction formation.   Reaction formation enables an individual to flee from disturbing feelings or desires by assuming their opposite. The following example indicates how this defense can be used by a person in counseling. A woman says to her counselor "Remember last week when I said I don't think counseling has helped me one bit; in fact, I thought it made me worse? Well, I gave that a lot of thought during the week and came to realize that for me even to have said that to you was proof of the tremendous amount of progress I've made. My only concern now is to adequately show my appreciation to you."

This woman may have scared herself with her honesty and anticipated being rejected by the counselor, just as her parents had rejected her when she was "too honest." She quickly recouped and did an about-face, guaranteeing that she not only would not be rejected but would be accepted more than ever.

The counselor can help this woman by responding "I think you said some very important things last week, and I'm afraid we're going to lose them if we just move to the next topic. I'm sure you had good reasons for what you said, and it would be helpful for us to go back and take a further look at them." This type of response will help the woman recognize how she typically switches from her real feelings to their opposite in order to avoid assuming responsibility for them.

Counselors can also use reaction formation. They can be overprotective to hide their deeper feelings of not caring. They can be optimistic to cover their feelings of discouragement. They can be overly accommodating to camouflage their feelings of dislike. They can be overly strong to hide their feelings of weakness. They can be overly active to compensate for their feelings of boredom. The problem is that these counselors' deeper feelings will subtly emerge and contaminate their counseling efforts.

Introjection.   Introjection occurs when a person acquires another person's values or opinions, even though they are contrary to his or her previously held attitudes. By doing this, the person becomes like the other in order to reduce anxiety and to feel safe.

A man in counseling may have good reason to feel that he is a homosexual, even though he feels very uncomfortable about it. His counselor, however, tells him that he does not think that the man is a homosexual but that, instead, he is suffering from a lag in psychosexual development. The counselor expresses this opinion with confidence and obviously wants to believe it. The man likes the counselor, fears him to a certain degree, and lacks the psychological strength to disagree with him. It does not take long for the man to adopt the counselor's opinion and launch out on what is likely to be a frustrating journey toward trying to acquire a heterosexual orientation.

This defense is likely to be seen a good deal in counseling, but it is passed off as "cooperation," "good motivation," and "positive transference."

Counselors can also use introjection. A person may angrily tell the counselor "We've got to do something now about my daughter's counselor because he is ruining her. I know you counselors all stick together; so I don't expect you to agree with me."

The counselor responds "Well, it's because I am a counselor that I am concerned about the methods of your daughter's counselor. Let's see if we can't draw up a sensible plan of action so that we can nip this situation in the bud."

The person in counseling in this situation is very strong and threatens the counselor. A counselor who did not introject could have said "I have two reactions to what you just said. One is that I'm angry that you think I would defend a counselor even if I thought he or she was wrong. The second is that you are emotionally involved at this point; so I think we should try to separate the facts from your feelings and perceptions. When we do this, you'll feel more confident that whatever you do will be appropriate and helpful." Instead, the counselor identified with the aggressive person and introjected his opinion to prevent the tension that an honest response would have created.

DEFENSE TACTICS

In addition to the classic defense mechanisms, people can use other tactics to avoid facing themselves, to keep people at a safe distance, and to defer accepting responsibility for their behavior. Although defense mechanisms and defense tactics share a common goal, they are different behaviors. Defense mechanisms serve a more intrapsychic purpose; that is, they protect persons from their threatening parts. Defense tactics also prevent others from discovering the threatening parts of the person. In other words, defense mechanisms are oriented more toward intrapersonal protection, and defense tactics are oriented more toward interpersonal protection.

One is likely to see the following defense tactics in counseling. As with defense mechanisms, people employing these behaviors may be completely unaware of their defensive function or only partially aware of the protective service that the behavior provides.

This discussion focuses on the person in counseling and not on the counselor because, although counselors can also use defense tactics, the ones discussed here are more likely to be used by the person in counseling.

Pedestaling

The person in counseling places the counselor on a pedestal. The person's attitude toward the counselor is "I admire, trust, and respect you greatly. Just tell me what to do, and I'll do it." As far as the person in counseling is concerned, he or she is simply realistically acknowledging the wisdom, benevolence, and expertise of the counselor. However, on a deeper level, pedestaling has three defensive functions.

1. Placing the counselor above the person makes it difficult for the counselor to confront the person directly. The dynamic is similar to that between an adoring son and his father. How can the father present anxiety-producing reality to his son who so looks up to him? When the father does, the son's reaction says "And I thought you really loved me." In the counseling relationship, the pedestaling person attempts to strike a deal with the counselor: "I'll admire and appreciate you as long as you don't do anything to increase my anxiety."

2. The person who is in an inferior position to the counselor defines her role as following through on the counselor's suggestions. The counselor who attempts to get the person to look for causes and solutions to her problem is met with the retort "*I* don't know the answers to these questions. That's why I came to *you—you're* the expert; *you're* supposed to tell *me* what to do."

3. Since this person has come to counseling to get answers to his problems, he is not interested in being "analyzed." This means that the counselor is not invited to question his motivations or feelings or to offer insights, interpretations, or any feedback that would create anxiety.

In a short time, the counselor discovers the limitations of trying to operate from a pedestal. Unwary counselors can be caught in this dynamic by allowing themselves to be bought off by respect and docility. They remain on their pedestal and offer suggestions. However, sooner or later they are faced with the reality that the person has not grown in any substantive way since counseling began.

Counselors who are going to be helpful remove themselves as early as possible from the pedestal. This best begins in the first session in a spirit that reorients the person to the proper role of the counselor. There may be a period during which the person will make repeated efforts to hoist the counselor back on the pedestal, but the counselor can strenuously resist these efforts while pointing out the reasons for the resistance.

Humor

Although humor can be healthy and have salutary effects, it is more often used as a defense in counseling. Humor can be used as a defensive behavior in three ways.

First, it can be used to derail an important dynamic in counseling. For example, just as the counselor brings the person to the brink of an important insight, he or she makes a humorous remark, thus derailing the dynamic. The counselor now has the choice of dealing with the defensive nature of the humor, for which she will be viewed as being "too serious," or she can participate in the humor, rationalizing that the person is not ready for the insight.

Second, humor can be used to express anger at the counselor. This usually takes the form of a "just kidding" joke. The person laughingly says to the counselor "Gee, you look more depressed than I do. Is there anything *I* can do for *you*? Ha, ha, I'm just kidding." By couching the anger in humor, the person does not have to take responsibility for the angry feelings and, at the same time, the counselor cannot respond in anger because the person *said* she was "just kidding." The counselor has the choice of letting the comment go, of facing the person with the defensive nature of the comment, or of laughing at the comment to prove that he is a "good sport."

Third, humor can be used to conceal a person's deep anxieties. The amount of humor and laughter some people exhibit during a session is directly correlated with the amount of anxiety they are feeling. They relate painful memories and events with laughter and a wide grin. They tell the counselor "and then my father hit my mother" as if it were the punch line of a joke. The artificial humor these people inject into situations protects them in an often unhelpful way from their painful feelings. These people work on the principle "If I don't laugh, I will cry."

Counselors can smile along with these people or gently confront them with the discrepancy between what they are saying and feeling and the humorous facade.

Agreeableness

Some people in counseling are very agreeable; that is, they agree with everything the counselor says and does, no matter how negative or unsubstantiated it is. They seem continually to nod their head in agreement, even before the counselor has said anything with which to agree or disagree. Agreeableness has three defensive functions.

First, it precludes any tension or conflict arising between the person and the counselor. This person has low stress tolerance and manages to escape the ordinary stresses of life by being agreeable. However, stress is an important catalyst for growth, and to the degree that people avoid everyday stress, they will remain stagnant or regress.

Second, agreeableness can successfully camouflage who the person really is. As long as the person agrees with the counselor, he or she need not make any personal declaration or revelation. The counselor's attempts to relate with the person are deflected by statements such as "I see," "I'd really like to help you, but I just don't know the answer," and "I hate to admit it, but I think you're right." The agreeable person's attitude toward the counselor is "You tell me who I am, and I'll agree with you" instead of "Let me tell you who I am, and I'll agree with you when I think you're right and disagree when I think you're wrong."

Third, agreeableness relieves the person from taking responsibility for decisions. As long as these people agree with and cooperate with the counselor, they do not have to make their own decisions, which may or may not please the counselor.

One indication that a person's agreeableness is a defense is when the agreement with the counselor does not manifest itself outside the counseling room. For example, a man heartily agrees that he should confront his boss with how he feels and may spend a whole session preparing for the confrontation. At the next session, the man does not mention the confrontation because he forgot about it as soon as he left the counselor's office. In other words, agreeable people feel that agreeing to something is as good as doing it, especially when it reduces their anxiety within the counseling session.

Counselors can initially be fooled by agreeable people because they appear to be open, cooperative, and motivated. The defensive function of the person's agreeableness is not manifest until the counselor recognizes the pervasiveness of the agreeableness and realizes that it is not matched by action.

Cuteness

Adults can be cute in a number of ways, all of which are vestiges of childhood behaviors that worked, and still work, to rescue them from facing the inappropriateness of their behavior. Cute behaviors are mostly nonverbal and involve the eyes, the mouth, the tilt of the head, and gestures. These nonverbal behaviors communicate messages such as:

> Oh, there goes silly me again.
> Gosh, do you really think I did that *on purpose?*
> I know it wasn't nice of me to do that, but it *was* funny.
> Oh, darn it—I tried *so* hard but messed things up.
> Oh, you're not going to be upset with me, are you?
> I know that sometimes I'm mischievous, but I don't mean to hurt anybody.
> Let's stop being so serious; let's play for a while.

Cute behavior performs the following defense functions. First, when these people perceive themselves as being cute, it hides the real destructiveness of their behavior. Instead of facing the damage they are doing to themselves and others, they tend to view their behavior in a semihumorous way. Since they don't quite take themselves seriously, their anxiety seldom reaches a point where it will motivate them to change their behavior.

Second, their cute behavior is meant to seduce the counselor into enjoying and protecting them, just as one does a child. They can offer a powerful invitation that reads "Come on, let's be cute together." The counselor is invited to play and flirt with the person. The purpose of this dynamic is to get counselors to abandon their role and allow these people to continue with their irresponsible behavior.

Third, cute behavior often places the counselor in a no-win situation. If the counselor accepts the invitation to indulge the cuteness, counseling will not be effective and, in fact, will not occur. If the counselor declines the invitation and attempts to point out the defensive function of the behavior, the person is likely to pout and accuse the counselor of being a "stuffed shirt" or of not liking the person.

Being confused

There are times when people in counseling are genuinely confused. However, much of the time confusion is a defense that serves four purposes:

1. Confusion can act as a smokescreen to protect the person from facing unpleasant reality. For example, a man reports obvious indications that his wife no longer loves or respects him and wishes to end the marriage. However, instead of being in touch with his hurt, fear, guilt,

and resentment, he reports only that he is "terribly confused by what's going on." His confusion acts as a buffer between himself and threatening feelings.

2. As long as a person in counseling is confused, he does not have to take any action. In the previous example, as long as the man can't figure out what's going on, he does not have to move in the direction of confronting the reality of his marital problem. Consequently, he has a vested interest in remaining confused for as long as possible.

3. The person's confusion can be contagious and cause the counselor to become confused also. Consequently, both people stumble through the fog being equally ineffectual and far removed from the real issues.

4. Prolonged confusion in counseling causes frustration in both the person and the counselor. The more confused they become, the more frustrated they become. They blame each other for the miasma in which both are caught. As they struggle with their frustrations and subtly or overtly blame each other, they become two stages removed from touching the issues that are causing the person's problem.

Acting stupid

Acting stupid is different from being ignorant. Acting stupid means that, on a deeper level, people know what they are doing and what consequences are likely to flow from their behavior. Being ignorant means that people genuinely are not capable of grasping the meaning and possible consequences of their behavior. One example of acting stupid is seen in a married man who spends an increasing amount of time with his unmarried secretary after work. Over a period of time, they date frequently, and although she assures him that she is not interested in marriage, she dates no one else. They become intensely involved both emotionally and sexually, and the woman begins to pressure the man to leave his wife and marry her or she will break off the relationship. This situation fills the man with anxiety and consternation, and it is this distress that brings him to counseling. He assures the counselor that he had no intention of getting into "this mess" and now wants the counselor to get him out of it. Although any objective observer with reasonable intelligence could have told this man that the situation could turn out in no other way, he is utterly surprised and is at a loss as to how the whole situation occurred.

This example illustrates the three defensive functions of acting stupid. First, it protects the person from anxiety-producing reality. The man wanted to face neither his deteriorating marriage nor the fact that he was actively and volitionally creating a romantic relationship with his secretary, the result of which could only be a source of great stress no matter how it turned out. As long as he acted stupid, he could have his cake and eat it too without paying for it.

Second, it allows people to avoid assuming responsibility for their behavior. When the situation caves in on top of them, these people can appear astonished and wonder what went wrong. The man mentioned in the example defines himself as a victim both of the woman and of circumstance. His question to the counselor is "How could this have happened to me?"

Third, acting stupid and its destructive results can focus on a bogus problem. The person defines his problem as one of naivete and stupidity. He asks the counselor to make him less naive and more intelligent; in other words, he wants to define the problem in intellectual terms. In fact, however, he is not naive or stupid, but wants things that he is neither able to admit to himself nor for which he is willing to accept responsibility.

Helplessness

Some people present themselves in counseling as helpless. They do this in one or all of three ways: They cannot figure out what their problem is; they don't know what is causing the problem; or they don't know what to do to solve the problem. Helplessness is a defense when it serves one or more of the following functions.

1. It induces the counselor to take over for the person. These people define the counselor's role as telling them what their problem is, what caused it, and how to solve it. By doing this, these people remove themselves as a creator or contributor to the problem and pass the responsibility for solving it to the counselor.

2. As long as these people remain helpless, they cannot move because no one, including the counselor, can successfully make them move in the direction of growth. So while these people protest that they want to solve their problems, they also ensure that things will remain exactly the same, which is the way they want them to be.

3. It can cause the counselor ultimately to agree with the person that he or she is helpless. The counselor may try budging the person in one direction or another, but to little or no avail. After repeated attempts and increasing frustration, the counselor may give up and agree that the person *is* helpless. This further reinforces the person's position, which is what he or she really wanted from counseling.

Being upset

Some people in counseling are genuinely upset and have a right to be. Others, however, use being upset as a defense. Being upset can function as a defense in two ways. It can provide sufficient distraction so that the person does not recognize what is causing the upset or what obvious steps must be taken to solve the problem. For example, a woman may be so upset that her husband is leaving her that all she has to be is upset. She does not have to consider her contributions to the problem; she does not have to think about what she must do now to help herself and her children adjust to the new situation. It is easier and safer for her to be upset than to face reality and handle it as well as possible.

Second, when people in counseling are using upset as a defense, they must be treated so delicately that the counselor is like a surgeon who must try to operate on a patient without making an incision. These people pretend that they are asking for help when they are actually telling the counselor to leave them alone. Attempts by the counselor to encourage these people to confront people and situations that are obstacles to their growth are met with some version of "Handle me with kid gloves or I'll just fall apart (or blow up)." People are left with the option of treating this person like a Ming vase or a keg of dynamite.

Religiosity

Religiosity is different from healthy religious belief. It can interfere with the person's making psychologically healthy decisions. These people do things that are psychologically destructive because they feel that their religion tells them to do so, or they refrain from making decisions that would be psychologically healthy because they feel that their religion forbids it. Hence, it is not they who are directing their lives, but their religion. These people use religion as a prison rather than as a freeing, loving influence in their lives. Their position in counseling is that they are suffering but there is nothing they can do about it since to go against their religious beliefs would substantially increase their suffering. Religiosity has four defense functions that protect people from further anxiety.

First, they may be waiting for God to send them an answer. They participate in counseling in a perfunctory way because they feel that the only real solution will come from God. The less they trust and use counseling, the more they regress and the more they call upon God for help, which further removes them from counseling. They can't allow counseling to help them because it would suggest to them that counseling can do more for them than God, and that thought would create intolerable anxiety. What appears to be deep faith in God is, in this case, actually a deep fear of facing a problem. If God directly intervenes, the person will get relief without having to face this reality.

Second, religion can be a defense when it allows a person to suppress "sinful" feelings such as anger, sex, jealousy, resentment, doubt, and distrust. These people feel that getting in touch with these feelings would make them worse than they already are. In fact, if they were not religious people, they would create another reason for not getting in touch with these feelings because they are so threatened by them.

Third, religion can be used as a defense against allowing the counselor to get close to them. Under the banner of "You must respect my religious beliefs," these people keep the counselor at a safe distance. The counselor who attempts to loosen the bonds of the person's unhealthy religious beliefs is met with some variation of the response "If you were as religious as I, you would understand my position."

Finally, these people often approach counseling looking for a counselor who shares the same religious beliefs, but they are unlikely to find one because their beliefs are opposed to sound psychological and spiritual health.

Decoying

Decoying means that the person presents superficial problems to the counselor in order to protect deeper ones. With these people, counselors must work their way through a medley of decoy problems until they finally reach the deepest and most important one.

For example, a college student's presenting problem is that he is unmotivated academically and socially. As this problem evaporates under examination, the next problem that enters the picture is that he has a problem with his father. The time and energy spent on this problem do not change his low motivation. The next problems that appear concern his girlfriend, his roommate, his studies, the death of a sibling years prior, his overweight, his poor self-concept, and finally, with great anguish, he reveals his homosexual anxieties. It is with the resolution of the last problem that he becomes motivated and reports taking a more active interest in studies and social activities. Counseling soon terminates because the man's presenting distress has been resolved. It could be that the counselor successfully worked through the decoy targets to the real one. It could also be, however, that the person's homosexual fears were a decoy problem and that he "got better" because the counselor was getting dangerously close to the real problem.

The real problem is that the young man believes that in order to be worthwhile he must be a great success professionally, marry a beautiful woman, and have a large family. Deep down, however, he does not want to be a great success. He would much prefer to have a nonprofessional job that would afford him a modest income and allow him a good deal of stress-free time to enjoy life. He also is very ambivalent about marriage and would prefer to remain single for a long time, if not forever.

He is faced with the choice of being "successful" and being unhappy or of living according to his deeper needs and values and feeling like a third-class citizen. As graduation approaches, his anxiety increases because graduation signals the start of the most important race in his life—a race that he can't win. Hence, the poorer he does in school, the longer he can put off entering the race.

This example illustrates the following functions of decoying:

1. It allows the man to think he is working to solve his problem while allowing him to hide it from himself and the counselor.
2. It allows the counselor to think that the positive changes in the man's behavior reflect a solution to the problem. This leads the counselor to agree with the man's assessment that he is ready to terminate counseling.
3. It allows the man to return to his symptoms shortly after he leaves counseling, so he can continue to forestall graduation.

SUMMARY

Defense mechanisms and defense tactics are prevalent in counseling. People bring to counseling the same defenses that they have employed throughout their lives and that worked sufficiently well to maintain them. People cannot be expected to abandon their defenses simply because they walk into a counseling room. Therefore, a great deal of time in counseling will be spent recognizing defenses and dealing with them, only to be met with a new barrage of defenses. The more defense mechanisms and defense tactics people employ, the longer counseling will take.

Because dealing with defenses is an important part of counseling, counselors can be aware of their role in this regard. They can be aware of the various disguises of defense mechanisms and tactics so that they can detect them as early as possible. Sometimes this is easy, especially when the defenses are unpolished and blatant. But many times defenses are almost imperceivable and hide beneath behavior that appears to be most cooperative and reasonable. With increasing experience, counselors will be able to detect the subtle type of defense more readily.

Counselors can help the person recognize the defensive nature of the behavior in ways that don't reinforce the defenses. This can be as challenging as telling a man he needs a hearing aid when he is convinced that he hears perfectly well. Defense mechanisms and tactics have become an integral part of many people's functioning; so they are often unrecognizable to the person. It is not helpful to assume automatically that people *know* they are using defenses and all the counselor needs is to call it to their attention. This could indicate to the person that the counselor is on a very different wavelength and that communicating with this counselor is likely to be impossible.

Counselors can also realize that they will get caught in the web of defense mechanisms and tactics and that this is true of all counselors. When counselors realize that they have been bound by the person's defense activities, they can begin to extricate themselves as quietly and calmly as possible. It is not helpful to burst forth from the chains with a flurry of activity and accusations, thinly veiled as "insights," for the person to consider. When counselors are sufficiently relaxed, they can communicate some variation of "I'm beginning to see something happening here, and I think it would be helpful for us to discuss it."

Finally, it is important that counselors learn to become increasingly familiar with their own defense mechanisms and defense tactics. Just as the person in counseling does not check defensive behavior at the door, neither does the counselor. As counselors grow in experience, they can begin to feel defenses welling up inside and say to themselves "Be careful, you're beginning to slide away from the real issue here by denying that it is important or by needing to be agreeable more than wanting to be helpful."

THOUGHT QUESTIONS

1. Of the seven defense mechanisms discussed in this chapter, which one do you think could most fool you? Why?
2. Of the seven defense mechanisms, which is your favorite? Under what specific circumstances are you likely to use it?
3. Of the ten defense tactics, which one would it take longest for you to spot in a person in counseling? Why?
4. Of the ten defense tactics, which one would you be most likely to use and under what circumstances?
5. There seems to be a subtle trend developing recently in counseling for counselors to assume that people *really do* know exactly what they are doing, even though they pretend that they don't. Why do you think this trend is occurring? What problems do you see with it?

CHAPTER 10

Resistance in Counseling

Resistance is present in most counseling relationships. Resistance means that the person in counseling and/or the counselor are less than fully committed to effecting positive behavioral changes. Resistance can be mild, which is analogous to foot dragging; it can be moderate—that is, the person is standing still—or it can be serious, as when a person moves backward.

Only the most naive counselor would think that being in counseling is an obvious sign that a person is dedicated to change. In reality, most people in counseling have ambivalent feelings toward change, and some people have a vested interest in not changing. Because resistance in counseling is common, it is important for counselors and people in counseling to understand the causes and signs of resistance.[1] This knowledge paves the way for appropriate responses.

REASONS FOR RESISTANCE

There are at least three reasons why a person in counseling resists cooperating with the counselor in his or her efforts to bring about growth in the person. First, growth is painful. Second, maladaptive behavior performs a service for the person in counseling. Third, countertherapeutic motives often bring a person to counseling.

[1]For another discussion of resistance, see Weiner (1975), pp. 160–201.

240

The pain of growth

The pain of growth in counseling is analogous to what a person in physiotherapy experiences when muscles are being stretched and exercised in new ways. There is almost always a price to pay for becoming stronger, and sometimes the price is dear. During the initial phase of counseling, it gradually becomes clear to the person that a good deal of hard, continuous work lies ahead. The person learns that there is no magic, no shortcuts. It is at this point that people often ask only half-kiddingly, "Isn't there just some pill you can give me to make things better?" or "Can't you just hypnotize me and get this all over with?"

In counseling, changing behavior means two things: stopping old behaviors and starting new ones. Both stopping and starting will create tension, and sometimes the tension will reach painful levels. When this occurs, the person will want to slow down, stop for a while, or quit. If it were possible to calibrate this starting and stopping with complete precision, the tension would never become painful. In reality, however, this is not possible, and perhaps it is good that it is not. If we could grow or regress painlessly, our behavior would be dangerously mercurial.

Starting new behaviors. It is typical that, as a result of counseling, persons may have to start some new behaviors. They may have to *be honest* with significant others. Most people find it difficult to be honest with one person, much less with many people. Honesty can create anxiety in both the person who expresses it and the person who receives it. So the person in counseling often will try to avoid opportunities to be honest with significant others. There is often a bargaining that takes place between the counselor and the person in counseling: "If I'm honest with my mother when I go home this weekend, can I wait a while before I'm honest with my father?" Such pleas reflect the pain involved in sharing deep thoughts, feelings, and questions with loved ones.

They may have to *become self-reliant.* One situation that often brings people into counseling is that they have been overreliant on others for advice and acceptance. They will often state "I'm so confused. My mother says that I should go to college; my father says I should work or go in the service first; and my fiancée says we should get married and move to Canada." When the counselor responds "What do *you* want to do?" the look on the person's face is exactly the same as it would have been had the counselor asked "What is the Doppler principle in physics?" Obviously, no one had ever asked this person what *he* wanted to do, and he had never asked himself. Some people have used others as crutches all their lives, and they find it painful to start the process of walking on their own.

They may have to *admit self-deceit.* Most self-deceit lies in the areas of feelings and motives. People deceive themselves into thinking that they feel one way when they actually feel another. A man may enter counseling certain that he adores his mother and gradually realize that he resents her greatly. A woman may feel that she loves her husband and may discover through counseling that she is very ambivalent toward him. These discoveries are painful because they often create guilt and because the person will have to act on the new insight.

The same is true for motives. A man may enter counseling saying he wishes to become a clergyman in order to serve God better. He soon discovers that he wants only to serve *himself* better. Now what is he going to do with his life, which had been so carefully planned? A woman may think she is withholding sex from her husband because she is angry at his excessive drinking, but she discovers that the reason is that she has become increasingly uninterested in sex. This can be a frightening discovery.

They may have to *reexamine basic beliefs and values.* Many people enter counseling unaware that the resolution of their frustrations and conflicts will require the reevaluation of a basic belief or value.

A man may have always uncritically accepted the idea that he would be happiest being married. After five years of marriage, this belief is being severely tested.

A woman may have always believed that she is a very skilled trial lawyer, but after three years of numerous failures, she must reexamine this belief.

A woman may have grown up with a particular concept of God. Because of the growth that is taking place in her, this image of God appears unrealistic, and she may even doubt the existence of God.

An adolescent has always believed his parents loved him dearly, but their recent behavior makes it necessary for him to reexamine the validity of this belief.

The scrutiny of basic beliefs and values is the cornerstone of existence. Changing beliefs and values can be very threatening. Such changes send shock waves through people and are understandably often resisted, sometimes with a vengeance.

Stopping old behaviors.   People in counseling may have to *stop a favorite behavior.* Some common favorite behaviors are getting drunk, having an affair, pitying oneself, impressing people, manipulating others, withdrawing from people, and doing nothing. Each of these can meet needs and reduce tension. When they have been used successfully for these purposes for years, it will be difficult to discontinue them. But it may become clear in counseling that such behaviors are self-destructive and, until they stop, little progress can be made. Favorite behaviors can become addictive and stopping them often causes painful withdrawal symptoms.

They may have to *stop pretending*. Many people who enter counseling are pretenders, although they would never define themselves as such. They pretend to be effective workers when, in fact, they are mediocre. They pretend that they are liked by many people when, in fact, their admirers are few. They pretend they know more than they do; that they are happier than they are; that they are braver, more religious, more caring, and more interested in changing than they are.

Perhaps an equal number of people are "negative pretenders"; that is, they pretend to be worse than they are. They pretend to be weaker than they are; less happy, competent, attractive, or intelligent; more sinful, fragile, depressed, scared, or hopeless than they really are. It is the task of the counselor to introduce reality to these individuals, and this pursuit is often fraught with anxiety for both the person and the counselor.

They may have to *terminate an important relationship or job*. When it becomes obvious that a relationship or job constitutes an unhealthy environment, the person must seriously consider terminating it. A relationship may be between the person and a parent, a fiancée, a spouse, or a friend. Breaking up relationships can be excruciatingly painful, so painful that some people would prefer to terminate the counseling relationship rather than the unhealthy personal one.

Quitting a job can also be traumatic. When a person has studied and worked for years to become a member of a profession and discovers that it was never the right profession for him or that he has outgrown it, a change can send strong reverberations throughout his entire self.

They may have to *stop making excuses*. It is a rare person in or out of counseling who accepts responsibility for personal difficulties and failures. People in counseling frequently make excuses for their shortcomings. A counselor asks a man why he thinks he's been divorced twice when he is not yet 25 years old, and the man replies "I just married a couple of lemons." A woman, when asked why she had an affair, responds "My husband was more interested in his work than in me." An adolescent boy explains his poor performance in school as due to his father's drinking problem, and the father blames his drinking problem on the son's rebellious behavior.

Excuses for problematic behavior will be clung to tenaciously because once the excuse is dropped, the person must accept responsibility for the behavior. And in accepting responsibility, he or she must do something active to rectify the situation. The man who married two "lemons" may find it easier to marry a third lemon and start an orchard than to spend two years in counseling finding out which of his needs drove him into such damaging decisions.

Even the psychologically strongest people would find the eight behavioral changes described anxiety producing, often to the point of pain. Since few people enjoy pain, most would not pursue these changes with total joy and dedication. If this is true for psychologically strong people, it is that much more true for psychologically insecure people. Sometimes counselors do not fully appreciate this fact, become frustrated, and assume the attitude "Look, just go out and do it—it's not that big a deal." It is a quirk of human nature that other people's pain does not seem painful to us. Yet honest counselors are aware of personal foot dragging on some changes that should be made in their own lives. This insight can breed empathy.

The functions of maladaptive behavior

People in counseling resist changing behavior for a second reason: they have a vested interest in maintaining maladaptive behavior. All behavior meets a need, and the more frequently a person participates in a behavior, the greater the need that is being met. Therefore, when people enter counseling with maladaptive behavior, there is always a compelling reason for it, a reason that will not be exorcised merely by the act of entering counseling. People will cling to maladaptive behavior until there is good reason to believe that the substitute behavior will be equally satisfying or anxiety reducing.

Maladaptive behavior can provide four psychological services for the person. These services are not healthy, but they play an important role in the person's dynamics. Throughout the following discussion, alcoholism will be used as one example of a maladaptive behavior that provides various services for the person.

Fulfilling psychological needs. Maladaptive behavior can fulfill a person's psychological needs, albeit in a destructive way. For example, the alcoholic may find that when he is intoxicated, he receives significantly more attention than when he is sober. The attention may be positive (for instance, his family may protect and nurture him), or it may be negative (for example, his family may scold and ridicule him). In either case, he learns that when he is intoxicated, others automatically pay attention to him. When he is sober, he is often ignored. This reflects how maladaptive behavior meets important psychological needs when a person lacks the competencies to get these needs met in constructive ways.

Providing distraction.   Maladaptive behavior can provide a distraction and can act as a decoy from more basic problems that would be even more painful to face. The alcoholic defines his problem as alcoholism. But his problems are deeper than that. His drinking is an effect, not a cause. He drinks because he feels painfully inadequate, is terrified of life, is filled with rage, has failed miserably, has fears about his sexuality, is permeated with guilt over long-repressed behavior, has grave doubts about God, or because of a combination of some or all of these issues. It is much simpler and easier for him to tie all these various problems into one package and call it "alcoholism." He will resist giving up the package for fear of discovering his problems are worse than he had thought.

Venting anger.   Maladaptive behavior can provide an effective, although destructive, outlet for anger. Often people who are not in touch with their anger or cannot communicate it directly and constructively allow their maladaptive behavior to be a messenger of the anger. In this way, they can deny their anger, but at the same time release it. The alcoholic who, when he is sober, is "the nicest guy in the world" becomes a dangerous weapon when he is intoxicated. What he says, does, and doesn't do damages his loved ones. He tells them he hates them. He may physically assault them. His foolish behavior in public embarrasses them. His unsteady employment forces them to go to work and to lend him money. When he becomes sober, he is deeply sorry, apologizes, and begs for forgiveness. In this way, his rampage costs him nothing. In fact, loved ones, to hide their feelings of resentment toward him, "overforgive" him and actually reward him for the destruction he has wrought. He will not give up his maladaptive behavior without a fight.

Atoning for guilt.   Maladaptive behavior can provide an effective but unhealthy way of atoning for guilt. Most, if not all, maladaptive behavior has a self-tormenting dimension. This serves to punish and cleanse the person. For example, when a little boy steals a cookie, he feels guilty. If he doesn't get caught or punished, the pressure of the guilt builds in him until he can no longer bear it. Finally, "for no good reason," he walks across the room and socks his sister in front of his parents. Predictably, the parents then sock him, and this punishment relieves much of the pressure of the guilt. The boy transfers the punishment meant for hitting his sister to his theft of the cookie. This dynamic continues since he still has not atoned for the guilt for hitting his sister. He will have to drive his bike carelessly, fall, and skin his knee to atone for that. This same dynamic is a part of most maladaptive behavior.

Because of his excessive drinking, the alcoholic often loses: family and friends, self-respect, the respect of others, money, jobs, intellectual acuity, sexual capacity, and health. On the surface, these appear to be tragedies. But on a deeper level, the person may experience a sense of relief and purification. Until this man can get in touch with his guilt feelings and atone for them in constructive ways, his only method of reducing the pressure of guilt is to punish himself through drinking. He will not surrender this safety valve easily.

Counselors who invite people in counseling to relinquish their maladaptive behavior must offer something in its place. The distance between getting needs met destructively and finally having learned to meet them constructively often resembles an endless desert. Sometimes the only solace a counselor can offer a person is to walk and sometimes crawl through the desert with him, holding him up when he wanes.

Countertherapeutic motives

The third reason that people in counseling are ambivalent about changing is that they enter counseling for motives other than positive behavioral change. The following are some of the other motives, both conscious and unconscious, that bring people into counseling.

To get permission not to change.   These people seek assurance from the counselor that they are fine just the way they are. Although they confidently tell the counselor of their willingness to do anything to make their lives less conflictual, their behavior in counseling suggests otherwise.

Under the pretense of searching for behaviors that need to be changed, they are not looking very earnestly. In fact, they may steer the counselor away from discovering maladaptive behavior. These people often voice some variation of the sentiment "Gee, this is disappointing. We turned that last topic upside down and every which way, and we found nothing to work on." When the counselor does discover a problematic area, it is invisible to the person, or the person insists that the behavior is not problematic. The counselor's suggestions for change are politely and subtly ignored, resisted, or declined. The person's hidden hope is that sooner or later the counselor will have to admit "Well, I've evaluated you thoroughly, and I have to give you a clean bill of health." This is the actual goal of counseling for these people.

To validate a decision. Some people have, whether they are aware of it or not, already made a decision to leave a marriage, change jobs, get married, have an abortion, quit school, or begin or end a relationship before they contact a counselor. They are merely bringing the decision to an expert for a stamp of approval.

These people may not be aware of what they are doing. On the surface, they are wrestling with the decision and are open to whatever the counselor has to say. On a deeper level, however, they are accepting only what the counselor says to support their decision, sifting out what doesn't agree. The counselor's attempts to give equal consideration to the other side of the issue are often met with well-disguised resistance. The person may respond "That's a good point. I hadn't thought of that. I'll have to give it some serious consideration." But the person returns to the next session proclaiming "I was so busy this week, I didn't have time to think about it"; "I thought about it and even discussed it with some of my friends, but we all agreed it was nothing to worry about"; or "Let's see. What *was* it we were talking about last week?"

To prove that someone else is to blame. The "someone else" may be a child, parent, spouse, friend, or boss. Counseling sessions are viewed as court appearances in which the judge (the counselor) will be swayed by a preponderance of the evidence to rule in favor of the person in counseling.

For example, parents may enter counseling with their 17-year-old son for the stated purpose of "improving our communication." But the real purpose is for the parents and the counselor to gang up on the boy and agree that he is the sole perpetrator of the family's problems. The counselor's attempts to improve communication are successful only when the communication provides evidence against the boy. When the communication focuses on other important areas or hints that the parents may share the responsibility for the family's problems, the parents are no longer interested in improving communication. At this point, the parents are likely to protest to the counselor "See, now *even you* are starting to think the way he does!"

To vent hostility on another. These individuals view counseling as an armory where they can obtain ammunition to vanquish their foes. A person may enter counseling with the implied message to family and/or friends "Look what you've finally done to me." This message is subtle, hidden beneath protestations such as "I know I'm the cause of so much conflict at home" or "My family and friends have been saints to put up with me for so long. I decided to give them a break and get some help."

Gradually, however, the real motive for entering counseling surfaces. The person returns home from counseling sessions sharing the rather benign insight "I thought it was all my fault. But now I'm learning you are part of the problem, too." After a while, the messages become less benign: "Dr. Smith says you are trying to mold me into someone I'm not." Then, "Dr. Smith wonders how I've maintained my sanity as well as I have living in this situation." Finally, "Dr. Smith says that you need counseling as much as I do, and if you don't get it, I'll have to move away."

No matter what the counselor says or does, it will end up as ammunition. The counselor is drafted as a part of the "hit team." Efforts to focus on this dynamic or undertake other issues are met with strong resistance.

To manipulate others. These individuals enter counseling to qualify as "psychologically infirm." They feel that if they can make "the clinic" an important part of their lives, people will start treating them better. Once they can present themselves as disabled, people will take better care of them, protect them from stress, relieve them of responsibility, and understand and forgive their misbehaviors. These people emit a fragile aura so that no one wants to be responsible for pushing them "over the brink."

When the counselor refuses to pamper these people, they react as a paralyzed person would when the doctor demands that he or she get up and walk. If the counselor gets enticed into treating the person as fragile, there will be no conflict. But the counselor who tries to erase the 'Handle with care" sign will be met with massive resistance.

To prove they are beyond help. People want to prove they are beyond help for two reasons. One is that they have several people tugging at them to become someone they don't want to, or can't, become. They figure if a doctor will pronounce them dead, everyone will leave them alone. The second reason is that if someone diagnoses them as "hopeless," they won't have to try any more.

These people paint only the gloomiest picture of themselves and their environment. They make it clear that if the counselor has any sense at all, the consensus will be that there is nothing to be done.

Attempts to resuscitate the person are scorned as a waste of time and met with bemused resistance. Every time the counselor spots a vital sign, the person quickly explains that it was merely an illusion.

To defeat the counselor.   Sometimes people have known the counselor as a teacher, lecturer, or writer and view him or her as a worthy opponent for their pathology. These individuals have identified with their internal aggressor; that is, they have become proponents of their pathology because they find it easier to join it than to fight it.

At other times these individuals symbolize the counselor as a hated parent, spouse, friend, society, or God. This dynamic is analogous to dressing up a punching bag to resemble a hated person, then attacking the bag as if it were that person.

In either case, the person's secret goal is to defeat and, in some cases, to ruin the counselor. Attempts will be made to outsmart, outfight, and outseduce the counselor. Obviously, the counselor's attempts to promote the person's growth will be used against him or her.

Although these people are difficult to work with, some of them can be helped. Think of the boy who picks a fight with a bigger boy, but the bigger boy holds his ground without fighting back. The smaller boy may begrudgingly respect the other boy at first and later even learn to like and admire him. The same dynamic is possible in counseling.

To satisfy others.   Some people have been manipulated into counseling against their will. A parent, spouse, friend, boss, or judge presents counseling as part of an ultimatum: "Either get help or I'll leave you" (or "you'll be fired" or "you'll go to jail"). This individual chooses counseling as the lesser evil.

Obviously, this is not an ideal situation, but it is not inherently unworkable. If the person's attitude is "Well, this can't hurt; so I might as well see what happens," it may be only a short distance to helping the person see the benefits of counseling.

If the person's attitude is "Well, I'm here. But you can't make me relate with you," the distance from this point to cooperation is significantly greater but not necessarily infinite. The counselor can take one of three positions:

I don't see people in counseling who don't come in on their own.

Well, I'll play along for a while until one of us gets tired.

As long as you're here, maybe we can agree on something worth working on.

The first and last positions are better than the second one, in which the counselor is functioning more as a baby-sitter than as a helper.

The unhelpful motive that brings a person into counseling need not be irreversible. Counselors can help people gradually realize what their deepest motive is and describe the negative consequences that follow from it. The counselor then can help the person replace the unhelpful motive with a more constructive one. Occasionally, a person loses all interest in counseling once the negative motive has been extracted. When this occurs, it is better to agree to discontinue counseling. The person can be assured, however, that the door is always open in the event that his or her motivation changes.

METHODS OF RESISTANCE

When people resist changes in counseling, there are often perceptible signs. The following indicators can reflect the presence of foot dragging, standing still, or regression in counseling. These indicators are a type of defense tactic, geared specifically to reduce the amount of time and opportunity that the counselor and the person in counseling have to focus on the person and to achieve the agreed upon goals of counseling. (Other defense tactics have been discussed in Chapter 9.)

Attitude toward appointments

Being late for appointments is a fairly reliable sign of resistance. By being late, the person loses precious minutes of an already limited amount of time. By the time the person catches his or her breath, explains the reasons for being late, apologizes, and listens to the counselor's reaction to the tardiness, another 10 or 15 minutes of counseling has elapsed. Elapsed time is not necessarily wasted time, however. If the counselor can help the person understand the meaning of being late for appointments and come one step closer to discovering the particular causes of resistance, the time could be well spent.

Other possible signs of resistance are failing and canceling appointments. A failed appointment means that the person simply did not come to the session, giving the counselor no forewarning. This usually is a sign of massive resistance. The dynamics underlying failed appointments usually include a good deal of anger along with fear.

Canceling appointments once in a while is expected in counseling. But if every fourth or sixth session is canceled, this could indicate resistance. A counselor can often get a clue as to the cause of the resistance by examining closely the content of the session prior to the failed or canceled appointment.

When a person in counseling suggests that the frequency of sessions taper off in the initial or middle phases of counseling, this could reflect resistance. Often it means that the person is beginning to get into some difficult areas or is feeling overburdened by the counselor's expectations.

Evading questions

An effective form of resistance is simply not answering questions. It is rare that someone will refuse outright to answer questions in counseling, but it is common for a person to decline to answer a question simply by answering one that was not asked. This can be so automatic that the person does not realize it has occurred.

For example, a counselor might ask "How are things going sexually between you and your husband?" The woman replies "Well, my husband's been away on business so much it seems that I never see him. That's something I've meant to talk about. I've found myself wondering if he needs to be away that much or if he's looking for excuses to get away." She continues tearfully "I even have to admit that I wonder what he does when he is away." The counselor takes the bait: "How do you mean, you wonder what he is doing?"

If this sequence continues, the session will end, and the counselor will have (1) not received an answer to the original question and (2) forgotten that the question was ever asked. It is helpful to listen to tapes of counseling sessions, count the number of unanswered questions, and draw a fairly accurate blueprint of the main areas of resistance.

Lulling

Lulling means that the person relates in a way that causes the counselor to become relaxed and drowsy. The dulcet tones, gentle mannerisms, and uninspiring subject matter have the same effect on the counselor as a massage. And, in a sense, a massage is being given. The person is rocking the counselor to sleep, thus significantly reducing the counselor's effectiveness.

Focusing attention on the counselor

As long as attention is focused on the counselor, it cannot be focused on the person in counseling. The focus may be positive; for example, the person may spend inordinate time telling the counselor what a wonderful person he or she is. This can place the counselor in an uncomfortable position. If the counselor lets it continue, this is not helpful. If the counselor interrupts and refocuses on the person, the counselor will appear unappreciative and rejecting. Nevertheless, it is the counselor's role to explain gently the importance of concentrating on the person and his or her concerns.

Attention can be focused on the counselor in a negative way. As soon as the counselor approaches a delicate area, the person may say "Why are you smirking?" The unwary counselor may spend the next ten minutes denying or defending a facial expression. Other similar comments that the person in counseling can make are the following:

Why do you always ask about sex?
You seem half-awake today. Didn't you get enough sleep last night?
It really bugs me when you just sit there with a deadpan look and your hands folded neatly on your lap.

The counselor who is not careful can be successfully detoured without even realizing what actually happened.

Entertaining the counselor

There are some people who are "fun" to see in counseling. They are intentionally or unintentionally humorous, affording the counselor one or two good laughs at each session. Some people actually bring a new joke each week for the counselor.

Other people are physically beautiful and entertain with their appearance. Just to sit in the same room with them and hear them talk is a spellbinding experience. Others are adroit psychologically and juggle insights and dynamics for the counselor in a dazzling way. Still others are dramatic and play the part of each person they mention, so they are actually performing a miniplay each week.

It is not terribly difficult for a counselor to get caught up in the entertainment and actually look forward to seeing the person as one anticipates seeing a good play or nightclub act. This may be a difficult resistance to deal with because it is very likely the person has used entertaining to skirt reality throughout life. For the counselor to "blow the whistle" on it will be very threatening. And the person's reaction can be threatening to the counselor.

Running in place

Running in place means that if a person is viewed from the ankles up, he appears to be running and covering great distances. But below the ankles he has not moved an inch.

Some people are very adroit at running in place. Each week they bring new insights to counseling. They easily establish rapport and tell the counselor that he or she is the first person to whom they have ever really opened up. They make it clear that the counselor is teaching them a great deal about themselves and human nature—things they never dreamed of. They place the counselor on an intermittent reinforcement schedule by assuring "This was the best week I've ever had"; or "This was a great session"; or "My roommate has seen so much progress in me, *she* wants to see you in counseling."

These statements are not necessarily indications of running in place. But if they are not matched by real and observable changes in behavior, they probably are. Counselors must focus on "below the ankles" and not get distracted by the straining muscles of the upper body and face and the trophies the person brings to show the counselor. A counselor might ask "Oh, what specifically has your roommate seen in you that makes her feel you are progressing well?" If the answer is "I don't know. I didn't ask her" or "I think she sees I'm happier," the counselor may be appropriately wary.

Forgetting

Forgetting is seen in statements such as "I never can remember what we talked about in a previous session"; "I was going to tell you about a conversation I had with my parents this week, but I've just blocked on the main point I wanted to tell you"; and "You're right. I was going to start filling out job applications this week, and I forgot all about it until you just mentioned it."

Anyone can forget, but forgetting in counseling takes on a particular meaning because the matters discussed in counseling usually rank quite high in importance in the person's life. Consequently, to forget matters that are central to a person's growth often indicates resistance. When the forgotten material is eventually remembered, it often gives the counselor some meaningful clues as to the nature of the pockets of resistance.

Relating conditionally

Sometimes people in counseling imply that they will "open up" if the counselor meets certain requirements, which are usually impossible to meet. A person implies that he or she will "let the counselor in" if he or she

will be gentle with the person;
will not reject the person;
will not respond with "a lot of Freudian stuff";
will not use the information to suggest taking a certain step—for example, getting a divorce.

These conditions are impossible to meet, and that's exactly the point. Even the counselor who wanted to will not be able to prove to the person's satisfaction that any of these conditions will be met. And after some information has been shared to test the counselor, the person can, for no good reason, grade him or her poorly: "See, I *told* you that you would think I'm crazy."

The most common condition that people put on opening up is that they must first trust the counselor. But how does one learn trust without opening up? This "Catch 22" condition can keep the person and the counselor distant for a year. Counselors will be chasing windmills if they enter into agreements as to how they will conduct themselves in counseling. A counselor can explain the underlying dynamics of such conditions, but sooner or later must stand firm: "This is who I am, and this is how I relate." It is up to the person to decide if that is good enough.

Controlling content

The person in counseling has full control over *what* is discussed in the session, no matter how much the counselor attempts to intervene. Sometimes people in counseling present counselors with a map that deftly excludes one or two very important territories. The counselor may realize after a year or two that the person has never mentioned a child who died, a first husband or wife, a grown child, or the subjects of sex, work, adolescent experiences, friends, or religion. Each session had been pregnant with what appeared to be relevant and pressing issues. Before the counselor realizes it, it's almost time to terminate, but he or she accidentally stumbles into an unexplored territory. Because this area is filled with important ramifications, it adds an entirely new dimension to counseling.

The person in counseling also controls what will be discussed in any specific session. The person may state at the beginning of a session "I know we agreed that we had to talk about my problems with my mother today, but I just had a fight with my roommates and that's all I can think about." The counselor who has been successfully decoyed responds "Well, then, maybe we should talk about that and leave your mother until next week."

The person in counseling also controls *how* he or she will communicate material to the counselor. A person can sneak important material by the counselor. For example, a person may offhandedly say "Oh, by the way, I didn't get the job at the telephone company, but the computer company asked me back for a second interview, and I'm kind of excited about that." The counselor responds "Oh, that's a good sign. What kind of work would you be doing if you got the job?" instead of asking "Do you know why you didn't get the job at the phone company?" If the counselor had asked that, the person would have replied "I was afraid you'd ask that. In the interview they asked me if I would take orders just as well from a man or woman, and I told them that I thought that question, in itself, was sexist. Afterwards, I realized I blew it.''

The person in counseling may underemphasize or overemphasize material as a way of controlling the distance between the counselor and the person's vulnerabilities.

The counselor is at the mercy of the person in counseling's ability and willingness to communicate relevant material. However, a counselor can be alert to the possibility that the person's fears are dictating the ebb and flow of information and therefore continually invite the person to be as specific and inclusive as possible.

Making excursions into the past

Some people spend great amounts of counseling time describing their past experiences. Even though the past is painful to the person, it is often less frightening than facing the present. One fairly accurate sign that describing the past may be an escape from the present is the person's inability to focus on the present for more than a few minutes. Before the counselor realizes it, the person has used some present situation to catapult the discussion back into the past. When the counselor attempts to hold the person in the present, he or she is likely to be accused of not being interested in the person but only in results.

Placing the counselor on the horns of a dilemma

This is seen when the person in counseling creates situations in which the counselor is "damned if he does and damned if he doesn't." A person may tell a counselor "I wish you would give me more feedback." When the counselor does, the person responds "If that's the kind of feedback you are going to give me, you can keep it."

Another person in counseling may say "I want to talk about my mother today, since I've had some really strong feelings about her this week." As the session nears the end, the person says "Is it time to go already? Why did you let me ramble on so long about my mother? I had several other things I wanted to discuss today!"

The counselor who is on the horns of a dilemma cannot move far in the direction of effectively helping the person. For example, the wary counselor who has gotten burned by previous "Gotchas!" may try to prevent falling into the same trap: "Before you start talking about your mother today, maybe you should decide how much of the session you want to spend on her so that we don't get caught short on time like we did last week." The person angrily responds "Look, this is very important to me! I can't *time* myself like you time a roast in the oven!"

Gotcha! Either way the counselor turns, he's skewered. The counselor must continually point out the motives and consequences of this dynamic until the person understands the reasons for it and chooses to stop it.

Counselors need to exercise great caution when considering how people resist in counseling. It is often too easy to overemphasize resistance, the result being that counselors view people in counseling as rivals. Struggles develop between the "growth motives" in the counselor and the "resistant motives" of the person in counseling, and counseling sessions become contests that are won or lost.

Counselors can also avoid becoming suspicious detectives, ever ferreting out pockets of resistance and, upon finding one, accusing the person as if he or she were purposely recalcitrant.

It is also helpful for counselors to understand that it is not always a sign of resistance when a person in counseling declines to accept or refuses to carry out a specific suggestion. People in counseling can resist growth, but they can also resist damage.

DEALING WITH RESISTANCE

Since a significant portion of a counselor's time is spent dealing with resistance, it is helpful for counselors not only to recognize it but to deal with it effectively. The following points can be kept in mind by counselors when they attempt to deal with resistance.

Relaxed vigilance

Some counselors seem to see resistance everywhere; others never seem to see it. An attitude of relaxed vigilance with regard to resistance is the most helpful one. It is unhelpful for a counselor to be picky. It is natural for some people to begin a session by remarking on the weather or asking the counselor how he or she is. A minute spent in "warm up" may be more adaptive than resistant. Obviously, if small talk continues for five and ten minutes into each session, resistance could well be an issue.

Along the same lines are friendly questions asking counselors if they are going away for their vacation, what courses they teach, or if they restrict their practice to certain types of individuals. Counselors sometimes create resistance by reacting to each casual statement as if it were resistance.

On the other hand, some counselors are not vigilant and rarely, if ever, see resistance. They view the person's avoidance behavior as "normal" or "within his or her rights as a patient." It could be that these counselors view resistance as a negative commentary on them; hence, they do not wish to see it. It could also be that they lack the strength or skills to deal with resistance. If they don't see it, they don't have to handle it.

Correct labeling

Before behavior is labeled and reacted to as resistance, it is important that the counselor be correct. Some behaviors that appear to be resistance are simply part of the vicissitudes of relating in counseling. For example, people can come late sometimes and can forget what they were going to talk about without it necessarily qualifying as resistance. Other behaviors that appear to be resistance may simply be appropriate reactions to some mistreatment by the counselor. For example, counselors who want to discuss the topic of sex because they need to, regardless of whether or not the person has more pressing issues with which to contend, are likely to meet with a healthy refusal that cannot correctly be called resistance.

It is helpful for counselors to accumulate sufficient data regarding resistance over a period of a few or several sessions so that they possess reasonable certitude that resistance exists. The data also should be concrete enough that the person in counseling can conceptualize and discuss them.

Differentiating between types

It is necessary to distinguish between content, characterological, and relational resistance. *Content resistance* means that the person in counseling resists discussing specific areas that are particularly threatening. Some common thoughts and feelings that are resisted are those involving hurt, anger, sex, jealousy, distrust, loneliness, dishonesty, and hypocrisy. Communication may progress smoothly until an especially threatening area emerges.

Characterological resistance refers to a type seen in people who have a basically defensive personality. They typically avoid ideas, feelings, insights, and situations that pose a threat. These individuals often have a preferred mode of defense; that is, they typically use intellectualization, withdrawal, attack, or some other specific avoidance behavior. They bring their character defenses into counseling as they would into any other relationship.

Relational resistance exists between the person in counseling and the counselor. It manifests itself in the person psychologically withdrawing from or attacking the counselor. The reason for this resistance is often found in feelings of hurt, fear, or anger toward the counselor. People may feel hurt because the counselor does not seem to genuinely care about them; or people may fear that they are becoming too dependent on the counselor; or they may feel angry at the counselor for not giving in to their wishes. Another type of relational resistance is *transference*, in which the person displaces positive or negative feelings from a significant other in his or her life onto the counselor.

It is important that counselors distinguish between the three types of resistance because to mistake one for the other leads to unnecessary problems.

Sharing

When the counselor feels confident that resistance is present to the degree that it is interfering with counseling, this information can be shared with the person. The counselor can share the behaviors upon which the belief is based and invite the person to discover what they mean. For example, a counselor might say "I've noticed that you've been late for our sessions four out of the past six times. Do you have any idea as to what this could mean?"

If the resistance is close to awareness, the person might reply "It probably means that I look forward to these sessions with the same degree of enthusiasm as I look forward to going to the dentist." This rather forthright reply opens the door to exploring the nature of the resistance.

People whose resistance is marked and deep will respond as they would to any threatening reality "I wasn't late the last four times. I was late twice, and you were late once!" Another person might respond "No, I don't have any idea what it means. But you obviously do; so why don't *you* tell me?" In these examples, the person is resistant to examining the resistance. This presents one of the more challenging situations in counseling. If the counselor backs off, the resistance is likely to incubate and become massive. If the counselor pursues the issue, a great deal of tension may arise. Each situation is different, but as a general rule, it is more helpful to pursue the issue in the most even-tempered, inviting way possible.

The counselor's attitude could be "Well, I see a problem here, and I think it would be good to see if we can agree on the accuracy of my observations first. Then we'll see if we can understand what the problem means." This attitude will be less threatening and more inviting than a statement such as "How can you say you don't see a problem when you've missed four out of the last six sessions! You say you want me to help you but, at the same time, you are tying my hands behind my back.''

It can also be helpful for a counselor to ask people how much progress they feel has occurred in the last few sessions. Often the person will be able to admit that something has happened to inhibit progress. Counselors can also compare what has been going on, or not going on, in recent sessions with the agreed upon counseling goals. The discrepancy can often be a point of enlightenment.

Sometimes, when resistance is massive and seemingly intransigent, a counselor must attack it directly. The counselor offers the person the option of working with the counselor in understanding and reducing the resistance or of terminating counseling until the person is ready to use it effectively.

A positive sign

It is helpful for counselors to understand that resistance to growth is part of the human condition and not a negative reflection on their skills. In fact, resistance is an indicator that counseling is moving forward but the person finds the progress threatening.

HOW AND WHY COUNSELORS RESIST

Typically, when resistance in counseling is discussed, it is the person in counseling who is resisting. In fact, however, the counselor can resist being fully cooperative with people seen in counseling. And when counselors are resistant, they are no more aware of it than people in counseling are of their resistance. Counselors who resist being fully cooperative are not necessarily bad counselors. One only need qualify as a human being to function on less than ideal levels. Perhaps the most persuasive evidence that counselors can resist is the fact that counselors often resent discussing that the possibility even exists; that is, they resist the concept of resistance in themselves. The following are some of the causes of resistance in counselors.

Need gratification

The counselor who is getting some basic needs met from the person in counseling does not want to discontinue getting those needs met.

Personal relationship.   The counselor finds the person attractive in one way or another and wants to foster a personal relationship as well as a professional one. The person in counseling may find this flattering and conspire with the counselor to draw out counseling as long as possible. Both discover a new problem each time counseling is about to terminate. The goal of counseling in this situation is not the growth of the person, but the continuance of the relationship between the counselor and the person in counseling.

Punishment.   A counselor may negatively symbolize the person in counseling in a specific way (that is, view the person as resembling a disliked parent, sibling, ex-spouse, or spouse). Or the counselor may negatively symbolize the person in a general way (that is, view the person as a typical "macho male," "castrating female," "upper-class snob," or member of a particular race). Although the majority of the counselor's motives are to help the person, part of the counselor wants to see the person suffer. It is as if the counselor were saying "I couldn't make my mother suffer for what she did to me, but I sure can make this person suffer." Under the ruse of being "honest," "strong," and "helpful," the counselor roughly pushes the person's nose in reality, destructively criticizes the person, and even encourages the person to take unreasonable risks that result in failure.

Control.   Sometimes a counselor's need to control is stronger than the need to be helpful. The counselor works on the premise "I have a set idea as to what you need to grow, and we will not deviate from that." The counselor may think that the person's growth hinges on getting a divorce, quitting a job, moving out of the parental home, getting sexually liberated, returning to or leaving religion, or facing a past experience more fully. The counselor's tunnel vision may interfere significantly with exploring other areas of the person's life that are equally, if not more, important. These counselors shrink the person to fit their narrow definition of what is helpful and unhelpful.

Conversion.   Sometimes counselors are on a philosophical bandwagon. They have found a particular theory or activity helpful and want to share its salutary benefits with the people they see in counseling. The theory could be that propounded by Freud, Adler, Frankl, Skinner, or Berne. The activity could be meditating, jogging, praying, or dieting. Although any and all of these theories and activities could be therapeutic, their level of helpfulness depends on each individual. Jung's thoughts may greatly benefit one person, but they may be of little or no help for another.

Counselors can realize that counseling is different from lecturing and proselytizing. If people want to understand a particular theory or practice, they should attend workshops and read books on it. This will be infinitely less expensive than most counseling and probably more informative. Theories and practices can get in the way of growth so that at the end of counseling the person has gained a working knowledge of a theory and/or technique but may not have grown much as a person. Unfortunately, the person does not realize this because he or she confuses intellectual understanding with personal growth.

Dislike for the person in counseling

Sometimes counselors dislike the person they see in counseling, just as people may dislike the counselor but continue in counseling. A disliked person may be seen because the counselor needs the income, because the person was assigned to the counselor by the clinic in which he or she works, or because the person has challenged the counselor in some way so that if the counselor terminates, the person in counseling wins some undeclared contest. Although the counselor tries hard to be professional, dislike for the person shows, and this significantly interferes with the growth process.

Signs of counselor resistance

The signs of resistance in the counselor are much the same as those seen in the person in counseling. The counselor may do any of the following:

1. Cancels appointments or comes late. (Counselors always have "good reasons" for being late; people in counseling seldom do.)
2. Talks *at* the person instead of listening *to* and talking *with* the person.
3. Daydreams and dozes off.
4. Talks about himself or herself instead of about the person in counseling.
5. Forgets pertinent information about the person.
6. Sets up impossible requirements.
7. Suddenly discovers that the person has "a special problem" and tries to refer the person to another counselor who specializes in the problem.
8. Refuses to consider as important the areas that the person perceives as important.
9. Is sarcastic or "buddy-buddy" with the person.
10. Introduces areas of discussion that are of interest to him or her but are not necessarily helpful to the person.

All these behaviors interfere with the growth of the person in counseling. Counselors are human beings, a fact both counselors and people in counseling forget too easily. It is important to realize that there is no such thing as being a "helpful" or "unhelpful" counselor. The concepts of helpful and unhelpful lie on the same continuum. At times a counselor may be very helpful to the person and yet be unhelpful in some instances. The same counselor may be helpful with one person but very unhelpful with another.

SUMMARY

Resistance in counseling is analogous to an emergency brake on an automobile. When a driver is not familiar with how it works, he may drive with the brake halfway on and not realize this until he eventually smells rubber burning. The same is true in counseling. A counselor who does not fully appreciate the dynamics of resistance is likely to progress at half-speed and not realize it until damage is done in the form of wasted time, needless frustration, and preventable confusion.

The counselor has to be equally open to the possibility that it is his or her foot that is on the brake or the foot of the person in counseling or *both* of their feet. The counselor who understands the nature of resistance, who realizes that "it comes with the territory," and who says, "Let's see what's holding us up" rather than "Why are you dragging your feet again?" will be in a good position to reduce resistance.

Resistance is almost never a one-time phenomenon in counseling. The road to growth is often pocketed with resistance, and each time a new path is explored, there may be fresh resistance. An effective counselor views resistance as a tool for insight and growth rather than as a bothersome enemy that must be destroyed once and for all.

THOUGHT QUESTIONS

1. A person with whom you have been working very hard in counseling misses key appointments and, when he does show up, accuses you of lacking sufficient interest in him.
   What is going on here?
   What is your "gut response" to his accusation?
   How *should* you respond?
   How *will* you respond?
2. "Running in place" is one of the most subtle forms of resistance. What are some clues that this is occurring, and what will you do with these clues?

3. Name three behaviors that you may manifest that the person in counseling *should* resist.
4. Of the five motives for resistance in counselors, to which one might you be most susceptible?
5. Counseling is probably the only profession in which a great number of people who seek its services don't really want them. Why do you want to enter such a profession?

CHAPTER 11

Problems That Counselors Face

Like any professional, the counselor must face problems that are sometimes slight and at other times serious. A counseling relationship is a microcosm of all that is good and all that is problematic in human nature. It is not the problems themselves that are the primary concern but how the counselor handles them. Problems handled well are priceless opportunities to show the person in counseling how to handle stress in constructive ways. All the talk in the world cannot have the effectiveness of a real-life situation. Conversely, when counselors handle problems poorly or allow problems to handle *them*, it can significantly interfere with the counseling relationship. In essence, the counselor is telling the person "Do as I say; don't do as I do." It is important that counselors and people in counseling recognize in advance the potential problems that await them. Realizing what these problems are, they can better appreciate their normalcy and can approach them with confidence. This chapter will discuss seven problems that are common in counseling relationships: boredom, hostility, counselor's mistakes, manipulation, suffering, unhelpful versus helpful relationships, and terminating.

BOREDOM

If counselors remain completely alert, energized, and committed, they should never be bored. In practice, however, counselors are human beings and do not always function on optimal levels. It seems better to admit the possibility of boredom as a factor in counseling and to deal with it constructively than to deny that it would ever occur except in the most mediocre counselors.

People in counseling have problems, and the greater or deeper their problems, the more they are robbed of uniqueness, individuality, and vibrancy. While existentially it is true that each person is unique, psychological problems tend to blunt individual differences. People who are depressed sound remarkably similar in counseling, even though in their well state, they are very different. The same can be said for people experiencing anxieties, phobias, paranoias, psychosomatic disorders, sexual, alcohol, and drug problems.

Beginning counselors seldom experience boredom because of the newness of their work. Each day they see a person with a different kind of problem, and they are trying out their newly acquired skills and responsibilities. But like any other behavior that is repeated, counseling can become boring. After a counselor sees 25 or 50 depressed people, he or she often can predict with fair accuracy what the person is going to say at any given time.

Problems created by boredom

One problem lies in the area of what boredom can do to the counseling relationship. Boredom moves the counselor away from the person, and the person feels the gradually increasing distance. Even the most disturbed people can sense when the counselor is bored and tuned out. The distance that boredom creates deprives the person in counseling of the sense of security and acceptance necessary in a counseling environment.

The second problem lies in how the counselor handles the boredom. Some counselors may daydream and substitute the reverie of fantasy for the rigor of counseling. If a teacher of 40 students can spot one who is daydreaming, so much more so can a person in counseling who is sitting 6 feet away from the only other person in the room.

Some counselors delude themselves into thinking they have become adroit at listening to a person with one ear and listening to their own thoughts with the other. They attempt to nod, grunt, smile, and frown at the right times to give the impression that their attention is fixed on the person. However, only the least sensitive people are fooled by this. Most people are aware of the attempted ruse and resent it, although they are often not strong enough to confront it and deal with it directly.

Other counselors may attempt to handle boredom by "stirring up the coals"—by jabbing at the person to add some zest to the session.

This may completely disrupt or cancel the flow of dynamics that the person needs to share with the counselor at that particular session.

A third danger is that the counselor will miss some important information while distracted by boredom. The counselor's nonreaction causes one of two situations. The person may feel that the information is important, but the counselor isn't astute enough to recognize it. Or the person may conclude that the information is not important, since the counselor did not react. If a counselor misses one or two important clues in each of three or four sessions, counseling will limp along, at best. In other words, the counselor's boredom leads him or her to miss important information, causing the sessions to become increasingly boring. As the counselor becomes *more* bored, so does the person. Eventually, counseling will grind to a deadening halt.

Solutions

If counselors find themselves bored, they can first ascertain whose problem it is. If the counselor is tired or distracted by outside concerns, the problem is the counselor's and he or she should then take appropriate action. In addition to rectifying the situation, the counselor might explain to the person in counseling "I'm sorry. I'm distracted today. Could you repeat the last of what you said so that I can catch up with you?" When a problem arises in counseling, it is very important for the person to know whose problem it is.

If a counselor feels that he or she is doing everything reasonable to be attentive but the person's presentation is sonorous, then the counselor can communicate this reaction. The counselor may state "The way you are talking and the things you are talking about make it difficult for me to concentrate on what you're saying. I care too much about you to lose emotional contact with you; so maybe we'd better see what's going on." Surprisingly, the person may well respond "You know, I *knew* you were getting bored. In fact, I'm boring *myself*. I'm glad you stopped me."

On the other hand, the person may respond in an obviously offended way "Well, I'm sorry. I didn't mean to *bore* you. I didn't realize that I was here to entertain you." The counselor can simply respond "I know what I said was difficult to hear. It was difficult for me to say, because I knew you might feel hurt. But I do feel that it's important for both of us to remain alert, and any time I'm losing my alertness, I have to tell you so that we can see what the problem is. I'm sure there will be times when I am talking and you drift off, and you must tell me, also."

Even more important than the counselor confronting the issue of boredom is helping the person understand its meaning and dynamics.

Boredom can be caused by a person being so repressed that little or no affect surfaces in the sessions. The person may be very frightened and thus may be reluctant to share any meaningful material that could evoke a negative reaction from the counselor. The person may live such a passive existence that he or she has few if any fresh experiences to share. The person may use boredom as resistance, which nullifies many of the counselor's abilities. Finally, the person can use boredom as a hostile weapon to frustrate the counselor.

Counselors can make some changes in the counseling sessions to counteract boredom. They may reschedule the person at a time when the counselor is more alert. They may see the person for two half-sessions a week instead of one whole one. They may have the person keep a journal and go over parts of it at each session. Sometimes it is helpful to take a more active, confrontive approach to cut through the person's lethargy. Group counseling can also be used as an adjunct to individual counseling as a means of igniting some affect within the person.

Counselors can also bore people in counseling. They can bore people with their bland, sedentary manner that causes a person to feel that he or she is talking to a wall or to a tape recorder. Counselors can also bore people when they overtalk, speaking at length about some dynamic that has come up in counseling, about their favorite theory, or about their personal life. Most people in counseling want to be polite; so they suffer in silence while the counselor expounds or relates stories that have the effect of a major tranquilizer. Since most people have only one counselor, they often think that all counselors must be this way and that listening politely as their counselor drones on is an integral part of the healing process.

Counselors who keep their reactions succinct and pithy and their questions short and clear will not be boring. Counselors can also be alert to signs of boredom in people: glazed, drowsy eyes; finger or toe tapping; bland, disinterested facial expressions. When these indications appear, counselors can address themselves to the signs and ascertain what they mean with a willingness to accept at least partial responsibility for the boredom.

HOSTILITY

Counselors generally perceive themselves as nice people. They help others and expect to be appreciated. But many people in counseling have pent-up hostility that must be regurgitated before they can continue to grow. Thus, they may often express hostility toward the counselor, which can confuse and frustrate the counselor. Understanding the person's hostility can help the counselor handle it more effectively.

Sources

The person in counseling's hostility may flow from several sources. It is often a cover-up for deep *fear*. The more some people are threatened, the more they attack, without ever realizing that they were frightened before they were angry. The anger mobilizes them and causes them to focus outward rather than inward, thus protecting the area of vulnerability from both others and themselves.

The more frightened persons are, the more they will view counseling as a threat. More specifically, the more they will view the counselor as a threat. People can be frightened that they will become too dependent on the counselor. Others may fear that the counselor will reject them; so they assume an "I'll reject you before you reject me" stance. People in counseling may also fear that the counselor will introduce them to disturbing parts of themselves, and they may use their anger to keep the counselor at a safe distance.

It is helpful for counselors to understand that most hostility directed at them is generated by fear. If counselors recognize this, they can duck beneath the anger and concentrate on the fears that are causing it.

Hostility stems also from *frustrated needs*. When people are semi-starved psychologically, they have very low resistance to stress. They are oversensitive to noxious stimuli. As one woman said, "What was once simply a leaky faucet now sounds like a crashing waterfall. What once sounded like one or two motorcycles driving by the house now sounds like a herd of motorcycles participating in some primitive struggle." These sounds that the woman once ignored now cause her to rage at the plumber for the leaky faucet and scream at the police about the intruding motorcycles.

These people will respond to the counselor's benign comments or questions with some variation of "How dare you think that about me!" The person's hypersensitivity will result in an overreaction in counseling as well as in other life situations.

Hostility can also be directed at a counselor who symbolizes some *external* or *internal conflict* for the person. The counselor may symbolize a feared or disliked parent, spouse, ex-spouse, or authority figure. The counselor may also symbolize an internal conflict when he or she represents a source of freedom to an overcontrolled person or represents an image of effectiveness to a person who feels inadequate.

Hostility can come from the *intense pressure* a person is feeling from other people and from within the self. The person is analogous to a balloon that is extended to its fullest. All it takes is the slightest poke, and the balloon will pop. As soon as the counselor creates the slightest bit of pressure, the person may explode at the counselor.

Finally, hostility toward the counselor may be *appropriate.* The counselor may be relating with the person in an unjust manner, which is resented. The counselor may not be trying very hard to help the person. The counselor may be continually focusing on the person's negative behavior and continually suspecting his or her motives. Less secure counselors rarely entertain this as a reason for the hostility they encounter. They gravitate to one of the previous four reasons, making the hostility the problem of the person in counseling, and not their own.

Dealing with hostility

It is important for the counselor to ascertain the correct cause of hostility and then to deal with it in the most educative way possible. When people learn what causes their hostility, they are in a better position to make it work for them instead of against them.

Among effective counseling relationships, it would be rare that a counselor would not encounter periodic hostility. Some counselors seem almost never to encounter direct hostility from the people they see in counseling. Such counselors may be "nice people" who skillfully and assiduously avoid confronting people in ways that could evoke hostility. They enter into a pact with the person in counseling that neither one will confront the other. The people who see these counselors often view counseling as a "pleasant experience" and their counselors as "awfully kind."

On the other hand, some counselors seem to be always in the midst of battles. Tapes of the counseling sessions sound like family feuds. These counselors reflexively react to the person's hostility with their own hostility, without ducking beneath it and addressing the causes. Their attitude is "Just because I'm your counselor doesn't mean you can push me around."

Counselors can be prepared to be the just and unjust target of hostility. Counselors who consciously or unconsciously avoid situations that will result in being targeted are like surgeons who want to operate successfully without getting blood on them.

In a sense, counselors are like sparring partners. They must absorb some punishment so that the other fighter's weaknesses can be diagnosed, but they don't permit themselves to be damaged. If the counselor acts like a punching bag that merely absorbs punishment, the person in counseling may feel a great release of tension, but will learn nothing about himself or herself.

Sometimes counselors can be hostile toward the people they see in counseling for the same reasons that people in counseling are hostile toward them. The people in counseling may pose some threat to the counselor's self-concept, or the counselor may be experiencing personal frustration and have a low tolerance for stress in counseling. The person in counseling may symbolize a disliked person or highlight a latent weakness in the counselor. Counselors who find themselves in frequent skirmishes with the people they see in counseling may wish to examine the possibility that they are part of the problem.

MISTAKES COUNSELORS CAN MAKE

All counselors make mistakes. The subject matter that counselors work with—namely, human behavior—is infinitely complex and subtle. It does not lend itself to precise measurement or standard treatment procedures, as does the body. Therefore, it is imperative that counselors realize they will make mistakes and be ready to admit and learn from them. With this awareness, the counselor can take a step toward diminishing their number.

Being weak

Problems occur in counseling when counselors are weak. Just as many problems with children can be traced to weak parents, many problems in counseling can be traced to weak counselors. Weak counselors allow themselves to be pressured by the person in counseling. They do not function according to their initial judgment, but accede to the person's opinions and wishes.

It is important to realize that there is such a thing as a weak counselor but also that a counselor may be strong with one person and weak with another. Strong counselors trust their judgments and stick to them unless the judgments are eventually proven unhelpful.

The following is an example of how a weak counselor can create a lot of problems for himself and the people in counseling. A counselor feels that marital group counseling is the counseling of choice for a woman who has come to him. When she refuses the recommendation, he agrees to see her in individual counseling. He also suggests that her husband join them immediately for conjoint sessions, but she insists she needs time in individual counseling to "get used to it" before her husband joins them. After some discussion, she convinces the counselor that this "makes sense." Eventually, the husband is invited to counseling, but he insists that he can come only on Saturdays, the counselor's day off. The counselor feels that as long as the husband is motivated to enter counseling, he might as well see them on Saturday mornings. He wants the couple to discuss their sexual relationship, which appears to be the heart of their problem. The husband refuses to discuss their sex life in front of "a stranger" and insists "there's nothing to discuss anyway."

The counselor convinces himself that the man needs more time; so he allows the couple to discuss superficial issues for a dozen sessions. Meanwhile, the couple has not made a payment for four months. The counselor does not want to broach this subject, because the husband's motivation for counseling is precarious and he may use the counselor's "money grabbing" as an excuse to pull out of counseling.

Between sessions, the counselor gets a call from the woman, who says she is extremely upset and is going to swallow a bottle of tranquilizers. Although the counselor would ordinarily call the police, he does not do so, because the woman's husband is a police officer and the couple would be embarrassed. Consequently, he goes to the couple's house and remains for two hours until the husband arrives.

Only the wife appears at the next session. Her husband hit her for "pulling the suicide routine." He announced he did not want any part of the "counseling scene" because it was ruining what little marriage they had. She tells the counselor that after he punched her, they talked more than they had in years and agreed that they could make the marriage work without counseling. She assures the counselor that they will pay off the bill someday, but she would appreciate it if he could be patient. The counselor assures her there is no rush.

In a sense, this counselor was fortunate. All he lost was 25 hours of his life and $1000. If the couple's dynamics had been slightly different, she might have committed suicide, or her husband might have killed her, or the couple could have sued him for anything they concocted. Had the counselor been strong enough to trust his judgment and set limits accordingly, the destruction would have been prevented, either because the couple would not have cooperated and quit or because the counselor's strength would have served as the adhesive the couple needed to grow.

Not admitting mistakes

Problems can increase in counseling when counselors don't admit mistakes. Although counselors are in a high-risk profession with regard to making mistakes, they seem as reluctant as anyone to admit them. One reason for this reluctance is the belief that effective counselors don't make mistakes, at least not serious ones. This being taken as truth, the counselor realizes the best way to preserve his or her self-concept as an effective counselor is not to admit mistakes. The truth is that even great counselors make mistakes, sometimes serious ones. It is not the presence or absence of mistakes that separates effective from poor counselors; it is their willingness to admit their mistakes both to themselves and to the people in counseling.

There are four ways that counselors can avoid admitting mistakes. One is never to take a risk. The counselor who only sits, nods, and makes reassuring sounds is unlikely to make an obvious mistake. Although these counselors do not view it as such, they are making one large mistake—the mistake of being afraid to take the risks with the person that are necessary for growth in counseling.

The second way to avoid admitting mistakes is to deny that problems exist in counseling. The person in counseling is getting more depressed, but this is seen as a "good sign." The counselor views his daydreaming through a quarter of each session as "only human, considering the time of day."

Third, counselors can blame any problems that arise on the person in counseling. Counselors assure themselves that if only the person were more cooperative, intelligent, motivated, or courageous, counseling would be progressing nicely.

The fourth way to avoid admitting mistakes is to believe the seductive myth that one does not "make mistakes" in counseling any more than one speaks of "mistakes" in lovemaking. This erroneous belief is based on the concept that there are only different levels of understanding and communication between the counselor and the person in counseling—levels that will naturally iron out on their own with care and warmth.

The fact is that counselors can make mistakes in counseling. They overinterpret or underinterpret situations; they react prematurely or too late; they are more directive or more nondirective than is helpful at the time; they get decoyed away from important issues; they interrupt too soon or not soon enough; they think they always know more about the person than the person does; they affirm and scold at the wrong times; they don't smile when they should, and they laugh when they shouldn't; they are tough when they should be gentle and gentle when they should be tough; they stand by the limits they set when they should be more flexible and are flexible when they should stand by the limits; and they daydream through important information.

Effective counselors will sit quietly for a few minutes after each session and examine it for any mistakes they might have made. They then try to discern why they made the mistakes—what need, fear, anger, insensitivity, or impatience momentarily took control. These counselors then plan how they will avoid the same mistake in the future.

Effective counselors also admit mistakes to the people in counseling. They do this for four reasons:

1. They are scrupulously honest, and honesty demands that this be done.
2. The person in counseling should be helped to separate what mistakes belong to whom so that the appropriate person can take responsibility and rectify them.
3. The counselor admits the mistake as a way of teaching the person in counseling the acceptability of mistakes and the importance of admitting them to others.
4. The counselor knows that the person in counseling probably realizes the counselor made a mistake and is watching to see if the counselor is secure enough to admit it.

MANIPULATION

Manipulation occurs when people employ veiled tactics to induce another person to meet their own needs rather than those of the other person or to neutralize the other person as a source of threat. The result is often detrimental to one or both people in the relationship. For example, a counselor induces a person to remain in counseling under the rationalization that the person needs to develop more competencies when, in fact, the counselor is getting personal needs met in the relationship.

It is important to distinguish between manipulating and maneuvering. In maneuvering, a reasonable amount of pressure is placed on a person in a forthright manner to encourage him or her to progress toward growth. For example, a counselor may place some pressure on an unemployed person to schedule job interviews. This situation is different from manipulation in two important ways. First, the pressure is forthright—that is, it is not veiled and there are no hidden motives. Second, the pressure is exerted in the best interests of the person in counseling and not of the counselor.

Manipulation of the counselor

People manipulate counselors for the following reasons.

To meet needs. The person in counseling is often semistarved or starved in a particular need. Often unconsciously, he or she sets up the counselor as the one who will satisfy this need. While it is legitimate for a person to get some needs partially met, it is unhealthy for a person to get many needs met in counseling. When this occurs, the person has no impetus to go out to other people who would be more appropriate and lasting need satisfiers.

People who are semistarved in the need to feel secure may manipulate the counselor into taking care of and protecting them. They can do this by inducing the counselor to make decisions for them; to represent and intercede for them in conflicts with parents, spouses, teachers, or bosses; to spend inordinate amounts of time with them (prolonged or extra sessions, phone calls, letters); and to give assurances and make promises that are unrealistic and inappropriate ("No matter what you do, I would never reject you").

A counselor who has strong needs to protect, nurture, guide, and be depended upon will be particularly susceptible to this person's manipulation. Under the rationalization that the person needs a "psychological bodyguard," the counselor assumes the crippling role of benevolent protector.

People with unmet needs for love may attempt to manipulate the counselor into loving them or at least having "special" feelings for them. These attempts may include being sexually seductive, ingratiating ("You're the best counselor I ever had"), overcooperative in a superficial way, or "dressing up for the counselor"—that is, discovering what qualities the counselor finds attractive and assuming these qualities to please him or her.

Counselors who are not receiving sufficient love in their own lives will be especially susceptible to these manipulations and may adopt a "my favorite patient" attitude toward the person. This can weaken the counselor and tint his or her perceptions. This counselor cannot entertain, even for a second, the possibility that the person in counseling is consciously or unconsciously using the counselor to their mutual detriment.

Sometimes people in counseling have destructive needs—for example, the need to be rejected. If they can get the counselor to reject them, they can prove that they are worthless, unlovable, and beyond hope. The "proof" acts as a license that enables them to indulge in more self-destructive behavior.

These individuals behave in abrasive ways toward the counselor. Typical provoking behaviors are coming late for, canceling, or failing appointments; making inordinate demands on the counselor for time, adjustments in fee, and goodwill; asking hostile questions of the counselor; aggravating the counselor by putting feet up on the desk or leaving in the middle of a session for an "important appointment"; and relating what goes on in counseling to friends and relatives in a derogatory way. These behaviors can eventually result in the counselor terminating the relationship.

To neutralize a threat.   Counselors, by definition, are a source of threat to people in counseling. The reason is that one of their main roles is to confront people with parts of reality they have a vested interest in avoiding. Such confrontations are anxiety producing and sometimes painful.

Analogously, a counselor is a toll collector on the road to growth. Reason says there is a price to pay for traveling on the road, but people in counseling often try to distract the toll collector and sneak by without paying. Some common and subtle ways the person attempts this are seen in the following ploys, although they are seldom articulated as boldly.

1. *Bribing:* "I'll work hard on this area (problems at work) if you don't face me with a more threatening area (problems in marriage)."
2. *Blackmailing:* "If you don't face me with my sexual fears, I won't face you with your phoniness."
3. *Distracting:* "Let's talk about sex today. You'll find that more interesting than talking about whether I've moved out of my parents' house yet."
4. *Seducing:* "I think if you could hold me really tight and I could feel your warmth and strength, it would do more for me (and you) than if we talk about my boring parents."
5. *Assaulting:* "Let's talk about whether you ever feel guilty just sitting there listening to people and making a fortune instead of why I get drunk three times a week."

Most counselors have an area that is particularly susceptible to manipulation. For example, a person in counseling could manipulate the counselor by making statements such as the following, which could tap a vulnerable area in the counselor.

I thought you'd be more *understanding* than that.

I thought counselors weren't supposed to be *judgmental*.

I know you're a *compassionate* person; so I'm not afraid to tell you that. . . .

I know you're a *reasonable* person and wouldn't make unreasonable demands on me.

You're the only person I can *trust* not to hurt me.

> You're somebody I could fall in *love* with, but I know it would be inappropriate.
>
> I know you *care* about me as a patient, but I don't think you care about me personally.
>
> How can you say that! I thought you were more *sophisticated* than that.
>
> I thought you had a *sense of humor*, but I guess you don't.
>
> You told me you wanted to be *helpful* to me, and now that I could use your help, you don't want to give it.

It is helpful for counselors to know what their vulnerable areas are so that they can diminish their manipulative potential.

Important points.   There are three important points to understand about people manipulating counselors. First, most of the time when people manipulate counselors, they are unaware of what they are doing. Their manipulative behavior is being guided by unconscious needs, feelings, and motives. When confronted with their manipulative behavior, people commonly react with genuine hurt, confusion, anger, and denial.

Second, it is counterproductive for the counselor to take a defensive attitude ("You can't manipulate me") toward people for two reasons. One is that people *can* manipulate counselors, especially people who have used manipulation as a survival technique for 20 or 40 years. The second is that such an attitude is analogous to a toll collector meeting each driver with the challenge "You can't sneak by me!" It will invite a challenge and/or put people on the defensive for no good reason.

Third, it is unhelpful to assume a cynical attitude toward people who manipulate counselors. Since *all* people manipulate counselors, cynicism would be an integral part of every counseling relationship. The helpful counselor can learn to handle manipulation without resorting to cynicism.

Manipulation by the counselor

Counselors can manipulate people who are in counseling. The following are some examples of how this can occur.

> A counselor wishes to terminate a woman because he has become bored or irritated by her. Instead of dealing with and communicating these feelings, he either leads the woman to believe that she is progressing significantly better than she is or tells her that she is not ready for the next phase and should take a vacation from counseling.

A counselor wishes to get into a personal relationship with the person in counseling to meet his own needs for affection and warmth. Using the rationale that the person needs to show warmth and affection, he offers himself as someone with whom she can practice.

A counselor feels that religion is contrary to psychological health. Without relating this belief to the person in counseling, she gradually weans him away from his religious beliefs, which have, until now, assumed a place of importance and support in his life.

A counselor needs to feel successful; so she encourages a person to apply to graduate school or accept a promotion under the pretext that this would be a good opportunity for growth. In fact, the counselor is using the person in counseling to meet her own needs to feel successful and is less interested in whether such a move would or would not be beneficial for the person.

The common denominators in these examples are that the counselor is not being honest with the person in counseling, is motivated primarily by personal needs, and is encouraging behavior that either is or could be detrimental to the person.

Counselors can remember that the most effective kinds of manipulation do not resemble manipulation. This axiom is as valid when applied to people in counseling as to counselors. Most counselors manipulate at one time or another. The point is that the more counselors realize that they are capable of harming a person in these ways, the more they can take steps to prevent it.

SUFFERING

Like manipulation, suffering can occur in counseling in two ways: the person in counseling can suffer and the counselor can suffer. Both situations can cause problems within the counseling relationship if they are not recognized and handled effectively.

Suffering by the person in counseling

Counselors, like most people, don't like to see others suffer. In fact, the desire to prevent suffering is a primary reason that many people choose to become counselors. Ironically, a common side effect of a counselor's work is that he or she *causes* suffering because suffering is an inherent part of personality growth. Counselors then are called upon to reconcile their desire to soothe hurt with the realization that most effective counseling necessarily entails suffering.

Counselors are instrumental causes (although not primary causes) in people's suffering for a number of reasons. They must introduce people to painful insights. Because of a counselor's probing, a mother discovers that she is jealous of her daughter, whom she loves dearly; a father discovers that his busy schedule has caused his son or daughter to feel unloved by him; a son gradually realizes that he has been exploited by a parent; a married person is led to the realization that his or her spouse has serious problems. These insights can be excruciatingly painful and can cause the spilling of much psychological blood.

Counselors can cause suffering when they must prod a person to grow, despite the person's strong needs to stagnate or regress. People will beg counselors to leave them alone, to allow them to regress, to succor rather than to save them. But an effective counselor can kindly but firmly encourage them to move in the direction of growth, despite their protests.

Counselors may cause suffering when they help a person let go of an important relationship. Sometimes the person in counseling has been rejected by a loved one but cannot let go. The person clings to the relationship as one would to a speeding bus, knowing that he will become battered if he hangs on and battered if he lets go. This can be a source of pain whatever the person decides to do. Sometimes the person agrees to let go if he can cling to the counselor. The counselor must decline this proposal, which adds to the person's suffering.

At other times the counselor can help a person break off an important relationship. The person feels like someone chopping off an infected hand. She knows she must do it, but it doesn't make it any easier. After the person breaks off the relationship, the counselor must suffer with the person, who is flooded with grief from one direction and guilt from the other.

Counselors who are unable to cause or to allow people to suffer can do damage. Some counselors are inclined to help the person "over the puddles," so that neither gets splashed or muddied. Or they prematurely apply first aid to stop the bleeding before it gets started.

Other counselors handle the person's suffering by becoming hardened and matter-of-fact about it. They cut, clamp, and suture with the cool detachment of a busy surgeon. They may even become counterphobic—that is, cause some unnecessary suffering in people as proof to themselves that they are not afraid to see people suffer.

Still other counselors become cynical about or angry at people who are suffering. They view the suffering as a manipulative ploy to force the counselor into doing something he or she does not wish to do, into feeling sorry for the person, or into feeling guilty for being instrumental in the suffering.

Effective counselors recognize that personality growth is earned and the price may be suffering. The more a counselor expects a person to grow, the more psychological bleeding will occur. The counselor must sit by and allow the person to bleed enough at any one time to release the toxins in the system, but not so much that the person becomes weak. When and how to allow bleeding and when and how to apply a tourniquet is a skill that must be developed over years of experience and is never fully mastered.[1]

Suffering by the counselor

Counselors also suffer in counseling, although in a different way than does the person. They realize that they must be instrumental in causing pain if the person is to grow, but they don't relish doing it. Although they understand the resentment of the person who is doing the suffering, they don't enjoy being the brunt of it. Counselors suffer when a person is suffering due to a loss of a loved one by death or by the termination of a relationship. This suffering lies in the counselor's feelings of helplessness because all he or she can do is offer empathy, which at the time appears to be an embarrassingly meager gift.

Counselors also can experience anguish when the person in counseling is psychologically bleeding due to the damage caused by other people, and all the counselor can do is stem a small portion of the profuse bleeding. The person in counseling cries out to the counselor for help, and the counselor feels as if he is just mopping up blood as the person hemorrhages. The counselor realizes that the bleeding will stop only as the person's natural healing process begins to function.

Inadvertently causing pain in the person in counseling also leads to suffering by the counselor. By some action or inaction, the counselor may be responsible for wounding the person and causing iatrogenic pain. This suffering is perhaps the most severe that counselors must endure because they realize they are the cause of a pain that may have little or no therapeutic value. To spend several precious counseling sessions helping a person deal with the suffering caused by the counselor can be both painful and humiliating.

Counselors can experience a sense of deep frustration when they are doing all they can for a person in counseling and the person prematurely terminates, telling the counselor that he or she has not been

[1]For further discussion of the role of suffering in counseling, see May (1967a), pp. 157–162.

helpful. Although part of the counselor assures himself or herself that the person is the problem, the lingering question remains: "What did I miss that I should have seen?" These counselors experience pain that stems from feeling that they did their best, but it wasn't good enough.

Generally, it is good for counselors to share their painful feelings with the person in counseling. It is important not to share them in guilt-producing or sympathy-provoking ways because this focuses attention on the counselor. The counselor can do this in a way that reflects both genuine empathy and supportive strength.

UNHELPFUL VERSUS HELPFUL RELATIONSHIPS

There are two types of unhelpful relationships in counseling; emotionally detached and emotionally attached. Both of these will be discussed in terms of their characteristics and effects on counseling and in contrast to the emotionally involved relationship, which is the healthy midpoint.

Emotionally detached relationships

Counselors who relate in an emotionally detached manner refrain from getting emotionally close to the person in counseling. They do not reveal personal data and opinions and do not become emotionally involved. Their main role is passive, reflective, and didactic.

Counselors relate in an emotionally detached manner either because they were trained in this fashion (a leftover from the medical model of treatment) or because they are frightened to "mix it up" with the people they see in counseling. Counselors who are distant cannot truly "get inside" the person. They cannot immerse themselves in the person's thoughts, feelings, and perceptions so that a real understanding and empathy can develop. This gives the person in counseling the impression that he or she is being *operated on* rather than *related with*.

When counselors are anonymous, they offer little personal data that is necessary to create a sense of trust and rapport. They expect people in counseling to share their most intimate and vulnerable areas with a virtual stranger. This is tantamount to asking a person to walk down an unfamiliar flight of stairs in the dark. Because of the counselor's anonymity, the person also cannot build a sense of identification with the counselor or with his or her mental health values.

When counselors are emotionally detached, their sole involvement is intellectual, which is insipid and uninspiring. People in counseling with this type of counselor often feel that they are treated as a patient and not as a person. It is difficult for someone to relate openly with a counselor when he or she cannot feel the counselor's concern, understanding, and acceptance.

People who need to relate to a counselor in an emotionally detached way use the counselor as a director, tutor, or mentor. They hold the counselor at a safe distance and thus prevent the development of understanding and empathy. Because these people relate in formal, polite, and respectful ways, the counselor finds it difficult to see what lies behind their social facade. People who relate intellectually rather than emotionally deprive the counselor of the opportunity to help them get in touch with, ventilate, and share important feelings. The counselor's attempts to personalize the relationship are met with resistance and admonishments that the person wants to "keep the relationship on a professional level."

Gradually, the effective counselor can help the person understand the important difference between a tutorial experience, which the person wants, and a therapeutic experience, which necessitates that the two people get close, involved, and equal. Progression from a role-to-role relationship to a person-to-person relationship can be swift with people who need simply to be oriented correctly to counseling. For those who have an emotional investment in remaining in a detached relationship, the change must be more gradual and gentle. As long as a relationship remains on an emotionally detached level, however, the effects of counseling are likely to be superficial and transient.

Emotionally attached relationships

A second problematic relationship occurs when the counselor and/or the person in counseling is emotionally attached. "Emotionally attached" means that the counselor and/or the person in counseling depends on the other for basic need fulfillment. The basic needs that are met in this type of relationship are the needs to feel secure, to receive and give love, and to be admired and needed. To the extent that these needs are not met outside of counseling and are met within the counseling relationship, emotional attachment will occur.

Because counseling is an emotionally intimate experience and because both the counselor and the person in counseling ordinarily grow to like and respect each other, there is a potential for emotional attachment. Whether or not the potential is actualized depends upon the sufficiency of need fulfillment outside of counseling.

Counselor to person. Emotional attachments can be "parental" (the counselor can relate as an overprotective parent), "fraternal" (the counselor can function as a best friend of the person in counseling), or romantic (the counselor can function as a lover or spouse).

Counselors can be alert to several signs that often indicate they are becoming emotionally attached to the person in counseling. Attachment is a possibility when the counselor

1. looks forward to seeing the person as a way of brightening up the day or week;
2. finds the significant people in his or her life lacking when compared with the person in counseling;
3. extends the time of the sessions, beginning early and/or ending late;
4. fantasizes about the person between sessions;
5. allows or encourages intersession contacts that are not permitted others (for example, phone calls, letters, or extra visits);
6. makes adjustments in fee that would not be made for others;
7. finds the sessions are more recreation than work;
8. is jealous of the other close relationships the person has and subtly downgrades or discourages them;
9. worries about the person between sessions in ways and to degrees that he or she does not worry about others.

The problems that arise from a counselor becoming emotionally attached to a person in counseling stem from the fact that such a relationship undermines the basic assumptions upon which counseling rests. The following assumptions are undermined when a counselor is emotionally attached to a person in counseling:

1. Counselors generally perceive reality more accurately than the person in counseling. Counselors who are emotionally attached get swept up in the person's perceptions; so the blind are leading the blind.

2. Counselors help the person in counseling make decisions that are to the person's benefit. Emotionally attached counselors angle people into decisions that will best meet the counselor's needs (for example, to continue in counseling when the person could function sufficiently on his or her own).

3. Counselors represent a strength that persons in counseling depend upon and from which they can draw. The attached counselor is inordinately vulnerable to manipulation and therefore is a weak foundation upon which to rely for support.

4. Counselors are able to remain stable, despite the mood shifts and crises of the person in counseling. The counselor who is emotionally attached must ride the moods and suffer the anguish of the person, thus

nullifying the counselor as a stable influence and source of objective feedback.

5. Counselors encourage people in counseling to relate with others in maximally fulfilling ways. Emotionally attached counselors may provide so much satisfaction and fulfillment that the person has little motivation to relate with people outside of counseling.

6. Counselors are strong proponents of reality. The attached counselor offers the person an unreal relationship. In fact, the counselor is not the mother, father, friend, lover, or spouse of the person in counseling. To pretend this is true is to violate reality, which will be to the eventual detriment of the person in counseling. The closer the relationship approaches termination, the more hurt, panic, and resentment the person in counseling will experience. Often the person must seek another counselor to undo the harm done by the first.

Person to counselor. A person in counseling can also become attached to a counselor without the counselor encouraging or even desiring it. This is understandable because sometimes the person feels that the counselor is the only one who accepts him or her.

The following are some typical signs of this kind of attachment:

1. The person wants a special relationship with the counselor; that is, the person wants to be the counselor's "favorite patient." These people often ask, directly or indirectly, if and how much the counselor likes them and how they rank with the other people the counselor sees.

2. The person wants intersession contacts (that is, phone calls, letters, or extra visits). Sometimes the person may make creative gifts for the counselor or bring presents, often of a personal nature.

3. The person's demeanor—verbal and nonverbal communication—reflects the signs of someone "falling in love." The person's eyes say "I love you," and the person lingers after the session in a way that says "I don't want to leave you."

4. The person feels hurt and rejected when confronted with an unpleasant reality by the counselor, especially the reality of the attachment to the counselor.

5. The person fantasizes about the counselor between sessions and sometimes makes the counselor an imaginary friend who is always there to protect and guide.

6. The person compares the counselor with the significant people in his or her life and judges the counselor to be superior to them: "If only I were married to you instead of Jim" or "If only you were my mother."

The following is a list of the problems that result when the person in counseling becomes emotionally attached to the counselor. The person may

1. lose interest in working on relationships outside of counseling because he or she has everything in the person of the counselor;
2. not be completely honest to avoid harming the relationship;
3. make it difficult for the counselor to set and enforce limits without feeling selfish or rejecting;
4. overperceive the counselor's care and understanding and underperceive the counselor's messages that he or she wants the person to become self-sufficient;
5. "get well" for the counselor and remain so only as long as the counselor treats him or her nicely; as soon as the counselor upsets the person or speaks of tapering off the sessions, the person "gets sick" again;
6. work halfheartedly at problems and concoct problems as counseling approaches termination in order to extend the relationship.

The effects of a person being emotionally attached to a counselor are detrimental to the counseling process and present a formidable challenge to the counselor. When emotional attachment is unilateral—that is, when the person in counseling becomes attached to the counselor despite the counselor's wishes—this cannot be prevented. However, the counselor can reduce and attempt to hold this attachment within reasonable limits. This can be done by setting limits and scrupulously abiding by them, despite pressure from the person to make exceptions. The counselor can relate in a totally honest fashion, refusing to modify needs, perceptions, values, or strengths to accommodate the inappropriate needs or fantasies of the person in counseling. The counselor also can deal openly with the manifestations of the emotional attachment, pointing out its nature and its detrimental effects.

The counselor must continually walk a thin line between being consumed by and rejecting the person. In the last analysis, however, it would be better for the person to terminate counseling or be terminated than to continue a kind of counseling that reinforces weaknesses and does serious damage.

Emotionally involved relationships

The only healthy relationship between a counselor and a person in counseling is an emotionally involved one, which lies equidistant between an emotionally detached and an emotionally attached relationship. In an emotionally involved relationship, the minds and hearts of the counselor and the person in counseling are *touching*, in contrast to being *distant* or *attached*.

The counselor and the person in counseling are close; so each is reasonably transparent to the other. They know each other well enough to trust and empathize with each other. They are emotionally intimate; so the feelings of one stimulate the feelings of the other, creating a vibrant relationship. Important learnings from this relationship can be generalized to other relationships.

As close as the counselor and the person in counseling are emotionally, however, they remain separate people with separate lives. They are equal partners in that each has equal rights, responsibilities, and freedoms. Both parties receive emotional resources from the relationship that allow them to become stronger. It is imperative that a counselor be emotionally involved in order to prevent the negative effects of the emotionally detached relationship. On the other hand, the counselor must avoid emotional attachment. This will free the counselor to be an effective helper.

TERMINATING COUNSELING

A counseling relationship, whether it lasts one or a hundred sessions, will terminate in one of three ways. First, counseling can terminate when the agreed upon goals have been achieved to a reasonable degree and the person is ready to launch out on his or her own. A second situation that arises is that the person in counseling wishes to terminate prematurely—to stop counseling before the goals have been met. Finally, the counselor may terminate the sessions even though the person in counseling wishes to continue.

Premature termination

When both a counselor and the person in counseling agree to terminate at the culmination of successful counseling, this does not present a problem. When a person in counseling wishes to terminate prematurely against the advice of the counselor, a problem is created. When this occurs, counselors can make one of two mistakes. First, they can immediately perceive this as a situation in which "fault" must be established. To them, it must be either the person's fault or the counselor's. Counselors who accept the blame may inappropriately berate themselves. More likely, however, counselors will blame the person in counseling and feel the need to point this out, which only compounds the problem.

The second mistake is to be cavalier about the situation. The counselor's attitude here is "Fine. I've got so many patients anyway, I can easily schedule somebody in your place."

The counselor's first response should be aimed at finding out *why* the person is saying he or she wishes to discontinue. Often, such a statement on the part of the person is, in actuality, communicating something different and is not meant to be translated literally. The following are some possible translations of what the premature termination by the person in counseling can mean:

1. An attempt to see if the counselor really cares about the person—to see how willingly the counselor acquiesces to the request
2. A test to see how secure the counselor is and how well he or she handles obstacles
3. An attempt to get the counselor to express some positive feelings toward the person, who feels only criticism from the counselor
4. A chance to try to hurt or punish the counselor for perceived or real injustices perpetrated by the counselor
5. A sign that the person is experiencing some very anxiety-producing feelings toward the counselor—fear, anger, sex, or dependency
6. An indication that the person intuits some frightening area arising in the near future and wishes to avoid it
7. An effect of defense mechanisms shifting, causing the person to feel euphoric and optimistic, whereas he or she was depressed and hopeless the week before
8. A fear that the counselor is going to reject the person (so the person chooses to reject the counselor first)
9. A sign that the person has found a "cure" elsewhere (for example, in love, religion, or a psychological "get rich quick" fad)
10. An indication that the person has not been truthful with the counselor in some important area and realizes that he or she must tell the truth or stop counseling
11. The person feels that the counselor is too strong or too weak and wishes to change counselors
12. The person feels that the counselor does not truly understand what the person is trying to say
13. The person feels that the counselor is laying "some trip" on him or her
14. The person feels that the counselor is incompetent

These are 14 typical issues that can be present, some or all of which can be explored in one way or another to establish the true reason for the person wishing to discontinue counseling. In the majority of cases, if this exploration can be done in a spirit of helpfulness and not as a threat or a dare, the person is led to understand what the real issue is and consequently is in a better position to make a good decision.

But what if the person still chooses to discontinue counseling? Every counselor, including the best, can expect that a few people will choose to discontinue counseling before its goals have been reached. There are three realizations that might be helpful. First, all counselors are imperfect and, therefore, occasionally will not be as helpful to a person as another counselor might have been. Counselors can freely admit this to themselves and to the person.

Second, not all people are equally ready for counseling, and not all people's readiness remains the same throughout counseling. A person's fear may increase during counseling and manifest itself in active resistance or a maudlin apathy. Either state may exist for a long time; so nothing is being accomplished. The counselor, in this case, is not at fault because he or she cannot work miracles. Therefore, it may be better for the person to discontinue counseling, at least for a while.

Third, the counselor may have been relating with the person in a potentially helpful way, but the person could not handle it. The person wanted a "special" relationship and, not finding it, chooses to look elsewhere. The criterion of an effective counselor is not that all people who begin counseling with him or her complete it. Analogously, a person's refusal to fill a prescription from a physician does not reflect on the physician's competence. Counselors can control only so many variables; the rest are controlled by the person and the people in the person's environment.

Whatever the case, the counselor's attitude and message to the person who actually discontinues counseling is important. A helpful attitude is seen in the statement "Well, I understand (or am trying to understand) why you feel the way you do. I think if you feel that strongly about it, you should take a rest from counseling. I hope you'll remember that the door is always open here for you. If you ever would like to talk, I would be happy to see you. I hope you do well, and I'll drop you a note in a while to keep in touch." This attitude need not cause the person to leave feeling guilty, either for making a mistake or for hurting the counselor's feelings. The person need not feel rejected because the counselor made it clear that he or she cared about the person and offered a standing invitation to return. The person need not be angry because the counselor obviously did what he or she could and was not angry at the person for leaving. Finally, the person need not feel hopeless, since the counselor did not connote that, without the counselor's help, he or she was doomed.

Counselor-initiated termination

Sometimes a counselor will wish to terminate a counseling relationship even though the person does not. There are both good and poor reasons for this desire. Some good reasons are the following:

1. Despite repeated efforts on the part of the counselor, the person has been entrenched for some time and shows little or no inclination to act in ways that will be helpful.
2. The person is using counseling in a destructive way; that is, he or she persistently relates to the counselor in an unhelpful way or uses counseling for motives other than growth.
3. Something has happened in the counseling relationship that causes the counselor to have strong feelings toward the person, either of attraction or antipathy. Thus the counselor feels it would be mutually beneficial to discontinue.
4. The person is as ready to terminate as he or she will ever be, but is still dependent on the counselor. The person would like to see the counselor forever, but the counselor clearly sees that it is time for the person to leave the nest.

The counselor may also wish to terminate counseling for poor reasons. One is the counselor is *angry* at the person in counseling. Because counselors are human, they will react angrily to people in counseling, just as people in counseling will react to them with anger. But if the counselor, in the midst of anger, terminates a counseling relationship, this can be damaging for both parties.

Sometimes the person in counseling can get a counselor so angry that he or she feels like saying "Look, if you're so unhappy with the way I do things, or if you're so cavalier about counseling, maybe it would be better if we stopped right now." It is doubtful that there has ever been a counselor who hasn't felt this sentiment. But *feeling* it and *acting it out* are two very different behaviors.

Counselors can remember that by terminating the person, they might well be playing into his or her dynamics. The person may seek rejection from the counselor to avoid the stress of counseling, to prove how truly incompetent the counselor is, or to show how hopeless the person in counseling is.

If counselors can articulate their anger in clear and strong ways, this should preclude the necessity of acting it out, unless the counselor wants to get rid of the person and is merely trumping up an excuse. People in counseling who are rejected by angry counselors learn either how totally unacceptable they are or how totally insecure counselors are. In either case, some lasting damage is likely to result.

As previously mentioned, a counselor may terminate a person who is doing ongoing violence to the counselor or to the relationship. Even then, the termination should be based on this dynamic and not solely on the anger of the counselor.

A second poor reason for termination is the counselor is *bored* with the person in counseling. Boredom may or may not be a just reason for termination of counseling by the counselor. If the person is boring as a part of intransigent resistance, then termination could be a reasonable solution. But if the person has a personality that is naturally bland and uninteresting, the counselor should reevaluate a decision to terminate for two reasons.

First, the person had the same personality when the counselor agreed to see him or her in counseling; so to terminate after this agreement may be unjust. Second, one of the reasons this person is in counseling is probably because of a boring personality. For a counselor to act toward this person just the way everyone else has is hardly the role of a helper. Rather than terminate the person, counselors can use their ingenuity to make the sessions more productive.

Regardless of the soundness of the reason, it is a very difficult situation for both the counselor and the person in counseling when the counselor chooses to terminate the sessions. There is no anxiety-free way to accomplish the termination. The counselor must possess the strength to say "As I've discussed with you on several occasions, I'm concerned about our situation, and I honestly feel that it has come to the point where it is in our best interests to stop seeing each other, at least for a while." The counselor may continue "I think it may be good for you to take a vacation from counseling for six months or a year and to clear out your system."

Depending on the circumstances, the parting may be relatively peaceful, but it also could be turbulent. Both the counselor and the person are likely to feel a mixture of failure, frustration, and resentment. This is why it is important to bring the subject of termination up early in the session so that feelings can be vented. Since the counselor should have discussed the possibility of terminating at least a few times prior to the session, both people should have been adequately prepared for it. All that is left is for both to learn a valuable lesson from the situation and to go on with living.

SUMMARY

Because counseling is a highly complex interaction, problems are bound to occur. Problems in themselves do not reflect the quality of the counseling relationship. Effective counselors, because they are astute and active, may address more sensitive issues and thus may experience more problems than less intuitive, less responsive counselors.

It is important, however, to distinguish between avoidable and unavoidable problems. Problems in a counseling relationship do not necessarily indicate that effective counseling is taking place. Counselors can create problems needlessly by sins of omission and commission. For example, a counselor may fail to offer support when it is needed, causing the person to feel that the counselor does not care. Or the counselor may confront the person on issues that are tangential to the goals of counseling, thus creating needless tension and resentment.

Whatever the quantity or quality of the problems that arise in counseling, it is necessary to evaluate each problem carefully to discern whether it is a tariff that must be paid for progressing in counseling or whether it is a problem that could have been avoided by a more prudent, secure, or skillful counselor.

THOUGHT QUESTIONS

1. Why do you suppose that boredom seems to be the behavior that counselors least acknowledge in themselves? What are the effects of refusing to acknowledge that a particular session or person is boring the counselor?
2. No matter how "therapeutic" counselors try to be, few enjoy being the target of hostility. A person says to you "How do you think you can help me? I have children older than you, and I noticed that your nails are bitten and you're overweight, which means you're not handling things so well yourself."

   What is your immediate reaction to this response?

   What do you feel like saying?

   What do you feel like doing?

   What *do* you say?

   What *do* you do?

3. What is the one quality you want people to see in you? Your answer will tell you the location of your largest manipulation button.
4. What is the one mistake you could make as a counselor that you would absolutely hate to admit?
5. In terms of emotional attachment, what kind of person could you see in counseling that would make it possible for you to become emotionally attached to him or her?

CHAPTER 12

Abnormal Behavior in Counseling

Although the number of essentially normal people who seek counseling is increasing, the majority of people in counseling experience symptoms of abnormal behavior. It is important, therefore, that counselors have a working knowledge of abnormal behavior. Because the field is extensive, it cannot be dealt with adequately in one chapter. However, some basic principles of abnormal behavior are particularly relevant to counselors. This chapter will deal with basic considerations regarding abnormal behavior, specific syndromes, and some medical aspects of abnormal behavior.

BASIC CONSIDERATIONS

Abnormal behavior significantly interferes with a person's psychological growth or with that of the people with whom the person relates. It has two dimensions. The first involves the *degree of impairment*. Abnormal behavior may impair a person's overall functioning to a mild, moderate, or severe degree. This scale of impairment is important in selecting candidates for counseling, in deciding how often to see the person, and in setting goals. For example, many people with severe symptoms may not be able to use counseling until the severity of their symptoms can be reduced by residential treatment and/or medications. The degree of impairment is also a factor in how often the counselor chooses to meet with the person. For example, the counselor may decide to meet weekly with a person who is mildly impaired and biweekly with a person who is moderately impaired. The degree of impairment also must be taken into account when establishing counseling goals. The goals of a person with severe impairment will likely be more modest than those of a person with mild or moderate impairment.

The second dimension of abnormal behavior is the *duration of the problem*. All other variables remaining the same, the longer a person has been behaving abnormally, the more unlearning and new learning must take place. This influences the length of counseling. Many people enter counseling with problems that have been present for years and assume that counseling should take only a few sessions. Often they so thoroughly assume this that they don't even mention it. Consequently, it is helpful for counselors to broach the subject of the possible length of treatment.

Using counseling

It's not necessarily true that the more distress people have, the more they will be motivated to use counseling well. More important than the amount of distress is the degree of psychological strength the person possesses. Some people have a fair degree of psychological strength. Although their distress is mild, they are willing to work as long and hard as necessary to change their behavior. Other people have only modest or little psychological strength. Despite their moderate or severe distress, they may feel that they are better off with their symptoms than without them.

Communication

Abnormal behavior is a way of communicating needs and feelings. For this reason, it is helpful to view it in an interpersonal context. A wife may be using her depression to communicate to her husband "I don't feel that you are meeting enough of my needs." An anxiety-ridden husband may be communicating to his wife "I feel that you are placing impossible demands on me." A phobic child may be communicating to his parents "I hate you, and I'm afraid if I go out of this house I'll never return." Counselors can help people translate their abnormal behavior into sentences that make sense and that lead to constructive action.

Symptom remission

When symptoms remit in counseling, it does not necessarily mean that counseling has accomplished its goal. Symptoms can remit for reasons other than the fact that the person has become stronger psychologically. Sometimes symptoms disappear when they have served their purpose by getting the person to seek counseling, by getting the attention of family members, or when pressure is temporarily relieved by talking with a counselor. Although the symptoms are no longer present, the person's behavior may continue to be maladaptive. It is important for counselors to understand this and be able to discuss it clearly with the people they see in counseling.

Assessing abnormality

Counselors can be careful not to simply take the word of the person in counseling as to how long the abnormal behavior and symptoms have been present. Some people significantly overestimate or underestimate the duration of problems as a part of their need to appear worse or better than they actually are.

The degree of seriousness of abnormal behavior is not always obvious. It is important for counselors to make an accurate assessment of the degree of disturbance so that appropriate referrals and treatment plans can be made. Some people present themselves in a highly agitated state and appear to be acutely disturbed. After a short time, however, it may become clear that the person is mildly or moderately disturbed, but far from severely impaired. Sometimes people consciously or unconsciously exaggerate their symptoms to impress the counselor with the seriousness of the situation. Other people typically overreact to situations as part of their personality.

On the other hand, people can appear to be very matter of fact and low keyed about their problems. They may assure the counselor that if he or she presently lacks the time to see them, they can return at a later date. It is important to remember, however, that many people who explode into a rampage of destructive behavior are described by others as appearing "perfectly normal" only moments prior. Counselors need to be keenly perceptive, astutely questioning, and totally listening to make reasonably accurate assessments of the extent of a person's disturbance.

There is no such thing as an abnormal person. While for purposes of brevity one may refer to "abnormal people," it is not a helpful practice. People may at times *behave* abnormally, but they are not abnormal. It is important to realize that no matter how impaired people's behavior is, they still behave normally in some areas. When people are defined as "abnormal," focus is placed on their weaknesses, which further contributes to their low self-esteem. People progress in counseling by focusing on what they can do as well as on what they can't do.

Everything that looks like abnormal behavior isn't, and everything that looks like normal behavior isn't. A man may suddenly quit his job and have no immediate means to support his family. At first glance, this may appear to be abnormal behavior. But under closer scrutiny, a counselor may discover that the man was placed in a situation in which he had to violate an important value or quit his job. His integrity was more important than what his friends would think or than his immediate comfort. Another man may have kept the job, and his decision is viewed as adaptive. The problem is that he has kept his job but lost a significant amount of self-respect, which gradually manifests itself in depression and sexually maladaptive behavior. As these examples indicate, counselors must be careful as to what they label normal and abnormal behavior.

It is important to diagnose abnormal behavior correctly. Some counselors do not relate comfortably to the idea of diagnosis. They may view it as labeling people in ways that will be detrimental to them; they may feel that diagnosis is identified with the medical model, which they reject; or they may feel that diagnoses are so unreliable as to be useless and harmful.

In a sense, all these positions have a degree of validity. To simply label a person and mistake this for treatment is harmful. To put specific diagnoses on records that will become a part of a person's life is not helpful. While diagnosis is a part of the medical model, it is not limited to this area. Diagnoses are important in many fields unrelated to medicine—for instance, in special education, automobile repair, and arson investigation. It is true that clinicians can give different diagnoses of the same person; however, this is true in all fields where judgments of people or performances are made. This is not a sufficient reason to abandon all judgments.

Diagnosis in counseling means that the counselor makes a clinical judgment as to the nature of the problem, develops hypotheses as to its cause, and formulates a counseling program that will have the best chance for success. Whether or not the counselor chooses to "officially diagnose" the person in terms of records or insurance forms is a matter to be discussed between the counselor and the person in counseling. The following example reflects some of the practical issues involved in diagnosis.

A woman seeks the help of a counselor because she is depressed following the death of her child. Is her depression a reaction to the loss of her child (an adjustment disorder), or did the death exacerbate a depression that is secondary to her dependent personality (personality disorder)? Is the death of the child only one of the several dynamics involved in her dysthymic disorder (a more serious affective disorder), or is her depression mostly caused by ingestion of reserpine, or by hypothyroidism, carcinoma of the pancreas, or a viral illness (organic affective syndrome)? These are not simply academic questions. It makes a critical difference that the diagnosis is correct because to treat a person for an adjustment disorder when in reality the person has a personality disorder or is experiencing organic dysfunctioning can make a great difference.[1]

Causality

Sufficient cause. It is important to distinguish between sufficient and contributing causes. A *sufficient cause* is an event that, by itself, causes abnormal symptoms—that is, no other cause is necessary. For a situation or event to be a sufficient cause, all people who experience it must react with abnormal behavior. For example, organic damage can be a sufficient cause for abnormal behavior. Serious damage to the central or autonomic nervous system alone can account for abnormal behavior, even in previously psychologically healthy people.

There are no nonorganic sufficient causes in abnormal behavior; that is, there is no psychosocial event that causes abnormal behavior in all those who experience it. There are some internal and external situations that have the potential to precipitate abnormal behavior, but they do not absolutely and categorically do so. For example, a concentration camp experience may have a high precipitative potential, but many people survived concentration camps symptom free. In fact, it seems that some people actually grew as a result of their experience.

Yet people commonly speak of causes being sufficient when, in fact, they are not. People say "His wife's death caused him to have a breakdown," "He went into a bad depression because he got fired," or "She went crazy because she heard her husband was unfaithful to her." For these to be sufficient causes for abnormal symptoms, everyone who experiences any of these situations would have to demonstrate abnormal behavior. Since few people experience abnormal symptoms as a result of any of these events, one must view them as contributing, but not sufficient causes.

This is not merely a theoretical distinction because to mistake contributing causes for sufficient ones will render the treatment superficial and ineffective. For example, to do grief counseling with a parent who is still depressed over the death of a child six months or a year later may be futile. The death of the child was a contributing cause, but the fact that the parent was and is unhappily married and had overinvested himself or herself in the child is another important contributing cause.

[1]For further discussion of this point, see Small (1972).

Counseling here would necessarily entail marital counseling to make the marriage stronger. If that doesn't seem to progress well, a third contributing cause—such as the individual's deep need to suffer in order to atone for earlier guilt-producing behavior—should be looked for.

Contributing cause. A *contributing cause* is an event that significantly creates stress in a person but does not, in itself, account for abnormal symptoms. Both external and internal situations can be contributing causes for abnormal symptoms. Some examples of external situations that can be contributing causes are a young man fails in school, loses his fiancée, or gets ejected from his parent's home. Examples of internal situations that can be contributing causes are a great deal of pent-up anger, emerging fears of homosexuality, and strong feelings of inadequacy.

Most abnormal symptoms stem from a combination of external and internal stresses—for example, inordinately strong dependency needs combined with the loss of a girlfriend, strong feelings of inadequacy plus a new promotion, inordinately strong sexual fears combined with entering marriage, deep fear of God plus the facing of imminent death.

Logic

It is helpful to understand some basic principles of logic as they apply to abnormal behavior. The fact that two events are related does not mean one has caused the other. For example, if a significant relationship between alcoholism in parents and antisocial behavior in their children were established, it would not mean that alcoholism in a parent *causes* antisocial behavior in children. If this were true, then the child could not be treated without first helping the parent to become nonalcoholic, a feat that may be impossible. It could be that alcoholic parents teach their children that the children are unlovable, and this causes the children to relate with others in unloving (antisocial) ways. If the children can be helped to feel lovable in spite of the messages that the parents give them, their psychological strength can be increased and their symptomatic behavior eliminated, or at least significantly reduced.

The fact that one event immediately follows another does not mean that the first event caused the second. A young woman moves away from home and gets an apartment with a female roommate. From the day she moves out of her home, she experiences anxiety symptoms. The "obvious" interpretation is that she is experiencing a separation anxiety caused by the abrupt breaking off of an over dependent relationship with her parents. However, the real cause of the anxiety attacks is her hidden fear that she may become emotionally and sexually attracted to her female roommate. To treat the separation anxiety as the cause of the symptoms will result in no symptomatic change.

The fact that one event can lead to a second event does not necessarily mean that the first event is the only possible cause of the second. For example, a person can reason as follows: Those who repress anger suffer from depression. Mr. Smith suffers from depression. Therefore he must be treated for repressed anger. But in fact, Mr. Smith is not repressing anger. He is depressed because he is lonely, feels helpless, has an endocrine dysfunction, or has a combination of all three. To treat Mr. Smith for repressed anger will lead to much wasted time and frustration.

Although these considerations may be academic in nature, the failure to understand them in a counseling setting can cause at least a good deal of wasted time and energy and at most a good deal of damage to the person seeking help.

SPECIFIC ABNORMAL SYNDROMES

The following are three types of abnormal behavior. These specific disorders were selected because they are commonly encountered in counseling.

Generalized anxiety disorder

Generalized anxiety disorder is characterized by generalized and persistent anxiety of at least one month's duration that is not associated with other specific disorders.[2] In the first stages of this disorder, it is typical for people to try to pin the anxiety to some external situation. For example, if exams are approaching, a student may assure himself that he is nervous about the exams, even though he has never been nervous in this way before. When the event that is supposed to be the precipitant passes, the anxiety remains or may even increase because it becomes clear that the source of anxiety is more ominous than was suspected.

Symptoms. The following are some typical symptoms of a generalized anxiety disorder.

1. *Motor tension.* The person experiences tremors of hands and feet, generalized agitation, fatigability, restlessness, and is continuously pacing and easily startled.

[2]American Psychiatric Association (1980), p. 232.

2. *Autonomic hyperactivity.* The person exhibits perspiring, palpitations, clammy hands; upset stomach, frequent urination, diarrhea; dizziness, light-headedness; shortness of breath, hyperventilation; weakness in knees, ringing in ears, inability to relax or sleep; muscular tension in neck, shoulders, and lower back.

3. *Apprehensive expectation.* The person feels that he or she is going to go crazy, die, do something of an aggressive or sexual nature that will cause public embarrassment, be arrested or confined to a mental hospital. The person may also fear similar events may happen to loved ones.

4. *Cognitive disruption.* The person feels confused and unable to concentrate, tends to be obsessed with anxious thoughts; experiences difficulty remembering; has little fantasy life except for morbid ruminations; has difficulty making decisions; reviews mistakes, real or imagined; when sleep is eventually possible, frightening dreams occur.

Some people who suffer from a generalized anxiety disorder experience *anxiety attacks*. These are recurring periods of acute panic that can last from a few seconds to an hour or more. These attacks are of sudden onset, mount to high intensity, and then subside. During the attack, many of the symptoms of anxiety previously mentioned can occur, but in terrifying intensity. These attacks can occur from several times a day to once a month or once every few years. When people experience their first anxiety attack, they may call a physician or ambulance because they feel that they are having a heart attack.

Anxiety in its milder and moderate forms is sometimes marked by analgesic behavior such as sleeping, drinking, or eating too much; working too hard; and taking tranquilizers. When people suddenly stop any of these behaviors, it is not unusual for them to experience raw anxiety that often causes them to revert to the analgesic behaviors.

People whose anxiety is of a more chronic than reactive nature often manifest the following behaviors: the inability to relax; rapid, loud, and rambling speech; inability to listen or comprehend directions; chronic irritability; low frustration tolerance; nervous laughter; inability to stop oneself from making foolish or hostile statements; and accident proneness.

Many people who experience anxiety-arousing conflicts feel trapped in their jobs and/or relationships. They lack the psychosocial competencies either to handle the unpleasant situation constructively or to extricate themselves successfully from it.

Causal factors.   Although there are many theoretical explanations of anxiety disorders, the following is a summary of the psychosocial explanations, since most counseling focuses on this dimension.

1. *Overly stringent conscience.* Sometimes anxious people repress normal aggressive and sexual feelings because they have been taught that merely entertaining such feelings, much less acting upon them, is psychologically and/or morally wrong. These people are placed in a bind. The more they repress these feelings, the more anxiety builds; the more the feelings approach consciousness, the more anxiety increases. Finally, the anxiety breaks through consciousness, but its sources remain repressed or enter consciousness in disguised forms.

2. *Anxiety-arousing conflicts.* These conflicts include the classic ones, especially approach-avoidance and avoidance-avoidance conflicts. A woman may have a strong desire to have an affair and an equally strong wish to perceive herself as a good wife. A man may be miserable being married but experience an equal amount of anxiety when he considers getting a divorce.

3. *Unrealistic expectations.* Some anxious people are laboring under unrealistic expectations placed on them by themselves or by loved ones. These expectations put great pressure on these people, which they dutifully accept without question. As the pressure mounts and the impossibility of meeting their expectations becomes more clear, anxiety symptoms surface.

4. *Self-alienation.* Some anxious people have lived according to the roles that others have assigned them for so long that they have almost completely broken with their true identity. Before the final break occurs and they completely lose themselves, the impending fracture creates massive anxiety, which floods them.

5. *Reactivation of prior stress.* People may find themselves in situations that rekindle long repressed ideas and feelings. For example, a man may have participated in sibling sex play with his sister 15 years prior and experienced guilt as a result. Now she plans to visit him during her vacation. As her visit approaches, he increasingly experiences anxiety symptoms to the degree that he must cancel his invitation. Because he has repressed his sexual behavior, along with the shame and guilt that accompanied it, he sees no connection between his symptoms and his sister's visit. Watching a movie, television, or a play, reading a book, or listening to music may present a subliminal cue that activates the anxiety around a prior experience without pulling the actual event into consciousness.

Counseling implications.   The following are some considerations that counselors may find helpful in working with people who are experiencing a generalized anxiety disorder. Counselors can remember that anxiety is contagious. Sometimes even experienced counselors get caught up in the anxiety of the person and make decisions that are premature and that they later regret. While anxiety disorders are obviously to be taken seriously, it may be helpful to know that, despite how acutely disturbed these people often appear, as with all neuroses, only 5% or less decompensate into psychosis.[3] Counselors will be more helpful if they can get some distance from the person's anxiety and deal with the problem without becoming anxious themselves.

The counselor can explain what is happening to the person in a clear, nonthreatening manner. Of all psychological disturbances, a generalized anxiety disorder is one of the most frightening and mystifying to people. They are electrified with anxiety and lack the slightest notion as to its cause. Consequently, they have anxiety about their anxiety, the combination of which can be paralyzing.

A counselor who understands the nature and dynamics of this disorder can offer at least tentative explanations and give assurances that none of the anticipated catastrophes is likely to occur. The fact that the counselor understands what is happening, has seen the syndrome many times before, and can offer realistic hope based on past experiences will render priceless support to the person.

Counselors who understand some of the more common causal factors can explore each one and render assistance in specific areas. For example, people with overly stringent consciences can be helped to understand the adaptive nature of feelings such as anger and sex and the damage caused by suppressing them. People experiencing anxiety-arousing conflicts can be helped to bring them into full awareness and to understand how to deal with them directly and constructively.

Anxious persons' fantasies and dreams often give clues as to the sources of their anxiety. For example, a man may go to sleep each night fantasizing that he received the report of his mother's death, or a woman may have a recurring dream that she is raped but finds herself enjoying it. The content of fantasies and dreams may provide a portal through which the causes of each person's anxiety may be discovered.

It is more helpful if counselors don't feel that they *must* discover the exact cause of the anxiety symptoms. If counselors place this imperative on themselves, their anxiety, coupled with that of the person, could become explosive. It would be helpful to learn the specific cause, but people can be greatly helped without such knowledge.

Sometimes the originating material is so deeply repressed that it

---

[3]Coleman, Butcher, & Carson (1980), p. 249.

will never be uncovered. The counselor still can help the person change cognitions about the anxiety, learn psychosocial competencies that will increase self-esteem, and show the person constructive outlets for the anxiety. Many people with anxiety disorders have successfully terminated counseling without ever discovering the specific cause of their anxiety.

Dysthymic disorder (depressive neurosis)

The affective disorder most commonly seen in counseling is *depression*. The basic feature in this disturbance involves depressed mood, loss of interest in everyday activities, and a diminishment or loss of pleasure in activities and relationships that once caused joy. These symptoms may be persistent or intermittent, separated by periods of normal functioning. This disorder usually begins in early adulthood and seldom requires hospitalization unless the person becomes suicidal.[4]

Symptoms. The following are some of the more common symptoms associated with depression. These symptoms can appear to a mild, moderate, or severe degree.

Emotional manifestations: dejected mood (feeling miserable, hopeless, blue, sad, lonely, unhappy, discouraged, ashamed, worried, useless, guilty); negative feelings toward the self (feeling stupid, sinful, worthless, ugly, perverted, selfish, crazy, weak, unlovable); reduction in gratification (things that were once pleasurable are now boring or even aggravating; these can include eating, sex, work, hobbies, and relationships).

Motivational manifestations: paralysis of will ("I can't go to work tomorrow"; "I can't get dressed today"; "I can't even talk to you"); avoidance wishes ("Leave me alone"; "I need to get away by myself"; "I just want to daydream"); suicidal wishes and tendencies ("I would be better off dead"; "I hope I don't wake up in the morning"; "I can see only one way out of this").

Physical manifestations: loss of appetite and weight loss; sleep disturbance (trouble going to sleep, waking in the middle of the night, waking too early); loss of sexual drive (less interested in sex, disinterested in sex, or repulsed by sex); psychomotor retardation (slowed speech, decelerated movement).

Cognitive manifestations: low self-evaluation ("I'm no good"; "I'm incompetent"; "I'm evil"); negative expectations ("I'll never feel

[4]American Psychiatric Association (1980), p. 220.

better"; "I'll never be able to return to work"; "Life is over for me"); self-blame ("It's all my fault"; "I deserve what is happening to me"; "I've caused my son's divorce"); impaired thinking (loss of concentration, memory loss, morbid ideation).

Causal factors. There are several theories about the causes of depression that deal with hereditary, biochemical, and psychosocial factors. Since most counselors focus on the psychosocial dimension, this section will list some of the more widely held concepts in this area.

1. *The experience of a significant loss.* Some common losses that can precipitate depression are the loss of or separation from a loved one and the loss of wealth or physical attractiveness. The common denominator in these losses is that they cause a person to feel less esteemed, important, and loved. These losses may be real, symbolic, or imaginary, but they can have the same damaging effect.

2. *Malignant interpretation of the loss.* Losses in themselves are not sufficient causes for depression; otherwise everyone who experienced a loss would become clinically depressed. An important variable in loss is how the person perceives its meaning. For example, one woman may have a mastectomy and continue to live her life as before. Another woman, interpreting the operation as causing her to be "no longer a woman," may react with depression. A man who loses his wife through death may view the event as the end of his life also, whereas another man, though grief stricken, recuperates and continues to live life well.

3. *Restricted sources of need fulfillment.* The more people put "all their eggs in one basket," the more problems arise when the basket falls. A woman who devotes her entire love and life to rearing her children may experience depression when the children leave home. A woman who lived for her career may become depressed when she retires. If these people had several sources of satisfaction, the loss of one or even two would not be shattering.

4. *Completion of a goal.* Some people set goals for themselves upon which rests almost their entire purpose in life. Everything in life revolves around the goal, and the pursuit of the goal is the person's main source of gratification. Once the person has reached the goal—for example, won a promotion or election, completed a book or play—there is nothing left but a large vacuum. This partially explains "promotion depression," in which the person feels depressed after winning a promotion, and "vacation depression," in which the person looks forward to a holiday, but experiences depression and irritability when it arrives.

5. *Learned helplessness.* This is the fatalistic belief that one cannot control important events in one's life. For example, a woman may la-

ment "My husband left me and I am incapable of living life on my own." These people have learned early in life that they are victims of circumstances, that life can be cruel, and that they might as well accept the fact that there's nothing they can do to change things. When life is good to them, they are happy; when life is cruel to them, they become and remain depressed.

6. *Strong anger that is not adequately or constructively expressed.* Sometimes it is less the loss itself that causes depression and more the anger at the loss. Some people tend to be self-blamers—"How could I have been so stupid?" "How could I have been so selfish?" Others blame those around them but cannot communicate the anger to these perceived causes of the loss and thus strangle on it. In either case, anger bloats these people to the degree that they can't move in any helpful direction.

7. *Excessive number of life responsibilities.* Some very conscientious and/or compulsive people assume almost an infinite number of family- and work-related responsibilities. After a while, two things become clear to them: they are exhausted and there are several important responsibilities remaining unmet. This combination fills them with a sense of frustration and hopelessness and shuts them down as a defense against the pain of trying to accomplish things that cannot be accomplished.

8. *Expiation of guilt.* People who feel that they are worthless or have committed serious sins may use depression as a form of self-punishment. They feel that they don't deserve to be happy because of who they are or what they have done. Consequently, they stop living as a fitting way to deprive themselves of happiness that they feel they do not deserve.

9. *Predisposing personality.* People who become depressed have a "fuse" in their personality that is ignited by the precipitating event. Without the fuse or without the precipitating event, no depression would ensue. The predisposing personality has three related cognitive sets. The first is a tendency to overinterpret events in a negative direction; normal setbacks and failures are perceived as traumatic. The second is low self-esteem. The persons view themselves as inadequate and worthless, and normal frustrations and failures prove to them that this negative self-concept is valid. Third, the persons view themselves as helpless and hopeless. When confronted with obstacles, they surrender. The combination of these negative cognitive sets causes a person to be inordinately vulnerable to stress, loss, and failure.[5]

---

[5]For a discussion of cognitive counseling for depression, see Beck (1976), p. 263, and Raimy (1975), p. 100.

Counseling implications. In the light of the previously mentioned symptoms and causes of depression, counselors can be aware of the following considerations.

Counselors can offer themselves as sources of understanding and appropriate empathy, especially since depressed people are often shunned by others, including loved ones.

Counselors can be familiar with the general causes of depression and help people strengthen the weaknesses that underlie them. For example, although counselors can't reinstate a loss, they can help people reinterpret it in more realistic ways. This will provide a stronger psychological foundation that will better absorb future stress.

Counselors can be aware of some of the traps they can fall into when helping depressed people. One trap is to "catch" the person's depression, so the counselor is swayed by the person's sense of hopelessness. This trap is easy to get caught in because the counselor's suggestions and plans are often met with several "good" reasons as to why each is unworkable. A second trap lies in becoming angry and frustrated with the depressed person. This reaction adds to the depression because the person already feels angry and frustrated, and these feelings in the counselor are interpreted as substantiating his or her own feelings of despair. A third trap is to reward the depression inadvertently. If counselors listen for hours on end to the feelings of depression without constructive, reality-oriented interpretations or plans on what to do with it, their patience, understanding, and empathy may be reinforcing the depression. The person may soon learn that it's more gratifying to have a "sympathetic ear" to talk to than to actively change the depressive behavior.

Counselors can understand that depression can be used as a way of expressing fear and anger. Many depressed people can't move because they are too frightened. Until the underlying fears are discovered and worked through, the depression will not lift. Depression can also be a very effective passive-aggressive behavior. A depressed person could be telling significant others "You've ruined my life; now I'm going to ruin yours." Until the anger can be conceptualized and effectively dealt with, the person has a vested interest in holding onto the depression.

Counselors can realize that the main goal of helping depressed people is not only to help them become undepressed, but to help them strengthen the preexisting weaknesses that made them vulnerable to depression.

Personality disorders

Personality disorders are characterized by personality characteristics that are relatively inflexible and maladaptive and cause at least mild impairment.[6]

Symptoms. People with personality disorders exhibit many of the following characteristics:

Maladaptive habits. These are long-standing and uninterrupted maladaptive habits of behavior that can be traced to early childhood or at least adolescence. They stem from flaws in the personality structure caused by failure to learn one or more important psychosocial competencies—for example, how to relate comfortably with people (schizoid personality), how to develop a sound value system (antisocial personality), or how to be self-reliant (dependent personality).

Resistance to change. The maladaptive behavior pattern is deeply ingrained and resistant to change.

Minimal distress. Minimum subjective distress is experienced more as a dull, continuing ache than as acute pain.

Problem to others. These disorders frequently cause more distress for others (spouses, parents, friends, coworkers) than for the person who has the disorder.

Lack of insight. People view themselves as normal and lack insight into the basic flaws in their personalities.

Inflexibility. The maladaptive behavior is inflexible and repetitive. The person employs the same defective behavior in all situations, failing to learn that what has not worked well in the past is unlikely to work well in the present.

Symptom dominance. People organize their lives around their symptoms. For example, schizoid people tend to choose associates and jobs that will allow them to remain essentially withdrawn emotionally.

Symptom variability. The symptoms may increase or decrease throughout life, depending on the nature and strength of stress at any particular time.

Secondary symptoms. The person may develop secondary symptoms as a result of the primary pathology. For example, a compulsive personality may develop ulcers or headaches; a schizoid personality may experience depression due to minimal need fulfillment.

Weak motivation. The motivation for counseling is usually tenuous. These people are often referred by relatives, friends, or

[6]American Psychiatric Association (1980), p. 305.

employers because their behavior has been socially disruptive. When they are self-referred, their goal is usually to rid themselves of a secondary symptom—such as headaches, depression, insomnia, loneliness, boredom, or scruples. However, they are seldom interested in changing the maladaptive behavior that is causing the secondary symptoms.

Causal factors. The psychosocial causality underlying personality disorders is that critically important psychosocial competencies were inadequately learned. The nature of the inadequately learned competency or competencies differs for each of the eleven personality disorders. Hence, causality can be discussed only in terms of each specific disorder.

Counseling implications. The following points regarding personality disorders may be helpful for counselors to consider.

It is likely that a significant number of people in counseling have personality disorders. Secondary symptoms frequently mask underlying personality disorders, which could give the false impression that counselors seldom see people with personality disorders. It is not atypical of dependent personalities, for example, to experience marked depression as a result of a fractured relationship. These individuals may seek counseling and offer depression as their chief complaint. Since the person reports feeling "fine, in fact, very good" prior to the breakup of the relationship, the counselor may automatically assume that the person is experiencing a posttraumatic stress reaction or an affective disorder precipitated by the loss of an important relationship.

People with personality disorders have a "string of beads" dynamic. The beads represent episodes where their maladaptive behavior gets them into trouble, and the string represents the basic personality flaw that causes and supports their symptoms. Counselors who do not take a careful history may devote their attention to the newest "bead" and ignore the string, which will continue to support symptoms long after the current therapeutic encounter.

People with personality disorders are often particularly challenging to work with in counseling. This is ordinarily true because their problem is deeply ingrained and causes them relatively little subjective anxiety, and they lack insight into their personality flaw or flaws.

Dependent personality. The *DSM III* lists eleven personality disorders. The dependent personality is frequently seen in counseling and can serve as an example of many of the other personality disorders.[7] The basic feature of this disorder is seen in people who passively allow others to assume responsibility for major areas of their lives because of a lack of self-confidence and an inability to be self-reliant. They subordinate their needs to those of others, on whom they depend in order to avoid accepting responsibility for their behavior.

Dependent personalities have many or all of the following symptoms, which are recognizable early in life. These people

1. exhibit excessive psychological dependence on others for attention, affirmation, and affection and suffer acute discomfort, even panic, at being alone;
2. subordinate their own needs, feelings, and values to the people on whom they depend (they psychologically prostitute themselves in order to gain acceptance);
3. induce others to make major decisions for them and often blame them if things fail to work out;
4. are willing to suffer great discomfort and even abuse in the service of getting dependency needs met;
5. view themselves as inadequate, incompetent, stupid, and helpless and use these self-deprecations to induce others to take over their lives;
6. depend on things as well as people (for example, pets, food, alcohol, or drugs);
7. repress and deny ideas and feelings that could evoke displeasure and jeopardize a relationship;
8. are exceedingly sensitive to signs of disapproval and rejection, often seeing signs when they don't exist;
9. cannot draw upon inner resources for comfort, stimulation, and gratification consequently, they often seek excitement and are easily bored;
10. capture people by manipulation, seduction, self-sacrifice, and by making themselves so useful or attractive that they won't be rejected;
11. tend to be naive and Pollyannaish, especially in relationships, because they don't want to see anything negative that would make them reconsider the merits of the relationship;
12. often experience secondary symptoms—such as depression, anxiety, hypochondriasis, and psychosomatic symptoms—when dependency needs are not met.

[7]American Psychiatric Association (1980), p. 324.

As with most personality disorders, the precise causal factors are based on speculation and inference. The following are some hypothesized causes of a dependent personality.

Parental attachment and overprotection. Parents greatly overmet these people's needs when they were children to the extent that they learned that other people can meet their needs more successfully than they can. Moreover, because these people were discouraged from becoming self-sufficient, they lack the psychosocial competencies for being instrumental in their own need fulfillment.

Weak self-identity. As a natural consequence of the first cause, these people are so reliant on others' definitions of who they are that they never develop a sound sense of who they are. Consequently, they not only must rely on others for need fulfillment but for a sense of identity, which is expressed in the attitude "I am no one without you." When relationships develop problems, severe anxiety is created because the situation threatens not only these people's need fulfillment but also their entire sense of self.

Rewarded dependent behavior. In order to be accepted and loved, these people behave in very pleasing, docile, and loving ways. As a result, they are often viewed as being helpful, polite, caring people who can be very loving and self-sacrificing. These behaviors are often rewarded by others; that is, their behaviors do the job they are supposed to do. Moreover, dependent people are rewarded because when they hand their lives over to others, they are relieved of the tremendous responsibility of making their own decisions.

As with all people with personality disorders, dependent personalities bring their disorder into the counseling relationship. Although this sounds obvious, sometimes counselors believe that people will check their disturbance at the door. Dependent people will appear to be "model patients" because they often seek help on their own and will do anything to help the counselor help them. But the main reason they look forward to counseling is that they view the counselor as a person who will be not only a benevolent but an expert caretaker. So while they appear to be motivated to use counseling, their deeper motivation is actually to use the counselor.

By adulthood, most people with dependent personalities have learned that they cannot hand over their lives to people in an obvious way, because that frightens people away from them. So with assurances such as "I know I have to do most of the work myself" and "I don't want you to manage my life; I just want some feedback from you," the dependent person begins to develop another dependency relationship.

Consequently, counselors can be careful not to allow these people to assign them the same caretaker role that they have assigned a medley of other people, the results of which brought them into counseling. While counselors need not be harsh in this regard, they can remain steadfast in their role as a counselor and not assume the role of mother, father, husband, or wife.

Counselors can take specific steps to see that the counseling relationship does not become simply another dependency relationship for the person.[8] The following are some relevant considerations.

Sometimes announcing to the person that counseling will be short term can be helpful. The message is that the person has only a set number of sessions to gain all he or she can from counseling, and this can cut down on the potential for becoming addicted to it.

Counselors can make it clear not only verbally but also behaviorally that they will make no decisions for the person and give the person no advice. Although the person can be free to discuss plans for action and get some meaningful feedback, the counselor does not act as a manager.

Counselors can focus on the person's dynamics and outside relationships rather than spend much time on the counseling relationship. One way of focusing on the person's dynamics is to assess the person's cognitions, especially those that deal with self-esteem, self-reliance, and the catastrophic expectation that drives the person to seek caretakers.

The focus can be on changing behavior rather than on learning how to develop newer and better dependency relationships. Counselors can often ask "How is what you did last week going to help you learn to stand on your own two feet?"

MEDICAL ASPECTS OF ABNORMAL BEHAVIOR

The body can affect the psyche in a number of ways. A basic working knowledge of this relationship will help counselors appropriately select people for counseling and make intelligent referrals when the possibility exists that nonpsychological factors may be causing or contributing to the abnormal behavior.

The following points may be helpful for counselors to remember when dealing with people with abnormal behavior and symptoms.

[8]For a more thorough discussion of this concept, see Leeman & Mulvey (1973).

Physical examination

It is always a good idea to refer a person for a thorough physical examination as part of the counseling evaluation. Ideally, it would be helpful to work with a physician who is attuned to the psychological as well as the medical components of disorders and medications. Equipped with this understanding, the physician is in a better position to gear the examination to discover or rule out factors that would affect the person's psychological behavior in problematic ways.

It is also important to understand that one examination at the beginning of counseling is not always sufficient. A counselor cannot realistically assume that the results of a medical examination done 6 or 18 months before are presently valid. This is particularly true in some disorders, such as anxiety and depression, in which the psychological stress can trigger biochemical reactions that, in turn, increase or change the person's symptoms. Also, a physical disorder may have been latent at the time of the first medical examination but become exacerbated during the intervening period, causing psychological problems that could be prevented with proper medical treatment.

Medications and abnormal behavior

It is also important for counselors to be aware of the relationship between medications and abnormal behavior. One situation that can arise in this regard is that a person in counseling is taking a nonpsychiatric medication. For example, while giving his history to the counselor, a man mentions that he is taking something to control his blood pressure. Since the "something" is unlikely to be a psychiatric medication, the counselor pays little attention to it. However, if the counselor had asked the man to bring the bottle of medication to the next visit, the counselor would have seen that the prescription was for Inderal. If the counselor had consulted the *Physician's Desk Reference*, he or she would have seen that the potential side effects of this medication include depression, fatigue, emotional lability, decrease in coordination of neuropsychological tasks, slightly clouded sensorium, disorientation for time and place, and hallucinations.[9]

If this man in counseling has depression as a chief complaint, it raises the following questions: Is the depression purely psychological in nature? Is it a side effect of the medication? Is it caused by the interaction between psychological and physical factors? Although such questions cannot always be easily answered, it is important that they be asked in order to prevent avoidable mistakes.

[9]*Physician's Desk Reference* (1981), pp. 613–614.

A second situation that can arise is when a person in counseling is taking psychiatric medication. It is important that counselors have a general knowledge of a medication's side effects. For example, Valium, a commonly prescribed tranquilizer, not only can reduce anxiety and tension but also has such potential negative side effects as confusion, depression, headaches, and changes in sexual energy. Paradoxical reactions are also possible side effects of this medication; these include acute hyperexcited states, anxiety, insomnia, and hallucinations.[10] Although these side effects may be uncommon, a counselor cannot assume that the medication is devoid of psychological side effects.

Counselors can be aware that sometimes physicians misprescribe a psychiatric medication because people may lack the ability to describe their symptoms clearly. Many depressed people describe themselves as "nervous" or "tense" because they lack the vocabulary or sophistication to be more precise. A physician who fails to take the time to make his or her own assessment of the person's subjective state may prescribe tranquilizers to help relieve the "tension." However, the tranquilizers may increase the person's existing depression, causing the person to want increased dosages because the dosage taken seems ineffective.

Another dimension of psychiatric medication that counselors can be aware of is the potential of a particular medication to create psychological or physical dependency. Table 12–1 lists some of the more commonly prescribed psychiatric medications and their potential for dependence.

A person in counseling may be on psychiatric and nonpsychiatric medications, the combination of which can cause psychological dysfunctioning.

Another situation can arise when a person enters counseling already taking one or more psychiatric medications. A counselor may request that the individual discontinue the medication because the counselor feels that it is unnecessary or that it is confusing the clinical picture. The counselor may also be philosophically opposed to people taking psychiatric medication except in cases when the medication will prevent or modify seriously disturbed behavior.

Whatever the reason for wanting the person to discontinue a medication, the counselor must be mindful that sudden discontinuance of medication can cause serious withdrawal symptoms in people who have become dependent on the drugs. For example, abrupt withdrawal from amphetamines (Benzedrine, Dexedrine, Methedrine) commonly results

[10]*Physician's Desk Reference* (1981), pp. 1531–1532.

TABLE 12–1. Dependence potential of common psychiatric medications.

Classification	Drug	Physiological dependence	Psychological dependence
Sedatives	Alcohol (ethanol)	Yes	Yes
	Barbiturates Nembutal (pentobarbital) Seconal (secobarbital) Veronal (barbital) Tuinal (secobarbital and amobarbital)	Yes	Yes
Stimulants	Amphetamines Benzedrine (amphetamine) Dexedrine (dextroamphetamine) Methedrine (methamphetamine)	No	Yes
Antianxiety drugs (minor tranquili- zers)	Librium (chlordiazepoxide) Miltown (meprobamate) Valium (diazepam) Others, such as Compoz (scopolamine)	Yes	Yes

From *Abnormal Psychology and Modern Life,* 6th Edition, by J. C. Coleman, J. N. Butcher, and R. C. Carson. Copyright ©1980, 1976, 1972, 1964 by Scott, Foresman, & Co. Reprinted by permission.

in feelings of depression that reach a peak in 48 to 72 hours and often remain intense for a day or two. Mild feelings of depression and listlessness may persist for weeks or even months after the last dose.

Serious withdrawal symptoms can also be seen in people who have become dependent on barbiturates (Nembutal, Seconal, Veronal, Tuinal). Some common withdrawal symptoms are anxiety, tremors, insomnia, vomiting, and rapid heart rate. Between the 16th hour and the 5th day, convulsions may occur, and an acute psychosis often develops.[11]

Withdrawal can also be a factor in people who discontinue the use of diet pills. Many diet pills have a fixed ratio combination of amphetamines and barbiturates. Since both these drugs are highly addictive, their sudden discontinuance can cause serious withdrawal symptoms.[12]

For these reasons, it is important that counselors refer people who are taking medications to a physician for medical evaluation. If the physician and counselor agree that withdrawal from the medication should be initiated, both professionals can work together to help the person taper off, both psychologically and physically, from the medication and so prevent potentially serious problems.

[11]Coleman et al. (1980), pp. 346, 348.
[12]Kunnes (1973).

While counselors need not be experts in pharmacology, it is important to have at least a general understanding of the effects of *any* medication on a person's psychological functioning. With this understanding, a more cautious attitude can result that will prevent avoidable errors.

Organically caused abnormal symptoms

It is helpful for counselors to have some familiarity with abnormal symptoms that can have nonpsychological causes. Endocrine dysfunctioning can cause symptoms that would bring a person to counseling. The following are some examples of psychological symptoms of endocrine disorders that might be seen in counseling.[13]

Hyperparathyroidism. In its milder form, it causes neurasthenic personality changes that are insidious: loss of initiative and interest, fatigue, depression, and memory disturbances. An unsuspecting counselor could diagnose this person as a dependent personality, a dysthymic disorder, or an adjustment disorder with depressed mood. In its more progressed form, this disease causes severe anxiety, paranoia, disorientation, and hallucinations, which could be mistaken for psychoses of a psychogenic nature.

Cushing's syndrome. Over 50% of people who have this disease experience the following symptoms: weakness, emotional lability, anxiety, and depression. Psychoses may be seen in one-half to two-thirds of all people with this disorder. The development of psychological symptoms may clearly antidate the physical manifestations; so a medical examination at the beginning of counseling may not detect its presence.

Addison's disease. Over 80% of people who have this disorder experience psychological symptoms. These include easy fatigability, apathy, and irritability. In its more severe form, Addison's disease causes marked depression, paranoia, delusions, and thought disorders.

Hypoglycemia. Some typical psychological symptoms of this disease are headaches, confusion, poor judgment, hysterical behavior, and schizophrenic-like and manic-depressive-like symptoms. People with reactive hypoglycemia manifest such symptoms as sweating, tachycardia, palpitations, and tremulousness, which could well be misdiagnosed as symptoms of a psychogenic anxiety disorder.

Hyperthyroidism. The common psychological symptoms of this

[13]Vinicor & Cooper (1979).

disorder are memory impairment, increased anxiety, irritability, aggressiveness, restlessness, and hyperactivity.

Myxedema. In its milder form, myxedema causes the following symptoms: depression, psychomotor retardation, memory failures, difficulty in concentrating and abstracting, and deterioration of intelligence. In its more severe form, the disorder causes confusion, delusions of persecution, and hallucinations.

Neurological dysfunctioning, like endocrine dysfunctioning, can cause symptoms that are the same as those seen in psychogenic disorders. Some common neurological disorders that can cause psychological symptoms are cerebral infections, encephalitis, neurosyphilis, vascular accidents, brain tumors, cerebral traumas, and degenerative disorders (presenility, Huntington's chorea, Parkinson's, Pick's and Alzheimer's disease).

The major symptoms that can occur as the result of neurological disorders are the following:

1. Disorientation in time, person, and place.
2. Memory impairment. (The person may have long-term memory loss but, more typically, has short-term memory loss and may confabulate to fill in the memory gaps. Memory impairment may be the most common symptom of brain disorders.)
3. Impairment of comprehension, calculation, knowledge, and learning.
4. Impairment of judgment. (The person cannot make appropriate decisions and may exercise poor judgment.)
5. Lability and shallowness of affect. (The person may shift quickly and inappropriately from apathy to hostility or from laughing to weeping.)
6. Emotional impairment. (The person emotionally overreacts with inappropriate laughing or crying, or a blunting of emotional responses occurs.)
7. Loss of impulse control. (The person is unable to inhibit inappropriate sexual and aggressive urges.)[14]

All these symptoms could also be those of a psychogenic disorder. No counselor, nonmedical or medical, is in a position to make these critical differential diagnoses alone. It is important to know how to make an appropriate referral to a professional, who may examine and refer the person on to other professionals so that all dimensions can be covered adequately.

[14]For further discussion of these symptoms, see Martin (1977), p. 581.

SUMMARY

It is not sufficient for counselors to have helpful personalities. If counselors are going to work with people who have psychological problems, they must also have an extensive working knowledge of abnormal behavior. An insidious and perilous assumption that some counselors harbor is that since abnormal problems are simply extensions of normal ones, the same understanding and approaches are relevant to both. The fallacy underlying this assumption is seen if it is applied to a more concrete situation. For example, while one can view a forest fire as simply an extension of a grass fire, the methods and skills required to fight the two are very different. A sound knowledge of abnormal behavior is necessary for counselors to be helpful to the people who need them most.

THOUGHT QUESTIONS

1. What aspect of seeing psychologically disturbed people in counseling is the most anxiety producing for you? Why?
2. What is your attitude toward formal diagnosis? If you think diagnosis is helpful, what about the real possibility that a diagnosis in some form will return to haunt the person later in life? If you think it is unhelpful, what will you do when the agency for which you work or the insurance company who will pay for the counseling requires a diagnosis?
3. What are some cautions counselors should keep in mind when working with dependent personalities?
4. What is your attitude about hospitalization and medications for people with psychological problems? How disturbed would a person have to be before you recommended hospitalization? What kind of symptoms would a person have to be experiencing before you referred the person for medications?
5. A person tells you "I'm more depressed now than before I started counseling." What will you respond to this?

CHAPTER 13

Crisis Intervention

Crisis intervention is a type of short-term counseling that is the treatment of choice when the person seeking help is experiencing a state of acute psychological disequilibrium. The person's symptoms are "hot" and need immediate and skilled attention.

Counselors are being called upon increasingly to deal with crisis situations. Whether this is because there are more crises occurring in our society, people are less prepared to deal with crisis, or people are more aware of the help available to them, crisis intervention has recently become a subspecialty in the field of counseling.

TRAUMAS AND CRISES

A *crisis* is a state of cognitive disorganization and affective turmoil that is caused by perceiving an event as so threatening that it leaves the person incapable of functioning effectively. Typically, crises are of short duration, lasting one day to a few weeks.

Most people in the midst of crisis use similar ways of communicating their cognitive disorganization. They may say "I'm so confused I don't know which way to turn" or "I think I'm going to lose my mind." They also express their affective turmoil in similar ways: "I'm absolutely terrified" or "I'm so distraught I can hardly see straight."

It is important to distinguish between a trauma and a crisis. A *trauma* is a powerful assault on the psychological well-being of a person and causes intense psychological pain (anxiety). A trauma may or may

317

not precipitate a crisis. Whether it does or not depends on the relationship between the trauma and the specific vulnerability of the person, on the person's perception of the trauma, on the person's ability to handle the pain that the trauma created, on the environmental (social and religious) supports available to the person, and on the psychological strength of the pretrauma personality.

In other words, a trauma is an objective event. A crisis is a subjective reaction to that event. It is only because this is true that crisis intervention can be effective, since no type of counseling can undo a trauma; it can only help the person experience the trauma differently and handle the psychological pain it produces more effectively.

The difference between a trauma and a crisis is evident in people's dramatically different reactions to the same trauma—for example, the death of a child. A parent may

1. grow in appreciation of the remaining children, feel closer to his or her spouse, and experience an increase in religious fervor;
2. be so overcome with grief that he or she commits suicide;
3. slip into an acute depression for several weeks;
4. get drunk for a month;
5. vow never to have another child;
6. immediately try to have another child;
7. initiate divorce proceedings;
8. insist on moving immediately to another home;
9. be relieved and grateful.

Preventive mental health focuses on the variables that turn traumas into crises, in order to prevent them. Crisis intervention focuses on the crisis in order to stop the psychological hemorrhaging before it does serious damage. Ideally, crisis intervention starts the person on a path so that he or she need never suffer another crisis, regardless of the traumas still to be experienced.

Types of traumas

There are four types of traumas that can precipitate a crisis: situational, developmental, intrapsychic, and existential. Each of these traumas can vary in intensity from mild to moderate to severe.

Situational traumas can include the death of a loved one, divorce, rape, loss of a job, serious financial reverses, discovery of a serious illness in oneself or a loved one, unwanted pregnancy, the discovery that a spouse has been unfaithful, the breakup of a close relationship or engagement, public embarrassment (such as being arrested or caught in a scandal), failure in business or school, and family stresses. Natural disasters are also situational traumas—for example, fires, earthquakes, hurricanes, and floods.

Developmental traumas can arise as a part of progressing through life's stages. These include traumas of childhood (birth of an unwanted sibling, peer rejection), adolescence (police, drug, or alcohol problems; sexual behaviors that cause shame and guilt; peer pressures to behave in ways that cause value conflict; dating pressures and stresses; academic or disciplinary problems at school), adulthood (stresses in dating, engagement, marriage, or parenthood; conflicts within the family and with in-laws and neighbors; dealing with the stresses of children leaving home; forced reduction of career expectations; waning attractiveness and sexual energy), and late life (retirement, failing health, loss of friends through death, loneliness, rejection by adult children, the specter of death). This is not meant to imply that all the events mentioned automatically cause a crisis. They *can* cause crises for certain people in specific situations.

Intrapsychic traumas are internal events that create great anxiety. They can include the gradual or sudden emergence of homosexual feelings, the realization that one hates a person one "should" love (a parent, child, spouse, or friend), the gradual or sudden awareness of profound identity confusion, the realization that one must leave a job or marriage to salvage one's sanity, the increasing intensity of thoughts regarding suicide or homicide, the arising of serious questions and doubts about one's religion or God.

It is typical that these types of intrapsychic thoughts and feelings are preconscious for some time and suddenly burst into consciousness when the person's defenses become overburdened with related or unrelated stresses. At this point the person may have a crisis reaction or carry the burden of the anxiety-producing realization for some time before it festers into a crisis reaction.

Existential traumas stem from the gradual or sudden recognition of a void, emptiness, or lack of meaning in one's life. Work, hobbies, social and love relationships, all of which were once compelling purposes and distractions, now seem vacuous and absurd. In a crisis reaction, the person feels a sense of emptiness that can create great anxiety and panic.

Benefits of crisis

The word *crisis* is frightening to most people and tends to have solely negative connotations. In fact, however, a crisis can have beneficial results in two ways. A crisis can be therapeutic when it brings both the beauty and ugliness in a person's life into sharper focus. A crisis at work may help a woman appreciate her family in ways she has never experienced. The death of a child may help parents appreciate their marriage relationship on a much deeper level. An existential crisis may lead a man to rearrange his values and priorities so that his life develops a fuller meaning than it would have possessed without the crisis.

A crisis can also introduce persons to the destructive elements in their lives that have been repressed and denied. For example, the explosion of serious marital problems may awaken the partners to the many ways they have been damaging themselves and sabotaging their relationship. This affords them an opportunity to recognize and evaluate the downward trend their marriage has been taking and to initiate steps to correct it or to terminate the relationship.

A crisis also can be therapeutic when people are helped to handle it successfully, learning cognitive and affective skills that will make them stronger psychologically. Many people look back on a crisis as "the best thing that ever happened" because they learned a good deal about themselves and life in general. As Aguilera and Messick state:

> The Chinese characters that represent the word "crisis" mean both danger and opportunity. Crisis is a *danger* because it threatens to overwhelm the individual or his family, and it may result in suicide or a psychotic break. It is also an *opportunity* because during times of crisis individuals are more receptive to therapeutic influences. Prompt and skillful intervention may not only prevent the development of a serious long-term disability but may also allow new coping patterns to emerge that can help the individual function at a higher level of equilibrium than before the crisis.[1]

HOW CRISIS INTERVENTION DIFFERS FROM OTHER TYPES OF COUNSELING

Crisis intervention differs from other kinds of counseling, including short-term, noncrisis counseling, in four important ways.

1. *Time.* Crisis intervention normally lasts from one to six sessions; short-term counseling of a noncrisis nature normally lasts from one to twenty sessions, and traditional counseling may last for hundreds of sessions.

2. *Focus.* In crisis intervention, attention is focused tightly on the present crisis. In other types of counseling, there is more time and psychological room to attend to other issues, such as the person's history, unconscious processes, interpretation, interpersonal conflicts, career stresses, communication problems, transference, counter-

[1]Aguilera & Messick (1978), p. 1.

transference, sexual and identity confusion, personality constrictions, and value conflicts.

3. *Active participation.* Crisis intervention demands more active participation than other kinds of counseling. A counselor is often called upon to be direct, to make suggestions, to give advice, to seek the support of family and friends actively and directly, to contact other referral sources and introduce the person to them, to work directly with legal counsel for the person or with police agencies that are involved in the situation, and to recommend environmental changes, such as taking a leave of absence from a job, temporarily moving out of a stressful family situation, or being hospitalized.

4. *Goal.* The goal of crisis intervention is to return the person to the level of precrisis adjustment. Precrisis adjustment is not pretrauma adjustment. In other words, if a woman is experiencing a crisis reaction to the death of her husband, she may still be very upset at the end of successful crisis intervention, but she is no longer in a crisis state. It would be unrealistic to expect crisis intervention to return this woman to the state of equilibrium she experienced prior to her husband's death.

RESPONSES AND SKILLS

Common crisis reactions

Although each person reacts to crisis differently, there are five common reactions.

Depression. People may react to crisis with a sense of profound sadness, grief, or hopelessness. Their attitude is "What's the use? Nothing makes any difference now anyway." The sadness is often accompanied by sobbing or obvious attempts to refrain from weeping; by a substantial lack of energy, which is manifested in "sitting and staring" behavior; by a marked preoccupation with the precipitating event and a reluctance to discuss different but relevant issues; by apathy, sleeplessness, loss of appetite, and a seeming inability to care for oneself; by veiled hints and sometimes explicit statements that reflect the feeling that life is no longer worth living.

Anxiety. People may feel overwhelmed by a sense of fear, dread, and apprehension. They report feeling that their tension is going to cause them to burst or disintegrate. They have an overabundance of unchanneled energy, which causes them to behave in an agitated manner: constant motion, which is seen in frequent sitting, then standing, then pacing; feverish attempts to reduce anxiety by smoking, drinking, eating, praying, phoning, taking medications, and talking to "anyone who can help."

Common physical symptoms that can accompany anxiety reactions include profuse perspiring, headaches, palpitations, chest pain, tremors, hyperventilation, dizziness, and shortness of breath.

Sometimes anxious people relive the trauma in thought, fantasy, dreams, nightmares, and speech. Ordinary problems become magnified, assume extra importance, and seem insurmountable. Daily chores become major obstacles and require great planning.

Shock.   People may be so stunned by the traumatic event that they feel numb and dazed. They partially dissociate themselves from the event, which leaves them with the feeling "This isn't really happening to me." The psychological distance they have placed between themselves and the event is reflected in their appearance, which is often zombielike. Their eyes look glazed; their speech has a "faraway" sound; they have trouble hearing and concentrating; they walk in a rather stiff, unsteady way. They seem to be helpless and are quite suggestible.

Violence.   Some people react to stress caused by the precipitating event with physical attacks on others or against themselves. They may attack, or threaten to attack, the person whom they perceive as the cause of the crisis (for example, an unfaithful spouse). They feel that the only way they can vent their fury and recapture their self-esteem is to hurt or destroy the person whom they perceive as having injured them.

People who historically have turned their hurt and anger inward would be more inclined to react with violence toward themselves. This violence could manifest itself in potentially self-destructive behavior, such as jumping in a car and driving at high rates of speed along winding roads or drinking or taking drugs until one lapses into unconsciousness. The self-directed violence may also manifest itself in direct ways by suicidal gestures, genuine attempts, or actual suicide.

Pseudoadaptive reactions.   This is the most subtle of all the crisis reactions. These individuals appear to be handling the trauma and the resultant stress well. In fact, they seem to be handling it *too well*. Their attitude toward the traumatic event is very philosophical or theological. Generally, their commentaries on the trauma are replete with platitudes that sound much more "taped" than well thought out and felt out. Some common "tapes" are "Everything in life happens for a reason; so I'm sure there is some good reason for this''; "God works in our lives in strange ways; I'm sure He's doing this so I will grow in my love for Him"; "This is my chance to show people what I am really made of."

The pseudoadaptive reaction is a very brittle defense buttressed by repression, denial, and reaction formation. These people rarely seek help on their own but present themselves to a counselor with statements such as "I'm handling this situation well, but my husband (friend, doctor, minister) suggested that it might be good to talk with you. So here I am." When the repressed feelings of fear, hurt, anger, or guilt incubate and spread, they are likely to inundate the brittle defense of the pseudoadaptive response and cause a major upheaval.

The pseudoadaptive reaction can be differentiated from a genuinely adaptive reaction in the following ways:

1. The pseudoadaptive reaction is a source of concern and not of relief to the people who know the person best.

2. In the pseudoadaptive response, the person does not reflect a healthy integration and resolution between the painful feelings and the positive and redeeming aspects of the crisis. The person ignores and intellectualizes the painful elements while concentrating on or exaggerating the salutary aspects of the crisis.

3. The person strongly resists any suggestions by the counselor that there may be some painful and unresolved feelings to which the person is not attending. When the counselor probes this area, he or she is likely to be accused of trying to create a problem where no problem exists.

Although there are no clearcut lines between a pseudoadaptive and a genuinely adaptive reaction to trauma, the counselor can be alert to the possibility that a person's seeming equanimity may be covering a welter of conflict.

Dealing with crisis reactions

When dealing with crisis reactions, it is helpful for the counselor and the person in counseling to be aware of the following factors.

Dealing with reality. At the time of the crisis reaction, the person is unable to deal adequately with reality. Depressed people are so sad that they can see only the negative aspects of their lives and have little energy to move psychologically. Anxious people are so frightened that they seem unable to concentrate on the reality of the situation and make helpful decisions. People who are in shock are sufficiently removed from the reality of the trauma that they are unable to take constructive steps to resolve it. Violent people are so intent on destruction that reality gets lost in their frenzy. Pseudoadaptive people are adapting so well to their hastily constructed defense system that they don't see any problem.

Counselors can help these people feel safe enough and hopeful enough to understand that there are more reality-oriented and constructive ways to deal with the trauma and resultant crisis.

Beneficial effects. Although none of the previously mentioned reactions are healthy, not all of them are necessarily maladaptive. Some are emergency reactions that temporarily help the person maintain equilibrium until resources can be gained to deal with the trauma more constructively. For example, the self-pity in depression may have some healing effect, especially in the absence of genuine compassion from significant others. Also, the general "shutting down" in depression can protect the person from further hurt while the psyche is recouping in an attempt to return to normal.

The dissociation inherent in shock can allow people to acclimate themselves gradually to the full impact of the trauma as they develop psychological, social, and spiritual resources along the way.

The intellectualization of the pseudoadaptive response can act as a buffer between the harsh reality of the trauma and the sudden and unmitigated painful feelings that were evoked. This gives the person time to assimilate emotionally what has been perceived intellectually.

Although undoubtedly some could argue that even the reactions of anxiety and violence have some temporarily beneficial purpose, these reactions seem to be the least helpful.

In any case, counselors can be careful not to rush in and remove psychological tourniquets that, while not skillfully applied, are still stopping the majority of the psychological bleeding until a certain amount of natural clotting can occur.

Attempts to help. All these reactions to crisis make it difficult for most significant others in the person's life to respond helpfully. Typically, family and loved ones try to comfort these people but soon become frustrated, if not outright antagonistic. This is especially true when the person in crisis reacts with depression, anxiety, or violence. After repeated and well-intentioned attempts to "pull these people out of it," family members often feel like telling them "Stop feeling so sorry for yourself. My husband died, and I didn't fall apart" or "I'm so sick and tired of you; I don't care what happens to you."

The result is that the person in crisis feels even more alone, alienated, and hopeless. Since counselors are susceptible to the same reactions, they can be aware of their own feelings of frustration or antagonism in attempting to help these individuals.

Creating further anxiety. Counselors in crisis intervention often have a dual role: to help the person through the original trauma and to help the person through the crisis that the trauma created. It is not helpful to lump what are often two psychodynamically different problems into one because one or both problems won't be resolved if this is done. Some crisis reactions create their own set of anxieties, separate from the original trauma. For example, a woman who has to deal with the death of a baby also has to deal with the personal problem of her depression and the interpersonal problem between herself and her husband caused by the depression. The man who reacts with violence to the discovery that his wife has been unfaithful also has to deal with a new problem—that is, the intense anxiety caused by deciding toward whom to direct the violence, what form the violence will take, and what the consequences of the violence will be. If this man acts out his violent feelings, the crisis this creates may be more dramatic than the one he is currently experiencing.

Delayed reactions. It is helpful to keep in mind that, while most crisis reactions follow immediately after the precipitating event, sometimes there can be a delayed reaction weeks or months after the initial trauma. While not usual, it is also not rare that a person may present himself or herself in a crisis state several months after the death of a loved one, the dissolution of a marriage, or the discovery of a serious illness. These people describe their symptoms as "coming out of the blue," and they appear to be genuinely perplexed. Their reactions are sometimes more intense than if they had experienced them at the time of the crisis for two reasons: first, the painful feelings have had time to ferment and thus are more powerful and, second, there appears to be no reason for the symptoms, making them all the more anxiety provoking.

Delayed reactions often occur when the original crisis was responded to with pseudoadaptive responses, but the painful feelings have finally eroded the defenses. While the painful feelings have broken through the defense, the traumatic quality of the original precipitating event may still be hidden. For example, the person may tell the counselor "Oh, I forgot to tell you at our last visit, but six months ago I had a heart transplant, and the doctor told me I could die at any time." After the counselor recoups from this "incidental" piece of information, he or she explores this area with the person but is assured it is of no real consequence because the person has "made his peace with both man and God."

Counselor skills in crisis intervention

Although it would be inaccurate to state that crisis intervention requires different qualities in a counselor than do other types of counseling, some qualities in a counselor are especially important. The following are particularly important for counselors who do, or plan to do, crisis intervention.

Realistic perspective. Counselors can keep a realistic perspective on their role in crisis intervention. This means that it is helpful for counselors to recognize both their strengths and their limitations in a crisis situation. Hopefully, their strengths include being able to help a person in crisis in ways that the person's family and friends cannot. On the other hand, there are some realistic limitations that counselors can acknowledge. One or all of the following factors may be present in any crisis intervention.

The first is that the person in crisis may not have possessed more than marginal psychological strength prior to the trauma. Hence, there may be a personality weakness that was present before the trauma about which the counselor can do little.

The second limiting factor is that traumas are objectively painful events, even though the pain may be increased by subjectively adding to it. Whatever the trauma, two elements are common. Traumas take away from the person something needed to function well—namely, a source of security, love, or self-esteem—and they add to the person something that significantly interferes with the person's functioning—namely, an overloading of stress. The crisis counselor cannot return to the person the psychological resource that the trauma took away; the counselor can only help by reducing the overload of stress and by providing other resources to soften the pain.

The third limitation is that the counselor has little or no control over the reactions of family and friends to the person in crisis. These reactions may run the gamut from healthy support, to unhealthy support, to antagonism, to outright rejection.

The counselor steps into the midst of this welter of psychological injury, painful feelings, psychological history, and family reactions. The situation is somewhat analogous to the fire fighter who is the first to arrive at the scene of a burning building that has people trapped inside. It is his duty to fight the fire as effectively as possible and to try to rescue the people. But the fire fighter must also recognize the limitations inherent in the situation and calibrate his expectations and behavior accordingly. If he does not, he may behave foolishly and/or inappropriately berate himself when he cannot save everyone. In short, counselors can define their role and area of responsibility and work within it.

Holistic orientation. The crisis intervention counselor must be holistic. A crisis is not a time for professional chauvinism or rivalry. In crisis intervention, counselors must accept all the help they can get. Sometimes it is appropriate to refer the person to a physician for psychiatric medications. It may be important to enlist the aid of a minister, priest, or rabbi, especially when the person communicates a need for spiritual comfort. Sometimes it is appropriate to refer the person to a counselor of the opposite sex of the initially contacted one. For example, a woman who has been raped may feel more comfortable with a female counselor, or a man whose wife has just left him may feel more at ease with a male counselor.

In some situations, referral to other agencies is appropriate, either as a final referral or as ancillary to the work of the primary counselor. A woman who is in a crisis because she has been raped may be referred to a rape crisis center; a man who is drinking heavily as a means of handling a crisis may be referred to a detoxification center or a substance abuse counselor as a first step in the intervention process. For this reason, it is important that counselors be familiar with the various kinds of professional and paraprofessional resources in the community.

Flexibility. Crisis intervention also requires flexibility. While a counselor may be disinclined to embrace people in counseling, being held may be the only behavior that communicates caring to a particular person in a particular circumstance. While setting limits and adhering to them is an important part of counseling, limits usually have to be more flexible in crisis intervention. Phone calls may be more appropriate; canceling or changing appointments may have more basis in reality; seeing the person in locations other than the counselor's office may, at times, be necessary; extending the length of sessions or increasing the agreed upon number may also be appropriate. Intervening in family interactions may be more appropriate than it ordinarily would be. Making direct suggestions in terms of whether a person should return to work immediately or whether a person should return to his or her parental home for a time may be more helpful than is usually the case.

Crisis intervention ordinarily is not the time for counselors to behave and react as they would in more typical counseling situations. Usually it is not the time for confrontation; for lengthy, nondirective volleys; for delving into the developmental precursors of the crisis reaction; for interpreting behaviors or dreams; or for worrying much about transference and countertransference. A crisis atmosphere is much like that in an emergency operating room. Surgeons do and say things that they may not ordinarily do or say in their normal practice. They do what must be done to keep the person alive, and it may not always follow the textbooks. Counselors who have a set and firmly entrenched way of doing things are likely to be less effective in a crisis intervention situation.

Balance between empathy and strength.   Counselors who do crisis intervention need a great deal of empathy, a great deal of strength, and a magnificent balance between the two. Some people are easy to feel empathy toward—for example, the parents whose child has just died or the young person who has just been told that she has a terminal illness. Other people are much more difficult to feel empathy toward—the man who is in a crisis because he has just been arrested for molesting children, including his own, and is now in an acute depression or the woman who is in a state of shock because she shot her husband when he called her some vile names.

Being human, counselors may initially react to some people's crisis with "Well, they deserve to suffer for what they did," "They asked for it, and they got it," or "They're just *creating* a crisis to get attention or to use as a weapon to hurt the people whom they feel have hurt them." There is just too much social conditioning for most counselors not to feel these sentiments at one time or another. Being aware of such reactions, the counselor is in a better position to control them and prevent them from unduly interfering with his or her attempts to help the person.

With people who, because of their personality or problem, do not evoke much empathy, counselors can attempt to tunnel beneath the barbed fence of unattractiveness and abrasiveness and reach the scared human being hiding behind it. This is one of the great challenges that face all counselors, and to meet it with a positive attitude is the mark of a good counselor.

If the negative sentiments are strong and lasting, it would be better to refer the person to another counselor. However, if the sentiments are less strong and short-lived, the counselor may feel these sentiments less strongly than anyone else in the individual's life and therefore be the best potential helper.

Empathy without strength to balance it can slide into sympathy and malleability, which interfere with effective therapy. Strength in counselors means that they maintain a healthy sense of separateness from the person and a willingness to stand by their decisions unless there is some compelling reason not to. A danger in crisis intervention is that the counselor may become so empathetic and immersed in the pain and pathos of the situation that he or she has no more objectivity or common sense than the person's family and friends. While counselors can empathize with the pain, they can also remember that the pain is not happening to them and that their main role is not to empathize but to help the person return to a more accurate perspective of the situation and develop the skills to handle it effectively.

THE INTERVENTION PROCESS

As is true with any type of counseling, crisis intervention must follow some process. This does not mean that there is only one prescribed way of doing crisis intervention, any more than there is only one way to practice counseling. It simply means that it is necessary to have a theme—that is, some basic guidelines, principles, and steps that will tie the process into a meaningful whole. Without this, crisis intervention would be comprised of scattered behaviors that are based more on intuition, good intentions, and panic than on sound counseling principles.

Deciding to do crisis intervention

The first consideration in the crisis intervention process is for the counselor to decide if he or she wants to get involved in a crisis intervention situation. Counselors can consider three factors in this regard.

The first is the qualifications and motivation of the counselor. Not all helpers are qualified to do crisis intervention. Some counselors are excellent in long-term treatment situations but have personalities that simply do not allow them to function well in crisis situations. When this is the case, it is better to refer the person in crisis to an appropriate counselor or agency.

A counselor who feels qualified to do crisis intervention may, for any number of reasons, be unmotivated to do so or at least may be unmotivated at a particular time. There is nothing that dictates that counselors must agree to see everyone who seeks their help.

The second factor is the amount of time required. Crisis intervention may take a great deal of a counselor's time over a period of a month. While the crisis intervention literature suggests most crisis intervention work takes four to six sessions, the person in crisis does not know this. In acute crisis situations, especially when the trauma is great and/or there is an underlying disturbance, a counselor may be required to spend 15 hours or more in a month's time on one situation. With this in mind, counselors must balance the amount of time required with other professional and personal responsibilities. Counselors who find more demands on their time than they had initially expected can find *themselves* in a semicrisis that creates resentment and diminishes their effectiveness as counselors.

Another part of the time dimension that counselors seldom consider is the possible legal ramifications involved in some crisis situations. People who are in crisis because of rape, assault, divorce, loss of a loved one through negligence, accidents, child molesting, loss of employment, or commission of a crime and arrest may eventually require court action to adjudicate the legal dimensions of the trauma. When this occurs, the counselor may be required to get involved in lengthy legal preparations and testimony, not to mention the stresses often involved when a mental health professional enters the legal arena.

The third factor is the nature of the crisis. Crisis intervention is often a more emotionally loaded situation than other types of counseling and hence may evoke strong feelings in the counselor. Will a counselor who has lost a child or spouse in death be the best helper for someone in a similar situation? Will a counselor who has been raped or had a loved one raped be the best person to help a rape victim or a rapist? Will a counselor who is experiencing painful marital stress or divorce be the best one to help a person in a similar situation? Although there are no obvious answers to these questions, counselors can legitimately ask themselves "Do I really want to go through this again?" and "Will I be the most objective and healthily detached counselor for this person?"

The most important step in the crisis intervention process is for the counselor knowingly to consent to give his or her utmost energy and skill to the process. When the consent is uninformed or ambivalent, the rest of the process will lean precariously on a shaky foundation.

Factors affecting a positive prognosis

The second consideration in the crisis intervention process is the question of what kinds of people in crisis do better than others in crisis intervention. As is true with all counseling, some people are able to use crisis intervention better than others. While research in this area is both scant and conflicting, experience can offer some reasonable guidelines. The following are some factors that can be considered.

Duration of the crisis reaction. The majority of people in crisis seek help between 10 and 14 days after the precipitating trauma.[2] This is considered a relatively short time for the existence of a crisis reaction, and all other variables remaining the same, the prognosis for resolving the crisis is good. However, some people exist within the broader parameters of a crisis reaction for six months or a year before eventually deciding to seek professional help. A reasonable assumption in this situation is that the crisis reaction may have done some rather serious damage to the person and that the person's maladaptive coping mechanisms have become entrenched by sheer repetition, even though they were basically ineffective. To expect that these people will be significantly helped in 4 to 6 or even 20 sessions may be unrealistic.

Severity of the trauma and resultant symptoms. In general, there seems to be some relationship between the nature of the trauma and the resultant symptoms. Ordinarily, reactions are less severe when the trauma is being expelled from school than when it involves the loss of a job, when the trauma concerns marital stress than when it involves divorce, when the trauma is the breakup of a dating relationship than when it involves the loss of a loved one, and when the trauma is discovering one's child is a homosexual than being told that one has less than a year to live.

However, because the severity of the crisis reaction is contingent not only on the nature of the trauma but also on several other factors, there is no one-to-one relationship between a trauma and the resultant crisis reaction. It is possible that one person may have a minor crisis reaction to the death of a loved one while another may have a serious crisis reaction to the breakup of a dating relationship.

Consequently, when considering prognosis in crisis intervention, counselors must consider *both* the nature of the trauma *and* the severity of the symptoms. It seems reasonable to assume in most cases that mild traumas that have mild crisis reactions will be resolved more quickly and effectively than serious traumas that precipitate severe crisis reactions, with other combinations falling between these two points on a scale of prognosis.

Pretrauma personality. All other factors remaining the same, the weaker the pretrauma personality, the more counseling time and effort will be required to effect a successful resolution to the crisis reaction. Some people who are experiencing a crisis had normal, if not somewhat

[2]Aguilera & Messick (1978), p. 65.

healthy, personalities prior to the trauma. The trauma hit them in a particularly vulnerable area and created a crisis reaction, despite the presence of many psychological and environmental resources. With these people, the prognosis may be good.

However, many people who experience a crisis reaction to trauma had less than strong and healthy personalities before the trauma. Crisis intervention with these people will be more difficult and may not be as successful.

Although crisis intervention is not the place for a long and detailed psychological history, an abbreviated one taken at an opportune time can give the counselor some clues as to the strength of the pretrauma personality. This information can help the counselor obtain a clearer picture and establish realistic goals. While there are no foolproof ways of assessing the pretrauma strength of the person in crisis, some criteria can be helpful.

First, if a person has a history of crisis reactions or has behaved in maladaptive ways over a period of time, there would be some evidence pointing to personality problems that were present before the trauma.

Second, if the person's crisis reaction appears to be obviously disproportionate to the trauma, this could be another indication of a disturbed personality. For example, if a person is considering suicide because she failed to get into graduate school or is acutely depressed over not being selected for a sorority, this ordinarily reflects more than a crisis reaction.

Another criterion is the duration of the crisis reaction. If a person is still acutely depressed six months after the death of a loved one or is experiencing acute anxiety symptoms six months after an automobile accident, one could reasonably expect there is more to the picture than a crisis reaction.

A fourth criterion is how the person uses the crisis reaction. People with relatively healthy personalities do not *use* crisis reactions at all. They experience them and want to get rid of them as quickly as possible. People with personality problems often use a crisis reaction for secondary gains. It is as if they have discovered a new and effective weapon and don't want to let go of it. They use the crisis reaction to elicit attention and sympathy past the point where it would be helpful or appropriate, to punish people whom they perceive as having caused the trauma or as having perpetrated injustices on them in the past, to escape facing some arduous or threatening responsibility at work or in marriage, or as a self-damaging tool that can further their veiled but ongoing efforts aimed at ultimate self-destruction.

How the person uses the crisis can be seen in reactions to others during the crisis and the tenacity with which the person holds onto the symptoms. It also can be seen in the person's motivation or lack of motivation to follow through on the counselor's suggestions and the willingness to accept the environmental supports offered.

If a person does have a pretrauma personality that is disturbed, this does not mean he or she is necessarily unsuitable for crisis intervention. It does mean, however, that the counselor should be aware of what he or she is dealing with and adjust counseling efforts, prognoses, and recommendations accordingly.

Quantity and quality of environmental supports.   In general, good environmental supports add significantly to a positive prognosis for crisis intervention. Environmental supports include family, friends, work, avocations, and religion. Some people in crisis receive a great deal of healthy support from family and friends who are willing to extend compassion, time, and material support in time of crisis. Other people receive a great deal of support, but it is unhealthy. Parents, friends, or loved ones try too hard to help, smothering the person and adding to the stress. One or more significant others may view the crisis period as an opportune time to take over the person's life or snatch him or her back into a dependency relationship. This response from the environment also increases stress in a person who is already overwhelmed with stress. Still others are rejected by significant others because of the nature of the trauma. For example, parents may disown an unmarried daughter who becomes pregnant or a husband may reject a wife who has been raped.

Some people have satisfying jobs and understanding bosses, which help absorb some of the stress; others have jobs they abhor and bosses who refuse to give them time off from work during the crisis period. Some people have avocations, such as hobbies, sports, and volunteer work, that serve to reduce stress and distract them from a constant reliving of the trauma. They also may have a strong religious belief and a spiritual director who provides helpful ways of perceiving and handling the trauma. Other people in crisis have no avocations and/or no religious beliefs; hence, they must carry the brunt of the trauma more fully.

In all cases, the decision as to whether a person is a suitable candidate for crisis intervention is the counselor's. In weighting the positive and less positive aspects of the aforementioned variables, counselors can decide whether to agree to work with a person in a crisis intervention framework or whether another framework or counselor would be more helpful.

Sequence of crisis intervention

The third consideration in the process of crisis intervention is the sequence of steps that counselors can follow in helping people resolve crises. Each counselor, person in counseling, and crisis is different; therefore, no universally effective sequence can be postulated. However, by having a sequence of steps in mind, counselors can have a framework that they can modify according to their needs and the particular situation. The following is a five-step sequence that reflects one way of therapeutically intervening in a crisis situation.

Step 1: Introduction. Step 1 consists of the counselor and the person in crisis introducing themselves to each other. This, of course, is not a social introduction, but a clinical one. It is the most important step in the sequence, because what happens at this point will have one of three effects: it will establish a positive tone to the relationship; it will establish a negative tone to the relationship; or it will terminate the relationship.

During the introductory part of the relationship, the counselor needs to obtain some specific information: the nature of the trauma; the kind and intensity of the crisis reaction; what the trauma and crisis reaction mean to the person; what the person has been doing to resolve the crisis; how the person has resolved crises in the past; what defenses the person is presently employing; what medications, if any, the person is taking; who referred the person and why; and why the person agreed to come for help.

On the other side, the counselor is introducing himself or herself, but not in the same way. The counselor's face, posture, voice, questions, manner of asking them, and method of listening and responding are introducing the counselor to the person. The messages the counselor can send include the following:

I understand; I care; I want to help; I am competent to help you.
I understand; but I can't afford to care right now.
I understand; I care; but I personally can't help you right now.
I understand; I care; I want to help; but I don't know what I'm doing.

It is important to recognize that it is not only the person who is being assessed and evaluated, but the counselor as well. At the end of the introduction step, there will be an explicit or implicit counseling agreement either to work together or not.

Sometimes people are so emotionally upset during the introduction period that it is necessary for them to vent feelings immediately. Counselors must walk the narrow line between stifling the feelings in the person and allowing the feelings to control the session so that important information cannot be gathered.

It is better if the person volunteers the necessary information without being asked question after question. If the person does not volunteer, the counselor may need to ask a series of information-gathering questions, even though this practice would not ordinarily be used in other types of counseling.

Step 2: Invitation.   After a counselor has reached an adequate understanding of the situation, it is important to invite ideas from the person as to how the person sees the counselor being of help. It is better to do this than compulsively to follow the next step in a prescribed outline. This does not mean the person in crisis always knows what is best for him or her. It simply means that people *can* know what is best for them, and it can be economical in terms of time and energy to ask before the counselor launches on a program of what he or she thinks will be helpful.

The main error Step 2 is meant to circumvent is the "This is what you need now" syndrome. The following are some verbal translations of this attitude:

1. "What you need now is some cognitive restructuring." Perhaps. But maybe the person is perceiving the trauma accurately. A woman may lament "My husband just died, and he was the only person in the world who loved me." It is possible this is true and that trying to "correct" her cognitions will only serve to present data that will prove her point. Maybe she does need some cognitive restructuring, but not at this particular time. Right now she needs some compassion or some ventilation of feelings.

2. "What you need now is to vent some painful feelings." Maybe. But it is possible that the person has vented feelings for a week and has gotten to a point of diminishing returns. He is simply regurgitating the same toxins day after day and is reinfecting himself. What he really needs now is to get at the source of the toxins and excise it.

3. "What you need now is to call upon your religious beliefs." Perhaps. But maybe the person is furious at God, whom she perceives as having taken her child or husband away. She views God as punishing her for past sins and as being a very cruel and vengeful being. To encourage her to appeal to her religious beliefs as a source of comfort is to further stoke up her hatred of God and the fear and guilt that the

hatred produces. Instead of reducing stress, appealing to her religious beliefs now could serve to increase it.

Contrary to what some of the literature states, experience indicates it is *people* who influence the sequence of reactions to the trauma, and not the trauma that influences the reactions of the people. Naturally, if a counselor "leads" a person through certain prescribed steps of grieving, for example, the person will go through these steps. But when people are left to grieve according to their personalities, they often grieve differently from one another. When counselors fail to understand this, they may tend to force people through a resolution sequence that does not consider the person's unique personality and situation.

When a person is asked how the counselor might help, it is unlikely that the person will respond with a clear set of directions. But the behavioral reaction to the invitation will often provide the answer. One person may need to ventilate deep feelings of fear, anger, shame, guilt, grief, hurt, and despair. Another person may need to be educated by the counselor as to what is happening to him and how other people fare who have experienced similar traumas. A third person may need some practical advice. A fourth may need to ask the counselor what the counselor thinks of her after she "spilled her guts." A fifth person may be more concerned about someone else involved in the trauma than about himself and may need to discuss this situation.

Once the person is able to communicate directly or indirectly his or her needs, the counselor can judge whether it would be helpful to meet them at this point. People in crisis are often astute as to what will most reduce stress for them. Sometimes, however, they are so confused and frightened that it is necessary for counselors to use their best judgment as to what issues need immediate attention. At other times, people will ask counselors to meet their needs in ways that would be inappropriate or unhelpful. For example, a person may tell a counselor: "I'd sure appreciate it if you could call the district attorney's office and see if you can talk them out of filing charges against me" or "Maybe if you called my husband and told him what his leaving has done to me, he may come back and we can give our marriage one more try."

Once the counselor has a reasonably clear idea what steps will most quickly and effectively begin to reduce the crisis reaction, he or she begins the work necessary to free the person to move on to the next steps in the sequence.

Step 3: Environmental support. The purpose of Step 3 is to garner some help for the person outside of counseling while he or she is trying to work things through in counseling.

The person's environment can be helpful in two ways. It can afford the person some understanding, compassion, and practical support, such as food, lodging, and money. It also can remove or diminish stress, at least temporarily, while the person recoups. For example, an employer may give the person some time off work; in-laws may take care of the children for a while; a student may be excused from school or assignments for a period of time; creditors may allow extra time to pay bills.

Counselors can help engender environmental supports by encouraging the person in crisis to use the supports available even though pride may be an obstacle. The counselor may invite family or friends to join some counseling sessions in order to reduce their anxiety about the crisis and to give them some ideas as to how they can be more helpful. The person may be encouraged to seek temporary changes in a work or school situation. The counselor may document the situation so that the person will be temporarily released from certain responsibilities.

When people are in the midst of a crisis, daily stresses can sometimes be unbearable and can significantly impede progress toward the successful resolution of the crisis.

Step 4: Action.   Step 4 includes planning for action, acting, and evaluating the action. By this step, the person should have progressed through whatever cognitive restructuring and emotional release was necessary to reduce the more acute aspects of the crisis reaction. The person is thinking more clearly and feeling more appropriately. The planning phase of the action step deals with the question "What can you do outside of this room that will help reduce your anxiety and provide a little light at the end of the tunnel?" The second question, which follows from the answer to the first, is "Exactly how are you going to accomplish this?"

More often than not, the answer to the first question will be "I don't know. If I knew, I wouldn't be here!" At this point, the counselor can patiently ask the person to list some options, regardless of how outlandish or impossible they sound. Sometimes the person is able to suggest some very plausible and helpful ideas. If, after a reasonable amount of time, the person genuinely cannot offer any options, the counselor may suggest some for consideration.

Counselors can be mindful of two points at this stage. One is that the proposed actions are not meant to resolve the crisis. A more realistic expectation is that each remedial activity will provide *some* symptomatic relief, and enough activities will provide *sufficient* relief so that, while the person continues to experience upset, he or she is no longer in a crisis state. This is in answer to the frequently heard response from the person in crisis to a suggestion from a counselor: "What good will *that* do—that won't solve anything."

A second point is that when two people earnestly struggle together to form some plan of action, it can be therapeutic in itself, even if no concrete plans are made during that particular session. Sometimes people leave such a session with the comment "Well, I still don't know what to do, but somehow I feel a little better."

Once some options for action are explored, the next phase is to try them out. What the actions are depends upon the nature of the trauma and the crisis. The trauma of failing in medical school will dictate different actions than that of an unwanted pregnancy, loss of a loved one, discovering that one's child is an addict, or being raped. If the proposed actions work to reduce stress, more options are explored in order to reduce symptoms further. If the actions don't bring about the desired result, new options are considered and acted upon.

Each action is evaluated. For the actions that worked, it is important to discover why they worked for future reference. It is equally important to find out why other options failed. Did the plan fail because it was a bad idea, or was it a good idea but poorly carried out? Successful actions are repeated and added to; unsuccessful ones are scuttled and replaced with effective ones.

It is important to realize that actions that work for one person may be unhelpful or even destructive to another. It is perilous to assume that what worked for the last rape victim will work for the next one. For example, it may be helpful for one person to share the crisis with parents, but for another this would be destructive. It may be helpful for one person to take a week off from work and disappear into the mountains, but this may be the worst thing someone else could do. It may be relatively easy for one woman to report to the police that she has been raped and very stressful for another.

Step 5: Termination.   Step 5 is meant to tie up any loose ends and to be educative. It is both past and future oriented. The counselor and the person summarize what was learned during the previous sessions. The person, who is now in a state closer to equilibrium, is encouraged to reflect on how he or she turned a trauma into a crisis. Usually there are one or two things that the person did that exacerbated the trauma into a crisis. The person may have viewed the trauma in an overly catastrophic way, waited too long to take some action to prevent the crisis reaction from developing, pretended to have feelings that really didn't exist, pretended not to have feelings that did exist, failed to use environmental supports wisely, underestimated his or her capacity to handle emergency situations, used defense mechanisms rather than adaptive behavior to handle the stress, or allowed himself or herself to get overly upset to garner some secondary gains.

This psychological reconnoitering is done with a positive spirit that asks "Let's see what we learned from this crisis that will help you next time a difficult situation arises." This invitation bridges the past and the future. The future dimension deals with the question "What will you do differently next time if a trauma arises?" The discussion that these questions engender can give people the feeling that they learned something valuable about themselves, people, and life in general from the crisis intervention. It may not be an overpowering insight, but simply one that says "Yeah. This isn't going to happen again, and I know exactly why it's not."

It is also at this time that the counselor may suggest further help in the form of short-term counseling of a noncrisis type or long-term counseling. It is helpful for counselors to approach this area with prudence. It may be that the person does not need any further professional help at this time, or the person may need further help, but this is not the time to approach the subject because the person is still quite tender psychologically and the suggestion would add further stress to the delicate post-crisis equilibrium. If this is the case, the counselor can set a definite time for a follow-up visit in the near future, at which time the recommendation can be made.

It may be that this is the exact time to recommend further help because the person needs it and the pain of the crisis is still fresh enough that the person would be willing to embark on any program that would help prevent a future occurrence. In any case, the termination should include an open invitation to return for "psychological refueling" any time the person feels the need.

Pitfalls

As counselors progress through these five steps, they will meet several potential pitfalls that are best avoided. The following are eight of the more common ones.

1. "Taking over" for the person in crisis. It is not helpful for counselors to assume control of and responsibility for the welfare of the person in crisis. The vast majority of people in crisis are still capable of leading their own lives, and if they are not, it is better to have family or friends take over the reins of the person's life.

2. Giving false assurance. A common social response to those in crisis is to assure them that things aren't as bad as they seem and that the future is bright. However, false assurance is not a therapeutic response. False assurance simply communicates to the person in crisis that the counselor does not clearly understand the situation. A realistic appraisal of the trauma is ultimately more helpful.

3. Focusing on the cause of crisis rather than on the resolution. It may be tempting for counselors to focus on questions such as "How did you get yourself into this mess anyway?" instead of "How are we going to get you some relief?" Analogously, while it is important to ascertain the cause of a fire, one must extinguish the fire first and only then seek its origin. It is only in the final step of the crisis intervention process that it could be appropriate to examine the factors contributing to the crisis.

4. Assuming the psychological meaning of the trauma. The same trauma can have many meanings to different people. A counselor may assume that a man is experiencing acute anxiety because he loved his deceased wife so deeply. In reality, however, his crisis reaction may be caused by his guilt for *not* feeling sad.

A woman who is dropped from medical school in her final year reacts with acute depression, and the counselor interprets this as meaning she is crestfallen that she will not be a physician. In fact, the woman never wanted to be a physician. All she wanted to do was make her physician father proud of her, and now she feels she has failed. Some very erroneous paths can be followed when counselors assume the meaning of a trauma to be different from what it actually is.

5. "Catching" the panic of the person in crisis. Anxiety can be very contagious, and even experienced counselors are not immune to it. A counselor may be handling a crisis situation well until the person mentions doing something drastic (running away, suicide, homicide, going crazy), and then the counselor panics and makes imprudent decisions. Panic can be prevented by working closely with a colleague in very difficult cases, by being mindful that counselors are not responsible for what happens to the person but only for doing the best they can in the situation, and by using environmental supports, such as getting other agencies involved, advising the family of the potential dangers, and hospitalization.

6. Underestimating or overestimating the situation. Underestimating means communicating the attitude "I realize you are terribly upset, but I work with these situations all the time, and it's no big deal." This conveys to the person in crisis that the counselor is cavalier about the biggest problem the person has probably ever encountered. Overes-

timating the crisis is to become as intense and worried as the person in crisis, which conveys the message "You *are* in serious trouble." This adds even more stress to a seemingly intolerable situation.

7. Failing to ask for help when it is needed. Some crisis situations are extremely complicated and intense. But some counselors feel that they will "lose face" if they call in one or more colleagues for consultation. Just as it takes more than one surgeon to do complicated surgery, it may take more than one counselor to handle a crisis situation.

8. Assuming that the principles that are valid in one type of crisis are equally valid when applied to all types of crises. While there are some general principles that underlie all crisis intervention, many crises also have a specific set of counseling principles.[3]

SUMMARY

It is important to put crisis intervention into a proper perspective. The question is not whether or not crisis intervention works, because the answer is the same as to the question of whether counseling in general works. Depending on the nature of the trauma, the severity of the crisis reaction, the pretrauma personality of the person, and the skills of the counselor, crisis intervention seems to work very well at times, very poorly at other times, and mostly falls between these two points. In some ways, it is a very difficult type of counseling to do because the stakes are usually high and the time is short. On the other hand, because the person in crisis is often suggestible and motivated to try anything, a minimal amount of intervention can bring about a maximum amount of relief.

A crisis is never inherently beneficial, and the field of mental health must do all it can to educate people how to avoid turning traumas into crises. However, good can come of a crisis in ways that may not have occurred in any other way in a particular individual. As Leitner and Stecher state:

> When forces of life push our daily existence to some edge whereupon we find ourselves in the midst of crisis, then we have a chance to emerge as changed beings. Growth implies change and change may imply growth. Emerging from a crisis can be a movement toward a new being-state, one that we may not have been capable of before the crisis. . . . Crises call for risking. People in crisis, under intense pressure, become introspective— they can look at themselves more deeply and honestly than in times of tranquility.[4]

[3]Readers who are interested in references that deal with specific types of crisis—such as grief, rape, suicide, and family and maturational crises—should see Aguilera & Messick (1978), Belkin (1980a), and Dixon (1979).
[4]Quoted in Belkin (1980a), p. 331.

THOUGHT QUESTIONS

1. What do you think is the most common mistake counselors make in doing crisis intervention?
2. What types of crises would you feel more comfortable dealing with, and what types would you feel less comfortable dealing with? Why?
3. What strengths do you possess that would make you particularly effective doing crisis intervention? What qualities do you need to strengthen in order to feel confident doing crisis intervention?
4. What thoughts and feelings would arise within you if a person you had seen for the first of several scheduled crisis intervention sessions committed suicide after the first meeting?
5. Under what specific circumstances would you feel it helpful to consult a colleague in a crisis intervention situation?

CHAPTER 14

Ethical
Considerations

Ethics are standards of conduct that assure that people are treated justly. In counseling, ethics means that the legal and human rights of the person are scrupulously protected by the counselor. Without this guarantee, people would be understandably reluctant to share crucial information with counselors.

In this chapter, four ethical issues particularly relevant to counseling will be discussed: the ethics of professional responsibility, confidentiality, imparting information, and the influence of the counselor.

PROFESSIONAL RESPONSIBILITY

Counselors have ethical responsibilities to the person in counseling and to themselves. Four responsibilities are particularly important.

Responding fully

As the word *responsibility* connotes, counselors must respond fully to the person during the counseling session. Responding fully means, from an ethical standpoint, that counselors do all in their power to be completely attentive to the person in counseling. They gauge their personal and professional lives in ways that guarantee maximum energy and attentiveness in counseling. They do not counsel people when their attention, energies, and motivation are blunted by personal responsibilities, social activities, or overscheduling of appointments.

After some experience, counselors learn to develop a schedule that provides for maximum efficiency. Some counselors can see eight people each day and do an effective job. Others find that four people or two people each day are the maximum, especially if they have other professional duties, such as teaching and consulting.

Pace is another important part of scheduling. Some counselors learn that they work better seeing people "back to back"—that is, three or four people in a row. Other counselors find that they need a break of 15 minutes to an hour between people.

The time of day is also a factor in scheduling. Some counselors learn that they are more attentive in the morning; hence, they schedule most people from early morning to early afternoon. Other counselors discover that they do better later in the day or in the evening.

Problems arise in the area of scheduling when counselors work for agencies, hence do not have a great deal of control over when they see people or how many people they see. The same problem can arise in private practice, where a counselor's income depends directly upon the number of people seen. When this is the case, counselors can rationalize seeing large numbers of people at any hour of the day or night, whether or not the counselors are physically and psychologically prepared to do effective work. One safeguard against this is to have a second source of income—such as teaching, research, or consultation—that will free the counselor to be more judicious about how many people are seen in counseling and when they are seen.

Responding fully also means that counselors are selective in terms of whom they choose to see in counseling. There is no ethical standard that says counselors must agree to see everyone who seeks their help. It is important for counselors to agree to work only with people with whom they have some reasonable expectation of success. People with problems outside the counselor's area of expertise should be referred elsewhere. For counselors to take on an "interesting case" may be unethical if the counselor knows, or should know, that other means of help have been more successful than those he or she can offer. For example, a counselor may never have worked with a "pain patient" and may decide this could be a chance to learn something new. The counselor does not consider that surgical intervention, biofeedback, hypnosis, or chemotherapy may be the treatment of choice.

Part of responsible selection requires that counselors realize the kinds of people with whom they work best. Hopefully, the more training, maturity, and professional experience a counselor has, the more types of personality he or she will be able to help. However, because counselors are human before they are anything else, they will find some personalities abrasive, distracting, and evoking less than helpful responses. Rather than enter into a professional relationship with this type of personality, which will likely eventuate in a negative experience for both, it is better to refer this individual to another source.

Responsible counselors willingly and commonly make referrals to other counselors. The reason for this is not that they are too busy, but that they recognize their own professional and personal limitations, as well as the kinds of personalities with which they work effectively.

Terminating appropriately

Another dimension of professional ethics is to terminate a counseling relationship when it is appropriate. This principle can be violated in two ways. A counselor can terminate a relationship prematurely for invalid reasons. The counselor may simply get bored, frustrated, or angry at the person and create some "acceptable" reason to terminate. Feelings of boredom, frustration, or anger are not uncommon and are often an integral part of counseling. It is the counselor's responsibility to deal with them, both intrapersonally and interpersonally, so that they can be used as an effective counseling instrument.

Counselors can also maintain a person too long in counseling. This is usually done because the counselor is getting some personal needs met. The counselor may find it pleasant, gratifying, or financially rewarding to see a person past the point where other, more responsible counselors would have successfully terminated treatment.

Evaluating the relationship

Professional ethics also takes into its purview the nature of the counseling relationship. A relationship can be more therapeutic than personal or more personal than therapeutic. A good relationship is therapeutic, but also judiciously personal—that is, the counselor and the person relate with each other as human beings, not simply as automatons programmed to act out a given role.

Sometimes relationships can become more personal than helpful. This can happen in one of two ways. The relationship can become an overdependent one that immediately or eventually serves as an obstacle to the goals of counseling. Or the relationship can become an angry, sadomasochistic one in which each partner is using the other in destructive ways. When a relationship takes on either of these characteristics, it is the counselor's responsibility to terminate. The responsibility to terminate is not shared by the counselor *and* the person because the person may be getting so many needs met that he or she sees no reason to terminate the relationship.

Counselors' responsibility to themselves

A final area of responsibility is that of counselors to themselves. Unfortunately, this is a dimension of ethics that is seldom discussed. It is important that counselors take care of themselves both psychologically and physically. Since counseling is primarily a giving process, counselors have to "get" in other areas of their lives. It is necessary for counselors to have rewarding relationships and leisure pursuits outside of counseling that create a sense of warmth and joy that the counselor brings to the relationship. It is also important for counselors to keep in good physical condition because, while counseling is a sedentary job, it demands an energy and freshness that only physical conditioning can provide. Counselors who sit all day only to go home and sit are very likely to become lethargic, easily bored, and impatient.

Counselors also have responsibilities to themselves in the counseling relationship. A counselor cannot assume the responsibility of being a manager, conservator, parent, or spouse to the person, nor is the counselor God. The counselor did not create the person's problem and is not responsible for curing him or her. Counselors have a limited role in the person in counseling's life, and that role should be clearly and unequivocally defined during the first three stages as well as continually underlined throughout the relationship.

There are times when a person in counseling may expect, and even demand, that a counselor provide time, energy, and services that lie outside the limits of a reasonable counseling agreement. Counselors who accede to these expectations and demands may well be doing damage to themselves, to the other people in their lives, and to the person in counseling. It is as much an ethical issue for counselors to take care of their own psychological health and exercise their own psychological rights as it is for them to safeguard the well-being of the people they see in counseling.

CONFIDENTIALITY

Confidentiality can be a very complex ethical issue because it deals with the twofold responsibility of the counselor: the counselor's responsibility to the person in counseling and to society at large. Sometimes these allegiances pull the counselor in opposite directions, creating a great deal of tension.

The basic principle of confidentiality is that, under ordinary circumstances, safeguarding information about a person in counseling is a serious obligation. This means that ordinarily counselors do not communicate, directly or indirectly, information that a person has shared within the context of a professional relationship.

Basic distinctions

The concepts of confidentiality and privileged communication are not synonymous. Privileged communication is the legal right that exists either by statute or common law that protects the person from having confidences revealed publicly during legal proceedings. It means that certain professionals cannot be legally compelled to testify as to the content of any professional communication between themselves and the people they see in counseling. As can be seen, privileged communication is relevant only to legal proceedings. Confidentiality, on the other hand, is a broader concept that imposes on the counselor the responsibility not to divulge information received in a professional capacity in court or in any other situation.[1]

Confidentiality is both a professional and legal issue. However, when a case involving privileged communication enters the courts, the legal interpretations of confidentiality supersede the professional ones. In other words, counselors may adhere conscientiously to the code of ethics of their profession, but the court may rule that such a code does not adequately fulfill the requirements of the law.

The rules governing privileged communication are not uniform throughout the United States or between federal and state jurisdictions. Different legal jurisdictions abide by different principles of privileged communication; so a counselor in California may face an entirely different situation than a counselor in Iowa, even though the case is the same. For this reason, it is important that counselors learn the exact nature of the rules of confidentiality that pertain in their state.

Which professions are covered by the privilege and which are not also differs from one state to another. In some states, many helping professions are covered; in others, very few are. In no states are paraprofessional counselors granted the right of privileged communication. It is important for counselors not to make the mistake of promising this privilege in jurisdictions where they do not have it.

Exceptions to privileged communication

The basic professional and legal problem with the issue of confidentiality is that there is no such thing as *absolute* confidentiality. The ruling bodies of the helping professions and the courts agree that there

[1]Stott (1981), pp. G1 and G2.

are circumstances that militate against absolute confidentiality. The California Evidence Code lists thirteen exceptions to the basic privileged communication rule.[2] Some of them are worth mentioning because many other states have the same exceptions.

Court appointees.   When a counselor is appointed by the court to examine a person, the report of which will be sent to the court and to no one else, the person in the professional relationship with the counselor cannot claim the privilege. The purpose of this exception is that it would be absurd for a court to order a mental health examination, only to have the person being examined claim privileged communication. The *ethical* issue that this exception raises is whether or not a person should be forced to undergo a mental health examination. The *professional* question it raises is what kind of evaluation can be done on a person who has a deeply vested interest in appearing more healthy or more disturbed than he or she really is.

Criminal trials.   Privileged communication cannot be claimed when the purpose of a professional relationship is to examine the sanity or psychological competence of the person in a criminal trial. Again the purpose of the exception is self-evident, but it raises the same ethical and professional issues as the previous one.

Reasonable cause.   Privileged communication does not hold in cases where the counselor has reasonable cause to believe that the person is in such a psychological state as to be dangerous to himself or to the person or property of another and that disclosure of the communication is necessary to prevent the threatened danger.

In practice, this is a particularly difficult exception, even though most people would agree it is philosophically sound. It is difficult because the concept of "reasonable cause" is so subjective. It is not uncommon for counselors to hear a person say "I'm going to kill my husband when I get home!" or "Sometimes I'm almost overcome by an urge to kill myself." People can make such comments lightly or halfjokingly and commit the act an hour later. Others can make such statements in very convincing ways and yet not commit the act.

A disheartening consequence of this exception is that counselors can be, and have been, successfully sued because, while they did not feel there was reasonable cause to inform the authorities or the victim-to-be, the court did. Perhaps the weakest part of the exception deals with the "property of another." The intent of the court undoubtedly is to

[2] Sections 911 to 1028.

prevent the burning and blowing up of buildings; however, the wording of the exception includes all property.

Child victimization.   If the counselor is in a professional relationship with a child under the age of 16 and has reasonable cause to believe that the child has been a victim of a crime, disclosure of communication is allowed as being in the best interest of the child.

The reasoning underlying this exception is that a child may be the victim of sexual assault by members of the family or friends. If this information is not brought to the attention of the authorities or the parents, when they are not the perpetrators, the child will continue to be a victim.

Psychological injury and litigation.   There is no privileged communication in civil cases where the person in the professional relationship with a counselor introduces his or her psychological condition into a civil litigation. In other words, a person who is, or has been, in counseling cannot claim psychological injury due to an event but not allow the court to determine if the injury was present or partially present before the event, was caused or only partially caused by the event, or affected the degree of psychological damage caused by the event.

The reasonableness of this exception, as with many exceptions, can be validly debated on both sides. In one sense, this exception appears to be reasonable. In another sense it does not, because if the claimant had not sought professional help, he or she would likely be in a more advantageous position because there would be no professionally obtained psychological information to divulge. In a sense, the claimant is being punished for having sought professional help.

Breach of duty.   There is no privileged communication in a case where the counselor is accused of a breach of duty. This means that if a counselor is sued for malpractice by a person he or she saw in counseling, the counselor cannot refuse to testify to the relevant issues by claiming privileged communication.

This exception demonstrates an important point—namely, that in all states privileged communication is granted to the *person receiving help*; it is *not* granted to the *counselor*. Although it is said that certain professionals are covered by the privilege, this only means that the people seeking help from these professionals can cause them to claim the privilege for them. In other words, the privilege is not meant to protect the professional but only the person the professional has examined or seen in counseling. This is the reason that a person who sues a counselor for malpractice can release the counselor of confidentiality.

Furthermore, especially in civil cases, counselors may be asked by claimants with whom they had or have a professional relationship to divulge information that the counselor feels will jeopardize the claimant's case or his or her overall psychological welfare. Although counselors may ethically choose not to reveal this information, legally they do not have that prerogative. The counselor who, under these circumstances, insists on silence can be fined and/or sentenced to jail for contempt of court.

General considerations

Confidentiality in a counseling relationship is not a constitutional right but rather a matter of local policy. Hence, what is considered to be privileged communication and which professionals may claim the privilege for the person they see in counseling are determined by local statute and custom, and sometimes they are simply determined by the presiding judge.

There is a general rule that a person who is or has been in counseling cannot discuss some privileged communication in court but decline to convey the remainder of the privileged information. Once the person voluntarily divulges *some* privileged communication, it opens the door to *all* relevant information.

In many states, when the person in counseling is judged to be psychologically incompetent or is under the age of 18, parents or legal guardians can waive the confidentiality privilege.

Depending on the specific jurisdiction, the fact alone that a person is in or has been in counseling may or may not be considered privileged communication. For example, in California, the attorney general has given the opinion that this fact is covered by privileged communication (53 opinion of the Attorney General 151, 1970).

In many states, communications occurring in the presence of a third party are not deemed to be privileged communications. Although this rule does not apply to the counselor's professional associates, it may well apply to family and group counseling situations.

If a counselor is compelled to testify by the court, he or she cannot be prosecuted for violation of professional ethics or sued for malpractice.

While it is easy for some mental health professionals to criticize the law and the courts, it is quite another thing to write laws that adequately protect everyone's rights and that are not so general or so restrictive that they are weaker or stronger than they should be in individual cases.

This is not to say that more cooperation between the courts and the mental health professions is not needed. It simply means that the issues are extremely complex and provide no easy solutions at this time.

Confidentiality in specific work situations

In addition to the basic principles of confidentiality, there are related issues of which counselors should be aware in specific work situations. Counselors who are employed by certain agencies may be required by that agency, and perhaps by state law, to divulge information regarding the people seen in counseling. Before taking a specific job, counselors should learn in detail the exceptions to the basic principles of confidentiality that will be required. Many counselors do not consider this factor and soon find themselves embroiled in great professional, political, and legal struggles.

Many school districts have policies that require counselors to divulge information regarding students in counseling. This information usually deals with drug and alcohol abuse, venereal disease and pregnancy, and behavior that would be grossly disruptive or harmful to the school. Some schools also have policies requiring counselors to obtain written consent from parents when behaviors in a sexual area are to be discussed.

In prison systems, the military, and industry, counselors are often required to pass on information gleaned from evaluations and counseling that relates to a person's potential for violence or ability to handle sensitive jobs. While such restraints are inimical to the counseling process, there are some situations in which they are understandable. For example, a counselor working in a prison may learn of escape plans that include taking hostages, and the lives of many people would be in jeopardy.

In a military situation, a counselor may learn that a person has a problem that will make him a serious risk to himself and others in his performance of duty. For example, a pilot confides that he experiences severe anxiety attacks and has almost lost control of his plane over populated areas on several occasions, but he refuses to tell his superiors or to transfer to another assignment. In these and similar cases, the counselor must weigh the importance of confidentiality with the overall welfare of the person in counseling, as well as that of society at large.

If counselors choose to work in situations in which confidentiality may be compromised, they must do three things. They should always tell the person of the limitations that are placed on confidentiality and underscore that fact during counseling. They must decide if they are going to adhere strictly to the policies of the agency, use their own judgment about confidentiality, or ignore the requirements completely. Counselors who lead agencies to believe that they are abiding by such restrictions, but in fact are not, may be creating another ethical problem for both themselves and their profession. Finally, if counselors decide in good faith that they must divulge some information, it should be done in ways that preserve as much as possible the dignity and welfare of the person in counseling.

Records and reports

Another dimension of confidentiality deals with consultations, reports, and recording the counseling sessions. Recording the session can be done by note taking, tape recording, or audiovisual taping. If any of these procedures is to be used, it is incumbent on the counselor to advise the person at the first meeting. If notes are taken, the counselor should explain how confidentiality will be preserved—for example, by using a code or pseudonym to protect the person's identity. If audio or visual tapes are employed, counselors can advise people that these devices will be used only by the counselor. If the counselor wishes to share them with others for consultation or teaching purposes, permission should be obtained from the person and the person should be disguised as much as possible. Included in this understanding is that counselors will *invite* the person to give permission but not attempt to persuade or pressure the person to do so.

With regard to consultation with other professionals, permission must be obtained from the person in counseling and the person's identity must be protected whenever possible.

Although it is not required, it is good practice to obtain permission to play recordings or consult professionals *in writing*. What seemed to be a clearly understood and freely given consent a year ago may be something counselors wish they had documented as they later defend themselves in court.

Test results and clinical data that are communicated in report form also fall under the rubric of confidentiality. Before counselors send a report, they must receive written permission from the person. If at all possible, it is helpful to let the person read the report and *then* sign the release form to prevent a situation in which the person states: "But I didn't know he was going to divulge *that* information."

People must be able to gain access to their personal information and know how it is used. They not only have the right to see any reports, but must have a process whereby they can correct or amend information. Counselors would do well to keep this in mind when deciding on the content and tone of records or reports.

Legally, a counselor does not have control over the report once it is sent to the recipient. For example, a counselor may send a report that is part of a job application to the head of personnel at a civil service agency. The head of personnel may then leave it on her desk for days for anyone to read, may file it in a place where there is public access, or may send a copy to a third party. For this reason, it is helpful to type in large print at the top of a report: "This report is confidential. The information therein is not to be communicated in any manner to anyone other than Alice R. Jones, to whom the report is sent." Although the legal standing of such a disclaimer is arguable, it demonstrates good faith on the part of the counselor and should be in his or her favor if a problem arises.

A similar problem arises with third-party payments for counseling—that is, when insurance companies, workman's compensation, or Medicare is paying for part of the counseling. Once a diagnosis or report is sent, the agency can send the information to whomever it desires.

Because there are so many exceptions to privileged communication and confidentiality, counselors must advise people which exceptions are relevant in their situation.[3] It could be that, once people fully comprehend the nature of the exceptions, they may decline to enter counseling. While this may be an unfortunate decision, it is the person's right and, in some situations, it could be a prudent decision.

CONVEYING RELEVANT INFORMATION TO THE PERSON IN COUNSELING

The counselor has an ethical responsibility to help the person make informed choices regarding counseling.

> Ethical principles require that clients be provided with sufficient information to make informed choices about entering and continuing in therapy. Knowledge of three areas provides the necessary background for such choices: (1) the procedures, goals, and possible side effects of therapy; (2) the qualifications, policies, and practices of the therapist; and (3) the available sources of help other than therapy. . . . It cannot be assumed that those who seek therapy do so with adequate knowledge of therapy or its alternatives. Thus, one of the initial responsibilities of therapists is ensuring their clients' rights to informed choices.[4]

This principle covers a number of areas.

[3]For examples of a client's rights statement, initial contract form, and informed consent form, see Everstein, Everstein, Heymann, True, Frey, Johnson, & Seiden (1980), pp. 832–833.
[4]Hare-Mustin, Marecek, Kaplan, & Liss-Levinson (1979), p. 5.

Counselor qualifications

There are legal qualifications that deal with the activities a counselor is allowed and disallowed by law to perform. And there are professional qualifications that, unfortunately, are less explicit. These deal with the areas of performance that the counselor's training and experience prepare him or her to do most effectively.

Many people who seek psychological help are naive about such considerations. They assume that every mental health professional is equally qualified to prescribe medication; possess hospital privileges; administer psychological tests; do individual, group, marital, and family counseling; help children, adolescents, young adults, the middle-aged, or elderly; and treat all psychological problems of all degrees of severity. Unfortunately, some professionals and paraprofessionals think the same thing. It is important to distinguish between legal and professional qualifications and convey this information to the person in counseling.

For example, when a state licenses a psychologist, it simply tells the people of the state that this person has met certain general standards and is not breaking the law by practicing psychology. This license does not imply that the psychologist is equally competent in all areas of psychology, any more than a medical license indicates that a physician is equally qualified in all medical specialties.

It is the individual counselor's responsibility to define his or her areas of expertise, which are commonly and appropriately quite narrow. Typically, as counselors mature, they realize more clearly their strengths and limitations, as well as their fields of interest and noninterest.

People who seek the aid of counselors have the right to know what the counselors' areas of specialty are and to ask for a referral if one counselor cannot adequately meet their needs. This in no way reflects on the counselor's competence, but simply indicates his or her area of expertise.

A serious ethical question arises when a counselor agrees to work with someone who has a problem that the counselor has seldom, if ever, treated, especially where there are other counselors in the community who are known to have experience with the person's problem. The concept of the counselor and the person both learning together can, at times, be carried too far. Counselors who wish to expand their areas of competence are encouraged to do so, but this should be done under the supervision of a colleague more practiced in the specialty.

Financial aspects

Counselors should inform people regarding the financial aspects of counseling. Counselors in private practice can advise people of their fees and payment schedules on the first visit. The person can be informed as to the amount of the fees, when they are to be paid (after each session or monthly), and if it is the counselor's practice to bill on a sliding scale under certain circumstances. Counselors who work in an agency should explain its fee schedule and the likelihood of any fee increases in the near future.

It is important for counselors to tell people the consequences of not making payments at the agreed upon times. Counselors should also tell people if they are planning to raise their fee during the period that the person is likely to be in counseling and, most important, if the counselor is legally permitted to accept third-party payments—for example, from insurance carriers, workman's compensation, or Medicare. None of these issues should be casually dealt with because they are important to the person and may appear as obstacles to therapeutic progress later in the relationship. In cases in which the counselor's fee would be an undue hardship on the person, the counselor has an ethical responsibility to help the person find appropriate help for fees that are more affordable.

Counseling consequences

It is the counselor's responsibility to inform people of the possible results and side effects of counseling. Many people enter counseling with a vision of its outcome. While these visions differ with regard to specifics, the main theme is that the person will be at least symptom-free and, hopefully, significantly more effective and happier than before counseling. However, it is often necessary for counselors to temper this vision with reality. In some cases, a reasonable counseling goal is to reduce symptom impairment from 80% to 50% or from 50% to 20%. Under specific circumstances, these gains could qualify as successful counseling.

Some people are likely to feel worse before they get better and should realize this before making the commitment to enter counseling. People should also be advised of the possible consequences of growing in counseling. Obviously, counselors cannot foresee the future, but astute counselors can evaluate a person and the environment in which the person lives and form some impressions as to what possible effects a person's growth may have on the person and those around him or her.

When certain side effects seem possible or likely, counselors should share their impressions at an appropriate time with the person so that the person knows exactly what he or she is doing and can freely choose to continue or discontinue counseling.

The following are some side effects that can stem from successful counseling, given a specific person and environment:

1. Growth in young people can create significant tension in their parents. The parents may deflect this tension back onto the children, making matters worse than ever.
2. Growth in one spouse but not in the other can cause disequilibrium in a marriage and may even fracture it.
3. Growth in a psychologically presexual person of any age can cause the surfacing of heterosexual or homosexual feelings that could be quite threatening.
4. Growth in a person can melt defenses, which allows hitherto repressed feelings of anger, fear, guilt, and depression to surface, sometimes with a vengeance.
5. Growth can markedly change a person's attitudes toward parents, marriage, spouse, children, divorce, careers, friends, and religion.
6. Growth can also drastically affect how significant others view the person in counseling. People who grow in independence may be viewed as ungrateful and selfish. Those who grow in assertiveness may be seen as disrespectful and arrogant. People who grow in honesty may be seen as less lovable and less attractive. Those who grow in warmth and tenderness may be seen as weak. People who change their religious attitudes may be seen as heretics or neurotic. Those who change their sexual behavior in one direction or another may be seen as "uptight" or "loose."

Many people who enter counseling have no clear understanding of what they are really doing. They could be admonished "Before you *ask* for it, be sure you *want* it." It is counselors' ethical responsibility to describe, as much as they reasonably can, some of the possible side effects each person might expect from counseling. This should not be done as a warning, but in the spirit of a tour guide who describes where the tour is going so that people don't suddenly find themselves in places where they don't want to be.

Time involved in counseling

Counselors should also inform people as to the approximate amount of time they can expect to be in counseling. Many people enter counseling thinking it will take only a few sessions or maybe six months at the longest. When their unarticulated but expected termination date passes, a difficult situation can arise. The person may feel that the fact that counseling is not finished by the expected time means that the counselor is ineffective or that counseling doesn't work.

If the person is paying a fee for counseling, the "extra" time can create a valid hardship. It could be that a person may have willingly agreed to a six-month program but would not have agreed to a two- or three-year one. Also, a suspicion may arise that the counselor is unnecessarily prolonging counseling for personal gain.

Counselors cannot make accurate predictions of how long counseling will take, but they can make approximations within several sessions for short-term counseling and several months for long-term counseling with some degree of accuracy.

Counselors should also tell people if they are planning to be absent for any period of time—for example, on a sabbatical or prolonged vacation—or if they may be moving from the area before counseling is completed. Sudden absences from counseling or premature termination by the counselor represent information that people need to know in order to make an intelligent decision.

Alternatives to counseling

It is the counselor's ethical responsibility to inform people regarding the alternatives to counseling. Counseling is not the only way people can be helped. When considering counseling for a person, counselors must take into account several variables, including the nature of the problem, the psychological resources of the person to use counseling well, the length of time counseling will take, the strength of the person's motivation to remain in counseling, the realistic gains that counseling may offer, and the amount of time and money the person can afford to spend. On the basis of the interaction of all these factors, a counselor may decide that the person needs counseling and is a good candidate, that the person needs counseling but is a poor candidate, or that the person does not need counseling but some other form of intervention.

People who are judged to be poor candidates for counseling or who need other kinds of help may be referred to such community programs as self-help programs; support groups for people with specific problems (for example, child abuse or battered wives); relaxation training; parents without partners; marriage encounter; peer counseling; courses in assertiveness, personal adjustment, sexuality, parent effectiveness, meditation, or group dynamics; centers and clinics that help people with weight-control problems, substance abuse, pregnancy, religious problems, or stress problems. Also, some people make good use of bibliotherapy (reading books that are relevant to the person's problem), chemotherapy (taking medications to relieve symptoms of anxiety or depression), biofeedback, and clinical hypnotherapy.

When and how alternatives to counseling are suggested and explained depends on each situation, but the counselor should exercise discretion. If the person is in an obviously anguished state, it may be more helpful to reduce some of the anguish over the period of a session or more than to deal immediately with the alternatives. It may be advisable to continue counseling while the person explores alternatives.

The manner in which the counselor discusses the alternatives is also important. Alternatives should be described without personal bias. For example, a person may ask if hypnosis would help, and the counselor, who has negative feelings about hypnosis, responds in a way that clearly reflects these feelings, even though hypnosis may prove to be reasonably effective in alleviating the person's symptoms.

Counselors can also be cautious that their referral does not erroneously connote that they simply don't want to see the person because he or she is not attractive, interesting, or financially solvent. Counselors can give sound reasons why an alternative method may be appropriate. This can convey to the person that the counselor is being forthright and is interested in getting the best help for the person at the most affordable fees.

Informing people concerning relevant issues in counseling is not a one-shot communication. It is often necessary to remind people of relevant issues throughout the counseling process and to inform them of new issues as they arise.

It is not only required ethical practice to inform people about relevant issues, but it is useful practically. The more surprises there are for the person in counseling, the more arduous the process will be for both the person and the counselor. It is better for a person to choose not to enter counseling on the basis of valid information than to terminate at a later date with feelings of regret, disappointment, and acrimony, toward both the counselor and counseling in general.

THE COUNSELOR'S INFLUENCE

It is important for counselors to recognize that they hold a position of influence in the counseling relationship. This is true for at least three reasons. One is that people who approach counseling for help often overestimate the counselor's knowledge, wisdom, and healing qualities. As a result, even the slightest nod of the head or casual remark can take on meanings of which the counselor is unaware. Second, counselors are more learned about mental health principles than people in counseling and, it is hoped, are psychologically healthier. Therefore, what counselors say and do is more persuasive than the actions of most, if not all, the significant others in the person's life. Third, people who are experiencing psychological pain are often suggestible and swayed by the influence of a person who presents himself or herself as someone who can help.

Many counselors forget the tremendous power they wield in counseling. They forget it because they are used to the concept and have more current, challenging problems to solve in their everyday counseling, because they enjoy being influential but feel guilty enjoying it and so repress the entire dynamic, or because they don't want to have to deal with the great responsibility that accompanies influence.

To be less than keenly aware of the influence counselors have is tantamount to being unaware that one is driving too fast. As the driver proceeds, he is naively unaware of the damage he has left in his path. It is for this reason that counseling influence is an ethical concern. Influence is not, in itself, antitherapeutic. In fact, if counselors had no influence, little learning would take place. However, counselors can allow themselves to be too influential or influential in damaging ways, and it is in these areas that great caution must be exercised. When a counselor's influence interferes with the proper goals of counseling, it becomes an ethical concern. The following areas are particularly relevant to the counselor's influence.

The counselor's personal needs

When the counselor's personal needs are inserted into counseling, they will enhance, impede, or reverse the counseling process. The following are seven counselor needs that can have ethical implications when they are present in counseling.

To control. When counselors exert inordinate control, they contaminate the decision-making processes of the person in counseling. Subtly, the person becomes attached to the counselor's decision-making mechanisms and becomes a psychological robot. Even though such control is benevolent, it undermines the person's attempts to define his or her own values and to make decisions accordingly. Counselors can rationalize their overcontrol by assuring themselves that their goals and the goals of the person are essentially the same and that they are only helping the person "get off the dime" and make some good decisions.

To be correct. When this need is overdriven, the counselor creates a dynamic in which he or she is always correct and the person in counseling is always wrong. This need manifests itself most clearly in situations in which the perceptions, interpretations, and values of the counselor and those of the person differ. When the counselor makes the person wrong, this reinforces the person's poor self-esteem and detracts from his or her self-confidence. It also subtly changes the therapeutic milieu from one in which a person can say and feel anything to one in which a person must be careful in order to reduce the risk of being wrong. Counselors can rationalize this need by assuring themselves that their role is to present reality to the person and that their view of reality is very likely to be more accurate than that of the person in counseling.

To rescue. This is an exaggerated, destructive version of the need to help. Counselors with the need to rescue pull people off psychological cliffs. However, when people are pulled off cliffs, they fail to learn the competencies necessary to rescue themselves, and they learn to expect someone always to be present to save them from facing the consequences of their behavior. Counselors can rationalize their rescue operations by assuring themselves that rescuing and helping are synonymous.

To be important. Counselors who need to be important in counseling subtly or overtly demand an allegiance that requires people to place them in a position of paramount importance. As a result, the person in counseling and the significant others in the person's life become dutiful subjects. This is one of the dynamics of the "guru" phenomenon in which people virtually hand over their lives and sometimes the lives of their families to the counselor. Counselors can rationalize their need by assuring themselves that they should be important in the person's life and that without this "transference" counseling cannot be successful.

To feel and receive affection. When counselors need to feel affection from the people they see in counseling, it can seriously impede progress. There is a difference between a person having some feelings of affection toward his or her counselor and a counselor *needing* the person's affection. When the counselor needs affection, the focus will subtly be placed on the relationship between the counselor and the person rather than on other, more important, issues. Also, the person in counseling may sense this need of the counselor and, at least unconsciously, choose to meet it as a means of neutralizing the counselor as a threat. Both these dynamics are inimical to good counseling. Counselors can rationalize this need by assuring themselves that a close relationship is the foundation of effective counseling.

To create tension. Some counselors continually inject tension into counseling even when it is inappropriate and destructive. Unduly creating tension has three effects that the counselor desires: it keeps a safe distance between the counselor and the person; it is an antidote to boredom; and, since the counselor is more skilled at handling tension, the counselor "wins" every confrontation. The person is a sparring partner for the counselor and learns nothing from the counselor except how to take punishment and how to avoid punches. Counselors can rationalize this need by assuring themselves that good counselors should generate tension because it is only through tension that people grow.

To make money. There is a difference between providing a service for which one gets paid and providing a service primarily for the purpose of getting paid. When the latter need is operative, people in counseling are treated as customers more than as human beings who need help. This need is manifested in the counselor who schedules too many people so that he or she is unable to be fully present at each counseling session, whose motivation is contingent on the amount of money the person is paying, and who charges higher fees than are necessary. Counselors can rationalize this need by assuring themselves that they have to make a living and that their fees are no higher than those of counselors who are far less effective.

It is important that counselors honestly appraise the nature and strength of their needs and discern whether such needs are enhancing or interfering with the counseling process. Basic personal needs that are healthy—for example, the need for affection—should be met primarily outside the counseling relationship. Needs that are basically unhealthy—such as the need to create tension—should be resolved so they will not affect the counseling relationship negatively.[5]

[5]For a fuller discussion of counselor needs and how they can affect counseling, see Hammer (1972), pp. 21–32.

Unresolved issues in the counselor

It cannot be overstressed that counselors are human beings. Although such a concept is self-evident, it is one that both people in counseling and counselors tend to forget with discouraging frequency. Even when the fact that counselors are only human is heartily agreed upon, there is often a subtle footnote that reads "Yes, but they fall in the top tenth percentile."

There are very few human beings, including counselors, who enjoy a complete resolution of all past conflicts from birth to the present. Instead of speaking in terms of resolved and unresolved issues, it is much more realistic to talk in terms of some conflicts being more resolved than others.

It is important for counselors to realize that unresolved areas do not continually manifest themselves. The unresolved areas may become operative only under certain conditions—for example, only when the counselor is fatigued, under stress, or relating with certain people. Unresolved issues may be latent and become activated by discrete, often unconscious, stimuli.

A counselor's unresolved conflicts become an ethical issue when they impede or reverse the counseling process. Realistically, there probably has never been a counseling relationship in which, at one time or another, the counselor's unresolved issues did not impede counseling. It is, however, the counselor's responsibility to recognize these areas of unresolved conflict, to control them, and to bring them to a state of further resolution. The following are two common unresolved issues.

Authority.　The counselor's life experiences with regard to authority may evoke primarily benevolent, angry or ambivalent feelings toward authority. Authority figures can be people older or younger than the counselor, or more intelligent, aggressive, powerful, of the same sex or opposite sex.

Unresolved issues with regard to authority can affect counseling in one or both of two ways. First, if the counselor who has a problem with authority views the person in counseling as an authority figure, he or she may react to the person in ways that are overly cautious, ingratiating, and docile on one hand or overly defensive, threatening, or aggressive on the other. Counselors with strongly ambivalent feelings toward authority vacillate from one end of the continuum to the other. Counselors who have a problem with authority may react with caution when a more certain, immediate response is appropriate, with defensiveness when an inquiring approach is more helpful, with anger when understanding would be more salutary. As a result, progress toward the goals of counseling becomes unnecessarily impeded.

Second, the counselor's problem with authority may manifest itself in how the counselor helps the person in counseling deal with authority in his or her life. For example, counselors who tend to be fearful of authority may suggest an overly passive and docile approach to authority. Counselors who tend to be antagonistic toward authority may influence people to take an inappropriately harsh or rebellious stance toward authority.

Sexuality. Sexuality, as an unresolved issue, has two dimensions: how a counselor relates with people of the same and opposite sex and how well childhood and adolescent sexual issues have been resolved. Some counselors relate equally well with both sexes. Others relate better with same-sexed people; still others relate better with opposite-sexed people.

Preferring to work with one sex more than another is no more of an ethical issue than preferring to work with children rather than adults. But to harbor beliefs about people based on their sex and to relate in counseling according to these beliefs is an ethical issue. For example, if a male counselor views the women he sees in counseling as typically manipulative and overemotional and a female counselor views the men she sees in counseling as typically childlike and insensitive, progress toward mental health goals may be substantially impaired. Unfortunately, because of their defense systems, counselors can blind themselves to their prejudices, fail to see how their biases negatively affect counseling, and blame the lack of progress in counseling on the person's "resistance" or on "negative transference."

The second dimension of sexuality as it relates to ethics in counseling concerns the presence of unresolved sexual issues from childhood and adolescence. Because of developmental experiences or lack of them, counselors can have weak spots in the area of sexuality. These can manifest themselves in a number of ways. Counselors may deny their own sexuality and/or the sexuality of the people they see in counseling. This can make sexuality a perennial nonissue in counseling when it is a factor that is always present and that may be a particular source of concern to a person. In this case, the counselor is inclined to view sexual conflicts always as "symptomatic" of some other, deeper problem and to choose to focus on the "real cause" rather than its "sexual manifestation."

Some counselors have the opposite problem; they focus unduly on their own sexuality and/or the sexuality of the person in counseling.

When this is the case, inordinate amounts of time can be spent dealing with sexual issues when other issues, which are at least as important, are ignored. To justify this preoccupation with sex, these counselors rationalize that all human dynamics are somehow integrally connected with sexuality. They may also use this rationalization to encourage people in counseling to participate in sexual activities both in and out of counseling as an integral part of their treatment program. Such practices can damage the person in counseling, the counseling relationship, and the profession in general.

The counselor's moral and religious values

All counselors possess moral values, and many of them also have religious values. Most of these values have been instilled since birth, are often strong, and their truth is viewed as "self-evident." These values affect every aspect of the counselor's life; therefore, their presence will also be felt in counseling.

Sometimes moral and religious values can be congruent with sound counseling practice, but at other times they are not. A problem arises when counselors' personal values cause them to react to people in ways that are countertherapeutic. Generally, the issues that are most amenable to moral or religious judgments are masturbation, premarital sex, living together without being married, extramarital sex, abortion, divorce, remarrying after divorce, homosexuality, spouse or child beating, child molesting, incest, and failing to live according to the tenets of one's religion.

One problem arises when the person in counseling behaves in ways that the counselor considers immoral, causing the counselor to view the person negatively. A negative view of the person may range from a condescending attitude ("You poor thing; you don't realize the wrongfulness of your behavior") to outright contempt ("You seem to be somewhat lacking in moral character").

Well-meaning counselors try to override these ingrained feelings with mental health values or with some variation of "hate the sin but love the sinner." These efforts are unlikely to succeed over a period of time, however, if the person continues to participate in the behavior either because he or she does not view it as immoral or does not consider the behavior in question a therapeutic issue. The person's casual attitude toward the behavior, added to the possibility of the person chiding the counselor about his or her differing values, may make it increasingly difficult for the counselor to maintain an accepting attitude. For this reason, there is worth to the idea that counselors should not see people who possess diametrically opposed values or who participate in behaviors that are morally repugnant to the counselor.

Does this mean that counselors should not have personal values or should put them on the shelf when they do counseling? Does it mean that counselors should *like* the behaviors of the people they see in counseling? The answer to both questions is no.

Counselors do have personal values and have no choice but to bring them into counseling. But they can realize that values are related to counseling in one of three ways: they have no effect on counseling; they have a positive effect and allow the counselor and person to relate in mutually accepting and freeing ways; or they have a negative effect, causing inordinate tension or antipathy between the counselor and the person. When the latter is true, counseling will be severely impaired, if not destroyed.

Counselors do not have to like or view as good all the behaviors of the people they see in counseling. A counselor may not like the fact that a person molests children, but he or she is not repulsed—that is, driven off from working in a close, caring, and effective way with the person. Counselors who are repulsed to the degree that it places a wedge in the relationship should refer the person elsewhere.

A second problem arises when the personal values of the counselor and those of the person clash. The counselor may wish to convert the person to his or her values or beliefs. A counselor who believes that masturbation is immoral may try to persuade the person to stop, even though there is no therapeutic reason to do so. Or a counselor may believe that religion is simply a neurotic defense that must be discarded if counseling is to be considered successful.

The practical problem is that some counselors do not see the difference between personal and counseling values; hence, they view moral, religious, and counseling values as synonymous, even when they are not. For example, a counselor may be convinced that until a married person discontinues extramarital relations, he or she cannot expect relief from anxiety or that until a woman admits the wrongdoing of having an abortion and works through the unconscious guilt associated with it, she cannot expect to be free of insomnia. In these cases, it is possible that the counselor's personal moral and religious values have become so intertwined with his or her mental health principles that the counselor may be infusing dynamics into the person when they simply are not present. When one of the main goals of counseling is introducing the person to phantom dynamics and resolving them, damage can be done to both the person and the therapeutic process.

A third problem arises when the person in counseling seems open to accepting the counselor's moral or religious values. The counselor feels that he or she has been given "permission" to teach personal values to the person. The person in counseling may have had little moral education or simply may be suggestible and willing to buy affirmation by assuming the counselor's values. At first this may seem like a benign process, but it may not be. Moral education can well be a valid part of counseling, but it should be moral education and not moral indoctrination. Moral education consists of objectively exploring with a person the rationale underlying various values and beliefs and the constructive and destructive aspects of certain behaviors. But it is the person in counseling who should freely and ultimately decide what values and beliefs are best suited for his or her overall growth. The values that the person chooses may be consonant or dissonant with those of the counselor, but the counselor's regard for the person remains unalterably positive and caring.[6]

SUMMARY

Professional ethics are rules of conduct that are meant to protect people in counseling, counselors, and the helping professions in general. Ethics in counseling covers a wide range of issues, from the more obvious ones (such as privileged communication) to the more subtle ones (such as paying full attention to a person during a counseling session). Adhering to a code of ethics does not ensure effective counseling, but violating ethics ensures ineffective counseling. It is counselors' professional responsibility to apprise themselves of the ethical issues in counseling and to communicate the relevant ones to the people they see in counseling. Only when people can feel that their human rights will be scrupulously safeguarded can the foundation of a counseling relationship be built.

THOUGHT QUESTIONS

1. What specific criteria would you use to guide you in deciding whether or not to inform authorities when a person states he may harm himself or another?
2. You obtain a "gentleman's agreement" from the parents of a teenage girl that whatever she tells you will be confidential and that the parents will not be privy to it. Later in counseling, the parents suspect that their daughter is sexually involved with her boyfriend and demand that you confirm or deny the accuracy of this suspicion.

[6]For a discussion of religion, mental health, and counseling, see May (1967a).

When you refuse, they threaten civil proceedings, in which they will likely prevail. What do you do?

3. Your values are such that you oppose abortion. A young woman you have been seeing in counseling for six months becomes pregnant and wants you to help her deal with the question as to whether to obtain an abortion. How will you handle this situation while preserving the quality of the counseling relationship?

4. After six months in counseling, a man says "I read the other day that, legally, I have access to all the information you have that pertains to me. I just thought it would be interesting to see the progress notes you keep on me." How do you respond?

5. Because counselors are human, it is unlikely that there is any experienced counselor who, at one time or another, has not failed to comply adequately with one or more of the several ethical principles discussed in this chapter. What are one or two principles that you should be especially careful about?

References and Recommended Readings

Adler, A. *Superiority and social interest*. Evanston, Ill.: Northwestern University Press, 1964.

Adler, G., & Myerson, P. G. (Eds.). *Confrontation in psychotherapy*. New York: Science House, 1973.

Aguilera, D., & Messick, J. *Crisis intervention* (3rd ed.). St. Louis: Mosby, 1978.

Allport, G. W. *Becoming*. New Haven, Conn.: Yale University Press, 1955.

American Psychiatric Association. *Diagnostic and statistical manual of mental disorders* (3rd ed.) (*DSM III*). Washington, D.C.: American Psychiatric Association, 1980.

American Psychological Association. Ethical standards of psychologists. Reprint from APA *Monitor*, March 1977. Washington, D.C.: American Psychological Association, 1977.

Ansbacher, H. L., & Ansbacher, R. R. (Eds.). *The individual psychology of Alfred Adler*. New York: Harper & Row, 1956.

Arbuckle, D. Existentialism in counseling: The humanist view. *Personnel and Guidance Journal*, 1965, *44*, 558–567.

Argelander, H. *The initial interview in psychotherapy*. New York: Human Sciences Press, 1976.

Arnold, M. B. *Emotion and personality* (2 vols.). New York: Columbia University Press, 1960.

Arnold, M. B. (Ed.). *Feelings and emotions*. New York: Academic Press, 1970.

Avnet, H. H. How effective is short-term therapy? In L. R. Wolberg (Ed.), *Short-term psychotherapy*. New York: Grune and Stratton, 1965.

Bach, G. R., & Goldberg, H. *Creative aggression*. New York: Avon, 1974.

Bandura, A. Self-efficacy: Towards a unifying theory of behavioral change. *Psychological Review*, 1977, *84*, 191–215.

Bannister, D. (Ed.). *Perspectives in personal construct theory*. New York: Academic Press, 1970.

Bassin, A., Bratter, T. E., & Rachin, R. L. (Eds.). *The reality therapy reader: A survey of the work of William Glasser*. New York: Harper & Row, 1976.

Baum, O. E. Countertransference. *Psychoanalytic Review*, 1972, *56*, 621–636.

Baum, O. E. Further thoughts on countertransference. *Psychoanalytic Review*, 1973, *60*, 127–140.

Beck, A. T. Reliability of psychiatric diagnosis. I. A critique of systematic studies. *American Journal of Psychiatry*, 1962, *119*, 210–216.

Beck, A. T. *Depression: Causes and treatment*. Philadelphia: University of Pennsylvania Press, 1967.

Beck, A. T. *Cognitive therapy and the emotional disorders*. New York: International Universities Press, 1976.

Beck, A., & Kovacs, M. A new fast therapy for depression. *Psychology Today*, January 1977, pp. 94–101.

Beier, E. G. *The silent language of psychotherapy*. Chicago: Aldine, 1966.

Belkin, G. S. *An introduction to counseling*. Dubuque, Iowa: Brown, 1980. (a)

Belkin, G. S. *Contemporary psychotherapies*. Chicago: Rand McNally, 1980. (b)

Benjamin, A. *The helping interview* (2nd ed.). Boston: Houghton Mifflin, 1974.

Bergin, A. E. The effects of psychotherapy: Negative results revisited. *Journal of Counseling Psychology*, 1963, *10*, 244–250.

Bergin, A. E. The evaluation of therapeutic outcomes. In A. E. Bergin & S. K. Garfield (Eds.), *Handbook of psychotherapy and behavior change*. New York: Wiley, 1971.

Bergin, A. E. Psychotherapy can be dangerous. *Psychology Today*, November 1975, pp. 96–104.

Binder, V., Binder, A., & Rimland, B. *Modern therapies*. Englewood Cliffs, N.J.: Prentice-Hall, 1976.

Blackham, G. J., & contributing authors. *Counseling: Theory, process, and practice*. Belmont, Calif.: Wadsworth, 1977.

Brammer, L. M. *The helping relationship process and skills* (2nd ed.). Englewood Cliffs, N.J.: Prentice-Hall, 1979.

Brill, N. I. *Working with people* (2nd ed.). Philadelphia: Lippincott, 1978.

Bry, A. *Inside psychotherapy*. New York: Basic Books, 1972.

Bugental, J. F. T. The person who is the psychotherapist. *Journal of Consulting Psychology*, 1964, *28*(3), 272–277.

Bugental, J. F. T. *Psychotherapy and process: The fundamentals of an existential-humanistic approach*. Menlo Park, Calif.: Addison-Wesley, 1978.

Bühler, C. Humanistic psychology as an education program. *American Psychologist*, 1969, *24*(8), 736–741.

Bühler, C. Basic theoretical concepts of humanistic psychology. *American Psychologist*, 1971, *26*(4), 385–387.

Burck, H. D., & Peterson, G. W. Needed! More evaluation, not research. *Personnel and Guidance Journal*, 1975, *53*(8), 563–569.

Burks, H. M., Jr., & Stefflre, B. *Theories of counseling* (3rd ed.). New York: McGraw-Hill, 1979.

Burton, A. *Modern humanistic psychotherapy*. San Francisco: Jossey-Bass, 1968.

Candland, D. K., Fell, J. P., Keen, E., Leshner, A. I., Tarpy, R. M., & Plutchik, R. *Emotion*. Monterey, Calif.: Brooks/Cole, 1977.

Carkhuff, R. R., & Anthony, W. A. *The skills of helping*. Amherst, Mass.: Human Resource Development Press, 1979.

Carkhuff, R. R., & Berenson, B. G. *Beyond counseling and therapy* (2nd ed.). New York: Holt, Rinehart & Winston, 1977.

Carkhuff, R. R., Pierce, R. M., & Cannon, J. R. *The art of helping.* Amherst, Mass.: Human Resource Development Press, 1977.

Carson, R. C. A & B therapist "types": A possible critical variable in psychotherapy. *Journal of Nervous and Mental Disease,* 1967, *144,* 47–54.

Chartier, G. M. A-B therapist variable: Real or imagined? *Psychological Bulletin,* 1971, *75,* 22–23.

Chessick, R. D. *Why psychotherapists fail.* New York: Science House, 1971.

Chessick, R. D. *Intensive psychotherapy.* New York: Jason Aronson, 1974.

Cole, N. J., Branch, C. H., & Allison, R. B. Some relationships between social class and the practice of dynamic psychotherapy. *American Journal of Psychiatry,* 1962, *118,* 1004–1012.

Coleman, J. C., Butcher, J. N., & Carson, R. C. *Abnormal psychology and modern life* (6th ed.). Palo Alto, Calif.: Scott, Foresman, 1980.

Combs, A. W., & Snygg, D. *Individual behavior* (2nd ed.). New York: Harper, 1959.

Corey, G. *Theory and practice of counseling and psychotherapy.* Monterey, Calif.: Brooks/Cole, 1977.

Corsini, R. J., & contributors. *Current psychotherapies* (2nd ed.). Itasca, Ill.: Peacock, 1979.

Craig, T., & Huffine, C. Correlates of patient attendance in an inner-city mental health clinic. *American Journal of Psychiatry,* 1976, *133,* 61–64.

Dewald, P. A. Reactions to the forced termination of therapy. *Psychiatric Quarterly,* 1965, *39,* 102–126.

Dixon, S. L. *Working with people in crisis.* St. Louis: Mosby, 1979.

Dollard, J., & Miller, N. E. *Personality and psychotherapy.* New York: McGraw-Hill, 1950.

Durlak, J. A. Myths concerning the nonprofessional therapist. *Professional psychology,* 1973, *4,* 300–304.

Egan, G. *The skilled helper* (2nd ed.). Monterey, Calif.: Brooks/Cole, 1982.

Ellis, A. *Reason and emotion in psychotherapy.* New York: Lyle Stuart, 1962.

Ellis, A. *Humanistic psychotherapy.* New York: Julian Press, 1973.

Ellis, A. Personality hypotheses of RET (rational emotive therapy) and other modes of cognitive-behavior therapy. *The Counseling Psychologist,* 1977, *7*(1), 2–42.

Emrick, C. D. A review of psychologically oriented treatment in alcoholism. *Journal of Studies on Alcohol,* 1975, *36,* 88–108.

Everstein, L., Everstein, D. S., Heymann, G., True, R. H., Frey, D. H., Johnson, H. G., & Seiden, R. H. Privacy and confidentiality in psychotherapy. *American Psychologist,* 1980, *35* (9), 828–840.

Ewing, C. P. *Crisis intervention as psychotherapy.* New York: Oxford University Press, 1978.

Eysenck, H. J. The effects of psychotherapy: An evaluation. *Journal of Consulting Psychology,* 1952, *16,* 319–324.

Eysenck, H. J. *The effects of psychotherapy.* New York: International Sciences Press, 1966.

Fierman, L. B. Myths in the practice of psychotherapy. *Archives of General Psychiatry,* 1965, *12,* 408–414.

Ford, D. H., & Urban, H. B. *Systems of psychotherapy: A comparative study.* New York: Wiley, 1963.

Forer, B. R. The therapeutic value of crisis. *Psychological Reports,* 1963, *13,* 275–281.

Frank, J. D. Therapeutic factors in psychotherapy. *American Journal of Psychotherapy,* 1971, *25,* 350–361.

Frank, J. D. *Persuasion and healing* (Rev. ed.). Baltimore: Johns Hopkins University Press, 1973.

Frank, J. D., Gliedman, L. H., Imber, S. D., Stone, A. R., & Nash, E. H. Patients' expectations and relearning as factors determining improvement in psychotherapy. *American Journal of Psychiatry*, 1959, *115*, 961–968.

Frankl, V. *Man's search for meaning*. New York: Washington Square Press, 1963.

Frankl, V. *Psychotherapy and existentialism: Selected papers on logotherapy*. New York: Simon and Schuster (Clarion Books), 1967.

Freud, S. On psychotherapy. In A. Strachey & J. Strachey (Trans.), *Collected papers* (vol. 1). London: Hogarth and the Institute of Psychoanalysis, 1950.

Freud, S. The psychopathology of everyday life. In J. Strachey (Ed.), *The standard edition of the complete psychological works of Sigmund Freud* (vol. 6). London: Hogarth, 1953.

Fromme, A. *The ability to love*. Hollywood, Calif.: Wilshire, 1972.

Gaines, J. *Fritz Perls: Here and now*. Millbrae, Calif.: Celestial Arts, 1979.

Garfield, S. L. *Psychotherapy: An eclectic approach*. New York: Wiley, 1980.

Garfield, S. L., & Kurtz, R. A study of eclectic views. *Journal of Consulting and Clinical Psychology*, 1977, *45*, 78–83.

Garfield, S. L., Prager, R. A., & Bergin, A. E. Evaluation of outcome in psychotherapy. *Journal of Consulting and Clinical Psychology*, 1971, *37*, 307–313.

Garfield, S. L., and Walpin, M. Expectations regarding psychotherapy. *Journal of Nervous and Mental Disease*, 1963, *137*, 353–362.

Garner, H. H. *Psychotherapy: Confrontation problem-solving techniques*. St. Louis: Warren H. Green, 1970.

Gaylin, W. *Feelings: Our vital signs*. New York: Harper & Row, 1979.

Gendlin, E. T. Initiating psychotherapy with "unmotivated" patients. *Psychiatric Quarterly*, 1961, *35*, 134–139.

Gilmore, J. V. *The productive personality*. San Francisco: Albion, 1974.

Gladstein, G. A. Is empathy important in counseling? *Personnel and Guidance Journal*, 1970, *48*, 823–826.

Glasser, W. *Reality therapy*. New York: Harper & Row, 1965.

Goldberg, C. *Therapeutic partnership: Ethical concerns in psychotherapy*. New York: Springer, 1977.

Goldman, L. A revolution in counseling research. *Journal of Counseling Psychology*, 1976, *23*(6), 543–552.

Goldstein, A. P. Therapist and client expectation of personality change in psychotherapy. *Journal of Counseling Psychology*, 1960, *7*, 180–184.

Gray, M. *Neuroses: A comprehensive and critical view*. New York: Van Nostrand Reinhold, 1978.

Greenspoon, J. *The sources of behavior: Abnormal and normal*. Monterey, Calif.: Brooks/Cole, 1976.

Greenwald, H. *Direct decision therapy*. San Diego, Calif.: Edits, 1973.

Gurman, A. S. Instability of therapeutic conditions in psychotherapy. *Journal of Counseling Psychology*, 1973, *20*, 16–24.

Gurman, A. S., & Razin, A. M. (Eds.). *Effective psychotherapy*. New York: Pergamon, 1977.

Hahn, M. E. Conceptual trends in counseling. *Personnel and Guidance Journal*, 1953, *31*, 232.

Haley, J. *Problem-solving therapy*. New York: Harper & Row, 1976.

Hammer, M. *The theory and practice of psychotherapy with specific disorders*. Springfield, Ill.: Charles C Thomas, 1972.

Hare-Mustin, R. T., Marecek, M., Kaplan, A. G., & Liss-Levinson, N. Rights of clients, responsibilities of therapists. *American Psychologist,* 1979, *34*(1), 3–16.

Harper, R. A. *The new psychotherapies.* Englewood Cliffs, N.J.: Prentice-Hall, 1975.

Harris, M. R., Kalis, B., & Freeman, E. Precipitating stress: An approach to brief therapy. *American Journal of Psychotherapy,* 1963, *17,* 465–471.

Hiltner, S. Hostility in counseling. *Pastoral Psychology,* 1950, *1*, 35–42.

Holt, W. E. The concept of motivation for treatment. *American Journal of Psychiatry,* 1967, *123,* 1388–1394.

Horney, K. *New ways in psychoanalysis.* New York: Norton, 1939.

Horney, K. *Our inner conflicts.* New York: Norton, 1945.

Izard, C. E. *Human emotions.* New York: Plenum, 1977.

Jourard, S. M., & Landsman, T. *Healthy personality* (4th ed.). New York: Macmillan, 1980.

Jung, C. G. *The development of personality* (1954). Collected Works, Vol. 17, Bollingen Series XX. Princeton, N.J.: Princeton University Press, 1964.

Karasu, T. B. Psychotherapies: An overview. *American Journal of Psychiatry,* 1977, *134*(8), 851–861.

Kardener, S. H. A methodological approach to crisis therapy. *American Journal of Psychotherapy,* 1975, *29,* 4–13.

Kelly, G. A. *The psychology of personal constructs.* New York: Norton, 1955.

Kelly, G. A. A brief introduction to personal construct theory. In D. Bannister (Ed.), *Perspectives in personal construct theory.* New York: Academic Press, 1970.

Kemp, G. C. Existential counseling. *The Counseling Psychologist,* 1971, *2*, 2–30.

Kemper, T. D. *A social interactional theory of emotions.* New York: Wiley, 1978.

Kiesler, D. J. Some myths of psychotherapy research and the search for a paradigm. *Psychological Bulletin,* 1966, *65*, 110–136.

Krumboltz, J. D. Future direction for counselor research. In J. M. Whietley (Ed.), *Research in counseling.* Columbus, Ohio: Merrill, 1967.

Kunnes, R. Double dealing in dope. *Human Behavior,* 1973, *2*(10), 22–27.

Lahey, B. B., & Ciminero, A. R. *Maladaptive behavior: An introduction to abnormal psychology.* Palo Alto, Calif.: Scott, Foresman, 1980.

Laing, R. D. *Knots.* New York: Vintage Books, 1970.

Lambert, M. J., Bergin, A., & Collins, J. Therapist-induced deterioration in psychotherapy. In A. Gurman & A. Razin (Eds.), *Effective psychotherapy: A handbook of research.* New York: Pergamon, 1977.

Langs, R. *The technique of psychoanalytic psychotherapy* (2 vols.). New York: Jason Aronson, 1974.

Leeman, C. P., & Mulvey, C. H. Brief psychotherapy of the dependent personality: Specific techniques. *Psychonometrics,* 1973, *25,* 36–42.

Levy, L. H. *Psychological interpretation.* New York: Holt, Rinehart & Winston, 1962.

Lichtenberg, J. D., & Slap, J. W. On the defense mechanism: A survey and synthesis. *Journal of the American Psychoanalytic Association,* 1972, *29*, 776–792.

Loughary, J. W., & Ripley, T. M. *Helping others help themselves.* New York: McGraw-Hill, 1979.

Luborsky, L., Chandler, M., Auerbach, A. H., Cohen, J., & Bachrach, H. M. Factors influencing the outcome of psychotherapy. *Psychological Bulletin,* 1971, *75*, 145–185.

Madow, L. *Anger: How to recognize and cope with it.* New York: Scribner's, 1972.

Mahoney, M. J. *Abnormal psychology.* New York: Harper & Row, 1980.

Mann, J. *Time-limited psychotherapy.* Cambridge, Mass.: Harvard University Press, 1973.

Marmor, J. The seductive psychotherapist. *Psychiatry Digest,* 1970, *31*(10), 10–16.

Marmor, J. Dynamic psychotherapy and behavior therapy: Are they irreconcilable? *Archives of General Psychiatry,* 1971, *24*, 22–28.

Martin, B. *Anxiety and neurotic disorders.* New York: Wiley, 1971.

Martin, B. *Abnormal psychology: Clinical and scientific perspectives.* New York: Holt, Rinehart & Winston, 1977.

Maslow, A. H. *Toward a psychology of being.* Princeton, N.J.: Van Nostrand Reinhold, 1968.

May, P. R. A. For better or for worse? Psychotherapy and variance change: A critical review of the literature. *Journal of Nervous and Mental Disease,* 1971, *152*, 184–192.

May, R. *The art of counseling.* Nashville: Abingdon Press, 1967. (a)

May, R. *Psychology and the human dilemma.* Princeton, N.J.: Van Nostrand, 1967. (b)

McNair, D. M., Lorr, M., & Callahan, D. M. Patient and therapist influences on quitting psychotherapy. *Journal of Consulting Psychology,* 1963, *27*, 10–17.

Meichenbaum, D. (Ed.). *Cognitive behavior modification: An integrative approach.* New York: Plenum, 1977.

Miller, G. R. *Explorations in interpersonal communication.* Beverly Hills, Calif.: Sage, 1976.

Millon, T. *Modern psychopathology.* Philadelphia: Saunders, 1969.

Mintz, J. What is "success" in psychotherapy? *Journal of Abnormal Psychology,* 1972, *80*, 11–19.

Morse, S. J., & Watson, R. I., Jr. *Psychotherapies: A comparative casebook.* New York: Holt, Rinehart & Winston, 1977.

Muench, G. A. An investigation of the efficacy of time-limited psychotherapy. *Journal of Counseling Psychology,* 1965, *12*, 294–299.

Mullen, J., & Abeles, N. Relationship of liking, empathy, and therapist's experience to outcome of therapy. *Journal of Counseling Psychology,* 1971, *18*, 39–43.

Okun, B. F. *Effective helping: Interviewing and counseling techniques* (2nd ed.). Monterey, Calif.: Brooks/Cole, 1982.

Osipow, S. H., Walsh, W. B., & Tosi, D. J. *A survey of counseling methods.* Homewood, Ill.: Dorsey, 1980.

Page, J. D. *Psychopathology: The science of understanding deviance.* Chicago: Aldine, 1975.

Perez, J. F. *Family counseling: Theory and practice.* New York: Van Nostrand, 1979.

Perls, F. S. *Gestalt therapy verbatim.* Lafayette, Calif.: Real People Press, 1969.

Phillips, E. L., & Wiener, D. N. *Short-term psychotherapy and structural behavior change.* New York: McGraw-Hill, 1966.

Physician's desk reference (35th ed.). Oradell, N.J.: Medical Economics Company, 1981.

Pietrofesa, J. J., Hoffman, A., Splete, H. H., & Pinto, D. V. *Counseling: Theory, research and practice.* Chicago: Rand McNally, 1978.

Pietrofesa, J. J., Leonard, G. E., & Van Hoose, W. *The authentic counselor* (2nd ed.). Chicago: Rand McNally, 1978.

Plutchik, R. *The emotions: Facts, theories, and a new model.* New York: Random House, 1962.

Rachman, S. *The meanings of fear.* New York: Penguin, 1974.

Raimy, V. *Misunderstandings of the self.* San Francisco: Jossey-Bass, 1975.

Rational-emotive therapy. *The Counseling Psychologist,* 1977, 7(1), 2–82.

Reik, T. *Listening with the third ear.* New York: Grove Press, 1948.

Reisman, J. M. *Toward the integration of psychotherapy.* New York: Wiley, 1971.

Reiss, S., Peterson, R. A., Eron, L. D., & Reiss, M. M. *Abnormality: Experimental and clinical approaches.* New York: Macmillan, 1977.

Rogers, C. R. *Client-centered therapy.* Boston: Houghton Mifflin, 1951.

Rogers, C. R. The necessary and sufficient conditions of therapeutic personality change. *Journal of Consulting Psychology,* 1957, 21, 95–103.

Rogers, C. R. *On becoming a person.* Boston: Houghton Mifflin, 1961.

Rubin, T. I. *The angry book.* New York: Collier, 1969.

Rubinstein, E. A., & Lorr, M. A. A comparison of terminators and remainers in outpatient psychotherapy. *Journal of Clinical Psychology,* 1956, 12, 345–349.

Ruesch, J. *Therapeutic communication.* New York: Norton, 1973.

Ryckman, R. M. *Theories of personality* (2nd ed.). Monterey, Calif.: Brooks/Cole, 1982.

Sahakian, W. S. (Ed.). *Psychotherapy and counseling* (2nd ed.). Chicago: Rand McNally, 1976.

Schmideberg, M. Values and goals in psychotherapy. *Psychiatric Quarterly,* 1958, 32, 333–365.

Schofield, W. *Psychotherapy: The purchase of friendship.* Englewood Cliffs, N.J.: Prentice-Hall, 1964.

Schofield, W. The psychotherapist as friend. *Humanitas,* 1970, 6, 211–223.

Seligman, M. E. P. *Helplessness: On depression, development and death.* San Francisco: W. H. Freeman, 1975.

Shave, D. W. *Communication breakdown: Cause and cure.* St. Louis: Warren H. Green, 1975.

Shlien, J. M. Time-limited psychotherapy: An experimental investigation of practical values and theoretical implications. *Journal of Counseling Psychology,* 1957, 4, 318–323.

Shlien, J. M., Mosak, H. H., & Dreikurs, R. Effect on time limits: A comparison of two psychotherapies. *Journal of Counseling Psychology,* 1962, 9, 31–34.

Shostrom, E. L. *Actualizing therapy.* San Diego, Calif.: Edits, 1976.

Singer, E. *Key concepts in psychotherapy.* New York: Random House, 1965.

Small, L. The uncommon importance of diagnosis. *Professional Psychology,* 1972, 3(2), 111–119.

Sprinthall, N. A. Fantasy and reality in research: How to move beyond the unproductive paradox. *Counselor Education and Supervision,* 1975, 14, 310–322.

Stott, R. L. *A summary of laws relating to the practice of psychology as a health profession in California and a discussion of relevant legal concepts and procedures* (3rd revision). Orange, Calif.: California State Psychological Association, 1981.

Strongman, K. T. *The psychology of emotion.* New York: Wiley, 1973.

Strongman, K. T. *Decent exposure: Living with your emotions.* New York: St. Martin's, 1974.

Strupp, H. H. Psychotherapy: Research and practice: An overview. In A. E. Bergin & S. K. Garfield (Eds.), *Handbook of psychotherapy and behavior change.* New York: Wiley, 1971.

Strupp, H. H. On the basic ingredients of psychotherapy. *Journal of Consulting and Clinical Psychology*, 1973, *41*, 1–8.

Strupp, H. H., Fox, R. E., & Lessler, K. *Patients view their psychotherapy.* Baltimore: Johns Hopkins University Press, 1969.

Strupp, H. H., Hadley, S. W., & Gomes-Schwartz, B. *Psychotherapy for better or worse: An analysis of the problem of negative effects.* New York: Jason Aronson, 1977.

Subotnik, L. Spontaneous remission: Fact or artifact? *Psychological Bulletin*, 1972, *77*, 32–48.

Sullivan, H. S. *The interpersonal theory of psychiatry.* New York: Norton, 1953.

Swenson, C. H. Commitment and the personality of the successful therapist. *Psychotherapy: Theory, Research, and Practice*, 1971, *8*, 31–36.

Szasz, T. *The myth of mental illness.* New York: Paul B. Hoeber, 1961.

Szasz, T. *The myth of psychotherapy.* Garden City, N.Y.: Anchor/Doubleday, 1978.

Train, G. F. Flight into health. *American Journal of Psychotherapy*, 1953, *7*, 463–483.

Truax, C. B., & Wargo, D. G. Psychotherapeutic encounters that change behavior for better or for worse. *American Journal of Psychotherapy*, 1966, *20*, 499–520.

Tyler, L. E. *The work of the counselor* (2nd ed.). New York: Appleton-Century-Crofts, 1961.

Vaihinger, H. *The philosophy of "as if."* New York: Harcourt Brace Jovanovich, 1924.

Vaimy, V. *Misunderstandings of the self.* San Francisco: Jossey-Bass, 1975.

Vinicor, F., & Cooper, J. Early recognition of endocrine disorders. *Hospital Medicine*, December 1979, pp. 38–47.

Viscott, D. *The language of feelings.* New York: Pocket Books, 1977.

Volberg, L. R. *Short-term psychotherapy.* New York: Grune and Stratton, 1965.

Vriend, J., & Dyer, W. W. Counseling the reluctant client. *Journal of Counseling Psychology*, 1973, *20*, 240–246.

Watzlawick, P., Beavin, J., & Jackson, D. D. *Pragmatics of human communication.* New York: Norton, 1967.

Weiner, I. B. *Principles of psychotherapy.* New York: Wiley, 1975.

Weitz, S. (Ed.). *Nonverbal communication.* New York: Oxford University Press, 1974.

Wexler, D. A., & Rice, L. N. (Eds.). *Innovations in client-centered therapy.* New York: Wiley, 1974.

Wicks, R. J. *Counseling strategies and intervention techniques for the human services.* Philadelphia: Lippincott, 1977.

Wolman, B. B. (Ed.). *Success and failure in psychoanalysis and psychotherapy.* New York: Macmillan, 1972.

Wylie, R. C. *The self-concept* (Rev. ed., 2 vols.). Lincoln: University of Nebraska Press, 1974.

Young, P. T. *Understanding your feelings and emotions.* Englewood Cliffs, N.J.: Prentice-Hall, 1975.

Zunin, L., & Zunin, N. *Contact: The first four minutes.* New York: Ballantine Books, 1972.

Name Index

Subject Index